A Thousand Coloured Dreams

JOSEPHINE ABAIJAH
and
THE LATE DR ERIC WRIGHT

Dellasta Pacific

DEDICATED TO THE MEMORY OF
DOCTOR ERIC WRIGHT

Dellasta Pacific
(c) Josephine Abaijah and the estate of the late Dr Eric Wright
First published 1991

National Library of Australia
Cataloguing-in-Publication data:

Abaijah, Josephine
   A thousand coloured dreams.
   ISBN 0 947138 32 3.
   I. Wright, Eric.   II. Title.

Edited by Cathy Oliver
Cover and text design by Ron Hampton
Typeset and printed by SRM Production Services Sdn. Bhd.
Selangor, Malaysia
Published by Dellasta Pacific, 3/6 Hamilton Place,
Mount Waverley, Victoria 3149
Correspondence to P O Box 777, Mount Waverley, Victoria 3149

Tribute to Josephine

We are all affected to a limited extent by the places we visit and the identities we meet during our lifetime, and our ideals and attitudes vary according to the impact such places and people have upon us. It is, however, extremely rare for a single individual to have a profound or permanent effect on anyone's life and to meet such a person is a privilege to be cherished. For such a person to be a woman, and to be born in a country in which women are generally regarded as an inferior necessity with few rights, is truly remarkable.

Such a person is Josephine Abaijah, and such is the influence she has unwittingly imposed on me since I first met her more than twenty years ago. At that time she was the frenetic, flag-waving leader of the Papua Besena Movement heading vocal rallies calling for the protection and preservation of her Papuan people and their way of life.

Her voice and her sentiments were embraced by her people in a manner which no Papuan leader either then, or since, has been able to surpass. Her supporters carried her inevitably into politics where she entered a new, but no less effective, phase as the first female Member of Parliament in Papua New Guinea. Since then she has devoted her life to the People and the country she loves and in so doing has provided the inspiration the National women of Papua New Guinea needed to assert their own influence on the development of the country.

She has gained the respect of her fellow politicians and community leaders in her own modest but persuasive manner. Although she has mellowed since her earlier firebrand days and is, perhaps, more likely to adopt a more moderate approach to achieve her ends today, she still has the Papuan fire in her eyes and it is not too difficult to set the sparks dancing.

Whatever the public perception of Josephine might be, there are few who would doubt her unbounded generosity, her warmth and her sincerity. As a fighter I have seen none more tenacious; as an orator I have seen none so persuasive; and as a woman there are few more beguiling. An enigma she may be, but she has, in her unique way, stamped her presence and personality not only on me but on the wonderful people she represents.

To have watched her influence develop over the years has been exhilarating. To have worked with her has been a rewarding and educational experience. To be able to call her a close friend is, to me, a supreme honour.

For her country and for her people I can only pray that Josephine realises all her Dreams.

Jeffrey R. J. Dickens.

Love is a tiara of a thousand coloured dreams

This story is based on my life but with the exceptions of 'Dr Dina' and my children, all of the characters in this work are fictitious and any resemblance between these characters and real persons is coincidental. The historic details and extracts have been reproduced in good faith, but are subject to the usual human errors that can occur.

Josephine Abaijah

Contents

Foreword

A Thousand Coloured Dreams is a love story, it's a part of history, it's the moving account of the life of a young Papuan girl who was destined to become a powerful leader in a male dominated society.

I commend this book to the women of our country who will be inspired by the struggle of one of their sisters to take her rightful place among our leaders.

I commend this book to the men of our country who will gain great insight into the valuable asset we have in our women – an asset that should be highly prized and encouraged at all levels.

Finally I commend this book to all our people, young and old as a valuable contribution to our literature and as a truthful account of the agony of Papua as she struggled against the iron will of a colonial power hostile to the Thousand Coloured Dreams of her people.

A. Doi CMG, MP
Ex Deputy Prime Minister
Papua New Guinea

PART ONE

Tambourines of the soft winds

1

Child of Papua

*O*n a tropical afternoon, in June 1961, I stood on the top of a shanty-crowded hill in the Australian colonial town of Port Moresby. I held a young baby to my breast and gazed beyond the vapourizing tin huts of the desperate and the poor of the town to the cool white sands, the gentle palms and the blue coral seas of my Papuan homeland.

I was homeless, destitute and very alone. My only possession in the world was the child who sucked my breast. My only asset was a dying, consumptive uncle who hoped to stay alive long enough to see his name live on through me and my son.

* * *

It all started at the native village of Wamira on the northeast coast of Papua. My mother, a young, grass-skirted bride of seventeen, was at full term in the village. My father, seven years older, was away working 'trade' for the Australian foreigners—the colonial masters who manipulated our lives, our thoughts and our gods to serve their own ends.

The pains of birth began as the *kokoroku* (cocks) welcomed the morning light as it crept through the motionless palms of the village. By high noon, Josephine Abaijah was ready to take her first look at colonial Papua.

My mother moved out of the palm thatched hut, which was to be my home, so that the tissues of creation would not defile the dwelling. By the time the labour was well progressed, she had taken up a position, squatting upright and unsupported, under a shady okari nut tree at the side of the village.

There were no midwives present. My mother carried out most of these duties herself. There were two scrutineers who had taken up their places nearby. One of these was my father's sister, there to look after the interests of his family. The other scrutineer was my mother's sister, there to protect the interests of the family of my mother.

At a late moment, banana leaves were cut and placed under my mother's squatting buttocks and a chewed up half towel, which was produced from the family treasures, was placed close by. And, so, I was unceremoniously pushed, by strong young muscles, out of the naked body of my mother on to banana leaves which separated me from the warm sands.

As a premature baby, my appearance was anything but impressive. Many of the wise people of the village shook their heads when they saw me, predicting my early departure to the next life. A white missionary, who lived at the edge of our village, was of the opinion that it would be wise to complete all church transactions with haste. It was hard enough for any baby to survive in a Papuan village without being two or three pounds short of weight to start with.

* * *

Nearly one year after I was born, my father, who was still away working for the foreigners, plucked up enough courage to tell his Australian master that his wife was dying and, thus, he had urgent need to visit his village. He dared not suggest anything so trivial as wanting to visit his young bride (whom he had scarcely seen) and to see his first-born child! After a long sea trip in a small island trading boat, my

father duly arrived in the village, and the family was re-
united for the first time since the early days of my parents'
marriage. My mother had felt the strain of single-handedly
caring for her small baby, who barely survived during the
early months, as well as doing heavy work in the village
gardens. She was not keen to face the future alone; and she
managed to get this message through to my father. So the
next time my father set off to work 'trade' for the foreigners,
he took us with him.

The time came for us to depart, and my parents, carrying
me in their arms, set off for a small wharf situated in a
neighbouring village. Unfortunately for my parents, at that
time a tribal fight was simmering between this village and
our home village. As my parents approached they were
attacked by hostile natives and, during the skirmish, an
attempt was made to stone me. My mother was able to shield
me with her body and take what stones came her way. The
issue at stake was who speared, and thus owned, a certain
wallaby killed in a recent joint village hunting expedition. In
a rich society, fighting over a dead animal could appear to be
an absurdity. But this could not be a trivial matter in a
society starved of meat and protein, where rules of conduct
had to be firmly established for large hunting expeditions
involving many families.

* * *

My father worked for a trading firm on Samarai Island—a
small trading post and government centre set among beautiful islands off the eastern tip of Papua. Here, the family
managed to establish a small territorial claim in a communal
'boy' house ('boy' was the Australian colloquial term for all
male Papuans). This building was a large, one-roomed shed
which served as a home for many Papuans from different
parts of the country. All of the people who shared this shed
as a home had one thing in common: they all served the
same foreign master for one dollar (ten shillings) a month
plus weekly subsistence rations of rice, two tins of corned
beef or fish, and a small amount of sugar, tea and tobacco.
For a wife and child an additional ration was allowed. All of
this was thrown together in an old sugar bag which served

as the store for the food. The only furniture provided for the family was a mat to sleep on, the sugar bag, and a small cardboard suitcase.

My mother was now about nineteen and had spent all of her life in her palm-thatched native village on the sands of Wamira. That life was clean and wholesome to her and not like now, breathing the stale air in the darkness at the end of a communal 'boy' house. Also, my father had been able to look after himself much better as a bachelor without responsibility, playing a cat and mouse game of master and servant unhindered by a family. These factors meant a change was in the air. Eventually, my father managed to gain work looking after a very small trade store on a picturesque south sea island called Misima, deep in the Coral Sea. A rich reward for faithful service.

My family found Misima much more to their liking. Here they could identify with the brown, grass-skirted people and loved the deep-blue sea, coral reefs, colourful flowers and graceful palms of our new home. My parents decided to settle here permanently. But the colonials not only bring their religion, their language and their materials with them when they colonise a country, they also bring their diseases and their wars. Pearl Harbour had been bombed and the Japanese armies were advancing across the Pacific. The drums of foreign wars were moving towards Papua.

Foreigners take their wars very seriously. They also expect others to do the same, especially so when the others are voiceless, colonial people under their control. It is impossible for them to concede that one set of colonials is much the same as another. Milne Bay and Samarai were preparing for war and all foreigners were to be evacuated from Misima. Papuans from other parts of Papua were to return to their home villages—but little thought was given as to how this was to be accomplished. The general idea was to proceed in a straight line to where the whites wanted to go and then to put the Papuans down at the nearest convenient spot en route. They were then to proceed to their homes without food or money, even though this could take many days' walking with children and personal belongings to carry and seas to cross.

Misima government station was closed down with the usual colonial drama. Lectures were delivered but not understood, flags were laid to rest like dead people and Misima government station quietly folded up and went to sleep for the duration — an event which probably affected nobody but the people who slept there. A small trading schooner was commandeered and a white colonial officer was placed in charge of the evacuation. A 'stiff upper lip' was the order of the day, and the Abaijah family was ordered to evacuate. Unknown to all then, the small schooner would carry us and other Papuans over several hundred kilometres of restless seas to the mainland of Papua.

There was only room on board for the people and some of the valuables of the Australians — so the natives were told to leave everything behind. The only property that the Abaijahs were allowed to take with them was their daughter, Josephine, now able to walk a few steps and still only protected by the old towel given at her birth.

One hundred and sixty kilometres from Milne Bay, word was received that Samarai had been bombed and that Japanese bombers were in the area. Our small schooner with its cargo of souls, did a right-angled turn and headed for the island of Dobu, in the D'Entrecasteaux group of islands, many kilometres off the mainland of Papua.

After battling with heavy seas for three days, we landed at Dobu. A wide sea and many kilometres separated us from our native village of Wamira. Needless to say, my parents were foodless and moneyless. Carrying me in their arms and begging for food and transport from villagers, my parents slowly made their way from island to island until, eventually, we arrived back at the wharf where I had been stoned a few months earlier. No more animosity or wallaby wars, as now the foreign war was the big news, as was our own arrival. Previously, news had come to the village that the Abaijah family had been wiped out by a Japanese bomb.

* * *

For the next few years, I lived the life of a small girl in the village where I was born. Growing up in a Papuan coastal village was a warm, agreeable experience which rooted a child's heart deep in the native soil. The blue waters of the warm Pacific reached almost to our front door, as our village of thirty or forty houses was on the beach. For four years, the sand was our floor and our bed, bundles of grass cut from old gardens our roof, and our walls the leaves of coconut palms. Our house' cost nothing to build but it was cool and dry. It consisted of one room in which everyone lived and shared everything in life including the smoke from the everlasting fire that smouldered in the middle. There are no secrets in a Papuan village and it is almost impossible to be alone. Procreation, recreation, eating, living and dying, for us all, took place on that few square metres of sand under the grass and coconut leaves, that we called home.

My memories are of hot tropical days and pleasant nights with cool breezes. We roamed free in the powerful sun with coconut leaf skirts our only clothing. Very few girls were rich enough to own a material dress or even a rag. Our brown skins became much darker in the hot sun but we had no colour consciousness. We felt closer to the hibiscus and the night breeze than we did to the pale, sweating Australians who occasionally appeared among us to observe how we were progressing towards civilization.

My days were spent swimming with the other children; in the gardens with my parents; or romping in the village. I grew to love the simple elementary beauty of natural things, the smell of grass, the warm colours of extravagant flowers and the warm touch of smooth brown skin.

Of my thirteen natural brothers and sisters, the next two girls were born during these four years. Like myself, they were pushed out of the body of my squatting mother, unattended, onto banana leaves on the warm sands of Papua. This ritual was to be repeated, at two yearly intervals, for the next twenty years.

Our family now had three girls and my parents had added responsibilities and were growing in status as their family increased. Being the eldest in the family, I was practically a fully developed mother before I was eight years old. About the only motherly duty that I did not perform with gusto and constancy was to produce a child myself and, after all, that act was of no great consequence.

Ever since my earliest days in Wamira, I have been deeply moved by the poverty of the village people. I doubt if my mother has spent more than twenty dollars in her whole life. If she were given a dollar now she would not know what to do with it and, probably, would look around for someone to give it to. The most vivid memories that I have of Wamira are of the rare occasions when we were given a small plate of plain boiled rice. These were tremendous occasions when I lovingly shepherded each grain to my mouth — events to be talked about and relived for years to come.

Life was hard on our few feet of sand. Food was just enough for existence; our gardens were several kilometres away; fish was scarce and only caught in the rivers; meat almost non-existent. Still, we had ourselves and we had the natural beauty of our native land.

My people had lived within the clammy grip of colonialism since the last century but my village had never experienced any form of material development. My people were considered so poor that the men were exempted from paying the one dollar a year tax which was extracted by the colonial ruler to pay for the practically non-existent services that were provided. But what the colonials did succeed in doing was to use our poverty to bait our young men away from the village to work for them for a dollar a month plus food, thus further weakening our own power to produce and develop. During the war years at Milne Bay, this became so bad that our married men, my father included, were released by the army to return to Wamira in order to save the village from disaster.

The most effective part of Australian colonial strategy was the open-handed invitation to Christian Missions to take over the country. This policy cost the Australians nothing and they knew that the good folk of the missions, and their overseas faithful, would be prepared to provide some of the services and development that the Australian government was reluctant to do at any cost to themselves. The missions provided us with our only education and they catered for some emotional development and wholeness through expression, love and beauty which were eagerly seized upon and internalised by the people.

The few years I spent in my own native village were important. I learned to speak my first Papuan language which is the close link with my family and my people. I stumbled through a primary experience with destructive poverty without knowing that there was any alternative. I learned to appreciate the elementary beauty of natural things and began to seek fulfilment through love, spirituality and self expression and not through a cult of material attainment.

When the war ended, my father gathered together his wife and three small daughters, and we turned our backs on our native village, never to return.

* * *

Once again we found ourselves on a small trading schooner headed for the island of Misima via the deep blue sea.

The waters off the east coast of Papua are full of sensuous magic. A scintillation of exquisite islands sprinkle in a riot of colour between the sea and the sky. But these waters are as fragile as they are beautiful, and our small, puking craft convulsed its way through three days and nights of violent torment before it slid to tranquility in the sand-locked, palm drenched, blue water of Misima Bay. Elegant, delicate and untamed.

For the next eighteen years, Misima was my family home. I acquired nine more brothers and sisters, which with my mother and father, meant fourteen mouths to feed and fourteen spaces to find on the floor at night for fourteen brown bodies on fourteen pandanus mats. It was poverty that drove my family away from our native village where the earth demanded too much sweat for the small bounty that it released. Looking back, it seems that my father made a wise choice. Feeding fourteen people, from the hard soil of my native village, would have been a tiresome, juiceless experience.

Misima is the kind of island dear to the hearts to those addicted to the magic, if not to the reality, of South Sea island romance. The island consists of mountain slopes and narrow coastal plains (where most of the population live) broken by clear, sharp streams fed by torrential rains which keep the island saturated. The rain comes quickly, hides the blue sky for a moment, refreshes the earth and quietly departs without any pause to spoil the day, but often splashing the sky with a vivid rainbow as a happy goodbye.

Compared with my native village, Misima was the promised land. An island of milk and honey or, more exactly, an island of plentiful fish, taro, bananas, yams, sweet potatoes, papaya, mangoes, tapioka and other wonders including royal rice and tinned corned beef which, after our early experience, never ceased to bring us pleasure. The wonders of Misima did not end with the food for here were grass-skirted, brown people like ourselves living in a much kinder environment than we had known.

My father was now a man of more importance. His job was to make a few dollars for a colonial master by selling canned meat from Australia, coloured cloth from China, fish from anywhere canned in Japan and a few other foods and trinkets. All this was designed to relieve the natives of the few dollars they acquired from selling copra or working for wages in the local economy which consisted of the government, missions and a foreign-owned gold mine. Food was so plentiful on Misima that my father could manage to feed his small but growing family and still remain relatively honest.

One of the wonders was our new house. We now lived in a real house on piers, with pit sawn timber floor and galvanized iron for the roof and walls. Our house still consisted of one room which served as bedroom, living room and kitchen but, each morning, the bedroom disappeared as mats were rolled up and neatly stacked in a corner. Even when our family eventually grew to fourteen souls, we were still living in grace and harmony in one room which served for all.

Our bathroom was a few sheets of iron nailed to old timber on the ground outside the house. Our toilet, at least for the records, was a public toilet which was over the sea about a half kilometre away. This is where we directed our foreign visitors but I never saw any Abaijah venturing into such dangerous territory after the sun had set. The public toilet also had another usefulness. It was a very good place to catch fish which did not taste any the worse for their curiosity!

In Misima we had come into much worldly wealth, and the

washing of our tin plates and dishes was an important daily ritual which was something akin to washing the first family car in a more affluent society. As the eldest child, I became the first to take over the jobs that my parents gradually devolved and one of the most important of these jobs was washing up. Usually, I took my load of valuables to a mountain stream that flowed near our house as it made its way to the sea. The plates were quickly cleaned, but then the pots had to be scrubbed with sand until they reached a state of gleaming freshness likely to be acceptable to my parents.

We also had another duty to perform. Near our house were a number of rocks which were the dwelling places of a group of long-haired, short, spirit people who needed to be placated to keep them at home and stop them creating disturbances by aimless wanderings around the place seeking their needs. We had to feed these spirit folk regularly. Once, when we became forgetful of our obligation, a terrible cyclone struck. In early evening, without warning, high winds and heavy rain came. These increased in intensity until our one-roomed house was swept away. Clutching one another, we managed to make our way to the small trade store where my father worked and there we sheltered until it, too, was swept away.

By this time a tidal wave had struck. The water was rising under the house and we were in danger of being swept off the few sticks still attached to the stumps. My mother and father, assisted by two policemen, decided to try to make it to the government station which was on higher ground. The small children were carried on the shoulders of the adults and the bigger children were half-carried, half-dragged along. We were blown from windbreak to windbreak through water, wind and flying missiles until, almost exhausted, we struggled into a roofless house on the government station. Here, the station people were sheltering while waiting for the cyclone to pass. We joined them and sought out a suitable windbreak for our family. Then, huddled together, we waited for the spirit people to end their wanderings and return to their homes.

In the cyclone we lost all of our possessions. Then, after a pause, we once again set about building our usual one-roomed house, this time using any old materials that we could collect or scrounge. And once again, we began collecting a few rags, pots and pans which were the status symbols of the new civilization that was pressing in on us.

* * *

One of my most constant employments, as a young girl, was fishing. We had many mouths to feed and, as far as fish were concerned, I was the one to feed them. I loved these fishing assignments as they made me free and one with the wind, the sea and the things of nature. When eight years old I was fishing with the elders and by ten years I was fishing on my own. For five years, after I was ten, I arose from my sleeping mat two hours before dawn, collected my gear and, alone and without light, I made my way to the sea. Most of my fishing in the predawn hours was done off a jetty or off rocks with which I was familiar.

Fishing excursions started the day before. Home from school, I had to work with my mother in the house as babies had to be nursed or fed, the house had to be cleaned and food had to be prepared for the evening meal. But every afternoon, half an hour could be found to go to the beach to collect the crustaceans that I used for bait. I grabbed the small creatures as they scampered away and pulled off their shells and legs in a twinkle and put them in a tin until I had a tinful of bait. The tin, line and hooks were then stored safely under the house and I went inside again in time to help with the preparation for the evening meal.

As regular as the cocks crowing, I awoke in the hours before dawn, straightened the skirt that I had slept in and picked my way to the open air where the consciousness of night and light slowly spread upon me. A small girl, dressed only in a light skirt, I clutched my line, hooks and bait and, alone with the night, I made my way to the sea. Some nights, the moon was a bright torch that illuminated the land and the sea with the harshness of day and at other times, an intimate and private darkness closed around me. For the five years that I experienced this nightly solitude, I knew little fear and my parents slept soundly into the light of day.

Reaching a suitable spot, I baited the hook and cast the line into the sea and, alert and confident, I waited for the first curious nibble. Sometimes the action was fast and rewarding while at other times, alertness spread to meditation, and meditation to dreams. Brown eyes shut as brown fingers wound a fish line to a toe and dangled a baitless hook into the dawn. Sometimes a fish was careless enough to hook itself and signal its misfortune by tugging on the line to my toe. As fish were caught, I stunned them on wood or rocks with a quick swing of the line, and threaded them onto a vine and placed them beside me as I continued my assignment to provide for the family for the day.

The nights were so quiet that listening to the beat of my heart I sometimes heard the beat of my soul. Still, five years was a long time for a small girl to spend in such silence and solitude. During my nightly vigils by the side of creation, I drifted in coloured dreams through the soft years from slight child to virgin woman. The sounds of the real night came as though through thunderous megaphones, and glowworms flashed like torches in the night. My dreams and my world were as private as the visions of a Bernadette and my thousand coloured dreams were drawn with pastels from the spirituality of my soul.

At times, my line was carried away by a spirited fish and fouled in rocks in the deep ocean pools. When morning came and the water cleared for day, I would slip into the sea and, with skirt still attached to my hips, I would swim to the bottom where with gentle care I would carefully free the hook as though plucking a precious pearl from its fleshy bed. While under the water, I was one with the fish, the rocks and the deep, unthinkingly preoccupied with my purpose. I was unafraid—like a small animal grazing near a feeding beast of prey—of the sharks that sometimes came my way and the crocodiles that occasionally floated by, in their search for prey.

Occasionally, a man from the Government station a kilometre away, would approach my privacy in the night. I would pick up his sounds long before he could see me and, quickly, I would gather my tools of trade and slide into the bush or between deep rocks. There, like a frightened animal, I would listen until the danger passed. Sometimes, I fell asleep in hiding, to find when morning came, that my bed was foreign material such as coconut husks washed up by the high tide or debris of the bush which I had shared with the crawling creatures of the night.

The colonials had long since taught us about Saturdays and Sundays. We could not think of becoming civilized unless we celebrated Saturdays by playing cricket or football and Sundays by worshipping in the House of God. Yet, on Sundays, some indisposition usually claimed its own attention. A useful by-product of these colonial innovations was that a young girl had more spare time on these days than on other days of the week. Thus, on Saturdays or Sundays, sometimes instead of fishing at night, I slipped off in a canoe to explore distant waters in my demanding obsession for hunting fish. I would be alone on the sea for hours probing every wild or lonely place where curiosity might be rewarded or profit gained. On these excursions, I used different techniques of catching fish which were suitable for use in the light of day. Filled with excitement, I turned to new challenges and I now speared fish, hunted turtles or gathered shellfish on the reefs and I became more aware that we must share the harvest of the sea with sharks and other creatures which must be respected.

There was another new experience, as now I sometimes met village people at sea who were similarly occupied to myself. A passing greeting brought me into a fellowship of interpersonal reality that I never experienced in the lonely spirituality of the night.

My fish hunting ended when I was fifteen, as at that age, I temporarily left Misima to attend school on the mainland of Papua. From then, until now, I have never hunted fish again and never split the sea for any useful purpose. My five year romance with the solitude of the night and the scent of fresh dawn was the most important spiritual experience of my early life and one which I sometimes tried to recapture when searching for purity or purpose in later years.

* * *

The new colonialism in Papua commenced a few years after the end of the Second World War but Australia's interest in Papua dated into the last century, and long before the Australian colonies talked the British motherland into declaring Papua a British protectorate. This the British did in the name of Her Majesty the Queen, when British flags were raised, British guns were fired and pious words were chanted about British abstractions such as honour, protection, trust and loyalty. Then, a few years later, Britain handed the 200 000 square kilometres, plus contained souls, to the Australian colonies as a birthday present following their federation as the Commonwealth of Australia.

Up to the time of the Abaijahs (the name of an Ethiopian King bestowed upon my father by a British missionary), Papua was administered by Australia with a big yawn. Then one day Australia suddenly woke up and decided that its colony of Papua was now an embarrassment because of the 'White Australia' policy and past neglect, and that it should be dumped forthwith as discreetly and as cheaply as possible.

In 1950, the first Government primary school was started in Misima. After decades of indifference the sudden haste to educate the Papuans became compelling and the school at Misima was started in the hastily erected bungalow of the headmaster-to-be. School started with an odd assortment of embarrassed children gleaned from many sources and amid wonders from the civilized world of toys, toilets and fat dogs. I was there on opening day adding to the confusion by being the only girl in my class. Indeed, I would be the only girl ever in my classes during the whole of my crash schooling programme in Papua.

After four years of schooling at Misima, I was singled out to be the recipient of another crash programme in education, this time on the mainland of Papua. After a further year of this, I was crash programmed once more into a girls' high school in Australia. I spent four years at school in Australia with an annual pilgrimage back to my native Papua and the things that I loved. When I went to school in Australia it was the first time that I had ever worn shoes, but, despite our cultural differences, I was treated with great kindness and gentleness by my contemporaries. At school, I was accepted unobtrusively and was even made a patrol leader in their 'Girl Guides' and given prizes for being 'Best Citizen' and such things.

For most of the time I was lonely for my home; for the

people of my own flesh and bone; for the lovely natural things among which I lived. One thing that I could not become accustomed to was the purposeless splashing in an artificial swimming pool, that the Australian girls called 'swimming'. I can still remember the swimming coach booming from the bottom of her chest, in a voice that would scare a hungry shark,

'Josephine, stop wasting time swimming around the bottom of the pool like a brown fish. Practise on the top of the water until you can swim properly like the other girls!'

But I had spent five years with the sea and my God through the deep nights and the clear dawns of my beautiful homeland. No purposeless swimming, in a concrete tub, could tear my soul from the deep rocks of a sky-tinted sea.

* * *

It was at the age of ten that sex first intruded itself upon my conscious being and compelled me to give serious thought to the business of being a girl. My eight-year old sister and I had attached ourselves to an attractive foreign woman — as was common with young Papuan girls. We regarded her as being the ultimate in dress, scent and grooming and her possessions were limited only by her desires. One day we decided to visit our fairy queen in her castle and present her with a bunch of beautiful flowers. After much discussion and choosing, we gathered a bunch of flowers suitable for such an occasion and tied it with a jungle strand. We then made our way to the house of the lady which was in the small settlement where the foreigners lived. As we approached, I, being the senior member of the family, held my sister's hand in my right hand and the bunch of flowers in my left. As was appropriate for Papuan girls, we shyly approached the house by the back door, but on arrival, instead of being greeted by our flower-scented lady we were greeted by the man of the house: a red-faced man, of big authority and big noises, who was employed to continue the process of civilizing the savages in some capacity or other.

We presented ourselves with courteous murmurs and briefly explained our mission. The red-faced man, with a voice like thunder, then ushered us into the house with unexpected enthusiasm but it soon became obvious, even to us, that he was more interested in the two little girls than in the bunch of flowers I was still clutching in my left hand.

We were taken into the kitchen which was full of every imaginable contraption and there we were told what nice little girls we were, how pretty our clothes were (the same for all occasions — a short cotton skirt with white briefs underneath) and how soft was our warm brown skin. Suddenly, to my amazement, the man knelt down on one knee in front of me and began to feel my thigh under my cotton skirt. His breath was hard and his eyes were wide like a wild pig, stuck in the bush with a spear in its throat. I was transfixed with terror and my muscles knotted like mangrove roots. I stood rigid, still clutching small sister with my right hand and the bunch of flowers with the other. After rubbing my thighs for a time, he forced a hand between them and started pushing his hand back and forth as though sawing a soft papaya with a blunt bamboo. I did not move. My skin grew tight on my body. My hands continued to grip their objects with fierce strength as the terrifying sawing continued with increasing intensity. At this stage, I would not have been surprised if the man had produced a stone or a betel nut from my thighs as I had seen magic men do after massaging some appropriate part of the anatomy of a person in torment. I expected the evil purpose of this attention soon to reveal itself in some disastrous finale but, to my great relief, the approach of the man's native cook, from another room, caused a sudden change in his mood and activity. I seized this chance to run from the house, and still clutching small sister in my right hand and the bunch of flowers in my left, I ran out of the house, over the soft grass to the safety to my own simple home.

After this experience, I became disturbed. For the first time, it slowly filtered into my mind that re-faced foreigners, whom I had thought were special creatures from some fabled land, indeed could be as dangerous as the spirits who can rob a girl of her soul and hide it in the branches of a high tree.

* * *

There were a few colonials who married or lived with Papuan

women but these men were mainly among those trading with Papuans or various kinds of farmers whose work, for the most part, isolated them from their own society. There were exceptions but for government officers, missionaries and ordinary men of commerce, marriage or sex with Papuans was largely proscribed. For practical purposes, all that the Australians knew about sex and marriage in traditional native societies came from the writings of European anthropologists. Optimists, who used these books as practical guides to romance in Papua, usually learned, from bitter experience, that it was unwise to believe everything one reads in books.

On Misima, there was the traditional pattern of sex and marriage as practised by the village people. My friends from the village had a clearly defined path to follow and free choice was limited as girls often had their marriages arranged for them by their parents. This sometimes took place at an early age, even soon after birth, and the first brush with sex for a girl often came after she had been signed, sealed and delivered. This was of small consequence to parents and others who were absorbed counting the profits and paying the costs. In Papua, as elsewhere, there was a solid economic basis to love. Patterns of behaviour for a girl were clearly defined and there were few alternatives. After marriage, a young girl passed from flower-adorned maiden to married village woman in a few short strides.

On the other hand, the small colonial population could always be counted on to provide new diversions which were a constant source of surprise. This was particularly so to the native people, like ourselves, who lived in the shadows of their unpredictable society. A colonial might satisfy his needs by a deal with the wife of his native cook. The native cook might then marry his ex-wife's sister to restore the status quo. His ex-wife then became his colonial boss and the recipient of his services as cook and man servant. After a few adjustments, it was business as usual with little disruption to the way of life. The master had a wife and the cook had his job. A new colonial master was often harder to come by than a new, dutiful wife.

One Australian wife of a government officer was inclined

to parade naked in front of her Papuan man servants. This was a grand finale to the ritual shower which was one of the marks of race superiority and an activity which helped to fill the empty days. Judging by the detailed descriptions of the events given by the Papuan man-servants concerned, it would be an injustice to them to say that they were unstirred by the experience. On the other hand, prudence, born of a long experience of the unpredictability of the colonial race, made them cautious as they glanced at the forbidden contours. But they dared not sip one drop of the proffered wine as the colonial goal was very close and six years or hanging was a big price to pay for a small cultural misunderstanding.

Some of the Australians lived by the book and would banish from decent society any fellow countryman who had anything to do with a native woman. Official letters and circulars made it abundantly clear that this was the order of the day. A law of the Australians made it illegal for a colonial to be alone with a native woman between sunset and sunrise. Also, it was illegal, on government stations or in towns, for Papuans to be out after 9 o'clock at night, unless they had a letter of permission signed by a colonial master. For many years, the gaols of Papua were full of Papuans who, like Cinderella, were beaten by the clock. Needless to say, there was no such restriction on the Australians and they moved about as they pleased.

Some Australians mixed freely with the natives and paid the penalty, but most of them rationed their contact to what they considered was consistent with the tolerance of their own society—which was slight—and what was not detrimental to their progress.

Many Australian wives found life in Papua a bore. The men enjoyed being big fish in a small pool. They got satisfaction out of a life of adventure in a primitive country or from lording it over the natives.

* * *

When I was sixteen I was almost arranged into marriage, by my parents, with a village boy of suitable family and connections. This all started when I was about thirteen. Nothing was said to me, but the parents of both families discussed the matter of my marriage in great detail and, over the years, various exchanges of food and valuables took place between them. I had nothing to do with the boy, but it slowly became apparent, because of the exchanges and the attention shown to me, that this was the boy I was to marry.

The thing came to a head when I was sixteen and home on holidays from school in Australia. During my absence, firm arrangements had been made by my parents and the parents of the boy that marriage was to take place during these holidays. I was to finish my schooling as a married woman of sixteen and I was to see my husband once a year when I came home. This was the Papuan way of solving the difficult problem of an absentee bride. Also, it was to solve the important matter of reconciling the many exchanges that had taken place over the years.

Up to a couple of weeks before the planned wedding, I was still uninformed of what was to take place because, to my father, this seemed to be an unnecessary triviality. In his world, a Papuan girl would do what her parents bid her, and in any case, what was there for a girl to do other than to marry a suitable man and settle down to produce children and sweet potatoes in a native village?

The alarm sounded when the boy started visiting my home more regularly. He would take up a point of vantage and gaze at me lovingly, which was the nearest approach a Papuan could make to looking like a love-sick suitor. But alarm turned to panic when it began to dawn on me that plans were in hand for the wedding ceremony to take place the following week. The marriage date suddenly became much clearer and closer to me than did the hungry gaze of the love-sick boy, across the floor of our one-roomed house which was shared by my several brothers and sisters and sundry visitors as well.

My panic gave me the strength to act. I mustered all my courage in my meek Papuan heart and blurted out to my parents that, if the marriage that was to take place next week involved me, they could count me out. I had no intention of creating history by being the only married woman in my school and I had no intention of creating a sensation among the good Church of England nuns who were in charge of my scholastic welfare, by growing more pregnant daily before their eyes. This was especially so as my major determination, at that time, was to become one of them.

My father became dumbfounded as my protest slowly took shape in his mind and he treated me as a brazen, rebellious daughter. My ex-husband-to-be broke down and made suitable public demonstrations of the depth of his grief and disappointment. The ramifications of this break with tradition went on for years and I was explained away as a casualty of the evils of the new colonialism that had come amongst us. As for me, I felt that a cloud over my life had been dispersed and I settled down to the important purpose of learning some of the secrets of the white man's world which unlocked all doors and provided everything.

* * *

At about the time that I was selected to go to the mainland of Papua for further education, I was alarmed to see one of my friends, a year or two my senior, become pregnant. This was the result of an affair with a man from another district which ended in a broken engagement and much more. This girl was not from the village, but lived in circumstances not unlike my own. I thought that it would be prudent to see that a similar thing did not happen to me, and as a Papuan girl, my thoughts turned to magic.

There is no privacy, ever, in a one-roomed house shared with several perceptive children. Sexual incidents involving outside people were freely discussed, but personal sex matters were never mentioned in the home or elsewhere. Such things were taken for granted. A girl soon learned the facts of life when she married a village boy and followed the traditional ways which the girls of the village had followed for thousands of years. Girls like myself, who lived on the edge of village society, could be absorbed back into traditional life in a twinkle.

I set about my small, private mission in a methodical manner and I reasoned that the best informed person on how not to become pregnant must be the prostitute from the government station, as she seemed to be immune to such inconveniences. On finding her, she told me in some detail that this end could best be achieved by having a woman who possessed suitable magic tie a special jungle strand around my body. After the purpose was achieved, the strand was to be kept and further treated when pregnancy would be desired by submerging in a certain pool.

Next, I communicated this information to my mother who did not regard my interest as unreasonable and undertook to see if such a service was available in any of the villages. Eventually, her efforts were rewarded. An old village woman who was skilled in such procedures agreed to provide the service, and a strand of jungle creeper was securely fastened around my middle, followed by various massaging and kneading exercises to suitably bind the essence of the vine to the relative parts of my body. I was instructed to sleep for two nights with the strand attached until the union of the essence with my body was complete. On the third day, the day that I was to leave Misima, the strand was removed and I was assured, with authority, that I was now protected against pregnancy.

During our trip to the mainland we slept one night at a school on the island of Logea. During the night there were disturbances in my body and I awoke to great alarm and greater embarrassment to find fluid pouring from my body: an extraordinary witness of the potency of the magic to which I had been exposed.

By seeking protection of this nature a Papuan girl did not necessarily mean that she was about to engage in an active sex life. It was just a part of becoming a woman. A Papuan girl feels that she will be exposed to the same forces and consequences as all other women and, if she is not living under the protection of traditional village life, where all consequences lead to the same ends, it is sensible to take precautions. In my case, an active sex life was far from my mind as I was fully concerned with preparations for the future.

* * *

When I returned to Misima for my last holiday, I was surprised to find that a white colonial doctor had taken over. He had been sent by the colonial administration to serve the sick at the government hospital on the station. Dr Parker was an enthusiastic ambassador for his country and was earnest and dedicated. Papua was one of the outlets for men and women of conviction to serve unprivileged man in his primitive environment. I attached myself to the new doctor and worked with him at the native hospital. On one of the medical rounds with him, a small village girl died in my arms. With all of my selfish privileges, I felt that I owed a debt to this little brown child who never had a chance. I decided to become a nurse or a doctor.

During the five years spent in the hours before dawn fishing for the family, I felt my god was always by my side and I developed a constant spirituality of purpose. Always, I heard spirit voices calling for me to go forward. The night never revealed the path that I had to follow but I was always sure that my destiny would lead me where the spirit finger pointed. I faced the dawn of every day with constancy and purpose. Child of Papua, woman of tomorrow.

At that time medical and nursing education were in their infancy but they were the most advanced courses available in the country. With practical assistance from Dr Parker and moral support from my parents, I set out on my last voyage, over the Coral sea, to the mainland of Papua. An inevitable journey into a new life. A timid thrust into the unknown.

2

The awakening

*P*ort Moresby: dry scale on the lush, rain drenched coast of Papua. Logical capital. Harbour for foreign ships. Land for foreign houses. Power for foreign machines. A short haul from Australia. Capital of hope, money and violence. Natural beauty unadorned. An unvirgined girl, from dainty Misima and lonely Australia, I arrived in Port Moresby with a heart wide open.

Due to the efforts of an Englishman, Dr Walter Strong, and an Australian, Dr Eric Wright, medical education in Papua was years ahead of any other like endeavour. Dr Strong was dead. He spent his final years in a Papuan village in the Central Province of Papua and died close to the things he loved. In death, he confirmed his eccentricity, to many Australians, by leaving money for the future university education of Papua students in Australia.

Because of the work of these men, I found myself, suitcase in hand, trudging up a goat track that led to the newly established Papuan Medical College in Port Moresby — my home for the next few years. I had never heard of the Papuan

Medical College before coming to Port Moresby, as it was only a year since its foundation. This was to be the first year for the education of medical doctors in Papua and New Guinea.

The first buildings that I came to were the temporary Halls of Residence for female students. Temporary, because everything was temporary at that stage of the Australian administration. For the immediate purpose of 'handing over', the Australians thought soft wood was as good as hard concrete; also it was more readily available. The Papuan Medical College and the Port Moresby General Hospital, which were a joint concern, were built on a stony rise overlooking a sea of swampy mud known as Boroko. The Halls of Residence were a few low wooden sheds behind a tall, chain wire fence. Modern, cement brick buildings were to come later.

Miss Hordern was the first Australian I met in my new world. I met her as I was making my way along the chain wire fence that enclosed the dormitories. It turned out that she was the colonial who directed and advised new students while they were settling in. She told me where to report and what to do and questioned me curtly about my education. Miss Hordern had stayed on in Papua because she had many Christian friends here and she wanted to help the natives. In the church circles she mixed in, everyone had a common interest in the natives. Saving the natives of Papua was an exciting adventure that engendered a sense of purpose into the participants that was not easily found elsewhere.

Miss Hordern took an instant dislike to me. She had never met a Papuan girl who had spent four years at a high school in Australia. To her I was some sort of a competitor. A threat to a Christian tradition of hundreds of years of balmy colonialism.

'Where did you go to school, Josephine?'

'My last school was in Queensland, Mrs, er . . er . . '

'Miss Hordern, thank you. What class did you go to, Josephine? Josephine, that is your name, isn't it?'

The rule was that all colonials were addressed by their surnames, suitably prefixed, while all natives were addressed by their given name, unadorned.

'Yes, I am Josephine. Josephine Abaijah, Miss Hordern,' I replied, chanting an old, familiar tune.

'And, what class did you say you went to, Josephine?'

'I did not go very far at school, Miss Hordern. I only completed four years at high school.'

Miss Hordern was obviously relieved, as the news could have been worse, and she continued her recitation in a softer voice.

'What did you think of Australia? Did you like Australia? You must have found the food strange after what you were used to?'

The conversation continued along familiar lines with appropriate nods and sounds of approval from me, until it spluttered to a quick end when I politely enquired of Miss Hordern, her schooling and her personal endeavours. This was the standard method of ending such conversations with foreigners after the time limit, demanded by custom, had been exceeded.

This was my first and last conversation with Miss Hordern. Despite years of contact and efforts on my part to be friendly, and a non-contestant, we remained enemies to the bitter end. This was my first meeting with a Miss Hordern in Port Moresby but, in the years to come, I found that the capital city of PNG was liberally sprinkled with such fading flowers of white colonialism.

As I left Miss Hodern, dejected and apprehensive, a loud masculine voice parted me from my bleak thoughts.

'Hey there! Miss Josephine Abaijah. You are Miss Abaijah?'

I defensively wheeled around to confront the owner of the loud voice who had addressed me in this unexpected manner. Before me stood a short man of medium build, blue eyes, fair hair and simply clad in colonial garb of white shirt and khaki shorts. By his exclusive attention to me and obvious confidence in what he was doing, he communicated to me that, in his scheme of things, I was important. Before I could fumble out some inadequate affirmative as to the correctness of my name, he boomed on:

'I'm Dr Dina, Dean of the Papuan Medical College. We've been expecting you. How do you like the place?' he shouted as he covered the wire fence and the wooden sheds with an expansive wave of his arms. 'You will like it after you get over the first shock. By the way, I hear you want to be a nurse. Forget about it. You are going to the medical school to train to be a doctor.'

I did not say a word but I felt that my veneer of Australian manners was melting away and that I was stripped down to my native brown skin. I felt warm, comfortable and wanted. Obviously disinterested in initial student responses, Dr Dina uninterruptedly continued:

'The first year of the first medical course ever, in this country, begins next week. I'll see you again tomorrow and, in the meantime, if there's anything at all you want, just give a shout and let me know.'

With a big wave and without waiting for any response from me, he turned and was gone. Gone also were Miss Hordern's hostility and rejection. Dr Dina's words continued to drum in my ears and I was glad that I had time to think, a very important element to a Papuan. My foreign veneer was stripped from me and I was a timid, naked Papuan girl. I was going to be a doctor and not a nurse. What difference did it make to me? The doctor seemed to have tickets on himself but he made me feel like a Papuan girl wants to feel and not like a miserable, third rate Australian. I felt that I was wanted and respected.

I was not sure of Dr Dina or his words but I was sure that this was no usual man. He knew me and took me for granted without letting me speak a word. I wondered if I would ever know him. At times in my life I had felt compulsions that made me feel that I had to make certain decisions and follow certain actions. A spirit or a voice worked within me and I had complete confidence in the direction. No matter what the sacrifice to me at the time, I could not deny it. This feeling came on me now and although I had never met this Dr Dina in any proper fashion, I knew, intuitively, that he was going to play an important part in my life. An empty spot in my heart had been tenanted. I was attracted to him, not as a man as I did not know him, but as a direction, a compulsion of the spirit.

* * *

My days at the Papuan Medical College passed easily, but

still, it was a strange experience. Ever since I had presented myself on the first day of the first Government school on Misima Island, everything that I attended was the first. A few of us had been suddenly caught on the crest of the wave of Australian decolonisation and we were carried on by an energy that we could not control. I lived in a peculiar world in which everything was a first. At no place was there any past. No successes, no failures, no honour rolls of past students or distinguished dead. No ends, only beginnings. We did not know where we were going and we scarcely knew where we came from. There was no history, no past, no heroes to salute or worship. Nobody had ever been there before us. We were a ghost army on patrol in an unknown land, marching toward tomorrow.

I was the first to do dozens of undistinguished things in my country from primary education to Parliament. Now I was a student on the first day of the first medical course ever in Papua and New Guinea. It was the 13th of February, 1960; a group of twenty bewildered Papuans and New Guineans made their way into the unfamiliar assembly hall for the opening ceremony.

On the platform, a few lecturers and administrative staff were assembled, most of them wearing shorts and open neck shirts. Gone were the days of white pith helmets, heavily starched long whites and coats which were standard dress for an earlier generation of white doctors. The age of informality was at hand but the floral shirts, careless dress and bare feet were still to arrive. As expected, the staff members were all foreigners. All such positions in PNG were invariably held by foreigners. The students sat in respectful silence, as far from the front as discretion permitted, waiting for the show to begin.

Dr Dina, the first dean of the first tertiary education institution in Papua and New Guinea, rose deliberately from his chair to give the first talk. His subject was 'An Introduction to the Study of Medicine', which he delivered in precise, well practised terms and, thankfully, with a familiar accent which was easy for us to understand.

'The students gathered here today are from many parts of Papua and New Guinea'. Dr Dina commenced his talk in low hesitant tones, a courtesy offering to humility which, to him, was an infrequent companion. But, he was soon into his stride challenging our sense with his own self confidence.

'Some of you have lived close to village life and the traditions of your people. Some of you are already seriously alienated from your native cultures because of the rapid changes which are now affecting us all.'

I thought of my beautiful Misima Island, the lovely things with which I lived, the sky-tinted waters of my warm lagoon and the four lonely Australian years softened by warm and friendly companions. It was only during my week in Port Moresby that I had experienced serious hostility and rejection. I was lonely. My eyes were moist. Should I run before someone manipulated me for evil which was alien to my mind, programmed as it was by soft sounds, vivid colours and warm brown bodies? But Dr Dina was still delivering his speech with confidence; I sat, shaking with apprehension.

'Papua and New Guinea are beautiful countries with picturesque villages and gentle people. The study of man, the purpose and meaning of all this beauty is also something of value. The study of medicine, in its fullest, is the study of man in his fullest — living man in a specific environment or the study of man as he adventures into new environments and the unknown.'

The student next to me, a jet black Buka, was fast asleep. I held my breath. I was terrified that he would create shame by crashing to the floor.

'Medicine is not a cupboard full of drugs and dressings but a house with many rooms.'

A pocketful of money crashed to the floor as a student claimed a handkerchief from his pocket.

'Every one of you can find a place in the study and practice of medicine. The purpose of my first talk with you is to welcome you to your new home and to your new family and I trust that God will bless our endeavours as we start on the great adventure of establishing medical education in Papua and New Guinea.

I wished that stupid man would stop crawling around looking for his money.

'Our first medical college is small, it is simple but those

things survive which have the flexibility to change and adapt to circumstances. Small may be beautiful!'

The student in front of me, a tall hungry looking youth, was eagerly fingering a stethoscope that he had obtained by mail order from Australia.

'Do not worry about where you stand now or what you know. Step by step, piece by piece, concept by concept, you will slowly build up the knowledge and expertise necessary to be a good doctor in your own country. A heart full of love or a heart full of hate.'

The sleepy Buka next to me crashed to the floor. My numbed senses were beyond reaction. Nobody took any notice and the voice droned on.

Dr Dina finished speaking and disappeared from the platform leaving the other staff members to take over. Nobody heard. Nobody understood. Each was occupied with his own thoughts. Then it was over. Twenty dazed students fumbled their way out of the assembly and made their way into the warm sun.

* * *

I sauntered away alone, sorting out my own mixed feelings. I had always lived among beautiful things and with warm friendly people but, in Port Moresby, things had been different. Something was happening to me. The people here were meaner, the soil was meaner and dry brown hills stood where lush tropic tropical abundance should have been.

I was depressed without knowing what depression was. Instinctively, I made my way to a delicate red hibiscus scrub growing in a small green oasis.

> Flower of desire, delicate rose
> Blushing in the mud.
> Lighten the light of my solitude.

I cupped the cool flower in my hands and traced its elegant swirl with my eyes, pleased to be relieved of my own disturbed feelings. Lifting the flower off its stalk I sat down on the soft grass.

'Hello, Josie! How are you these days?'

I started out of my dreams and looked up to see Manu, a Papuan, whom I had casually met on trips to and from Australia for school.

'I saw you at the meeting just now. I'm glad you're here. It seems pretty dull don't you think?'

Manu lounged down on the grass beside me. These were Australian manners for sure. No Misima boy had ever acted like this. Indeed, it was not very proper for a boy to speak to a girl in public at all.

Defensively, I straightened myself and said,

'You are Manu Tau, one of the boys from St. Joseph's?'

Taking the hibiscus out of my hand he continued with enthusiasm,

'Yes. Remember the good times we had coming back from Australia?'

I could not remember any good times and was thinking what to say next when Manu relieved me of the responsibility by continuing his conversation.

'It's good to meet someone who talks the same language as yourself. You know what I mean? I hope we'll be good friends?'

'I'm sure we can be good friends,' I returned, 'but, I am sorry I don't know what you mean.'

'Well, you know,' said Manu, scratching the ground with his finger. 'Some of the fellows doing this medical course, they're real kanakas. I think some of them are straight out of the trees. They really don't know what day it is. You know what? The fellow who sleeps next to me chews betel nut and spits all over the place like a real kanaka. The kids who went to Australia would leave some of these for dead. Some of them sleep in their clothes and have never heard of pyjamas. I hope I'm not around if any of them ever become doctors. You can tell the kids from Australia. They're cleaner and they talk proper English. Do you know what? I've forgotten a lot of my own language. Anyhow, these village languages are of no use anymore. English is the only thing for the future.'

I thought that Manu Tau and I were both inflicted with the same illness, loneliness. He was thinking aloud and I was talking to a flower.

Long ago, the habit of agreeing with everything that a man said had been laid to rest, so I said,

'I don't see myself as any different to any other Papuan just because I've been to Australia. My parents have never worn pyjamas and would never waste money on such foolishness but they are just as clean as I am. I want to remain a true, natural Papuan and feel the same as they do. I don't want to become a miserable imitation of an Australian rejected by them and rejected by us too. I cannot stand loneliness. I must belong.'

Manu was not going to be talked down by a woman. His Papuan heart was but slightly shadowed by his Australian experience so he came back more aggressively.

'You are only kidding yourself, Josie. You just want all the money and good things of civilized society and want to drink your mother's *susu* (milk) as well. If you want to live the life of a natural Papuan like your mother or father, why don't you go back to the village and dig sweet potatoes in the sun all your life.'

Offended by the aggression and, perhaps, by the truth in his remarks, I swung to the attack. Here, I was not being lectured to by a colonial, to whom there must be no reply, but to a Papuan who was no better than I was. A Papuan who had invited himself to talk to me and who was displaying some manners that I found offensive.

'What about yourself? You're just as bad. It's rubbish saying you don't remember your own language. You were already grown up when you went to Australia. All you're trying to do is to turn your back on your own people. You're trying to make an exclusive club for those who have been to Australia.'

By this time I had risen to my feet, ready to take my leave. Manu had done likewise but for a different purpose. The conversation had not gone to his liking. Girls did not talk to him like that and this was a new experience. He had been looking forward to a pleasant relationship with an Australian educated girl who spoke the same language as himself and who was willing to join the club. He was disappointed but he was not going to take defeat so easily.

'I had better go. It's nearly lunch time,' I said, clipping another hibiscus and putting it carelessly in my hair.

'I'll see you at the next class, Josie.'

'Sure, see you,' I said and quickened my pace as I made towards the female students' home. I felt much better now. At least I belonged. I took the hibiscus out of my hair as I passed through the gates of the home.

> Flower of desire, delicate rose
> Blushing in the mud.
> Lighten the light of my solitude.

* * *

Dr Dina had experience in both Papua and New Guinea. His experience in Papua extended back to when he worked with Dr Strong to establish the first Native Medical Assistant training in the country. He spoke three Papuan languages and was able to identify closely with the people. His present work caused some jealousy or apprehension among aspiring colonials. Some of them did not want to see any advances made unless their own name was attached to it and others had dreams of personal academic grandeur. But most of them were just reactionaries who were very comfortable in their colonial world and did not welcome change. But Dr Dina was usually a step ahead of their moves. As he established the various courses, he always managed to keep enough people on side to see him through the six years that it took to establish medical and nursing education in Papua and New Guinea. Some top colonial officials, including the Australian minister, supported the development, and several doctors were behind it all the way.

For the first year only a few lecturers were required. These were mostly foreign doctors and science teachers collected together by Dr Dina from different sources.

The introduction of medical education for doctors in Papua and New Guinea was not just a question of establishing a school of medicine in the Papuan Medical College. It also involved the introduction of all of the ancillary training necessary to run a major hospital, and several rural services where doctors could be educated and trained. It also required vast changes to nursing and other services within the teaching hospital. 'It was no use relying forever on foreigners'. A constant battle raged about the introduction of student nurses and clinical supervisors into the wards to replace the untrained orderlies who were firmly entrenched. Some Australian doctors and nurses resisted the development of nursing education but, after two or three years, the obvious became more obvious and they grew tired of fighting or bowed out.

During our introduction to medicine we experienced one novelty that I did not appreciate. Dr Dina decided that the medical students should work in the hospital wards early in the course, so that we could become familiar with what was going on around us. This was all right until some foreigners decided that the lady medical students should dress as student nurses while in the wards, as otherwise, we might disturb some of the more timid male patients. The fatal day arrived and I was dressed in a nurse's uniform. I felt like a cheat and a fraud. Like a mud man at a fancy dress ball.

I was too timid to oppose Dr Dina's orders. A Papuan girl is conditioned to obey authority without question. Self-consciously I made my way to the hospital. The wards were full of patients and, at night, there were more people on the floors and on the grounds outside than there were in beds. At times a patient would sleep on a concrete floor while a relative slept in the bed. The rough fibro walls were liberally splattered with red betel-nut spit and the nurses complained that there was no running water at the wards to wash their hands. In some wards double-bunked beds had been installed in an effort to beat the restriction on numbers by spreading upwards.

My dreams of nursing had been shattered long before this but I was not prepared for the native toilets. The toilets were at floor level and were supposed to flush, but some were blocked and not working. The place was littered with human waste and the walls were painted with it. People cleaned themselves as best they could in the unfamiliar surroundings. Some athletic types performed extraordinary contortions and cleaned themselves directly on any object that did not move.

This was an elaborate native hospital of the 1960s and, except for the toilets which were probably the worst, better than most. It boasted modern operating theatres, capable surgeons and a range of specialist services.

About two hundred yards from the cluster of buildings of the native hospital was a trim cottage hospital, complete with modern conveniences, and intended for the use of the colonial population. The professional staff were foreigners. I only caught a glimpse of its mysterious interior when I carried a bunch of flowers to a lady. Attached to this hospital were X-ray and pathology departments which served both natives and Europeans. In between the two establishments, suitable architectural barriers had been erected, such as a morgue, workshop, boiler room and stores.

* * *

The medical students were in the lecture room to meet a new doctor, and to discuss the hospital experience. Students were lounging on their chairs, talking in ones and twos, or hurriedly brushing up on notes for their own presentation.

Manu was there with the others. Big hair, light skin, island shirt and loud talk. He liked to talk to me in private but, in public, it was rather unmanly to take too much notice of a girl. Manu was older than I was but he reminded me of some of my younger brothers, boasting about a tree they had climbed or a football game they had won. At times Manu would locate me on his mental radar screen and then carry on a lively conversation with other male students but, I suspected, partly for my benefit as well. I had a difficult time adjusting to life in Port Moresby and many of the values that I had previously taken for granted were being challenged. Manu's extravagent statements and unusual ideas helped me to look at myself less seriously. I was not impressed by many of Manu's arguments but, still, he was no fool. A clown can make you cry with laughter while a fool can make you cry with pain. Above all, Manu treated me gently. He made no demands and I found our talks a relaxation in a new, strained world. At the time I could not have tolerated any relationship in which my sensitive emotions had to be defended against assault of any sort. I wanted to swim free, completely unrestrained, staying cool in the warm waters of desire flowing over me.

By now, Dr Dina had taken up his accustomed place on the raised platform at the head of the class. He was fond of conducting his classes sitting down, saying that he did not see any reason why he should not enjoy some of the privileges enjoyed by the students. The new doctor, Dr Sidney, was self-consciously fidgeting on a seat alongside Dr Dina.

'May I introduce Dr Sidney who has joined the staff and will be responsible for the teaching of community health. Now, I invite you to make comments about the short hospital experience that you have just completed.'

The students looked from one to the other each hoping that someone else would speak first. A serious looking boy from the New Guinea islands began to speak.

'Many of the people I spoke to said the food was no good. The people are accustomed to eating hard foods in the villages. When they come to hospital they are given wet, soft foods to eat. They do not like to eat these new foods when they are sick. They want the hard foods like sweet potatoes, yams, and taro that they eat in the villages. People don't want to have strange tasting food when they are sick.'

Most of the early speakers repeated complaints that they had heard.

'The people would prefer to die in the village rather than be cut up in the hospital.'

'The hospital is filthy. The government should look after it better.'

'It was a waste of time. We did not know what we were looking at or what we were supposed to do.'

So it went on for about fifteen minutes. Dr Dina and Dr Sidney made no comments. The students were then called on to present their ideas on different aspects of the hospital. Each student had been given a subject a few days previously. These presentations covered first impressions of medicine and hospitals, and some of them had been thoughtfully prepared. Dr Dina and Dr Sidney commented briefly after each speaker.

My turn eventually arrived. I was terrified. My subject was 'The patient and his personal feelings'. My mouth was dry and the words came slowly. For about ten minutes I read out a lot of things I had copied from an article I had found in the library. As I stumbled towards the end I felt compelled to lift my head and say a few words of my own.

'Now, when I think of people and some of the problems

that affect them, I feel that life is full of sun and shadows, happiness and sorrow. The shadows can make the sun more beautiful and dull moments are the contrasts of happiness. Good experiences can be satisfying and our spirits are high. Bad experiences can dampen our spirits and make the heart grow cold. Sickness can be a bad experience which gives contrast to life and, also, it can make life more beautiful.'

'I used to think that life had to be lived only in happiness and with beautiful things, as that was the only life I had known. Now I have a new feeling and I am not sure that beautiful things and contentment are the only important things. I now have a feeling that I want to be free. Free to express myself in faith or humility. Free to live in equality. Once I thought that my feelings ended with warmth, beauty and the approval of foreigners. Now I don't want these alone if it means that my mind remains in slavery and other people control my thoughts. When I read what I have copied from others I feel deprived, but when I speak for myself my heart grows warm. I feel pleasure after the pain.'

I sat down. My eyes were wet and I was full of emotion. I could not cope. Relieved but frightened I waited in shame for Dr Dina to pronounce his judgement. But, to my surprise, when it came it was not the voice of Dr Dina thundering from exalted heights, but the voice of Dr Sidney meekly proclaiming,

'I must apologise for being a cause of the problems voiced by Miss Abaijah. Colonial problems spring from human needs and human personalities and they are just as fundamental and just as complex. All of you not only carry the bonds of colonialism, from which you must seek your own release but also, in this country, populations will increase, slums will be built, foreign vices will be introduced, diseases and tensions will develop, and Papuans and New Guineans will demand the 'cargo' that will destroy their native style of living and make them toiling slaves. Still, generations will live and die and within the reality of their own lives, as master or slave, they must seek their own happiness, their own harmony. Change is inevitable. It may not be pleasant. It may scar our minds or it may be the pain that lightens our fulfilment.'

The meeting was over and I was tired. I wanted room to think, I wanted to hear Dr Dina speak, as he was strong and direct and I trusted him. Still, I was pleased that Dr Sidney had answered. His meek voice was a gentle breeze across the lagoon, not a thunderstorm. He seemed to understand what I was talking about when I did not understand myself. I badly needed a strong shoulder to lean on just now. I hoped I would meet Dr Sidney. Would he be interested in me like Dr Dina was? Dr Dina was too tough, too active, too practical to lean on, but he gave me the strength and security that I needed. A hand touched my shoulder.

'Excuse me, Miss Abaijah, may I meet you before you leave?'

I was too upset to reply.

'May I congratulate you on your presentation,' said Dr Sidney, 'it was fine. Dr Dina was impressed also. He said a few words from the heart are better than volumes from books.'

Recovering slowly I smiled and said,

'Thank you for being kind to me. I would have died if anyone had scolded me then.'

As Dr Sidney moved off I called after him, 'Goodbye, Dr Sidney. See you.'

I walked up the concrete path leading to the home. Manu ran up alongside of me as he often did. I could not open my mouth. I silently pursued my course as though he was not there. When we reached the gate, we parted.

'See you later, Josie!'

'See you later, Manu!'

3

Conflict

*L*iving in Port Moresby was like learning life in a foreign country. The lagoons, the palms and the fresh rivers had gone, and in their place streamed motor cars, dust and purpose. Friends were exchanged for strangers and peace for violence. The races rubbed shoulders but shared no common ground. Neighbours were hidden dangers like the submerged rocks of a lagoon. Loneliness was not a horror to hide from but an art to be acquired. Beauty came in pay packets and not from God. The sweet frangipani was here, not as the sensual fragrance of a woman in love but as a spray in a can.

Sunday. The day all Papuans dress and go out. Breath and flesh must mingle or the spirit dies. If there is nothing more pressing to do, there is always Church.

Sunday. The day Australians want to spend in loneliness. Lonely barbeques in the jungle, lonely picnics on the sand or, best of all, lonely newspapers in lonely houses. The Australians used newspapers like we used people. To them the paper was warm and friendly. They did not go to church or mingle with the people, but stayed in their homes and read the newspaper. There they found new cars, grand furniture and an unbelievable array of gadgets to buy, and, enticing deals for new houses on strange land; like buying a Papuan bride, but cold bricks not warm flesh was the prize.

The queue to the newspaper shop was a hundred metres long and every soul a foreigner. For a few cents plus air freight, they would buy their culture and their entertainment for the day. But, today, the Qantas plane from Australia was late and the colonials were angry. There was nowhere to park the cars and there was no relief from the stinking heat.

'Good morning, Miss Abaijah, I didn't expect to see you here.'

I defensively glanced to the side. It was Dr Sidney waiting in the queue for the Sunday newspapers to arrive. Dr Sidney had that freshly-showered look common to many foreigners here. Short shorts, a sky-blue, servant-ironed shirt, and plastic sandals completed the material adornments. He seemed anxious to talk to me so I hesitated while I summed up the situation. A Papuan girl must give consideration to every possible consequence for every encounter, especially with people from foreign tribes. There were disapproving looks from some of the foreigners who did not think it was proper conduct to be friendly with a Papuan girl in public. Others were just angry because the papers were late. Most of them were sure that kanaka inefficiency must be the cause of their inconvenience.

I had formed the opinion that a feature of the behaviour of some colonials, in Port Moresby, was that they either wanted to seduce you or to insult you. So, some of the first skills that I had to acquire were defensive measures to divert both of these unpleasant excesses. Even the women wanted you to behave like their shadow or to treat you with great ignore. And, of course, a native girl was too unsanitary for too intimate an association. For many years the ocean at white Ela Beach was reserved for foreigners and the Pacific Ocean kept 'pure' for Europeans.

'Good morning, Dr Sidney,' I replied pleasanty, 'I'm on my way to Church.'

The anonymity and discomfort of a newspaper queue encourages tense nerves and expressions of opinions which would be unwise at the government office the next day. A tall, hungry looking man was growling to a short, half-blind man next to him:

'These bloody kanakas must be the stupidest, laziest bastards on God's earth. They haven't even got enough energy to go to the airport to pick up a few papers. God knows how long we'll be here.'

'The plane might be late,' ventured the half-blind one, timidly.

'I don't think so,' said the tall one, 'I heard the plane about an hour ago. You can't trust a bloody kanaka to do anything properly except eat and sleep.'

The timid one was nervous and Dr Sidney was nervous too; our conversation had been interrupted by this boisterous competition.

'You should not take these Europeans seriously,' said Dr Sidney. Australians referred to themselves as Europeans, as though they were slightly ashamed of being Australian-made.

'Most of them mean well, but talking like that is a bit of a boost for their ego. They shout out the same sort of abuse to themselves at football matches back home.'

I smiled at Dr Sidney because I liked him. He was friendly and something attracted me to him, but I was not sure yet how I felt.

'Don't worry,' I said. 'I have become used to this sort of talk since coming to Port Moresby. I really don't get upset about it. That is, after I got over the first shock.'

'But, it must make you bitter sometimes,' consoled Dr Sidney as he pressed my hand gently.

'I suppose it does,' I said, drawing my hand away and putting my bible in it. 'Before I came to Moresby I thought white people were great. People to be looked up to. It hurts me to be rejected and I really am ashamed to be always thought of as being dirty and stupid. I want to like everybody and be liked.'

I was embarrassed by my long reply but I wanted to tell Dr Sidney how I felt. It gave me relief. It was friendly and intimate. But I must leave now. I was beginning to feel uneasy.

'Goodbye, Dr Sidney. See you.'

'Goodbye, Miss Abaijah. I wish I had half your luck. I'll change places with you any day.'

'Okay, we'll see,' and I left the long white line of foreigners to wait for their newspapers and continued on my way to Church.

* * *

I sat in the Church of England at Boroko, in the residential area of Port Moresby where most of the colonials lived. Going to Church on Sundays was a natural part of life. It gave balance to the days and filled some of our basic needs for expression and warmth. While I sat waiting for the service to start my mind strayed to former days.

When I was growing up on Misima Island, I always attended the Methodist church. The early colonials divided Papua into religious zones so the Christian religion of a Papuan was largely determined by the place where he or she was born. The islands off the East coast of Papua were in the Methodist zone so everyone there was a Methodist. But Wamira village was Church of England. Although I spoke both the Wedau and Misima languages, I regarded myself as Misima as I remembered little of Wamira and the Misima people claimed me as their own. But, when the time came for me to go to school in Australia, the colonials decided that, as I was born in Wamira village, it was fit and proper for me to attend a Church of England school.

Sunday church on Misima Island was a big event and everybody looked forward to Sundays with pleasure. They dressed in their best plumes and leisurely walked over the lawns and along the flower lined paths to the church. Everybody mingled with everybody and sang and laughed as one. The fat, *rami*-draped native pastor, was king for an hour or two. He exhorted us, in our own living tongue and with the vivid parables from native life, to be virtuous in the service of God and generous in our support of the church. And, the people lustily praised the Lord in deep throated harmonies.

'Iesu be praised, a friend is dead.'
'Iesu be praised, a new church is rising.'
'Iesu be praised, a son has been born.'

'Iesu be praised, our gaoled deacon, who walked after
the 9 o'clock curfew, has returned and is cleansed.'
'Iesu be praised, the lagoon is full and the pastor is
fat.'
'Hallelujah Christ is highest,
Hallelujah our new bell rings,
Hallelujah heaven's flowering,
Hallelujah shout and give.'

Grass skirts swirled, ramis tightened and voices rolled
through the generations.

Christ is King come and adore him.
Christ is King and his gift is love.

I glanced up from my holy book and was ashamed at what
I saw. That cheeky Geva boy was smiling at me. Had he no
shame in the House of God? I glanced again and he was still
beaming. *Hemarai* (shame), my body was burning. *Hemarai*,
I wished he would stop staring at me. He would not have
shamed me in the public gaze. He would not have dared to
take such liberties if the people's distraction had been less
complete. I would teach him a lesson. I would never talk to
him again!

The service finished and the prosperous pastor made his
way to the sand at the Church step and beamed on us all as
we streamed out. He was conscious that his thriving person
augered well for us all. 'God's in his heaven, the pastor is fat
and all's well with the world.' Out into the glorious warm
shade of the palms. People were everywhere talking and
laughing. Never ever a person alone. We wandered down to
the beach, around by the lagoon, across the fresh stream,
past the rocks where the midget spirits lived, and home.

Sunday at home was like a church without a pastor.
People, people, always people. Betel-nut chewing, red spit,
laughter, talking, guitars, singing, mats unwrapped and
uninterrupted sleep.

* * *

'All men are sinners,' boomed the tall, well-endowed Englishman who held sway as priest at the tiny, wooden, iron-

roofed Church of England at Boroko. 'Great is our evil and great are the sins of the world,' the priest shouted as he rested his protesting muscles on the edge of the pulpit like a pregnant woman washing clothes. The tin roof of the little church made it like a copra drier and holy sweat ran down the face of the preacher and half the congregation. If only I could sweat, too, I would not be so ashamed of my sins. The preacher and the people must have been sweating because of their sins but my skin was as dry as a cool papaya. I was too ashamed to look around and so I stared straight ahead. I never knew before how evil I was and how much I had offended God: the God who walked by my side always, who worked miracles for me and was my constant companion and friend.

The fraught preacher became nervous when his hawk-like glance brushed my person and, as he looked at me with yellow eyes, I was nervous too. At times he broke into two or three sentences of baby talk to ensure that the message of sin and damnation reached down to me, the lowliest of the poor sinners before him.

The service eventually finished and I respectfully waited for the twenty or so foreigners to leave the church first. I then crept out as unobtrusively and apologetically as possible. Once in the grounds, I was surprised to see that the small, bare church ground was already devoid of people. Everyone was hurriedly making for their Japanese motor cars parked in the street below. With a sense of relief, I pointed my person in a straight line for the medical college, about two kilometres away, and I was preparing to take off with haste when, to my dismay, a small group of church elders emerged from the shade of the church building and blocked my way. One of them, a tall, superior-looking woman, separated herself from the rest of the group and headed me off.

'Hello, Josephine,' she said with an affected English accent that was difficult for me to understand.

'I know you are Josephine Abaijah, the eldest daughter of Abaijah,' she continued. 'You don't mind me calling you Josephine, do you? You know I was at Wamira when your dear mother and father were married. Your mother was such a lovely girl. I think you must take after your father, you know.'

There is no need to do any talking when you are conversing with this type of colonial. They do not really expect you to contribute anything to a conversation and they just babble on, regardless, pursuing their own particular purpose.

'I am Miss Harris from the Mission. You may have heard of me?'

I had not heard of Miss Harris, but I had no intention of telling her so. I guessed that she was some sort of a social worker, a general 'do gooder' as they were affectionately known.

'Good morning, Miss Harris. It is a lovely day, isn't it? I am pleased to meet you here. You must know all about Papua after all of the years you have spent here.'

I had long ago learned that mild flattery was the only accepted form of conversation with many 'do gooders' here. Any expressions of original ideas or opinions, by a Papuan, were greeted like words from a talking donkey.

'Dear Josephine, I have devoted my life to the Papuan people. I love them dearly. They are such uncomplicated, gentle people. My first years in Papua were spent in Boianai and I have been in love with the country ever since.'

'Do you speak my language, Wedau, Miss Harris?' I enquired. Some of them did speak it to some extent and they loved to show their ability.

'No, I can't speak Wedau properly but I would love to learn, Josephine. I must some day but there never seems to be enough time for everything.'

I was getting uneasy as I knew from experience that this long preamble was leading up to something unpleasant.

'Please, don't think I'm rude, Josephine,' the English accent had slipped a bit, 'but what I have to say is for your own good. They thought that I could talk to you like your mother but I find it very unpleasant.'

I felt terrible. I must have committed some terrible offence in this strange church.

'You see, Josephine, we don't encourage natives to come to this church.' The English accent had disappeared so I could now clearly understand her talk. 'Really, it is only a very small matter. I don't know what all the fuss is about. You see, we encourage the natives to go to the church at Koki. Koki is a native place. You will meet your own people there. This church at Boroko is more suitable for Europeans. You see, the people here really have different interests from yours. You do understand what I am saying, dear Josephine?'

'Yes, I understand you, Miss Harris. I have just returned from Australia and I had a lovely time with the Church of England there. The priest was lovely to me and we were great friends. I thought it might be the same here. I'm sorry I made such a stupid mistake, Miss Harris. I won't come again. Goodbye.'

Miss Harris was in tears and, for once, was unable to speak. This gave me the opportunity I wanted. I turned away and walked, through the colonial homes of Port Moresby which covered the swamps of Boroko, until I reached the medical college which was now my only home.

I made my way to the shed I shared with twenty other girls and threw myself on my wooden bench and cried.

> Warm, deep, placid, clean,
> Rainbows flow in rainbow streams.
> Sun, clouds, earth, sky,
> Rainbows live and rainbows die.

* * *

There was trouble in the hospital grounds. Not that that was anything unusual. This time it was due to the death of a boy who had died from snake bite poison after being bitten while hunting wild pigs in heavy jungle.

This boy had been carried a long distance on a stretcher made of saplings and jungle twine and finished his journey to the Port Moresby hospital, bumping on the back of a truck over rough rural roads. When he arrived in hospital he was in a critical condition and his breathing was partially paralysed. He died while the nurse was pumping a rubber apparatus that gave him air. When he died, the village people were very upset and some of them blamed the nurse for the misadventure, while others blamed the hospital administration. But all of them blamed some sort of hostile magic for the death. Unfortunately, on top of this, the hospital authorities would not release the boy's body for burial as they wanted a *post mortem* carried out.

The village people felt all deaths deeply and the whole community shared in the loss. The sudden death of a young man, at the gate of full manhood, provoked a very emotional reaction not only with the family involved but also with the whole village community as well. A loss to one family was a loss to every family and the strength of the community was the strength of the village. Everyone lived in the gaze of every person in the village, so the loss was a loss to all.

Their son had died and they needed to pour out their grief in unfettered emotion and love. They wanted to handle the body as in life and decorate it with familiar beauty. The boy's body would then be put to rest with the things he loved, in the warm soil of his native home. But, instead, the doctors wanted to cut the top off his head to search his brain and cut his body up. The people would then be told that he died of snake poison, something that they already knew as did everyone from every village in the district. But the doctors would say nothing about the magic that made that particular snake poison their particular boy, which was the problem of their gravest concern.

Things were near riot proportions by the time I arrived: a large number of people had assembled outside the morgue, and native trucks barred the way as the people threatened violence if anyone touched their son. Talking to weeping women, at the edge of the crowd, I learned what the confrontation was about. I was also told that the people would kill anyone who cut open the body of their son or denied to him the rights of traditional burial. Several men were arguing with the police, who were out in force with their white police masters. Villagers were shouting in Motu, and the police were shouting in Pidgin English. Neither party could understand a word of the other, so noise was the important element. The police liked to make Papuans talk in Pidgin English, a colonial language used in ex-German New Guinea, but these village people did not understand.

One woman had slashed her body in protest and was bleeding freely as she sat on the ground and others were threatening to do the same. Men were calling for the body of the boy and were threatening death to anyone who obstructed them from claiming the body of their son. Two young girls of about 17 years, who were close relatives of the dead boy, had sharp knives in their hands and were threatening to plunge them into their breasts, while others restrained them and wrestled the knives from their hands.

The dialogue between the Australian police and the village people was meaningless sound. What did the stupid Papuans know about the due process of law or the value of scientific investigation? What did the stupid colonials know about the needs of a Papuan boy to rest unmolested in the warm soil of his own land, with the sound of the laughter of life and close to the eternal beauty of his native home?

A pair of unseen hands pushed me against a blue uniform and this seemed to encourage a tall Australian policeman to recite to me,

'You can't take the body away from here until the doctors say so. I don't know when that'll be. Tomorrow is Saturday and that's a bad day, so's Sunday. Tell these people there's no need to worry. The body will be kept in the 'ice box'. They must be sensible and keep order or we'll have to arrest them. There's nothing they can do now.'

As things turned out, this event had an important effect on my life. For the first time I became involved in a direct confrontation with colonial authorities and, for the first time, I was called upon to speak on behalf of village people. It was my first political adventure.

As a good colonial subject, I was most respectful of foreign authority. I looked up at the police officer and timidly suggested:

'Please, sir, these people cannot understand English and they want me to speak for them. They want to know why they have to wait until Monday before they can take their dead son. They are sad now, not on Monday, so they want their boy now.'

The tall police officer looked me over as though I was a small pup that had got itself under his feet. But, before he could think of an appropriate answer, a younger Australian officer pushed forward and took over the conversation.

'*Yu meri bilong we?*' (Where do you come from, woman?). I knew what the younger man was saying but I could not reply in Pidgin.

'I am a student at the medical college here and I am sorry I cannot speak Pidgin. Could you please talk to me in English?' My words seemed to infuriate the man and his face went red as he shouted,

'Like hell I will,' but he continued just the same. 'You Papuans give me the irrits. You should be kicked in the behind and made to bloody well learn Pidgin whether you like it or not. I need a kanaka with a 'big head' right now like I need a hole in the head. *Nau, yu save gut, sapos yu laik tok long police master yu mus lanim tok kanaka pas taim. Save gut, Your Royal Highness.*' (Now, you savvy good, suppose you like talk to a white police officer you must learn to talk pidgin first time. Savvy good, Your Royal Highness.')

The crowd had grown quiet. They could not follow the gist of the conversation but they thought that their case was now being put and they were surprised at the animated responses I had evoked.

The older policeman, who had given a good imitation of a dead log up to now, suddenly joined the conversation again,

'I don't mind talking to you in English, Miss. What is it you want to say?'

I had never stood up to a colonial officer before and I had always been encouraged to believe that it was never a question of right or wrong. It was just a matter of shut-up and do what you are told. If a native became involved in an incident with a colonial officer in Papua, it was possible that the officer would change his hat and become his judge. This would not happen with the police in Port Moresby but, still, speaking up to a foreign police officer was an awesome experience for an inexperienced Papuan girl.

'Please, sir, these people just want to take their boy home. He is dead and nothing more can be done for him here.'

The tall, stern policeman was acting very properly and patiently now. His experience prompted him to treat the diminutive, English speaking native girl with caution. He was not going to let his hot-headed young colleague call the tune any more.

'I've already told you that the body cannot be released until the doctors give permission.'

I felt that I must do my best for the people so I continued with my pleas. But, while I was talking, I noticed that a strange change had come over the crowd and the village people were slowly melting away.

'Thank you for talking to me, sir. I'm only speaking for the people. These village people say that if the doctors were not sure that he was dying of snake poison, when he was alive, then they should not have treated him for snake bite poison. The people just want to take their son while he is freshly dead, with the same body that he had in life and bury him properly in their own way.'

Something was definitely wrong. The people had vanished like a brief tropical twilight. The tall, stern policeman had become aware of the change of mood and had turned around to assess the situation. He was no longer taking any notice of me. A voice behind me whispered,

'*Kekeni, rakatania. Hanua taudia ese, mase tauna idia guia vadaeni. Rakatania! Lao, kerere ia vara garina.*' (Miss, leave it. The village people have taken the body away in a truck. Leave it, get away or you might get into trouble?')

Accustomed to Papuan ways, I determined that the villagers, with the help of their Papuan friends inside the hospital, had taken the body from under the noses of the police and it was now bumping through the night towards the village. The police were guarding an empty morgue.

The night would know no quiet and the people would know no sleep until their son was at rest in his native soil. They would then commence the long preparation for the feast of the thousands that would see the last rite for the dead boy who had been killed by an evil magic just as he was to take the final step into manhood. After this his spirit would be free with the spirits of his clan and the spirits of his tribe.

I now became frightened. I had visions of being arrested so I also slipped away into the night. As I went, I furtively glanced in the direction of the tall, stern policeman. I thought I saw him smile but, for me, no more risks. Now that there was enough distance between me and the police for me to run, run I did. Over the hard brown Moresby clay, as I once ran over the soft green grass of Misima.

I lay face down on my wooden bench. What had happened to me? I did not know then, but I now know that I had taken the first step on the long road to politics. I was ashamed of speaking up against the white police but I was proud to be identified with the village people. Was not authority dry, dead, colonial Port Moresby and the villagers the colour, the sounds, the scent of my native home? I loved that beauty and I missed it so much. I loved those village people. How could I live without them? Growing to a woman in Port Moresby had not been as joyful as I had expected it to be. Port Moresby belonged to foreigners and the virus of white colonialism, while the villages belonged to happiness and harmony. The warmth and rhythm of rural Papua was the warmth and rhythm of my childhood, deeply branded on my soul.

Was this new excitement good or bad? Time might tell. I thought of the boy who had died so young. I was so pleased he was not cut up like a pig. Restless and hot, I fell asleep.

* * *

As the year moved on, I found myself thinking about Dr Dina and Dr Sidney a lot as I was encouraged by their understanding and interest in me. Dr Sidney was a single man from a comfortable middle-class professional family. He had been to the right schools and had a comfortable journey through university. He knew the 'right' people and belonged to good societies but he steered clear of the pub and the club and did not mix easily with the underdogs of his own society. He tried hard to talk nonchalantly about sport and common things but his soft, unpractised hands made it likely that he was more at home with the book than the bat. Polite, quiet, reliable and readily approachable, he was the perfect. gentleman. I felt that we were the subjects for his service to humanity but that he was too moulded in propriety to be one of us.

Dr Dina was the tamed rascal. From working class Sydney, he gave his occupation as a 'professional foreigner'. He was older and more experienced than Dr Sidney. He had children of his own and complex family relationships that only a Papuan could entertain or comprehend. I mixed easily within the family consortium and thrived on relationships which were almost as complex as my own. His children told me in confidence that he was a placid, quiet and gentle man who never raised a hand against them. On the other hand, a few of his white contemporaries whispered to me that he was a real cad and that there were far nicer types around. Tough, uncompromising and unpredictable they said. He left school after one year of high school, and worked his way through universities, built houses in his spare time, and specialised in getting things done.

I felt secure with Dr Dina. With him, I was an equal and my self-esteem was high. I was something of value. These were strange new feelings for a Papuan girl who had been nurtured to feel that the slave mentality of colonialism was the only reality and that the colonial master was superior in every way.

It should not have been hard to choose between the two foreigners who figured large in my new life but why was there a need for a Papuan girl to make a choice at all? My dreams were getting out of hand. I found it hard to differentiate between dreams and reality. Where was the curtain drawn when day disrobed and dipped into the night? Hushed in the hazy twilight, I was touched by an inscrutable spirituality that was master to my waking mind. I must listen to the voice that controlled my destiny. I must follow certain paths.

* * *

I was sitting on the verandah of a thatched house, in a coastal village a distance from the town. The house consisted of one room which served all purposes for a family of ten. At the rear, was a small partition that marked off a place for an open fire while, at the front, beyond the open doorway was a verandah which was the main meeting place for visitors. Cool and protected, it looked out over the white sands of the village. Most village activities took place on this white sand. Children played, dancers danced, politicians shouted, lovers glanced, women were beaten, God was praised and sly grog traded. All was seen in the lazy gaze of the village with no detail trivial enough to be overlooked or important enough to raise an eyebrow.

The villagers were in a happy mood and I was there to

enjoy the fun and to heal a few of my own wounds. Pigs, wallabies, fish, turtles, nuts, fruits, vegetables, bandicoots, fowls, sago and foreign rice, flour and meat had been arriving in this village during the past few days.

There were protesting pigs, carried upside down with feet lashed around poles. Turtles flapped in the light air, resting on their shells immobile, helpless and exposed. Domestic fowls, legs tied with jungle twine, dozed away the balance of life while dead *kepoka* (bush hens) were scorched to stop decay. Yams, taro, sugar cane, papaya, green oranges, pineapples, watermelons, tapioka, sago flour, bananas, bread fruit, avocado and the rest were crowded on temporary platforms on the sand with the ubiquitous banana leaf for plate and covering. And still the lazy glances of the people that missed nothing and the eyebrows that never raised.

Girls had the aroma of love, oils of beauty, garlands of fragrance, grass skirts low on naked hips, tatooed breasts in sensuous garlands and flaming hibiscus in burnished hair. All of the men and women were gaily adorned. The young children mimicked the adults in small groups around the edge of the major activity and everyone had an equal right to be involved. Happiness and laughter did not belong to any particular group, and everyone participate according to his or her mood.

Usually I danced with the people but this time it was different. Manu was sitting with me on the open verandah watching the feasting and dancing. A Papuan girl had to be in a certain mood before she would let her hair 'up' and dance in front of an uncertain suitor whom she was not trying to impress.

Lately, Manu had become much more serious and he was now talking about marriage and life together, subjects that brought me no pleasure. I was defensive about these new developments. But, after six months in Moresby, I was slowly learning to talk about unpleasant matters that I preferred to ignore. In the past, while I was growing up, matters ignored usually disappeared. Now, other people were insisting that some things had to be faced and I was learning to deal with this crudity. Manu was beginning to feel the strain of our undetermined relationship and was in an argumentative mood. At that moment, he was venting his feelings on the staff of the medical college.

'They're all right,' Manu said tersely, 'but they are just the do-gooders who you find everywhere. They get a big kick out of up-lifting someone. It makes them feel good. In any case, what they are doing is just a part of the panic to get out of the country. If they were genuine they would have started this sort of education fifty or a hundred years ago. In the past they did not show any interest in our progress. Why all the panic now? They thought that all of the good jobs were for them and they had no interest in teaching us anything. It only took a few years of schooling here and a few years at high school in Australia to prepare us. This could have been done fifty or a hundred years ago.'

I did not believe that this was entirely true and Manu was threatening my image of Dr Dina and others I trusted. Friends who were my only hope in the new world.

'I don't believe you and I don't want to discuss the matter any more. I came here to be happy not to be morbid about colonialism and its past sins.'

Manu met aggression with aggression, but then he would suddenly take control of himself, cool down and try to cool me down at the same time. But, now he had been offended and he reacted,

'You don't want to discuss anything that is unpleasant to yourself. You don't want to face life and solve its problems. You just want to live on dreams.'

I thought for a moment, turned to look towards the people on the sand, and said,

'I was a lot happier when I lived on dreams than I am now. What is so important about analysing everything that the colonials do? You and I were born to be colonial slaves. Why don't you accept it and make your own happiness within that? You and I are nobodies. At least the village people are free in their own traditions. We are nothing but coloured, third rate Australians trying to grab at the things that they are dangling before our eyes. We will always be nobodies so let us break through to our own happiness as we are. If we don't we will be failures because we will die cold and lonely and be buried in Port Moresby slime. Even in death, I don't want to be a fake or a freak. I want to be me.'

I was upset but Manu was becoming accustomed to my outbursts and sat silent. I was born to be happy and to love without question. Now, I was forced to accept alternatives to happiness and adapt to a reality in which happiness was only a reflection of other moods of life.

'Don't worry about it, Josie,' Manu soothed. 'I don't know why I always go off the deep end when I'm with you. I guess I'm just trying to show off most of the time. I'd feel much more secure if I could turn your thoughts to mine. I would feel there were no barriers between us then. You see, Josie, I love you. I suppose you will laugh at me for saying that and that it's just cheap talk. But, no matter what you say or think, I've never said that to any other girl. And I don't think I ever will.'

I looked away at the dancers, while I searched for a suitable answer. I was caught in my own sea trap and could not swim out. Once I could hide in the cave of silence but not any more. I had encouraged Manu to this point and now I had to explain my presence. I needed companionship and Manu had given this to me, but being in love was something I had chosen to ignore. I turned my gaze slowly to Manu and held his eyes in mine. Every moment was important to me as I fought for the right answer. He was a grown man but to me he was a small boy. A surrogate brother, which was a ruse, adopted by Papuan girls, to classify a male companion into a category in which sex was taboo. Someone to keep them company on special occasions, do odd jobs and act for them outside of the wall of restrictions that was built around their own lives. Messengers who were rewarded with smiles. The closer they came to being a brother the more distant they became as a lover.

'It's very nice of you to talk to me like this,' I said cautiously. I did not believe in the western idea that being in love was a spiritual experience sparkling with heavenly dew. Being in love, to a Papuan girl, could be brutally physical, terminal and complete. It was with these ideas that I continued to frame my reply.

'Manu,' I said quietly as I was taking great liberties talking in this manner. 'I wish I could say that I loved you but I do not know what love is. Not the way that you mean it. Love to a Papuan girl means marriage, children and life as a married woman. Are you asking me to have physical love with you, marry you, have your children and give up my life to serve yours?'

The drums were incessant like the beat of my heart, the dance was swaying like the mist in my brain, the dancers were lovers touching and parting, the laughter was life fostered for feeling and the drummers drummed on with the passions of night. Relief was a lover's deep breath by my side but love was a luxury I could not afford. A satisfaction that could only be paid for in sorrow. The price was too high for a coward to pay.

'I love you too, Manu, but not in the way of the foreigners. I love you like a brother and more than a friend but I cannot give myself to physical love. I hope some day we can love without fear. If we love together it will be the fresh love of flesh to flesh, seed to seed. I could not stand us ending in physical love and sour dreams. Love to me is the beginning, not the end.'

Manu did not flare up like he usually did when I opposed his views but this was not a usual conversation. I had never talked about sex to any man. How could I get out of the situation that I had caused without offence to Manu or damage to myself? I needed time to think. I always needed time to think. I must think about the alternatives. I must have room to breathe.

Manu said nothing. Was he satisfied or was he concealing a damaging aggression? He put some food, that he had been nibbling, back on the bowl, slowly got to his feet, walked down the complaining steps and mingled with the crowd. A part of me was walking with him. The dancers slowed and the music quietened. I sat alone.

Later in the evening, I caught a glimpse of Manu on the beach, boisterously drinking alcohol with some of the young doubtfuls of the village. I had to exercise severe caution so I sought out some village women returning to Moresby to accompany me home. I had to slip away like a bamboo shoot between protecting palms until I was delivered into the arms of the only lover I would know this night — my dry, wooden bed. And, tomorrow would be another day.

4

A sensuous moment

*P*apua is a country of about 140 000 square kilometres. At
this time it was controlled as a colony of Australia and
jointly administered by that country, and the ex-German
colony of New Guinea, a United Nations trust territory.
Students at the Papuan Medical College were from both
countries. All colonial officials, including Ministers and Administrators, referred to the natives as Papuans or New
Guineans respectively, or collectively as Papuans and New
Guineans.

We, the first year students, were on our way to take part
in a field exercise in the northern district of Papua which
was no great distance from Port Moresby but situated on the
other side of the island.

Hauled towards the clouds in reliable aircraft, piloted by
'European' pilots, it was only about fifteen minutes before we
were skimming the tallest trees of the lowest gap in the
mountains of the Owen Stanley Range. Clear of the gap, it
was only another half-an-hour and we were racing towards a
small jungle airstrip that was moving swiftly towards us.

Our exercise, in the northern district, was to rub shoulders with the rural people and to do elementary surveys into aspects of their community life.

Manu was with the other students. We still met and talked about a variety of things but the mood had changed. Arguments were fewer but our relationship was more substantial and more matter-of-fact. I presumed less, the brother-sister relationship had ended and a vulnerable, cautious friendship had taken its place. We seldom talked together when we were with the other students, as neither of us now wanted to give the impression of a relationship that did not exist. Yet, now that Manu was no longer my brother, I felt more vulnerable to intimacy and I countered this with a consistent courtesy and smiling good humour: well practised virtues that had earned me citizen and class honours at school in Australia.

Despite these artificial barriers, I now regarded Manu as a possible life partner and avoided anything that I thought might offend him. Growing apart had allowed for more objectivity; emotions were out and cold reality was in. I was happy with the new honesty but felt a need for the warmer intimacy I had known in family life. When the young blood cooled, Manu was happier too. Growing up was not easy for either of us.

Dr Sidney was in charge of the exercise as he was teaching community medicine and he was laying the foundations. He was a gentle man and from this he drew his strength. His non-aggressive manner made it difficult for the students to fight with him, and the person of the moment, in his presence, occupied his full attention. His teaching method was to expose the students to experiences and to allow them to form their own conclusions. Every thought expressed was searched for meaning in the total context of man and medicine. The mind was not an empty bucket to be filled with facts and figures but a living tissue that grew on experience, reflection and association.

The northern district was different to both Wamira and Misima Island. It was fertile beyond belief and food that was won with back breaking toil in my native village grew wild in the jungles, free for the picking. Torrential mountain rivers tore through fertile volcanic plains and jungle filled forests, as they sparkled to the sea. With intensive farming and adequate cultivation, this land could have fed the whole of Papua with plenty to spare for the Church, the planters and the 'Europeans'. Instead we found a poorly nourished, depressed people suffering from the creeping sickness of colonial disregard. Their history, under colonial rule, was as rich and varied as their land and their sufferings as acute as the dazzling rivers that cut their soil. Like the other students, I was assigned to the task of probing into their privacy, their historical past and their present purpose. There was plenty to report.

This brought me face to face with a new experience. Misima Island was an island paradise, a 'Paradesia' slumbering through a slight colonial presence that touched it lightly. By contrast, this district had seen an inferno of upheavals caused by violent storms of natural disasters and colonial intrusions. Foreign miners searched the sparkling rivers for yellow gold. They were as crude as the metal they came for and they challenged the mysterious land with a gun, a spade and a pair of hands. They died as they lived, rough and hard, and they took a bit of the country or the people with them as they fell. These fortune hunters were not invited here but they came and wrote their own rules. Many people suffered and many people died. Malaria parasites invaded their friendly blood, dysentery germs fed on their blistered bowels, and death and degradation constantly stalked their friendless camps. Quarter men fought half men and nothing was stronger than a lead bullet and the people of the northern district never forgot.

Later, foreigners decided that they were aggrieved enough to fight a war and the northern district of Papua was in the eye of the storm. It was the gateway to the Owen Stanley Ranges and the back door to Australia.

The war was a white man's war but the natives were threatened by both sides. The atrocities of the gold mining days were vividly retold and it was recalled that civilized man, with a spike and a gun, was a very dangerous person to harbour on your soil.

The northern district natives were involved in the death

and destruction of a foreign war. These native troops became known as 'The Fuzzy Wuzzy Angels'. They were sometimes facing one way, sometimes facing the other, but always in the wrong and always suffering. Foreign soldiers perished and the natives perished, foreigners starved and the natives starved, foreigners fought disease and lost and the natives died from the same germs. The natives were threatened on every side and might was right. Some could not distinguish between one army and another but loyalty to one was death from the other. Food was destroyed, villages wiped out and garden lands ruined.

In 1943, in the northern district of Papua, a group of miserable village Papuans, who were caught facing the wrong way during the war, were roughly rounded up and brought to summary justice. This occurred at an out-post near the Kokoda trail, on the slopes of a sleeping volcano called Mt. Lamington. And there, Papuans were executed by the Australian army for their part in the war. These miserable natives were exalted to the ultimate in colonial status, that of Australian citizen and Commonwealth subject and then, as Australian citizens and Commonwealth subjects, they were tried for treason. Some of the wretched men were gaoled for ten to fourteen years but one group of twenty two was condemned to be hanged.

For several days before the executions village people were rounded up as the hangings were to be a public spectacle. This was achieved with difficulty. When the appointed hour arrived the men were publicaly hanged in front of 3000 village people. The Japanese had been defeated and the Australians had regained control of Papua, but blood-smeared women paraded their feelings at the executions and the natives were sullen and unimpressed. Papuans, who were Australian citizens, had learnt a lesson by a liberal display of death. It was the army but many of the men behind the uniforms were the old officers of the colonial administration. No Australian citizen in Australia was ever forcibly paraded for public hanging.

The war was gone, the 'Fuzzy Wuzzy Angels' forgotten; the Papuans of the northern district settled down to cope with the rains and the floods, unwanted coffee, foreign settlers, malnutrition and the white death. For the Australians the incident was closed and the flame was out. But the white man's war had left its mark, and in some red hearts the flame burnt on.

* * *

January 21, 1951, Mt Lamington blew up and Higaturu, the site of the war time public hangings, was destroyed and never built again. Higaturu was high on the slopes of a volcanic mountain and the area was thick with jungle growth. The jungle was cut by a few human tracks and many clear mountain streams and there was one rough motor road joining the outpost with the plains and Buna on the coast. Higaturu was a typical outpost of empire, and the local centre of colonial administration in the area. There was also an important mission station and the rich fertile land supported a large Papuan village population.

For a week before the fatal day, there were unusual rumblings and tremors coming from the mountain and the people were worried. The government was confident but the people were packed, ready for a speedy departure. Then, without further warning, the side of the mountain blew off. When the fatal blast came everyone was on the move. The foreigners were running for their vehicles, the villagers were running out of their houses and the dogs were running in. All were struck by the one fatal blast, the same second for death for 4000 villagers, officials and missionaries. Every standing object was flattened. All of the trees around were like parallel matches — the giants and the twigs. On Higaturu nothing stood but twisted steel and smashed wood. Vehicles were in trees and bodies were everywhere — everyone running. Nobody in the severe blast survived but, at the edge of the blast, the people were blown over, got up again and walked away.

Then came the burning rain. The air became filled with hot, lethal, powdery dust and many people who survived at the edge of the blast were later killed by the cloud of burning dust. The dust was blown far and wide and rained on the fertile plains, subsided and came to rest. But the people were still disturbed. The colonials explained what had happened, the missionaries explained what had happened, and the people listened and obeyed as they always had.

* * *

We were meeting in a Government rest-house for the last meeting of our field exercise. A government rest-house is a native-type building, built in a native village for the convenience of visiting administration officials. They usually had one inside room for sleeping, a simple back room with an open fireplace for a kitchen, and an open verandah in front where visitors were entertained. The rest-houses were made of native materials collected from the bush: the roof was of grass or layers of palms, the walls of thatched palms or split stems and the floors of any material that would stand the weight of half a dozen people at a time. They were cool, sometimes rainproof and provided comfortable quarters for sleeping snakes.

The students were seated on the floor of the rest-house verandah. Dr Sidney and Dr Dina were seated on wooden packing cases against one wall. Dr Dina had come over from Port Moresby for the day to hear our final reports and, I suspect, to get away from the Moresby grind. Dr Sidney had used the week to introduce us to some of the realities of village life in this part of Papua and to establish his quiet, confident style as an effective teaching method.

Between us, we had been forced to scratch the surface of community life, and to unravel some of the experiences that had shaped their present wants. Dr Dina was the first to talk:

'I have a sentimental attachment for this district of Papua and New Guinea. It was close to here that we started the first training school for medical assistants in this country. I was working close to here when I resigned from the old Papuan administration and commenced medical studies in Australia. It was close to here that Mt Lamington blew up and I was one of those who saw the death and destruction. Miners, wars, volcanoes and tornadoes have all been unexpected visitors here.

'With the help of one or two native medical assistants on each government station, I was supposed to cover the medical services for about half of Papua and supervise the work of the native medical assistants as well. I decided that I was wasting my time and that the only way that I could contribute was to prepare Papuans to look after their own people. This is why the medical training for medical assistants was started near here and why medical education for Papuan and New Guinean doctors has been started now.

'Up to the end of the last war, there was only a token medical service in Papua. There was a Government Medical Officer in two or three main centres and a very occasional missionary doctor elsewhere. In between there was a small handful of European and native medical assistants. It was the thousands of kilometres of 'in-between' that I saw, and what I saw convinced me that the medical education of the people of this country was our most urgent medical need.

'I performed thousands of life-saving and restorative operations on Papuans, under all kinds of primitive conditions. Scrotums that dragged along the ground, cysts the size of watermelons and limbs ulcerated through the bone. Malaria was unchecked, tuberculosis was rife, nutrition was poor and numerous native and introduced diseases were the normal burden of the people. We did what we could and the others were left to die. This is why the population has remained so low. With surgery we had two rules, the patient had to survive and there had to be enough anaesthetic to finish the job. Bad risk patients were not operated on as a fatality did great harm. Those who looked bad risks were allowed to die in their villages without any help from me.

'I am telling you this so that you may know a little more of the history of the people you are studying and what has made them what they are. They have lived very close to suffering and death. I also hope that this knowledge will help you to realise why we regard you as very important people and why we accept the establishment of medical education in Papua and New Guinea as our primary task.'

There was a great contrast in styles between Dr Dina and Dr Sidney. Dr Dina was in the thick of it with the students. Everyone had to participate to survive and students' comments were met with laughter, encouragement or challenge. We were like children at play, sometimes laughing, sometimes crying, but always learning. There was room for everyone's ideas and all were equal.

Dr Sidney was different. He exposed us to ourselves. He fought aggression with a gentle touch and encouraged us to leave the protection of our own shells and venture into a world that was in the palm of his own hand. We were exposed to experiences and formed our own conclusions, solved our own problems or learned to live with them.

* * *

We were seated in a Dakota aircraft returning to Port Moresby. We were flying by the side of Mt Lamington, the restless volcano, and over the fertile plains of Orokaiva as we fought for elevation to clear the Owen Stanley Range before the descent to Port Moresby and home.

When we joined the plane at the outstation airstrip, I was surprised when a middle-aged Papuan man edged a student out of the way, with a smart bump to the thigh, and sat in the vacant seat alongside me. It was not long before my fellow passenger made himself known to me and, addressing me in Motu, said,

'I am Dibura, the uncle of Manu Tau. Manu is the son of my third sister.'

'*Namo* (Good),' I said, using a conventional reply, 'do you live in the northern district?'

'No, I have been visiting relatives in the northern district. I live in the same village as Manu's father. I am taking some food and betel nuts back to the village.'

'Did you see Manu?' I enquired, wondering why Manu's uncle had chosen to sit with me rather than with his nephew.

Manu's uncle started to chew betel nut as a preliminary to introducing the main theme of his conversation.

'Manu's father wanted him to be a pastor or a teacher and did not want him to study to be a doctor.'

'*Namo* (Good),' I agreed. 'It is very good to be a pastor or a teacher. That kind of work is good.'

'Manu is a young man. He thinks he knows what is good but young men do not know anything.'

'*Oibe* (yes),' I agreed. I was likely to agree no matter what he said as I was speaking to an elder.

Manu's uncle had started to chew a pepper leaf that he had fished from another pocket beneath his rami.

'Manu's father was angry when he heard that Manu had become friendly with you. He said it was your fault that Manu would not listen to his talk.'

I suddenly became tense. This was more than a friendly chat and I felt like telling Manu's uncle that, as far as I was concerned, Manu could go to hell. Instead, I concealed my aggression and murmured,

'*Lau* (me)? What has it got to do with me what Manu does?'

'You know. The behaviour of village people. They talk a lot. Manu's grandfather was a German half-caste from near Samarai. That is why he has a light skin. Manu's relatives think that Manu has been educated like a white man. Manu knows all of the customs of the white people. Manu's relatives think he should not marry a native girl — he should marry a white woman.'

I was surprised beyond belief. I had expected almost anything but not this. In my small experience I had known of white men who had married native women but I had never thought of a white woman marrying a native man. There were exceptions but I could not see Manu as one of these. White people are rich natives are poor. How could a Papuan man buy all of the fine clothes, luxuries, grand houses and motor cars that white women use? If a white woman married a native man where would they live? Would she become a village native or would he become a white man in a grand house? I then turned sharply to Manu's uncle and said,

'Manu can marry who he likes. I am not stopping him. I have nothing to do with Manu or what he does.'

The plane had just cleared the trees of the gap in the Owen Stanley Range, and had started its descent to Moresby. Everybody in the plane was relieved except me.

'It will be good if you leave Manu alone,' said Manu's uncle, his mouth full of red spit and nowhere to deposit it. He looked at the wall of the plane, hesitated, and changed his mind.

I picked a textbook out of the bag at my feet and stared blankly at the pages until the plane touched down.

For the next two weeks there were violent storms. The

rain poured down in sheets. Bright skies every morning and deluges of water every afternoon and the earth struggled to stay afloat. The foreigners put on extra clothes to protect their bodies while the villagers took theirs off to protect their clothes. Between downpours roofs were mended, cars dried and house dug out of the mud.

Manu started sending me letters to which I did not reply. He wanted to see me urgently. What had happened? He must know. He loved me. The earth knew no beauty like mine. Why won't I talk to him? Love hides in the shadow of our desires.

The lectures usually ended in the rain. A short run and I was home. Home to the laughter of carefree girls. No men could enter here and I was secure from the world.

The rain thundered on the fibro roof and water cascaded through the grounds. It was wonderful to be free like the rain. If I could have stood naked in the storm, as I did on Misima Island, I would have been relieved. Water-filled hair, wet clothes and a shower had to do instead. It was wonderful to be alone. White or native, what was the difference? It was good weather to think in.

The rains cleared, the earth flowered and Port Moresby showed its finest colours in a short flight before it embraced the primordial brown of the long, hard dry. It was Spring— Moresby's special kind of Spring: hotter than the hottest summer, clearer than the desert sky, and the fresh display of the departing rains.

* * *

The end of the rains in Port Moresby was the signal for additional activities for the medical students in the surrounding rural areas. The road system outside of the town was primitive, and rain largely dictated when these roads could be used. For much of the year it was not possible to travel by road the hundred or so kilometres to the nearest government sub-district station. Our first rural project in this area was to study the road systems, such as existed, and their effects on living standards and health.

A convoy of three 4-wheel drive vehicles from the administration transport pool was assembled, and we set off to examine, at first hand, the road to Rigo and the surrounding villages.

The outward journey was accomplished with no more than the expected happening — rivers up to the engine, mud up to the axles, and mangrove roots, like giant limbs, stretching across the track. Near Gaire village, about 50 kilometres from Port Moresby, there was a sheet of water about two kilometres wide and 30–45 centimetres deep but, with two or three tows and much pushing, we eventually made it and continued on our way.

On arrival at our destination no time was spent on postmortems of the trip, and we were soon assigned to our activities in groups of twos and threes. It was at this stage that personal disaster struck. One group of villagers who could be reached by road, had to be visited by Motu speakers, as there was no other means of communicating with them, and Dr Sidney asked me if I would tackle this assignment with Mr Manu Tau, who was nearest to a local native as he came from the same district.

This was the very situation that I had been trying to avoid. Since being told that Manu was to marry a white woman and that his father thought that I was not good enough for him, I had been avoiding him like the plague. It had been my custom, in the past, to avoid embarrassment by turning my back on it or hiding in deep silences. Physical danger I could look in the eye but, in matters of the mind, I was still a coward. Colonialism had endowed me with a beggar's mind. I could take but I could not give. I had learnt to run but I had not learnt to stand and face the music. I was caught in a cage with a threatening obsession. A dancer who could not dance, a singer who could not sing, a lover who could not submit, a woman who could not run. To look beyond the night and beyond the dawn I had to stand and be threatened.

I was angry with Dr Sidney for exposing me to this situation. A typical do-gooder trying too hard to think. These ignorant colonials know nothing. But, now I had sold myself to the colonial cause and the master had spoken.

'That's all right, Dr Sidney, I'll go with Manu Tau and do the survey. But can we have a Motu driver, please? I cannot speak to some drivers and I'll need a driver whom I can talk to — I don't want Mr Tau to have all the say.' Following this request Dr Sidney selected a driver who could speak Motu. As it happened, this driver was a distant relative of mine and could speak my own native village language as well. Thus, Mr Manu Tau, the driver and I set off to complete our assignment.

The day passed peacefully enough and the matter of our estrangement was not discussed. I worked energetically on the assignment while Manu loafed most of the time, carelessly chewing betel nut and talking with the few villagers who remained in the village. Exchanging news between villages was an important pastime of the rural people and Manu was in no mood for taking work seriously.

Our return trip to the station took longer than expected because of local rain and we arrived late. I was then dismayed to find out that Dr Sidney and the rest of the party had already left for the return trip to Port Moresby! They had been prompted to leave on time by the news of rain in the Gaire area, and this meant the possibility of rising swamp water making the return trip to Moresby impossible.

I learned that Dr Sidney had only left about half-an-hour before, and as we had an experienced driver, we should be able to catch the others if we started at once. So, mainly at my insistence, we decided to give it a go. The worst that was likely to happen was that we would have to walk to a village to get somewhere to sleep or, alternatively, to spend the night in a swamp and wait until we were rescued the next day.

The roads were rough and tough. It was not a matter of racing a vehicle from one point to another, but one of skill in driving so that unnecessary damage did not occur and the machine did not become bogged. Time was saved by not making mistakes and to arrive was the achievement.

As we raced towards the Gaire swamps, which were about half way to Port Moresby, there were plenty of signs that the other vehicles were only just ahead. We entered the swamps, about two kilometres of axle deep water, at about 6 p.m. We caught a brief glimpse of a vehicle ahead but, in another moment, it was gone. Our first mistake was wet spark plugs which delayed us long enough to impress on us that there was no chance of wishing our way through such an expanse of water. Also there was only about half an hour of light left which did not help. One more mishap would finish the day. There was ample time to bump our way over the mangrove roots and get through the swamps providing we could see the road, keep hard steel off the ground, the wheels out of the heavy slime, and the water out of the engine. If anything went wrong, the night would close around us and nothing further could be done until the dawn.

I talked to my God without embarrassment as I always did. We were aware that the foolishness was mine but my God of love embraced his foolish children and waited with them through the lonely nights.

The land cruiser hauled its steel frame centimetre by centimetre across the swamp and mud. The engine roared with power, the clutch burned in protest, the water rose and fell, firm hands skimmed the spinning wheel and careful eyes directed. And where was the road? Always, where was the road? The light was leaving the heavy jungle and the one thought of all was where the road was hidden.

Manu and I walked ahead of the front wheels. The engine roared in the lowest of its eight gears with four wheels fighting for traction. How much water could the engine take?

Then the end came. A back wheel slipped into a deep rut, made by the bogged wheel of a large truck, and the axle was fast in the mud. We were stuck. Forward and reverse, pushing and pulling. Useless cries to the silent night. We all knew that we had gambled and lost. There would be no relief before the dawn, and now the dark that we would share with the sounds and creatures of the night.

We would huddle on the seat with the windows closed to listen to mosquitoes whining through our thin protection and prepare to fidget half-conscious through the night. I had done the same thing before and would repeat it many times in the years ahead. I occupied a seat against the window and began to arrange my affairs for the night. The main preparation was to retrieve a cotton sheet from my bag to wrap around me to seal off the mosquitoes. This sheet was my constant companion on rural excursions. It was my sunshade and my blanket and it also served as a notice to the restless, that the affairs of the day were ended.

* * *

As the night deepened, I noticed twinkling lights in the direction of the beach, which was only a kilometre or so away. At first I thought that the lights were glowworms, but later I became convinced that the lights were kerosene lamps and open fires of a native village. The only coastal village in that area was Gaire so, as far as I was concerned, Gaire village it was. The friendly village of Gaire was the last home of the pioneer English doctor, Walter Strong, who died in its warm arms. A village like the villages of Misima. As close to home as I could get.

With village lights so close at hand I was determined not to spend the night in the swamp. I insisted that I was going to walk to Gaire even if I had to walk on my own. I was more familiar with the night and the dangers of the swamps than were my companions and the reaching of friendly people was reward enough for any risks involved. When Manu realised that I was determined to act on my words, and there was nothing he could do to force me to change my mind, he consented readily enough to join me in the adventure, even though, to him, it was a short but hazardous journey. We said goodbye to the driver with instructions to him to wait for us in the morning, collected a flash light and a few other other essentials, and set off into the night.

As the result of my childhood experiences, I could protect myself and could spend the night in a mangrove swamp just as easily as I could in the crowded cabin of a bogged land cruiser. But no matter how familiar you are with swamps and black nights, they are always worse than expected.

I knew from experience earlier in the year, where the local streams were, and that it was fairly level ground between the road and the village. I was confident that the water would not get out of hand and that the water would not be above knee deep for most of the way. The area was thick with exposed roots that would give plenty of support and I did not consider that there was any prospect of getting into any serious trouble on that account. There were a few crocodiles in the area near the larger rivers but I did not think that there would be any chance of any of them being near here. The larger swamps and the bigger rivers were quite a distance away.

To my surprise, these opinions were not shared by Manu and he found it hard to control his feelings and to retain his self-control. I made my way through the swamps with confidence. Now and then the water was deep but, mostly, it was not above our knees. Sometimes a small rise provided temporary relief but, usually, this quickly gave way to water again. Poor Manu did not fare so well and he often stumbled and fell. For him, every step in the water was a step into eternity and the submerged, stout roots were vicious arms threatening him. I had taken it for granted that Manu would know the swamps and the night like I did but I had made a mistake, and I was deeply concerned about him. I had no intention of exposing his manliness to such a beating. I talked easily and pleasantly and minimised the difficulties in an effort to give him confidence and quieten his fears.

The village lights were coming closer and there was no turning back. Manu fell badly two or three times and his shorts and shirt were saturated with swamp water. He had gathered a few cuts from unfriendly trees and was gravely unhappy. Since our first meeting, I had enjoyed our companionship together but never felt any great tenderness towards him. Manu was always acting the big man and I was always defending myself against his aggression. Now it was different. Manu was at such an obvious disadvantage that there was certainly no need to be defensive. As he splashed and fell through the black swamp, his manliness was threatened. He was frightened and ashamed. Once or twice he mentioned poisonous snakes. I never thought of such a possibility, but then this was near his village not mine.

I had a desire to hold him up in the water and to support him in his unsteady walk. I wanted to point out the roots to avoid and the ones to use but I dared not embarrass him further. I fell against him to show him that I was as unsteady as he and I held his hand for comfort and laughed aloud at the dangers of the night. I had made a mistake in subjecting Manu to this ridicule. It was not in my nature to do this intentionally.

The village lights were beginning to take shape and

Manu's confidence began to return as the threatening experience dropped behind him. I had dropped some of my usual barriers and attempted to make amends for his wounded pride by personal gestures of interest and affection.

Eventually, we stumbled up to the first village house and we were greeted by friendly people. The villagers did not seem surprised that we had become bogged and had walked through the swamp. Manu had not yet fully regained his composure and the attitude of the villagers shamed him more. He was not confident enough to assert himself, so I carried on with our greetings and put out feelers about somewhere to sleep for the night.

Usually, a man like Manu would look up a friend or someone he knew in the village who would provide somewhere for him to sleep. But Manu and I having been thrown together by this unusual experience, made our way to the pastor's house together.

The native pastor greeted us with a friendly smile. He introduced us to his family and spoke a few words about groups of village women who were sitting around the house.

The village was on the white sands of Gaire beach and the home of the village pastor was one of the few neutral places where everyone could meet. Tonight was no exception. The women were dressed in clean cotton frocks, thrown over such undergarments as they possessed, which indicated that their assembly had the authority of the Church. A Papuan girl, educated in Australia, was still a curiosity though many of the women associated me with their own daughters who were just beginning to have educational opportunities.

I identified easily with these people and was happy with them. I had discarded my wet dress for a cotton T-shirt that I carried in my small plastic bag and a coloured grass skirt that had been given to me by the pastor's wife. I was happy and secure and the morning seemed far away.

Manu was still recovering from his ordeal in the swamp. He sat apart from the others, on the top step of the pastor's house and looked out over the sand to the sea beyond.

It took little prompting to turn the mood of the women from discussion on village netball to singing and dancing. Any excuse was good enough to dissolve a formal meeting into laughter, song and dance. A leader called a tune, a note was taken and a song began. The spirit gathered strength as the song took flight and winged to the stars through the Gaire night. As the mood deepened, the spirit moved the women and brown feet rose to the rhythm of love and laughter and to the hunger and pain of their native land.

Two women arrived carrying bowls of steaming food and tropical delicacies; fish, eggs, taro, yams and sweet potatoes, together with pineapple and bananas. At the sight of the food, the women dispersed to their homes, some along the warm sands and some to canoes for the short crossing to their sea houses.

The pastor brought two young village girls from the back of the house to introduce to us. They would look after our wants and clear the food away when the meal was over. He also pointed to two bedrooms, close together, where Manu and I could sleep. The pastor then took his leave for the night, reminding us that village life started at dawn and that this would be the best time of the day to raise the necessary help.

Manu remained silent as I squatted on the mat opposite him. He selected some food and began to eat. I wondered how deep had been the hurt to his pride. As the author of Manu's misadventure and humiliation, I felt a tenderness towards him that I had never felt before. In an effort to relieve the tension between us I made an attempt to talk to him.

'I hope we will be able to get enough men to push us through the swamp tomorrow. I wonder how many we need?' I said, trying to make conversation. Manu's reply came back quick and firm which relieved me of some of my anxiety.

Our meal was finished and we were satisfied. The girls cleared the remains, arranged for our comfort and were gone. Manu and I were now alone, squatting on the pandanus mat, very conscious of our closeness and of the barrier that had come between us. In the softer mood that had come over me, it seemed too abrupt to leave suddenly and secure myself for the night. Manu gave no indication of leaving so we talked on. Suddenly, the matter of our recent differences was raised and I was forced to face the issue.

'Why have you been avoiding me lately, Josie, what's wrong?'

Weighing my words carefully, I said,

'There's nothing wrong. It's just that I think that there is no future for us and that we should not play with love or keep pretending.'

Manu, relieved that we were talking together again, also spoke carefully.

'I didn't know that we were playing at anything. I've told you that I love you. I've never forced myself on you or opposed your wishes. Can't you give us a chance to develop something? Love cannot grow without nourishment.

I did not want to have a long discussion on these matters so I decided to come to the point.

'Who wants to nourish love? I want to become a doctor and that has nothing to do with nourishing love. I could have stayed in the village and married years ago and had two or three children by now if that was all I wanted. You don't know how difficult it is to be a girl. Friendship may end in love, but love will never end in friendship. Not for me. Love is the end of equality.'

Manu remained silent as he searched for a suitable answer. He could not reconcile my needs while serving his own. In the romantic night love was sex, but beyond the dawn it was total, complemental life.

Manu looked up and still playing for time, said, 'But, lately we have not even been friends. You don't answer my letters and you don't talk to me like before.'

'I'm sorry, Manu,' I quickly replied, 'but I was hurt by what one of your relatives told me.'

Manu changed his mood and looked up sharply,

'And what was that?'

I looked him straight in the eyes and said,

'Your family says that you are going to marry a white woman and your father says that I'm not good enough for you. I'm just a native girl and I'm spoiling your life.'

'What stupid bastard told you that?'

'Your uncle for one. The one who travelled with us from the northern district.'

'Those people should mind their own business. They have nothing to do with my life.'

'I've been hurt enough in Port Moresby without being told that I'm not good enough for you and that I'm ruining your life. I came to Moresby full of love and pleasant dreams but now I have no pride left. I feel dirty and unwanted.'

I was crying and wiping my eyes with the white T-shirt I was wearing.

Manu moved closer to me, cupped my hand in his and gently said,

'Don't cry, Josie. There's no need for you to do that. You should not take any notice of what these people say about you. You are a queen, Josie. The only girl I have ever loved. Trust me, Josie, I will always stand by you.'

I felt weak and dependent. I had never cried like this in front of a man before. I had always presented a calm, tough front. But the strains of the day were telling. I had taken as much as I could stand alone. On that lonely night, Manu was the only friend I had.

'I have really lost my pride with foreigners calling me names. People I don't know treating me like a dog. I can't swim somewhere because it is for whites. I can't do this and that because I'm a native. Now your father tells me that I'm not good enough for you, that I am ruining your life. When I came to Moresby I did not have a care in the world. Now look at me. I really have no confidence left.'

Manu held my hand tighter.

'My parents don't know anything about you. What they say about you is what they would say about any girl that they did not pick out for me. They have curious ideas. A distant relative of mine was a German from Samarai. Some village fortune teller told my parents, that after I went to school in Australia, I would become a big man. You know we were among the first to go to Australia for education. He told them that I would marry a white woman. Some sort of a white queen, I guess. It's all fantasy.'

'And what am I, some sort of a black queen? Before I came to this rotten town I did not know that there was such a thing as black and white.'

Manu continued earnestly,

'Look, Josie, I'm not going to marry my mother or my father. I'm in love with you and it's you I'll marry if you will only give me a chance.'

Manu had made advances to me beyond anything I would

have allowed in the past. He was holding my arm on his thigh and had his other arm around my back.

We sat in silence. I felt his warm body against mine. Some of my pride had been restored. A glow of tenderness towards Manu had taken possession of me. Was this the beginning of love? Time would tell.

Manu leant closer to me and said quietly,

'Josie, I will come to you in half an hour. We need each other now.' Then he rose and was gone.

I sat silently with my thoughts. After five minutes, I got up and went to the room, opened the door and went inside. With mixed feelings of excitement and misgivings, I looked at the wooden bolt, hesitated, did not touch it and left the door unlocked.

The first thought that came to my mind was pain and the second thought was pregnancy. I had had sex before at Misima during the excitement of a Christmas carol singing festival. It was painful and it had been an unpleasant experience but this should be different. I was better prepared for love. It would be easier. Pregnancy, that was another thing. Like all Papuans girls I firmly believed that pregnancy could not occur with one experience. Repeated sex was necessary to have a child. There was often a long wait between marriage and the eagerly awaited first-born child.

I also firmly believed that I could not become pregnant under any circumstances as I was firmly protected by a powerful magic spell. I could not conceive until the spell was broken with substantial rituals. With such thoughts I lay on the wooden bed, moved some flowers nearer to me and waited.

It was not long before telltale sounds alerted me to the opening of the door and the presence of Manu in my room. I heard the door bolted with firm intent. I could see Manu clearly in the soft light, but he had to stand for a short time to accustom himself to the furnishings of the room.

He came to me and I turned and put out my hand to meet him. It was better to be as one in our first embrace rather than give the impression that he was forcing his will on me.

Manu was excited and trembling. He had experienced extremes this day and his control was not all that it might have been.

He removed his native rami, his only clothing, and was in bed beside me, soon satisfying the hunger long denied. He smothered my own emotions in the heavy restrictions of his powerful arms. Young impulses could not long be denied as my few remaining clothes were removed with fumbling hands. Manu could not control his feelings beyond this stage. He was on top of me and I was ready to receive him. I could not breathe and could scarcely move but I tried to assist him as best I could. It was painful, but not as painful as before and, when this was lost, we were given to love. Flesh to flesh, seed to seed, Love was final. I had given myself freely and was prepared to receive the passion of his body in mine. Then, suddenly, without warning, I was filled with the seed of his desire. Manu slowly slipped from my body, lay by my side and went to sleep.

Left with my thoughts I relived the events of the evening. I had been full of tenderness and freely gave myself to physical love. Love is final, but, for me, this was not complete. I shook Manu and firmly insisted that he return to his own bed. He was satisfied. He touched me gently and left. I followed him to the door and firmly replaced the bolt. Back in bed I dreamed of love and hope and I wondered what they were all about. In the next room Manu was sleeping soundly.

I was awake before the dawn as had been my custom on Misima. At first light, I called Manu and, after eating some food provided by the pastor's wife, we enlisted a number of village men, who had been leaving for their gardens, to help us in our plight. We gave our thanks and took our leave.

Using the village paths, there was no difficulty in reaching the mud-bogged vehicle. The driver was relieved to see us and fifteen pairs of strong hands made short work of shifting the land cruiser. The villagers walked and pushed with us and saw us safely through the swamp.

* * *

When we arrived back at the college we knew that it was all over. At the end of the year, Manu left the medical college and followed his father's wishes. I never met him again.

But for me, the first moon came and there was no sign. I had no concern as the magic of my ancestors was active in me. The second moon came and still no sign. The old woman was confident that the essence was potent beyond mortal power. The third moon came and the seed was still in my womb. Manu had seeded his manhood in my body through his own failure. He achieved through weaknesss what he could not achieve through strength.

In secret, I went to an Indian nurse, who was wise in such things. Was there a child in my body? She collected some urine and injected it into the back of a male toad. The next day, I returned in mortal dread to hear what I already knew.

'Yes, my dear,' said the understanding nurse. You are most certainly pregnant.'

I was depressed beyond belief. The thought of not bearing the child never entered my head. There was no decision to be made. I had never had experience in these things. I was pregnant and I was going to have a child.

The sun went deep in the clouds, my body was cold, my work was a burden, I could not carry on. I would have to move out into a new world of relatives and villagers and turn my back on the ambitions and happiness that had brought me so far. I must now retrace my steps back to obscurity.

I got word to Manu that I was pregnant, hoping that my child would have a father's name, that it was not too late to complement Manu's life with mine. If Manu had any interest in my final capitulation he showed no sign. I expected it. I was alone.

* * *

When the year ended, I slipped away from the college and entered the world of tin sheds, neglect, wife bashings and malnutrition. There to wait until my child was born. Then, together, another day.

Dr Dina was the only one I had courage to face. I told him the truth. He was gentle and pleasant and told me that it was not the end of the world and that some day I would be proud of my child. He said he would be behind me in anything I decided for the future.

'Remember, Josephine, you are never alone. Just give the call and you will have someone beside you. If you need me, I'll see you through no matter what you decide.'

A relative, with a number of children, had a tin shed in a

slum settlement among the poor and lonely of the big town. The shed was made of sheets of tin nailed to scraps of wood. The almost flat roof was made of the same materials and leaked when it rained. The floor was dirt and the furniture little more than a few packing cases. I was allocated a small sleeping bench and a hole for a window at one end of the building. The rest of the single-roomed house was shared by all. At night, as the temperature cooled, the tin exploded against its restraints like rifles in the night.

My most constant friend now was an uncle, far advanced with tuberculosis, who wanted to give my baby his name if nobody better came along. He did not expect to live long and he would be honoured to leave my child with his name.

The months went by and I moved further and further away from the artificial affluence created by the fever of Australian decolonisation and moved deeper and deeper into the desperate poverty and deprivation of the people of the slums. I had no money and no means of income. My father was in gaol, on Misima, serving a six month sentence for some misdemeanour and my mother, denied house and support, was desperately trying to feed her many children.

As it came close to the time of my confinement, I found the tin shed hot and breathless at night. One by one, the children fell asleep on their mats on the dirt floor. I listened to their familiar breathing and to the changing sounds as cockroaches, rats and vermin took over the night. Then, sleep at last.

The deep night came and I was startled out of a shallow dream by the tin sheets exploding in the night. As I reached consciousness I was sitting on the edge of my wooden bench, crying. My baby was moving in my body. I was afraid and alone. Where was the carefree young love now that I embraced so warmly a short time ago? Where were the eager plans for tomorrow? All were dead. Dead like the dry stones, from time beyond comprehension, that lined the road that I must travel. The young girl of a thousand coloured dreams was gone. Here was a lonely woman, lost, afraid of creation, and afraid of life.

'Oh, God, always by my side, don't desert me now. Dear God, creator of heaven and earth, have mercy on your poor servant who is lost with the vermin of the night and cannot reach the dawn but through Thee.'

I had learned the meaning of happiness. Happiness was life. There was no other life. Now I knew what loneliness was. I had not known that it existed. Deep-seated, destructive loneliness that only my belly could relieve. Then, no marriage, no future, lost in the brutality and obscenity of thoughtless poverty. A heavy price for a girl to pay for a belief in ancient magic and a glimpse of romantic love.

PART TWO

Beyond the fantasies of love

1

The Bare Brown Rock

*P*ort Moresby was scorched brown and the high sun went unchallenged in the cloudless sky. The tin shack was drenched with heat. My baby son, two weeks old, was dehydrated and crying from thirst. I took him in my arms, went to the cooler shade of the bread-fruit tree and satisfied his needs. I looked down at this little creature in my arms. How often had I done the same with my mother's children! But this baby was mine. I felt there should be a proper mother somewhere as I did not seem to be real. But he was mine and the two of us were going to see it through together. My womb was empty, my breasts were full and I was a functioning human being again. I felt some purpose grasp me once more.

Depression slipped away as I cared for my baby. Breast milk was the only milk I could afford, as I had not owned one cent for weeks past. Scraps of rags served my baby's needs and young breasts could easily satisfy. The drives that had brought me to Port Moresby had subsided but I felt the awakening of a new urge — the urge to survive.

I had salvaged a few clothes from my affluent student days

and these, together with my son's rags, occupied my furniture which consisted of one small suitcase. I depended on the charity of my host relative for survival. I was destitute like the bare brown rock on which I lived.

For the first time since my confinement, which took place at a gentle Roman Catholic Hospital situated near my slum home, I had an interested look at my clothes. With my baby swinging in a string bag tied to a branch of a tree, I inspected my belongings. The battle gear for combat with the world. The rags that stood between me and starvation; tenderness and brutality; lust and love.

There was an innocent, apple green, three-tiered skirt with matching blouse. It was made for a school dance when my innocence matched my clothes. My eyes filled again as they often did of late. I would keep it for that extra special occasion, if such an occasion ever came again. My resolve was to escape from the slum that was claiming me as its own. My relative was sorely pressed for space and for food and the small bench that I occupied would have provided space for three or four children. The heat burned my body black and my spirit dry. Strange persons eyed me regularly as prospective merchandise and my host complained of the nature of the people who suddenly became solicitous of the well-being of his family.

Unpleasant creatures occupied my nights. A hairy monster with slotted teeth and furrowed arm appeared regularly at the hole in the tin wall where I slept with my baby. The creature was not a dream, it was a living, breathing thing, a part of the torture of my soul. My relatives complained of my screams in the night and also of a white robed spirit that they regularly saw sleeping by my side. This was a dangerous demon, known to the people of my tribe, and a bad one to attract into the shack. The demon made no demands but it was indestructibly constant. In order to continue breathing at night, I had to open the hole in the wall of the hut that served as a window. This attracted several frights and mis-adventures and, at times, I felt that death was only a short step away.

Friday nights were danger nights for the women of the slums, particularly on the pay-day fortnight. Poor, denied men, filled with bitterness and cheap alcohol, could become belligerent at the slightest provocation in the kingdom of their tin shacks. Sometimes women were ruthlessly bashed until they mercifully escaped into unconsciousness. Still, despite such excesses, many of the families of the slums handled their poverty with dignity and were fulfilled within the thin measure that affluent Moresby allowed for their survival.

* * *

On two occasions during the first month of my new life, I made arrangements for my baby and ventured out into the world as far as my legs would take me. There was no money for public transport fares so I had to walk. When I saw people drinking cool drinks I was alarmed at their extravagance and I eyed the ripening tropical fruits with thoughts of paradise.

On my second excursion I ventured over Korobosea hill, down to Boroko where the masters lived, past the European and the Native hospitals and on to the Papuan Medical College. The second year for medical studies had already begun and there was a new group of students starting their first year. Most of my memories of Port Moresby flowed from here and tears were in my eyes again — a frequent condition I could no longer control. What had this place done to me? My dreams, my pride, my baby. What had colonial Port Moresby done to me? It had made me feel black, dirty and rejected.

Not much more than a year ago, a timid Papuan girl, with a heart full of love, bravely walked up this path into the future. Now, a timid woman hung in the shadows and wept alone. I looked towards my red hibiscus tree where I had spent many hours with Manu but it was dead. Moresby mud had done its work. Gone was Manu, gone were my flowers, gone were my dreams and dead was my song.

> Flower of desire, delicate rose
> Blushing in the mud.
> Lighten the light of my solitude.

Students came out of the lecture room, parrots in courting. Girls ran to their quarters, sprinkling provocative laughter. No Dr Dina, no Dr Sidney, no hope. Only that doctor from the hospital who slept on the examination couch during lectures. Hurriedly, I slipped away towards the evening slum and my baby. Compassion would be fed when I held him in my arms.

* * *

Then, a week later, a new miracle. Dr Dina's confident voice charged through the tin shack like a loud-speaker.

'Hello Josephine, great to see you again. How is your beautiful baby? Excuse me for barging in but I thought it was time I came to see you.'

A voice from beyond, a new hope born.

'Hello Dr Dina, it's so nice of you to come and see me,' I said, overcome with gratitude.

'I should have come long ago. But you know what I'm like. Quick to talk and slow to act.'

I picked my son up in my arms and took him to my friend.

'He's great, Josephine. He is a he, isn't he? The only trouble is there are many hes in the world already.'

I wished he would stay all day. I wished he would talk all day. I really needed a friend. With a pair of strong arms around me my heart could beat again. I loved the beauty of free things, the passion of tempered loyalty, the warmth of friendship possessed.

'Do you like my home, Dr Dina?' I said, waving to my bench at the end of the tin hut.

'Not bad for a start, Josephine. But this is not your home. Your home is among the beautiful colours and shapes of Misima. You told me so. I always remember what you once told me. You said the frangipani of Misima had the fragrance of a woman in love. We never forget beautiful things. Love is a beautiful thing. So is a baby. Have you ever been in love?'

'I don't know, Dr Dina, perhaps I was for a moment. But it was a red hibiscus love, the flower of desire; it had no scent. Some day I will find a frangipani love and it will be final and complete.'

'I'm sure you will, Josephine,' said Dr Dina, sitting on my sleep bench for there were no chairs. 'And you will be the most beautiful frangipani on the tree.'

The warmth was coming back into my heart. It was beating again. Dr Dina always talked like that. He played with words like a game of tennis. He returned the shots and challenged your imagery to match his own.

I looked at my friend and said with a smile, 'I shall not be much of a frangipani now. The fragrance has gone and there is just the stale smell of a fallen flower.'

'I suppose you are a fallen flower, Josephine. Does that worry you?' asked Dr Dina, helping himself to a solitary banana that had been given to me by a hopeful garbage 'boy' as he passed my window, on his way to work. This was my diploma to eat and sleep with the least of God's equal people. I had not yet accustomed myself to salvaging the nutritious garbage from the opulent society I had recently offended, and I was still pondering the origin of the fruit as I replied,

'I don't know if it worries me or not. On many things I no longer have any feelings. I saw a priest from Koki and he looked the other way. But I was contemptible before he came along; Moresby saw to that. You can't offend a pig with mud. Even you left me for dead.' I continued, showing off my school girl slang. 'Nobody from the college has been to see me. A fallen flower is a lonely thing. Bathed in sensuous glory it gives in passionate wonder and falls in grey moult to the ground. I am not worried about being a fallen flower, I'm worried about being lonely.'

I was not as bitter as I sounded. I was just fighting back and this was a good place to start. I don't know what I would have done if Dr Dina had breezed off without leaving some hope behind. I dared not think.

'The flower falls and the seed grows, Josephine. Life is always beautiful. The colours of God's canvas cannot be matched by man. You and I are part of the cycle of life. You have been privileged more than I because, through the will of God, your body has been touched for greater purpose.'

'The will of God is fine in sermons but it is a different thing when you have to live with it.'

'I'm glad to see you in such fine form. It gives me heart to carry on. First you want to fight me and now you want to fight God. Take it easy. You should learn to fight your enemies one at a time and always keep a majority of one.'

Dr Dina put his strong arms around me.

'I love you, Josie. You are the most wonderful girl in the world, and the most beautiful.

For a moment, life stood still. Those were the words I wanted to hear. The arms I needed so much. But the love Dr Dina mouthed was not the kind of love I planned for me, final and complete. I was not finished with Dr Dina yet. He released his grip and I started to breathe again. Did he read my thoughts? Perhaps he underestimated the warmth of my young, firm body. I hoped it was one ball over the net he could not hit back. It would teach him a lesson. He was speaking again now, but not so detached.

'Fight back all the way.' I noticed that there was no paternal Josephine this time, but my mind was on other things and his voice droned on.

'Mediocrity feeds on tasteless happiness and suburban bliss. God's world does not end in a three-bedroomed house in a colonial dump, or its substitute, the local club. It also reaches to the mountain tops and by the forest streams. Live it and love it. Learn what God gave you your senses for. Don't be mediocre, it's too dull. Trust in God and reach for the stars. It's much more fun.'

'Yes, Dr Dina, I shall trust in God and reach for the stars. And if I can't reach them I can call on you. You told me I could count on you any time. I will count on you too. Remember, always have a majority of one.'

'Josephine, may I say something without interruption? I am proposing to the Government that they employ you as my secretary at the Papuan Medical College in place of the foreign woman who is leaving soon. I expect a major confrontation, but I think that we can beat them. There are one or two who really believe in native advancement who can help. If necessary, I'll fire the big guns and that should do the trick. Will you take the job, Josephine, if I can work it? You'll be my private secretary, secretary of the Faculty Board, secretary of the Board of Studies, secretary of the Examination Boards and all that jazz. What about it?'

'Yes, I'll take it, Dr Dina,' I said trying to suppress my excitement.

'Okay, Josephine, wait for me. I should know in about a week's time.'

Then he was gone. Always the same, blowing in and blowing out and a tornado in between. I wondered if he ever slept. I don't think he could stop his mind.

The first colour of a new spring. The first smile God had given in a long time. The unfurling flower of a woman reaching for a star. I took my baby in my arms and my heart was full of love. I was no fallen flower, for I now had the strength of two. My son and I, we would make it together. A firm body and a suitcase of old rags. What more did I need to fight my way out of this colonial dump? I will not eat their refuse; they will have to kill me first.

Beyond that day the sun was cooler, the stars brighter, the fibres sweeter. I think, I saw a baby smile.

* * *

My most constant companion and supporter during this experience was my uncle. He was my closest blood relative and almost a true uncle, for, in European terms, he was a first cousin of my father.

His native name was Dagaiana. This being a bit of a mouthful for strangers, he was known just as Robert. To me he was Uncle. A gaunt man, he carried the drama of the years in his drawn face. He had a slight stoop and was more at home squatting, cross-legged, on the floor than he was standing. He worked for a large colonial firm that supplied meat to the foreigners of the town. Uncle Robert was nearing the end of his working career, but life without work was an unknown dimension to him and the prospect of not working frightened him. He was the type of Papuan who the masters described as a 'good, reliable native', or, after they had had two or three beers, as 'a bloody good boy'.

During the war he used his skills with cold efficiency in the service of his masters, but when the knife dropped, the next enemy he had to face was destitution. He had lived to serve the colonial master and in doing this he gave up a series of lost causes, including his village identity, his marriage and the establishment of a family of his own. He was a man of retiring nature. I found him easy to talk with and he showed me a lot of kindness and affection. He now had little left to serve so he was happy when he found me in need of a service he could provide. He offered to share with me whatever shelter he could scrounge, and he wanted my son to bear his name.

In Papuan custom, it was the first or given name of the father that passed on to the next generation. There were no permanent family names or surnames. So I named my son Robert, which was in keeping with the tradition. I added to Robert my father's first name, Abaijah. Thus, my son was Robert Abaijah. A reasonable compromise to the two worlds that I lived between. Western culture had pressed its cause and had won a victory. By now, my father's Christian name, Abaijah, had become the permanent surname of my family.

Uncle Robert visited me in the early evenings after he had finished work and at the weekends. It was not so lonely when he was there as it made me feel that I belonged somewhere in the scheme of things. Slight matters that previously I would have laughed away, were now treated as of serious consequence. Uncle could not offer me a roof yet, but he would shift heaven and earth to provide one in the future. Papuans are a race of unfulfilled optimists. In the meantime, the strategy was to cling to my bench in the tin shed on the bare brown rocks.

I wondered what it would be like to own some money of my own. In my present world, money was food given by friends and space for a sleeping mat. In some ways I was proud of my life without money. I was being cleansed of some of the dirt gathered in my previous colonial experience. Still, the food I ate cost a few cents and there are not enough to go around. I ate almost anything that anyone handed me so that I would eat less from the common bowl. But I would have to face the world with my baby soon. My father was locked up and growing fat on Government rice and my mother was unreachable on Misima, having a hard time feeding her ten children while my father was in gaol. We had no relatives in the town with enough food to feed two extra mouths.

'*Egwalau* (hello), Uncle,' I said happily as my uncle approached on his usual visit. I had extra news for him today.

'I am later than usual today,' returned my uncle, 'I had to walk a long way to get here. I did not want to spend money on bus fares today.'

I walked away to get baby Robert and called over my shoulder as I went, 'You should not have done that. The bag you are carrying seems very heavy, even for a strong man like you.'

Uncle Robert loved to nurse baby Robert and this was the main pleasure of his visits. The best way to welcome him was to pass the baby to him. I exchanged the baby for Uncle's sugar bag of food and said,

'What have you got for us today? It seems heavier than usual.'

'Just the usual—meat for you and a tin of milk for Robert. But I was lucky today, I was able to get some better meat for a change.'

My uncle's loyalty to his masters did not extend to allowing his niece and baby to starve while he cut meat all day for the well-fed colonials.

'I might be able to get a job next week, Uncle,' I said. 'My old boss, Dr Dina, came to see me and said he wanted me to work in his office. It will be great if I get it. What should I do with Robert during the day if I have to go to work, Uncle? You know, I have never worked for white people before. If I get this job, it will be the first work I have ever had.'

Uncle was surprised by the news of my job and I thought that he looked sad. His drawn face began to show the tension in his muscles. He was probably sad because he realised that he could not help us in the way that he wanted to. It was only the masters who had plenty of money to throw around. This was his last chance to patch up his own broken life and he desperately wanted to succeed. When poverty throws the dice, they are always loaded. The winner is a foregone conclusion.

'When did he come, Niece? What did he say to you?' Uncle did not want to commit himself until he had heard more.

I was so happy about my own chance to become independent that I had completely overlooked the possibility that anyone else could be affected as well. I had been so alone that I did not see the man beside me. I had committed a part of somebody else's happiness to my own life. I must walk more cautiously in the future and I spoke with less enthusiasm now.

'I really don't know what the work is. I have never worked before. I think it's some sort of work like a clerk. Dr Dina is a good man and I am not afraid to work for him. It's at the Papuan Medical College. I can walk from here. It's over the hill by Korobosea so there will be no need to catch a bus. That can save money and we might be able to find some sort of a house where we can live.'

My uncle shared sleeping quarters with others at the back of the butcher shop. This provided little more than a bed for himself to sleep on. Engrossed in my own problems, I had taken him for granted and had forgotten that he had needs of his own. The plans that I had so easily discussed with him had become an important part of his life.

My uncle was now ready to reply. We always talked together in our own native tongue.

'I think it's too soon for you to work yet. You feed Robert with your breasts and he is too young to be left with other people. Our relative here may not want to look after him. It is a big job looking after a baby. Also, when you get work from Europeans you should look around at several jobs first. It's most important to take the best job the first time. These Europeans have a system among themselves and sometimes they won't take workers from other companies. They gang up against Papuans so that they can do what they like with us. Sometimes you have to go away until they forget about you. Be very careful, Niece, before you take your first job.'

I was disturbed by the reply. I began to doubt people again. My distasteful experiences with colonialism began to come back to me. Foreigners could not be trusted. They were either do-gooders who wanted to own you or others thinking only of their own interests. That was for sure. But was Dr Dina like that? I had never thought of him in that way. I did not want to discuss the matter any more.

'It's all right, Uncle, I will be very careful before I take a job. I will also see that Robert can drink milk from a bottle first. This sweet condensed milk will be all right. You don't need to keep it cold. I will have to give part of my wages to a woman to look after Robert properly. There are many poor women who want money. I shall feed him my breast in the morning and after I come home from work.'

My uncle's face had softened again. He had won decorations fighting in the foreign war against the Japanese. He could march on Anzac Day with a chest covered with medals — with empty bones underneath. Still he was an ex-service man and that was something to be proud of. 'A great Papuan'. 'One of the best'. He had suffered in the war and half of his lungs had been cut out because of tuberculosis. My son bore part of his name and I gave a touch of reality to his wasted dreams.

After sharing some food with me, Uncle took his leave. He had to walk the five kilometres back to his shed. I was glad he had come tonight. We could both see clearer now.

The dry grass was burning fiercely yet again on the hillsides around us. The smoke was rolling over the slums and up the valleys. A crimson fierceness was forming low in the sky. There would be no sleep tonight. I would have to watch my baby.

* * *

Uncle Robert had reconciled himself to me working at the Papuan Medical College as Dr Dina's secretary and arrangements had been made with a relative to look after baby Robert while I was away at work. I had raised enough money to buy a tin of milk. A cousin produced a few teats and bottles. Uncle Robert knew somebody who had a small plastic jug, and I parted with a white cotton blouse to provide clean cloth. Three bottles of milk mixture were wrapped in the clean cloth provided by the discarded garment and were placed in a cool place in the hut. Instructions were repeated until thoroughly understood and my own appearance received unaccustomed attention. The big day had arrived and Josephine Abaijah, mother of Robert Abaijah, set off to meet the world.

I climbed to the top of a rocky hill to the village of Korobosea, looking down on foreign Boroko. This was my first day at work and excitement had winged me from my home earlier than propriety demanded. So I rested at the village. I thought I might look foolish if I arrived at work too early. I wished I was not so excited.

Korobosea village was on a small ridge of land on the crest of a hill that the town had forgotten. The village consisted of twenty or thirty small houses built side by side along a crest that was shaped like an elongated hull of a ship. The home of a missionary was at the bulkhead. The good earth of the village was solid brown rock with the exception of the mission which had a small carpet of green grass.

The trouble with Korobosea, in the heart of colonial Port Moresby, was that it existed. In the past, the Papuans of Korobosea owned most of suburban Boroko and plenty more. Now they owned almost nothing. Like the twisted and the maimed of a war, the people remained visible and un-answered.

From one side of the ridge, the people looked down on the slums where I lived and, from the other side, on lucrative, orderly colonialism. Real estate worth millions of dollars now owned by foreigners. I walked to the house of a villager I knew and sat down on the top step leading to his house.

'Hello, Isaac,' I said to the thin, rami clad man sitting on the floor of the house, carving a stick for the tourist market. 'It's a bit cold this morning?'

'That is so *natugu* (my daughter). It is very cold.'

Isaac Tom was a man of note in his community but, like many other men from the village, he found it difficult to obtain work as many people from other areas of Papua and New Guinea had come to Port Moresby in recent times.

Among other things, Isaac was a village poet. He had written several prophetic songs and poems but neither of these credits brought any material benefits. Now, being un-employed, he carved small souvenirs which were sold to curio conscious travellers. His wife with a hungry look and his daughter with a friendly smile disposed of the goods in the foreign settlements. If the food situation was bad and sales were poor, they could be boosted by the young daughter wearing a grass skirt and a frangipani lei. A dollar or two for a glimpse of brown beauty and for a forgotten licentious smile of young cupidity. I stood up and crossed the narrow verandah to read from a yellow piece of paper.

> Clouded, brooding mountain ranges;
> Streaming jungle lethargy,
> Lovely, lonely coral islands;
> Azure sky and bluer sea.
> Gleaming, swaying, brown breasted maidens;
> Graceful ballet, palms in sand,
> Beauty unsophisticated;
> Drums beat, drum beat, night spent land.

I was reading the translation of a poem on an aged piece of typing paper, transfixed with splinters of bamboo on the front of Isaac's house.

'Have you written any poems lately?' I asked. 'I think your poems are beautiful. I love beautiful things. They make my body warm with feelings. Beautiful words are the drum beats of beautiful thoughts.'

'Not all poems are beautiful,' said the gentle poet, as he paused from his carving to look at me. 'Some songs are sad. Now when I start to make a happy song it always turns sad.'

He put his carving down and fished a sheet of torn school paper from his pocket.

'I started to write this but the words are locked up in my stomach. They won't come out.'

I took the sheet of paper and glanced at the few scribbled words of an unfinished poem written in his native language.

> The soul of a man...
> The feet of a man...
> The love of a man...
> But the heart of a man beats deep in his land.

Several minutes passed. I looked at my watch and then at the piece of paper in my hand. I must go soon, I thought. I took up a ball-point pen that Uncle Robert had given to me and began to write on the paper.

> The soul of a man seeks a heaven to fly;
> The feet of a man seek a journey to travel;

> The love of a man seeks a passion that passes;
> But the heart of a man beats deep in his land.

I read the completed lines and handed them back to my friend. His heart cried but his eyes were too dry for tears. Without looking up he said,

'Thank you *bada herea, natugu* (thank you very much, my daughter). May God walk with you. The streets are not safe for our girls anymore. Walk carefully.'

'I shall be careful,' I replied. 'It is very sad about our land, Isaac. You can only write what is in your stomach. Your stomach is dry. Thoughts of your lost land are all that is in it. I am going to work now, *bamahuta* (goodbye).'

Isaac looked from the paper to his native land below. An alien garden and memories. I must not be bitter so early in the new day. Things will be different now. With a fresh sense of joy I completed the walk to the place of my new occupation.

So it came to pass that, eighteen months after my initial entry to the Papuan Medical College as a medical student, I entered it for the second time. I was no longer an innocent girl from Misima with my eyes full of wonder and my heart on the moon. Now, innocence was life, wonder was the smile of a baby and my heart was closer to the dead brown rocks of my new home than to the moon.

The long dry had finished, the rains came and then the mendacious spring.

2

To rise again

My wages from the colonial government bought me out of
the brown slums of Kaugere to a new housing settlement at
Hohola. Hohola was a colonial delousing centre where better
(richer) class natives were mixed with a few (marginal)
whites as a basic drill in cultural advancement.

My friendship with Dr Dina had deepened. I needed his
friendship because I had the typical, dependent mentality of
a colonial slave; and he needed mine because he was bored
with scoring points off those who tried to stop the inevitable.
To him, today was already history. Everything happened in
the future — and I was tomorrow. I was an interesting catch
for a bored professional. Life would have been simpler if I
had advanced, in an orderly manner, to mediocrity and
obscurity as I most certainly would have done if baby Robert
had not intervened. But Dr Dina insisted that it was my
good luck that he did. He would not have it any other way.
The price of his friendship was that I had to reach for the
stars. At times, I longed for an ordinary home, an ordinary
job and to love an ordinary man. And with luck and a well-

practised smile, I might even land a three-bedroomed house among the foreigners. Then Dr Dina would burst in on my dreams.

'What on Earth do you want to do that for, Josephine?' he would shout. 'It's no good reaching for the stars and then snivelling around looking for mediocre suburban comforts.'

'It's okay, Doctor.' I had advanced to the stage of calling him Doctor. 'I wasn't dreaming about anything. I'm happy doing what I am doing.'

What I was doing was washing and feeding baby Robert in the morning, dashing off to work to be entertained by Dr Dina and his dramatics for most of the day, off to the basketball courts for exercise and relaxation, then back to my slum home at dusk to be a mother until the next day.

* * *

The sports were basketball and netball. We practised five days a week and played in competitions at the week-ends. Needless to say, Dr Dina was coach. It did not take long to learn a few of the tricks that made a competitor good in these sports. I learnt these tricks from him so well that I won a medal in the trials and a place in the team for the fledgling Olympics of the Pacific, the South Pacific Games.

The time for the games in Fiji came around. The trip came at a good time for me as it helped me to repair some of my damaged self-esteem. I was chosen as vice-captain of one of the women's teams; the captain and the team manager were both Australian.

Trouble started before we left when it was suggested by a junior Australian official, at a meeting, that the pants of our sports uniform should be black instead of green.

'Black pants, Miss Daniels,' I gasped. 'Why black pants? Why not keep to the uniform green that we have?'

I thought that the combination of green and black on brown skin would be generously unflattering and, by now, had enough courage to say so.

'Well, we thought that with menstruation, Josephine, black would be a more suitable colour.'

One of Dr Dina's favourite expletives, 'What the hell!' jumped to my mind but it was subdued just in time.

'What has black pants got to do with menstruation, Miss Daniels?' I asked as calmly as I could.

'Well, Josephine,' Miss Daniels discreetly explained as an aside to me, 'Some of the girls may not be very experienced. Green might show the stains and this could be embarrassing during a game.'

'Please, Miss Daniels, Papuan girls don't have black blood. They have red blood like everybody else. The colour of the pants has got nothing to do with menstruation. We wear white, green or any other colour we like. We don't put on black pants just because of menstruation any more than the women of any other race do. I think that we will make fools of ourselves if we wear black just for that reason.'

The discussion was becoming embarrassing to Miss Daniels, who was not accustomed to being questioned by a native. By this time, another kangaroo had taken over and, then and there, decided that the question should be put. The Australians raised their hands first and, with the exception of myself, all the Papuan girls followed suit. It would be an understatement to say that I was surprised at the response. We broke up and began to walk home and I turned to my friends and angrily asked,

'Why did you follow that stupid idea?'

'Don't be angry, Josie, the white women will make all of the decisions no matter what we say. If we go against them we might not be picked for anything again.'

I was learning. It was my first lesson in politics. Money is power and government by personal patronage was the next lesson in decolonisation. An acceptable substitute for democracy.

Suva was a pageant of the Pacific. Men and women from all of the island countries were there. Some wore picturesque costumes and everyone seemed happy. It was good to have weather like home and the countryside was like our own. We played our games and won a medal. We met many people and made some friends. But, still, something was wrong. Several of the other Papuan girls felt it too. To us, everybody seemed to belong to something but we had no identity of our own. Although the Papuan girls belonged together within the team, the whole Papuan and New Guinean contingent was dominated by Australians and Chinese. We were smothered in alien cultures. We could not feel or express our own.

As the games went on the girls became withdrawn and subdued. We spent most of our time in practice and in our dormitories. Outside, foreigners were in charge of our feelings. I was no longer capable of feeling proud that I was an 'Australian' or anything else. I was happy to march with the others in friendly fellowship but I now realised that Papua was my home and my only identity. Anything else was a fake.

* * *

The weeks that followed the Suva games brought a fresh worry. Since leaving the slums at Kaugere, baby Robert and I had shared a house with Uncle Robert at Hohola: first a house rented from a Papuan, who had no better use for it, and later, one of the houses leased by the colonial government to some of its favoured native servants. The favour in my case came from direct frontal attacks on the authorities by Dr Dina, rather than from any sympathy for my own needs. My status with the colonials, who decided who lived where, was that of a temporary female on probation. These gentlemen made several complaints about my continued presence in a government house and, eventually, insisted that I live elsewhere.

Hohola was built like an Australian penal settlement of the early convict days and the roads were reminiscent of the same period. Most of the day, we lived in a cloud of fine dust that settled on everything. Some of the roads in Port Moresby were sealed but these were not for us. The houses were constructed with grey cement brick walls, concrete floor and corrugated iron roof. There were no internal doors or linings as, by analogy with village family homes, such things were unnecessary for natives. A kitchen and laundry were indicated more by declaration than content and one or two low partitions suggested where the beds should be. Uncle Robert occupied one of these sleeping cubicles and I occupied the other. As a special mark of respect, Uncle parted with one of his thin cotton native *ramis* and hung it as a curtain in front of my cubicle.

Our main misery was the toilet. In common with many

other houses in the area, the water table and poor drainage caused regular malfunction of poorly-designed septic tanks. Raw sewage regularly floated around the garden and, at times, back into the house. When this became unbearable, the administration sent out a modified water truck which sucked the waste into its interior and disgorged it elsewhere. Then we had a few days of relief. There was no other way of waste disposal so we had to learn to live with it. The toilet was out of bounds to visitors who had to be schooled to take their troubles elsewhere.

Still, it was a great improvement on the Kaugere slums and we were happy there except, during heavy rains, when everything disappeared under water for a day or two until the water table subsided again to the level of the concrete floor. We had electric light that operated on a ten cent coin metre attached to the outside wall and a water tap of our own. Luxuries beyond dreams in the slums.

Uncle Robert was especially happy. This was the nearest thing to a home that he had known and, together with baby Robert, we made some sort of a family. For me, it was not a home as I had known it but, as a single mother in Port Moresby, it was more than I had a right to expect. Uncle Robert adored the baby and was pleased that he had his name. The intensity of his attentions was a measure of the emotional deprivation he had suffered by turning his back on his natural way of life to spend his years in 'boy houses' provided by the masters. For myself, caring for baby Robert was similar to the care that I had given to many of my brothers and sisters during their first years. Uncle Robert did not approve of my casual attitude to my motherly role, which he put down to poor family upbringing and the bad influence of an Australian education. He did not like the idea of my leaving the baby with Papuan mothers while I was at work and he now had a vague idea that some day he might be able to stop working and look after the house himself.

Uncle Robert and I were both earning a few dollars and a little fresh meat from the butcher shop found its way to our saucepan. I was beginning to show the effects of better nourishment and, for the first time, tipped the scale at 100 pounds.

I was accustomed to living in small one-roomed houses but that was in my secure family at Misima. Port Moresby was a different proposition. A house in Port Moresby could be more like a hotel than a home and people of many cultures and dispositions shared the same land. We were never short of visitors to keep us company. Visitors in homeless Port Moresby were like flies in summer. If a door or a window was left open, they swarmed in and their removal called for firm resolve and strenuous methods! Many pleasant village customs had to be drastically modified in the light of the reality of life in the town.

* * *

Uncle Robert was sick. While I was away in Suva he contracted pneumonia and had not been well since. Dr Sidney was also a practising doctor in the town and he promptly offered to treat my uncle. Dr Sidney was a true do-gooder. He defended the good intentions of his fellow Australians with the same quiet earnestness that he defended his right to care for the underprivileged of the world. It was essential nourishment for his soul.

He came to my house in the late afternoon, carrying a small case and, as ever, sporting that freshly showered look.

'Good afternoon, Dr Sidney, it was nice of you to come to see my uncle.'

'Hello, Josephine. I am glad to have the opportunity to help your uncle and to help you, too. You have enough worries looking after your big family without having sickness in the home. Where is your uncle?'

'He's in there, Dr Sidney,' I said. Papuans had a habit of constantly repeating the surname of a person they wanted to impress. 'I shall open the window so you can see.'

'Why don't you open the window all of the time?' Dr Sidney scolded, 'After all of my good teaching about fresh air and sunlight!'

'Sorry. We Papuans are stupid. When we are sick we like to close the windows. A villager lives in the open air all of the time so when he is sick he wants the windows closed. He feels more comfortable. Otherwise he is thinking of cold air, spirits, enemies and all sorts of things. This is one of the reasons why the people do not like the hospital. It is too open. Remember you not only told us about fresh air but you also told us about following the customs of the people.' I wanted to change the subject, so I asked,

'How is the medical course going, now? It makes me sad when I think about it.'

'Much the same, Josephine. It has its ups and downs. It's not the same for me now that you are not there. You were my most interesting student.'

I thought that he could have added that it was a pity that I had fallen from grace so soon but, instead, Dr Sidney went into the dark cubicle to examine my uncle.

After a time he emerged from the darkness with a lighted torch in his hand. Dr Sidney always gave warning of his thoughts with his facial expression and this prepared the listener for what he had to say. Now, his face was grave.

'I am sorry to have to give you bad news,' said Dr Sidney. 'Your uncle seems to be quite sick. He has had part of his lungs removed in the past and now he seems to have had an inflammation of the lung that has not healed properly. Unresolved pneumonia. I could treat him here but it might be dangerous. It would be much better if he went to hospital.'

'Do you think he will be all right? He should go to hospital if he needs to. We should not take any risks. That way we will be doing the best for him. Will you treat him in hospital?'

'In hospital he will have to be treated by Dr Taylor who is in charge of the medical ward, but that will not make any difference. I can still go and see him. I shall take him with me now, Josephine. It will be better. Who will look after you? Will you be here on your own?'

'No, I have my baby. I shall be all right. I can get someone to stay with me.'

Dr Sidney looked at me intently before speaking again.

'You can stay at my place if that would be better for you. There are servants there who can do some of the work for you. Also, you would be safe there.'

'No, not this time, thank you just the same,' I quickly replied. 'Perhaps I shall be able to accept your offer some other time. I shall be all right now.'

Dr Sidney unexpectedly took my hand in his. 'Be very

careful. A young girl with your background should not be exposed to the danger of living alone like this.'

I thought to myself that I had no intention of exposing myself to any danger that I could avoid and said,

'I shall sleep at the home of a relative tonight. Tomorrow, I shall get organised and arrange for somebody suitable to stay with me.'

We helped Uncle into Dr Sidney's car and then they were gone. After the car disappeared, the brave front dropped and the tears came. I was alone. My thought raced. 'I shall have to hurry if I am going to beat the dark. I can't live in this house alone. That's for sure. Many strange natives now live in Port Moresby and everyone tells stories of attacks and worse.' House-breaking had become common. Port Moresby was becoming a dangerous town. Girls no longer walked away from their homes alone at night.

I gathered up my baby, a few clothes and some food and made my way to a Misima family who lived about two kilometres away. I carried a mat with me. I would ask them for space on the floor for the night. Being village people they would not let me down.

The following days were full of worry and I visited Uncle Robert in hospital twice a day. With the help of friends in the hospital compound, I managed to cook some native food for him every day. He was so appreciative of familiar food that this became a duty. He told me that he would die if he was not nourished with good native food.

I could no longer cope. Transport, my baby, my sick companion, my Hohola home, my work. At this stage, Dr Dina took over and I collapsed in his arms. He could do anything he liked and I would agree. He could go anywhere and I would follow. After my recent experiences, I was too weak to stand alone. I could not discuss anything with him. I just wanted him to make the decisions for me and alter them if anything went wrong. Dr Dina told me that he wasted half of his life on discussions at meetings so that when he was away from them, he wanted to make a few decisions on his own! He was decisive and confident and right now I needed his strength.

I could not accept the help Dr Sidney offered because, with

all of his gentleness and good intentions, I felt that the
clammy hand of colonial intent was present all of the time. I
was secondary to the principles he served. Colonialism had
distorted my dreams of beauty and friendship. I could not
embrace them again. That part of me was dead. I was
conditioned to foreigners and I liked to be with them. I
looked for a familiar love but something had gone wrong.

Dr Dina did not offend me in that way. Perhaps it was
because he was so detached. He was more interested in
justice than in causes and, for good or bad, what he did for
me was selfish and personal between us. He had no special
objections as to when or where he worked for me or in whose
time. Dr Dina worked on priorities. If the priority was high,
you made it, and if it was low, you did not exist. With me,
just about everything but his scheduled lectures were secondary. His car was at my disposal, accommodation was
arranged with a suitable family in the hospital grounds, food
was purchased, my baby was looked after. There was food for
the stomach, music for loneliness and church for the soul.
Not a question asked but nothing overlooked. I could now
cope with the responsibility of looking after my two Roberts.
The warmth came back to my body and I could feel again.

'Thank you, Dr Dina.' I said gratefully.

'Rubbish, Josephine. What are you talking about? Don't
thank me, thank yourself for being worth it. The strongest
athlete or the weakest animal may need help some time. A
person stumbles, is held up for a moment and then, off
again. It's your turn today, it'll be my turn tomorrow.'

I could not thank Dr Dina. He demanded some other
satisfaction of my debt. I should hate him. I don't know why I
stay here. There's no escape from his demands. I'll thank
God instead. He always listens to me. He knows how weak I
am.

'Dear God, always by my side, thank you for your understanding. I was cold and could not feel but now the warmth
is flowing in my body. I was blind and you guided my feet.
You have restored my courage. I can now travel on. 'Curse
Dr Dina! He demanded more than I have to give.'

The days passed. Uncle Robert did not improve and I
devoted myself to his care and to the care of my baby. I was

depressed by the failure of my companion to respond. I felt
that I could make no sacrifice severe enough to express the
depth of my concern. I came closer to him as I felt the full
impact of his lonely life. I confided in him, talked of our
future and tried to breathe emotional life into his tired
heart. Then suddenly, unexpectedly, Uncle Robert was dead.

'God have mercy on his soul. May his spirit rest with the
spirits of our ancestors in our warm Papuan soil. Gentle
companion of my lonely days. We are parted and I am here,
alone. You gave more than you had to give, hope when you
had so little, security when you had none yourself and love
when I had none to return.'

* * *

I was my uncle's closest relative in Port Moresby at the time
of his death. I decided that I would try to raise the money to
return his body to our own native village, as was his wish. I
would try to do it on my own but, if I failed, I was sure that
Dr Dina would help. I was not at the hospital when my uncle
died and I did not hear the news until the next day. When I
heard of his death, I went with a relative, from the hospital
staff, to see his body in the hospital morgue. I had not fully
accepted that he was dead. I saw the body. My uncle had
been claimed in death. I could not relate what I saw to the
considerate man who stood by me in life. His frozen body had
no place in my memories.

When I introduced the matter of his burial, my relative
told me that he thought some Australians were going to bury
my uncle and that we would not be involved. I did not
believe this so I got in touch with some people around the
town to find out more about it. What I learned was that the
Australians had taken over and that we did not exist. I was
amazed and it took a long time for the news to sink in. I had
attended many burials and in every case it was the relatives
of the dead person who were the main ones involved. What
did these Australians have to do with my uncle? He never
talked to me about any Australians when we spent our lives
together, and they certainly never came to see him.

My upbringing was such that when a colonial walked
towards me, I always stepped aside, and if I walked in their

company I always walked a step or two behind. My father invariably walked behind any Australian he accompanied as a matter of second nature and he was uncomfortable in their presence unless he could be continuously demonstrating his inferior status by constant flattery. I wanted to claim my uncle and bury him myself but the force of my years made me bow my head and wait to see what happened. I did not want Dr Dina to know what was taking place. I did not want to be embarrassed by any trouble over the body of my dead uncle.

The Australians who were going to bury my uncle were his white employers and the Australian Returned Soldiers' League. It seemed that my uncle had earned great merit in the eyes of both of these institutions by serving them well in life, so, in death, they had a duty to show their respect and appreciation. In life, they gave him a few medals and, now that he was dead, they would honour him with a civilised burial. I asked these strangers when and where Uncle Robert was to be buried and if I could attend. I was sure that the people I asked had never heard of him until after his death.

His funeral took place on a Saturday afternoon, after the shops had closed for the week-end. For a lonely man who had few, if any, close friends in life, I was astounded to see so many come to honour him in death. As my father's daughter, I apologetically attached myself to the rear of the funeral cavalcade which was headed by several cars driven by Australians. As I travelled along at the end of the procession, my thoughts went to the long, lonely walks he made without car, friends or money and now, in death, there were cars to burn. It was better when we shared our poverty together.

Uncle was to be buried at the old cemetery near Hanuabada village and almost on the spot where Commodore Erskine, in 1884, proclaimed our country a British protectorate in the name of her most gracious Majesty. I was happy that Uncle Robert was going to rest in sight of a Papuan village with cool green trees around and wind blowing in from the sea.

When I finally reached the graveside there were more surprises. One of these was that I could not get near enough to see the grave where Uncle was to be buried. Everybody crowded around the site in social order. This meant that the

Australians occupied the inner circle and I was on the outer looking at tomorrow's laundry.

Unknown to me, Dr Sidney had also attached himself to the funeral. This was the sort of thoughtful act that was characteristic of him. Now, he attached himself to me at the back of the other mourners. In the crowd, there was not a tear, a cry or a murmur. I, too, was frozen. My thoughts strayed from Uncle to Dr Dina. I now needed him more than ever. I had asked him to come with me to the funeral but he replied that there was no need for him to rehearse death. He provided transport for me and then bowed out.

I could see nothing at the graveside and I was beginning to panic. I must assert myself enough to be able to see Uncle buried. I would be ashamed if he visited me later, as a spirit, and I had not even seen him buried. I appealed to Dr Sidney and told him that I could not push all of the foreigners out of the way to get to my uncle.

Dr Sidney saw my predicament and suddenly realised that I had been excluded from this foreign service. Like the chivalrous crusader that he was, Dr Sidney became aggressive in a manner foreign to his nature. He handled his compatriots roughly and pushed them aside, explaining to them the importance of my presence. We arrived together at the graveside, but I was totally unprepared for the spectacle before me.

My uncle's coffin was completely wrapped in a large Australian flag. A red, white and blue Union Jack and a Southern Cross on a blue background. I gasped in surprise. Dr Sidney, thinking that I cried in grief, put a firm hand on my shoulder while I hurriedly withdrew. I must have stumbled onto a foreign secret ritual. Maybe this was not a proper place for a native woman — I was the only one present. For a confused moment I thought that I might be at the wrong funeral. I should have stayed at the back where I belonged.

Dr Sidney, caught unaware by my sudden retreat, slipped back to join me. My uncle's flag-wrapped coffin was lowered into the grave with 'European' precision. Not a hitch. Not a murmur. I had never seen a Papuan funeral like this one. My uncle was in there. He was a Papuan but he was buried like a foreigner! Would Uncle have been proud of this silent tribute? He had told me that he wanted to return to his own village to be buried.

The earth thudded dully on the casket as I stood in stunned silence. I wanted the ceremony to end quickly. I did not feel well and I wanted to go home to be alone with my thoughts. I looked at all of the foreigners around the grave. I would come back and visit him properly when all of these people had gone.

In our short life together Uncle had never mentioned the foreign war to me. I must have been too busy talking about myself. I had seen his medals and he left them to me. But when I went to collect his things after his death, all of the medals were missing.

The grave was filled in and the rounded earth was covered with expensive flowers. I started to walk away from the grave and Dr Sidney walked with me. I was lost with my thoughts.

We reached Dr Sidney's car and he turned to confront me.

'Didn't you have anything to do with how your uncle was buried? You should have arranged it how you wanted it.'

'I'm a coward in such things, Dr Sidney. When the Australians took over I was too frightened to say anything.'

'Why didn't you tell me or tell Dr Dina. Either of us could have helped you.'

'I was frightened to tell Dr Dina. I thought that he might get angry and cause trouble. I'm a Papuan. I hate trouble, especially where foreigners are concerned. They are the masters and we are the servants. We were each born to our own roles. Some Papuans believe that this is God's purpose for us. I am ashamed of myself for being such a coward.'

'Nonsense,' said Dr Sidney very angrily. I had never heard him speak so loudly before. Perhaps I should not have brought God into it.

'God made everybody equal,' said Dr Sidney. 'There are no masters and no servants in the eyes of God. These Australians are only trying to show respect to a man who must have earned it while he was alive. I never saw a Papuan so honoured by them before.'

I started to take my leave and turned towards Dr Dina's

car. 'Goodbye, Dr Sidney, and thank you very much for coming along. I did not feel so alone. I really did not think that it would turn out like this.'

Dr Sidney wanted to talk on but my thoughts were elsewhere. Baby Robert had not come to the ceremony as he may have become possessed by spirits which are active during these events. When I arrived home I wanted to go straight to him but I had to shower first. We cannot go to a child after such an event until we have bathed. We must not take risks. Everything must be washed off first and clean clothes put on. No harm must come to the young ones. Then I went to my baby. I still belonged. We lived to rise again.

* * *

After Uncle Robert's death I sent money to my parents. I wanted them to come to Port Moresby together with the children. Times were hard for them since my father came out of gaol. The whites would not employ him. He was so like Uncle Robert. He had spent his life serving the foreigners and now he was destitute. All of this made me feel that I could no longer cope on my own yet I still wanted to retain my independence. I did not want to be tied to someone who would marry me and every time he looked at my child see a secret lover. I did not want to give up. I wanted to try to walk with Dr Dina. Also, I needed my parents and I hoped that they might need me.

The family arrived in Port Moresby and it was like old times again. My parents and my younger brothers and sisters were with me. I had more responsibility and I felt much older. At Misima, I depended on my parents but now a lot depended on me. I was the wage earner and I provided the house. There were no native gardens in Port Moresby and food was hard to come by.

Robert was no longer Baby Robert. He was growing bigger now. With my mother home his care was no problem. My parents had twelve children with another one on the way. Eventually, they collected another four adopted children to make seventeen in all. My extra one was hardly noticed. The

Abaijahs were good breeding stock. My own experience left me in no doubt about that.

* * *

Things were going smoothly. Work with Dina was good, though it had its rough side as well as its smooth. Some colonials regarded our union as an unholy one. It just wasn't done. A man in such a position should not be so friendly with a Papuan girl. Natives should be kept in their place and their place was not consorting with an eccentric professional. Things must have been going too smoothly because the next confrontation did not take long to appear. Three or four times I had been told by the colonials that I had to vacate the government house that I was occupying. It was not proper for a single girl to occupy a house. Each time Dr Dina told me to ignore them.

'Take no notice of them. They would like you to go without any fuss but it's much harder if they have to do something about it. Just do nothing. They will go on leave soon and forget all about you.'

But this time it was war, and I had to go. I could not occupy a government house. I was a temporary female and I had to go. At least that was the excuse the colonial officials used to get rid of an unwelcome tenant. Now it was a matter of pride. Them or us. There was no room for compromise. Confronted with the inevitable, Dr Dina acted in a characteristic manner.

'Why don't you build your own house, Josephine? That is what the village people do'

'How can I build a house, Dr Dina? I have no money to build a house in Port Moresby or anywhere else.'

'Who is talking about money? You don't need money. What you need is the desire and the character to succeed.'

'Do you really think I could build a house in Port Moresby?'

Dr Dina never joked about such things. I knew enough about him by now to take the suggestion seriously.

'Look, Jo.' Jo was the intimate touch kept for special occasions. 'I not only think you have the courage and character to build your own house but it's about time that you started to build your own life as well. In ten or fifteen years

you could be President of your country if you really tried
hard enough.'

These were the words I longed to hear. Some of the courage
I had brought to the Papau Medical College had returned to
me. I thought this time I had the strength to see it through. I
wanted to have the chance to prove it.

'Tell me what I should do. You are the only man I can
trust. I will not let you down again.'

'You never let anyone down but yourself. You had a baby.
So what? That's not the end of the world. It altered the
circumstances of your life, that's all. One thing a woman
should do is to have a child and when she proves to herself
that she can do it, she should then proceed to preserve
and build the quality of her life. Life at all ages can be a
wonderful experience. Actively prepare for the next stage,
don't sit back and moan about it.'

I did not reply. Papuans often do not reply to people they
know well. If any other man had said these things to me I
would have dismissed them as empty talk. I had never heard
Dr Dina take words lightly or indulge in idle boasting. I was
optimistic that I was on the march again. But I must not
expect too much. A house of my own in Port Moresby sounded
an impossibility but I would tell my parents, to cheer them
up.

With my family in Port Moresby, destitute except for my
support, my responsibilities were greatly increased. Decisions
now involved their welfare as well as my own. The colonial
administration had ordered me to vacate my house either
because I was a single girl or because a colonial ghost had
followed the family to town. I was a single girl but with a
large family. Father, mother, Josephine, Robert, Mita,
Rodney, Paul, Rowland, Ronald, Neville, Linda, Edna,
Jennifer, Coleman, and the others coming and going. I had to
house and feed all on the income I earned from the colonial
administration. The colonials found the number of people
around my house offensive. Dr Dina was right. The only
solution was to build a house of my own.

My idea was a slum house in a squatter settlement, like
the one I lived in when Robert was born. One made of
discarded timber and old iron, salvaged from the rubbish

dumps that received the rotting remains of the demolished houses of the town. We would have to leave Hohola and return to the slums, to leave our electric light and water tap behind. Perhaps it did not matter. I was working and we were together. It should be okay. The other poor people survived so I supposed that we could.

'Those foreigners must really hate me. They won't let up until they grind me into the dirt. There is nothing I can do. They control everything. My father made a mistake when he turned his back on the village to spend his life working for the masters. Village Papuans are better off than we are. At least they have a house to live in.' These were the thoughts that occupied my mind when Dr Dina next spoke about the house. As it turned out, his thoughts on the matter were very different from mine. When he told me his plans it took me time to control my thoughts and talk sensibly. He must have thought that I was an inexperienced child. I was sure that he was talking nonsense.

Dr Dina's plan was to stall the housing committee as long as possible with promises and hard luck stories.

'Let them take court action against you if they are game to. It all takes time. It would look bad for them too. Especially with a story like yours. While this is going on, lease the best land still available in Hohola and make sure it's close enough to work to walk if necessary and far enough from the main traffic not to be suffocated with dust. Then, all you have to do is be the first Papuan to get a government loan to build a house of your own design. Not a slum house in a shanty town but a fine home of expensive foreign materials and good Papuan timber. We'll build the house ourselves to make up the difference between the loan and the real value. Buy the materials with the money from the loan and build the house ourselves. Don't talk about it in case someone panics. Just do it.'

Then, before my disbelieving eyes, it all began to happen. We prevailed on the housing committee to stay their hand for a short time and we managed to have this extended two or three times. Suddenly, and by mysterious means, I found myself the lessee of a block of land in a suitable location. A loan was arranged with progressive payments. Dr Dina knew how to draw the plans and build the house: in the past, it had been a part of the job. Build or perish. Family muscle would supply the unskilled labour, and friends would supply specialist know-how.

Working together we built the house. It absorbed all of our spare time and we developed our skills as we went along. In six months I had a fine new home on an elevated site at Hohola. It was just off the main road and a mansion compared with anything I had known. I had plenty of family to fill it with and, with the endless succession of brothers, sisters and their issues to care for, I have kept it filled ever since.

Dr Dina called it drive and character. I thought that it was hard work and white man's magic. No money and I now had a house! They told me that I had a debt but I could not feel it. Dr Dina said to forget about it.

'Improve your job and encourage inflation and it will pay for itself.'

I did not know what he was talking about and told him so. And I was told that it was time that I studied the economics of survival in a savage society — his own. That is what I set out to do.

* * *

The time had arrived for the first graduation of general trained nurses in the Territory of Papua and New Guinea and the Australian Minister for the Territories had come from Canberra to introduce the new order.

The day dawned blue, as always, in Port Moresby but this day was to witness a special event. The graduating nurses had been preparing for this day for the past three years. They were up early and went together to the small United Church at Boroko to pray, as was the custom of the people. After the service they returned to the College where Dr Dina presented each graduand with a graduation badge which was the status symbol of their new profession.

The first of the bright new generation passed on their three-starred epaulets to the students nurse who were to follow. A last meal together and then the nurses dressed in white uniforms for the first time and prepared to meet the Australians and their Government Minister. The private dedication had ended; now for the public ceremony.

The old lecture room, where I had studied as a medical

student, was packed with Australians and hundreds of students. Relatives and friends of the graduands were outside, competing for space around the louvered windows. Everyone was in a pleasant mood. The raised platform at one end accommodated the Minister, Dr Dina and an appropriate assortment of departmental heads and colonial officials. The students sang 'The Lord is my Shepherd'. Several of the Australians had tears in their eyes. It was their turn to cry and many lips muttered that they never thought that they would have lived to see the day. The Australian Government Minister, in emotional tones, gave a fatherly address and greeted the new order.

It was a beautiful day; a day for gentle thoughts. The old and the new blended in graceful dignity and the Australians were well-pleased with their efforts. This was their day. Dr Dina, the author of their pride and satisfaction, had slipped away. He did not want to intrude on the privacy of their achievements.

For me, split between two worlds, it was an experience of mixed emotions. I had been chosen to be the witness to the bitterness of the struggle as well as the celebration. In the end it was as simple as it was inevitable. Why did they wait so long? Why was I the witness to the first of so many things that my parents could not have dreamt of?

* * *

The colonials manipulated our popular titles as often as political expediency dictated. The people of New Guinea were variously known as *kanaka, monkey*, and *meri* (mary), while we were known as 'boy' and *hahine* (woman) and, unofficially, various slang labels stuck. Later, we were collectively known as natives, indiginies, Papuans or New Guineans, Papuans and New Guineans, Papua New Guineans, nationals and naturals.

Pidgin English was introduced by the Germans as the colonial language for German New Guinea. Pidgin English was unknown in Papua until after the Second World War when the Australians introduced it to Papua as their new colonial language. Previously, we had no trouble communi-

cating in Motu or simple English. Now we had to learn
pidgin.

Dispela sis i wankain olsem mit.

This fella cheese is one kind all the same meat.

Cheese is similar to meat.

By the time that they tried to pidginise me, I was already
speaking four languages in my daily conversations. I decided
that I could live without it.

By now I had become an urban dweller. I was responsible
for a large household and responsible for my own future. The
picturesque villages and romantic surroundings of my growing years were now but memories. I grasped at the beauty of
natural things but I was continually bombarded by the
noises of a materialistic culture that was slowly absorbing
all of the attention of my senses.

I slipped from childhood to physical maturity with graceful
ease and unpractised love. I changed from light-hearted girl
to sensuous woman with the scars of broken dreams, the
emptiness of unfulfilled love and the unresolved hatred of
the rejections of an indifferent colonialism. Part of me was
dead, but I felt the growth of a new determination to accept
the challenge to restore the essentials of my old values in a
hostile new environment. I sought a solution to loneliness
through sport and the companionship I needed. I expressed
myself through the extravagances of the new materialism.
My basic needs rested deep in the roots of my family. My
hours were filled with purpose. If I was trying to forget, I had
found an answer.

Peggy was an Australian girl who worked in our library.
She was two years older than I was. She was blonde, petite
and a constant weight-watcher. Casually attractive to her
own satisfaction, she did not appear to carry any colour
consciousness and hastily assumed that my needs were the
same as her own. She usually visited me during her lunch
break when she had nothing better to do. The visits were
never reciprocated but she did not seem to mind. We talked
together for half an hour or strolled across the hospital
grounds to the Red Cross kiosk.

At first her conversations were stimulating as they gave

me a glimpse of the mysterious world of foreign women. I
wondered if she was typical of other Australians here. She
assured me that she was and she told me that most of the
girls who came up here were looking for husbands while a lot of
the men were running away from wives.

She did not seem to be looking for companionship. It had
something to do with emotional and material security. To
achieve this, there had to be a constant rejection of life as it
was. A restless unfulfilment that provided the energy to
search for the right person to fill the void. It seemed to be
absolutely necessary to be unsatisfied, as satisfaction was
capitulation. She told me weird stories of sexual misadven-
tures of Australian women here. An Australian girl, who
became pregnant to a house 'boy' on her parents' plantation
and, subsequently, nearly killed herself trying to put things
right. Peggy loved to talk about the latest things in contra-
ception, Siamese twins and sex change operations.

Eventually, I tired of the constant repetition. Things
central to her life were marginal to mine. I avoided complications as these distracted my purpose, but Peggy embraced
complications as they were the currents that carried her on
her unchartered course. The world of my mother and her
thirteen children was simple and straightforward. Peggy's
was complicated, technical and time absorbing.

Peggy and I were spending our lunch break together for
the last time. She was going overseas for a holiday as she
had saved up enough money to continue the search elsewhere. We sat on the same spot where I had sat with Manu
years before. The red hibiscus had gone but the grass had
expanded into lawns and Indian flame trees shaded us.

'What do you think about white women marrying Papuans?'
I asked Peggy as I thought about Manu. Peggy hesitated as
she had never thought of such a possibility. But she was an
expert in such matters and would give an expert's opinion.
She thought for a while and said,

'I have never considered it before.' It must have been the
only possibility she had not considered. 'It might be okay for
a white girl to marry a native man. It depends on what she
wants to get out of life. Some stupid girls might want to live
in a native village but they would not be normal. Just

showing off. Trying to annoy someone. Really, I don't think it would last.'

'What about the towns?' I asked, thinking that Peggy was trying to evade the questions.

'I can't see it,' said Peggy. 'The Papuans work for almost nothing. The woman would have to keep the man. I don't suppose the man would mind that. I don't know about the woman. I don't think so. Not for me, anyhow.'

'What about later?' I persisted. 'We might become an independent country some day. It might be different then.'

'I'm not so sure. My father says independence might come here in 50 years. It might happen some day. I wouldn't like to get married on that assumption,' Peggy said tersely. 'It might be okay if a native had big pay and was a big shot. I know money isn't everything but you can't live without it. I don't fancy it myself. I don't know what my mother would say if I took her home a couple of black grandchildren. Life is complicated enough without looking for trouble.'

'Do you know, Peggy, before I came to Port Moresby I didn't know that I was black. We only call people black when they are really black. It's the name of a colour, not a social class. I really got shocked when the Australians in Port Moresby started to call me 'black'. What do Australians mean by black?'

Peggy was having a hard day. We had never talked like this before. Her favourite topics were men and clothes. Today, it was her turn to talk about something different.

'I guess they mean anybody who is dark.'

'I'm not sure about that,' I replied. 'Many Australians are dark, too. They sometimes spend all day in the sun making themselves darker. They say this makes them handsome, attractive or something. What do you think about colour, Peggy?'

'I don't think about it, Jo. I just say that I would not marry a Papuan. I want to live my own way and that takes money. Facts are facts and we should face the facts, not run away from them. 'What do *you* think about colour, Jo?' asked Peggy, turning the question in my direction.

'I was always taught to be proud of brown skin. We like it better than white or black. That's because we develop our own sense of beauty in our own country. When colour means more than colour it can make problems. This is one of the facts we must face, I guess.'

We were back at the office so I turned to Peggy and said,

'Good luck, Peggy, have a nice time. We might not meet again. I shall remember our lunches together.'

'Goodbye, Jo, I'll always remember you, too. Especially our talk today. It was beaut. It's good to sweep the cobwebs away sometimes. I spend too much time thinking about myself, that's my trouble. Look after yourself. I hope I come back some day.'

'Do you think you will come back?'

'No, I don't think so.'

3

Fished out

*F*ollowing my fall as a medical student, Dr Dina, had 'fished me out' of the Kaugere slums and made me secretary to the Dean and to half a dozen faculty and study boards at the Papuan Medical College because 'I was the only educated native who was desperate enough to take the job; being a girl the material was more interesting; and, after a year of association, we were still reasonably good friends.'

Dr Dina influenced me at a time when I was vulnerable to his unorthodox charms. On the first occasion, I was an unsuspecting medical student facing a bright new world. On the second occasion, I was a lonely woman disillusioned with innocence, cowed by failure and recuperating on the bare brown rocks of the Kaugere slums. On both occasions, his gentle touch was servant to his schemes to snare me into a future carefully selected for style and fit. Now, my failure formed the rock to build on, and my disillusionment was the author of a new determination. Willingly I gave myself to a personal intimacy that, for constancy and purpose, surpassed any measure of expectation.

My induction into the economics of a 'savage society' was coming to an end.

'Throw away your typewriter and take up the pen,' Dina persisted. 'A pen is lighter than a typewriter. With it you can travel further. Don't make yourself too useful to other people until you are in a position to use them to your own advantage. The same as you have manipulated me.'

'You finished your education with a High School Certificate. That's not good enough. It's just a beginning. You now have to matriculate. You have to improve your capacity to earn money. You have to pay for your home and buy a car. That means a softer job with more pay. Matriculation is society's 'Learners' Permit' to personal advancement. If you're lucky you can make it by other means but, with your record, I wouldn't advise you to try. Forget everything else, Jo. There's only one thing for you and that's matriculation.'

'When, Dr Dina?' I asked cautiously. I had to speak sparingly when this mood was upon him.

'Now, of course. What other time is there? Now is the only time that we have any control over.'

'How am I going to matriculate now?' I asked firmly. 'That's impossible. I have to work and keep a family.'

'Nothing's impossible, Jo.' Jo was my steady name now. I sometimes called him Doctor.

'I have debts, Doctor,' I persisted. 'I have a house to pay off. Now I have a car to pay off. It's not possible to matriculate and work at the same time.'

'You have half a house to pay off. You already paid for half your house with our labour. You can't matriculate without wheels. The car will matriculate you. You have to save time somehow. That's why I talked you into buying that old Volkswagen. It will keep you poor but you will survive. You are not alone. I will make sure you don't get into too much trouble. The car will save you time and that's how you'll matriculate.'

'I've forgotten everything I learned at school,' I said defensively. 'I could not study like that again. That part of me is finished.'

'That's an advantage,' persisted Dr Dina enthusiastically. He always enjoyed his own philosophies. 'It's an advantage to know nothing before you start. You can study subjects as a whole and not limb by limb. Another advantage is that you are mature. It will be much easier than before. Children can waste half of their time fighting themselves. At least you are past that stage.'

'I can't argue against you for long. You know that,' I replied, but I also had a secret ambition to study further. Anyhow, you are usually right. If you say that this is best then I shall try, but don't be surprised if I am a big flop.'

'It is best and you must, Jo, otherwise you will be left behind. You think now that the High School Certificate is a good education because no Papuans were educated to that standard before. But others who will follow will go to matriculation and university. They will leave you for dead. Your education was never completed. Everyone was in too much of a hurry.'

I had come a long way and I did not want to turn back. If Dr Dina said that I was going to matriculate then I was going to matriculate. There was no further discussion. Foreigners were plentiful in Port Moresby and there was a demand for Australian matriculation examinations. The structure for study was there. All that remained was the work. By taking one or two subjects at a time, and working at night and in my other spare time, I completed the studies in three years. Dr Dina wanted it done in two. But he was not human: I had my work, home and soul to look after as well.

Why English, logic, economics, physiology, modern history and the history of the Pacific and South East Asia? I did not have the faintest idea. Most of the subjects were new to me so I had to start from scratch. Dr Dina said that this was an advantage. Nobody knew what was in the mind of Dr Dina as he planned so far ahead. It was no use asking. It was better to wait for the purpose to reveal itself even though this might take ten or fifteen years..

Sometimes I found it necessary to stand up and fight. Previously, I did not believe that it was possible to spend so much time with one person and still survive. Priorities were set and time was made available day or night. No questions, no thanks. Just work and purpose.

I still had a house, a car, a family and no money. I now
thought that I had a reasonable education or, as I was told,
the beginnings of an education. A 'Learner's Permit' to
personal advancement. There was nothing unusual about
this in a normal society but it was very unusual under
Australian colonialism. I was the first Papuan girl to do
many common things. What was to come next? I dared not
raise the question.

* * *

Of all our people, I alone was witness to the foundations of
medical education in Papua and New Guinea, the first tertiary education established in the country. The beauty of
innocence belonged to another world; it could not survive
here. Civilization was intruding to the edges of every sensi-
bility. Its own rules were scribbled over the tablets of God
until neither could be read or understood. So each man
wrote his own rules and lived in his own image.

I learned that the missionaries only worked with people
such as us. They were foreign in their own countries. Their
service was especially for us. In their own countries many
people used churches only for extremes. Birth, death and
sickness in between. The white man's churches were lightly
used while the brown churches of Papua overflowed with
song.

It was a day of breathless blue sky and scorching sun. I
was with Dr Dina attending a native church service in the
northern district. An English missionary exhorted the people
to give generously of their money so that more and bigger
churches could be maintained or built. The villagers gave
generously of their prayers, but, of money, they had little
and the priest was flushed with anger. Much of the money
was coming from overseas while the prayers were coming
from Papua. His mind was distorted by the imbalance that
he had devoted his life to redress.

When the service was over, the priest and the people
poured from the loose-thatched walls of the church to the
lush lawns outside which were fenced with tropical, flowering shrubs. The church was under the shadow of Mt
Lamington, the sleeping giant. There was no imbalance of

nature here. The volcano, the rain and the sun had combined in generosity to produce an earth bursting with life and beauty.

For some time it had been obvious that we could not continue to keep my large, expanding family in Port Moresby indefinitely. The house at Hohola was good but it was bursting at the seams and, at night, every available space was taken up by a sleeping mat. Food in Port Moresby was expensive and transport and other services cost a lot of money for a large family. My father had become restless because, without money or work, he felt that his position as head of the family was threatened. I had taken over. He was a man of rural Papua and he could not understand the austerity and isolation of the big town.

So we were now looking for a permanent solution for the accommodation of my family in the shape of a block of farm land. We needed another home where the family could grow their own food. Also, I had to be free of some family responsibilities if I was going to advance. The family had become too dependent on me and on my continued employment in Port Moresby. A rural home in the northern district, over the mountain range from Port Moresby, was to be the answer.

The land here was very fertile and small 20-acre settler blocks were available for purchase. My family could set themselves up as farmers which is what they had always wanted to be. My parents would keep some of the children with them and I would keep some of them with me. The children could be transferred between the farm and Port Moresby as circumstances changed. Our total family of natural and adopted children was seventeen. We were an industry on our own. I could send money from Port Moresby and they could send native vegetables to me. Everybody would gain and the family would put down roots in rural Papua once again.

After leaving the church we set off in a borrowed 4-wheel drive vehicle to visit some foreign plantations and native-owned settler blocks in search of suitable land for a farm of our own. The Australians lived proudly on their plantations but, in some ways, they were worse off than the natives. Some of them were returned soldiers, who were settled on land to develop cocoa plantations with the help of generous loans. The scheme was for the white returned soldiers to develop large cocoa plantations and then to repay the loans out of their profits. It did not work and many went broke.

So the rural area of Sangara had become a mixture of native villagers, white plantation settlers and outside Papuans and New Guineans on small 20-acre blocks of land. This was the melting pot. It melted but it did not produce much more than subsistence farmers and a lot of bad debts. But the parasites thrived and steadily ate their way through the plantations and now there was plenty of land for sale.

We arrived at one white plantation where a bearded migrant from Europe looked us over and invited us into his house. He lived on his estate like a feudal lord. Everything was spic and span, with polished furniture and well-kept lawns. The planter seemed to be in a constant state of agitation which I thought could have been a show put on for our benefit. Every few minutes he gave his native servant a new command.

'Boy! Cigarette,' he shouted and a native servant, who constantly hovered in the background, lifted a packet of cigarettes out of his master's shirt pocket and placed a cigarette in his master's mouth. The native servant, who was a well-fed boy of about sixteen years, then lit the cigarette and returned to the background.

'Boy! Pencil.'

'Boy! Move the chair.'

'Boy! Bring the brandy.'

'Boy! Take off my boots.'

'Boy! A cup of tea for the lady.'

The cry of 'boy' seemed to sound every few minutes — and I was the lady — a concession to changing times!

I had long since withdrawn from colonial situations such as these and took no notice of them. I was withdrawn and protected so they no longer touched me. I watched but did not see. Like a law of diminishing returns, each insult was less effective than the last. I had reached a dangerous stage. I could criticise as well as be criticised and respect for white foreigners was being replaced by intolerance for their weaknesses. The slave mentality of my colonial inheritance was slowly fading away.

'Yes,' said the planter in reply to our query. 'I know where there's a good block of land. We are particular about the type of natives we get around here.' Then turning to Dr Dina, he said, 'That girl with you looks a decent type. Much better than some of the *kanakas* we see around here.' Then, after a pause, he said, 'There's one decent block I know. It's owned by a man who wants to take his family to Moresby. It's twenty acres, has a good fresh stream flowing through it, is fully planted with cocoa and has a good site for a house.' The planter paused to look at Dr Dina and, after winking knowingly, continued. 'There's a native house there now. You'll have to pull it down. It's spoiling a good site. Good houses improve values and keep the *kanakas* out.'

The planter paused to get his native servant to produce another cigarette. Travelling with Dr Dina, I had become accustomed to being treated like a *taukurokuro* (white). He made no compromises in the presence of foreigners and the usual reaction to this was to accept me without comment. Usually, when I was with Dr Dina, foreigners did not modify their conversation because of me. If I could not take it, I should not masquerade as one of them. Dr Dina said it was better to know the worst spoken about us natives than to walk around in a dream.

By the time we took our leave, our host had become more friendly. He was now keen to have us in the district and filled us in on the details likely to be of use in finalising the purchase of the land.

When we found the block we were pleased with what we saw. It was exactly what we had been looking for. It was on the main road that joined the coast at Buna with Kokoda in the foothills of the Owen Stanley Range. It had good flat land for buildings in the front and the rest was fully planted with cocoa. Some of the trees were four or five years old and were bearing, while some were recent plantings. There was a small, clear stream, some metres wide, that flowed across the block and which had been dammed with loose rocks to give deep water for drinking and washing.

We were satisfied. It was easy to settle on a price and, after brief negotiations, the deal was closed. The owner, who had cleared the land and planted the cocoa, thought that he had done well.

When we travelled in rural Papua we usually slept in native houses. Except for the materials, this home was not really like a native house. It was more like a 'boy' house on a plantation with a row of single rooms opening onto a wide verandah in front. It was my job to handle the accommodation so I approached the man of the house with my request. I was told that there was plenty of room in the house if the *taubada* (big man) did not mind.

Dina and I sat together on the mat-padded verandah and looked at the surrounds of my future family home. It was growing dark already and giant sentinel trees that had escaped the axe, ringed our periscope to the sky and the wondrous beauty of the stars. Papuan foods were plentiful here, and to culture-starved strangers from Port Moresby, a tin of corned beef and native foods could be a banquet.

As we finished a meal provided by our hosts, clouds rolled down from the mountains and the closed heavens opened up to charge the streams and the land with water for another day. Then, belching light and thunder, they demanded respect and silence while the spirits retreated to the mountains to gather for the night. This was the dangerous cycle of the rain spirits that my family would witness down the years. If the spirits were distracted they could hold fast in the mountains until our waters ran dry. If they were angered, they could so fill the earth with water that the food rotted in the ground and humans had to seek food from the jungle trees and watch as children became sick and died.

With the meal and the storm over, our beds were prepared for the night. We had been warned that hungry rats might distract us during the night by sampling our hands and feet! Sometimes in Misima, I had woken up with sore hands and feet from rat bites, so I did not have to be warned twice. With this in mind, we prepared a capsule consisting of mosquito nets and native mats so that, when the time came for sleep, we could retreat inside and hope a toe, a finger or worse did not touch the side. The family of our Papuan hosts were preparing for early sleep as they would be up at dawn, but Dr Dina and I had important things to discuss.

The clouds cleared and revealed a small moon, bright enough for our needs, so we sat and talked. We had found a home for my family in a rural area. It was far away from beautiful Misima island but near enough to my native village of Wamira for me to feel at home.

'After years in Port Moresby this is paradise,' I said, as we sat in village-made cane chairs on the verandah, looking out into the night.

'It took you a long time to get around to a place like this,' Dr Dina said.

'I could not face it before,' I replied, 'I had to cleanse myself first. I had turned my back on so much that this represents. I could not come to terms with rural Papua again until I had come to terms with myself.'

'It's more than five years since you came to the Papuan Medical College. I thought that you had turned your back on rural life.'

'I never turned my back on rural life. I just let myself down and could not face my past,' and, changing the subject, said, 'Do you think we can build a house here, like we did at Hohola? I don't want my family to return to the houses they lived in before. They deserve something better. I suppose that is what you call turning my back on the past.'

'What sort of house, Jo? A native material house or a foreign house?'

'A decent native material house will do. The only trouble is it won't last long. They have to be renewed every few years. I am strong now. We can build a house if you help me. In the future I might not be able to do it.'

'We can do it if we take our time,' said Dr Dina, 'we'll get the foundations done first. There are no building regulations here. We can build to the same plan that we used in Port Moresby. We can start as soon as you own the land. It won't be as easy as Port Moresby as we have to fly here and that takes time and money.'

'That's great,' I said, 'I can't wait to start. I might be able to get an additional job and earn some more money. The people say the Government might lend $600.00 to develop the plantation. We might be able to get that.'

Dr Dina shook his head. 'No, no more debts. You have all the debts you can handle. You might lose the lot if you go too far.'

'Okay, I'll have to depend on you. I don't really understand about money and you taught me what little I know about building. At least I'm strong now and I can hammer a nail.'

'Forget about the nails, Jo. We won't make the mistakes we made at Hohola. First, we'll make high two and a half metre concrete piers, and a smooth concrete floor at ground level. That will take a while. In the meantime, your family will have to live in this native house. It's a bit of a wreck. It will have to be repaired. But that should not take long.'

So the conversation went on until the subject of the new house and the family shifting to Sangara had been exhausted. It was then that Dr Dina introduced a new subject, the thought of which kept me awake for the rest of the night. I expected the Papuan Medical College and Dr Dina to go on forever. With Dr Dina's companionship I could not be bored but old colours were unfolding to new purposes. I was deeply involved. Happy, fulfilled and confident, I was developing a new set of values to replace the unrelieved naivety that had brought me to harm.

'Do you know, Jo' Dr Dina said seriously, 'the Papuan Medical College will fold up soon?'

I thought that I had not heard correctly and I asked, 'What do you mean 'fold up'? The Papuan Medical College can't fold up.'

'No,' said Dr Dina, 'the PMC cannot fold up but we can. Our jobs will fold up soon. We have to look for new jobs.'

'I don't believe it,' I said. 'You built this thing up. There would have been nothing without you.'

'There would have been something without me,' said Dr Dina. 'It would have been a few years later and twice the fuss. It could have been done fifty years ago. But now it's just a part of decolonisation. That is the price that you have to pay for working for a government. If you fail, nobody worries. They might even transfer you to a better job. But, if you succeed, the success belongs to everyone but you. There's always someone higher up to take the credit. In any case, Jo, I am bored with this work now. We will soon have the first graduation of doctors. There are hundreds of qualified nurses. Six schools of nursing and all of the other courses are thriving. It's all downhill from here in. Just routine management. Anyone can do it now. The opportunities are gathering on the sidelines. They see the signs and they will move soon.'

I was staggered. I never thought of a PMC without Dr Dina.

'What are we going to do?' I asked, wondering if he was joking or serious.

'What do you want to do?' he answered cheerfully.

'I want to stay with you. You are everything I need. I have not thought of life without you. You know I'm a coward. I'm frightened of life.'

'I need you, Jo, just as much as you need me. More. I need meaning to what I am doing. You are the only meaning around here now.'

Dr Dina had more than a year of accumulated leave coming to him. This was against the rules. He must leave soon. Others were waiting for the opportunity to move in. I did not care what I did but we had to stay together. I had been taught to reach for the stars. I had been taught to expect success. I was not going to quit now. I liked the feeling.

I was in love with Dr Dina. A love that had to do with breathing, feeling and living. A love of warmth and strength. A love of success, self-esteem and equality. A love I had learned at his hands. A primary experience in living. I could not let him go. I knew him as intimately as he knew me. It was now my turn to fish him out with a few schemes of my own. If he suggested us breaking up I would fail until he came running back to save me. He could not stand failure and I would be the biggest failure he had ever known. A failure of the heart, the body, the soul. I would be a mental and a moral wreck. He could not stand that. I would always need him and I would always let him know. I would fight back and I would win. I had not closed my eyes all of the time during the six years that I had known him. I didn't care how much I would hurt him. It might teach him how I feel. If he were to dump me now, he should have left me in the slums when I was with my own kind and not shown me the stars. It was not the stars that I wanted, it was him. I wanted him to show them to me. I wanted to rest secure in his body, in his arms and in his mind. He had so much strength, he had plenty to spare for me. I not only learned his strengths and praised them liberally, but I also learned his weaknesses and kept them to myself for use on a rainy day. To me, the clouds were gathering, now.

At Sangara every day was a rainy day and I was not going to build Sangara without him. I had tried love as a one night stand and it had died before the dawn. This time it would not die so easily. The one thing that Dr Dina could not stand was failure of anything that he had touched, and that included me. We talked into the night. The rats had a bad night but the mosquitoes did well. I did well, also.

I did not have to do much more than hint at my weaknesses to convince Dr Dina that it would be a bad time for us to go our separate ways for, as he said, we had been through so much together. He had set his mind on returning to clinical medicine but, before the night was finished, clinical medicine was out for the time being and we had decided to see the next six years through together. A lot could happen in six years.

I was pleased that I had learned something to my advantage and he was pleased to have been forced into a promising adventure with a Papuan girl. Two people, poles apart, bound together by a loyalty to the qualities that they had developed in each other. A willingness to share what we had to share. An exercise in loving and reaching for the stars.

* * *

We planned to part and to quickly and separately qualify ourselves in the discipline of Health Education, a much neglected and little sought after branch of medicine, as it did not bring high returns in the medical market-place. I was to gain a Diploma in Health Education at London University under the eye of a woman of influence. Dr Dina would study for a Masters degree at the University of the Philippines under the eyes of some of the favourites of the World Health Organisation headquarters at Manila, who looked after the needs of South East Asia and the Pacific. In this way, we would effectively cover all likely sources of expert health education consultants who would be likely to advise the colonial government on the direction that health education should take in PNG.

Dr Dina was to continue his work as Dean of the Papuan Medical College until the first group of medical students graduated as doctors. He decided that the examiners would be chosen from local specialists, as well as three professors from medical schools in Australia, to examine the subjects of medicine, tropical medicine, obstetrics and gynaecology. There was a lot of work to be done and only a few months to go.

Back in Port Moresby I had my first setback. Dr Dina said that there was a World Health Organisation fellowship in Health Education going begging for a year of study at London University with all expenses paid. He also said that I was the best qualified of anyone likely to apply because the colour of my skin should now be working for me and not against me as was the case in the past.

I applied for the fellowship, was interviewed and was bundled out like a naughty schoolgirl who had strayed into the wrong class. The colonials who conducted the interview talked twice as much as I did. They gave me the impression that they had decided that I could not be given such a fellowship as it would be a waste of time giving a fellowship to a single girl. If I skipped off later, the good WHO money would have been wasted. As it was the fellowship lapsed and nobody got it.

I meekly protested that I had had numerous opportunities to get married and had not succumbed yet. Also, married women made very successful health educators. A few notes were scribbled on official memoranda and expressions toughened. One of the colonials chastised me for not developing my health education career through official channels. He found the silence of my intentions about becoming a health educator disturbing.

I whispered, in my most submissive voice, that I thought that I was well qualified for a career in health education and was unaware that I had to seek anyone else's permission to follow such a career. My presence, in front of them, was indication of my intentions. I was disappointed that they were not pleased, especially as I was a Papuan who wanted to help my people. I had learned at the PMC that this was a standard declaration expected of all Papuans requesting education — a declaration of loyalty to the decolonisation policy. I also meekly pointed out that I thought that my six years of work and study at the Papuan Medical College should merit some consideration, as should the recommendations of Dr Dina and others covering my ability and experience.

I left the office, rejected and depressed. All of our plans had been destroyed already. I did not know that I could feel like this again. I thought that I had developed bullet-proof skin. But here I was again with the old feelings of inferiority and rejection that had harmed me during my first contact with colonial indifference. There must have been some other reason why, after six years, they still would not give me any opportunity for further training.

During the whole of my time at the PMC I was treated with suspicion and caution by the white bureaucracy. Progress, within the colonial public service, was painful and laboriously slow. I was either in competition with colonials or a brazen hussy who was getting too much as it was. Until I played things Dr Dina's way and forced them to promote me, I simply got no encouragement or advancement of any sort. When I told Dr Dina the sad news he became very quiet. He had been sure that this fellowship would be my ticket to London. He did not enjoy being so wrong. His subdued voice was a sure sign of concern. The quieter he became, the deeper was his hurt. In extremes he did not talk at all.

After a long pause he asked,

'What do you want to do, Jo?'

My reply came quickly,

'I want to go to the Administrator and complain. The Administrator has just announced that he was there to serve the Papuans and New Guineans and that he would do everything in his power to see that we would advance.'

Dr Dina never opposed any suggestions that I made unless it was clearly leading to self-destruction.

'Yes, Jo, that's a good idea,' he agreed, 'you go now while you feel like this. He might learn something.'

I arrived at Konedobu, the high seat of the colonial government. The Administrator was busy but he condescended to see me. I was ushered into one of the largest offices I had ever seen. It was as big as my house at Hohola.

As I entered the office, a signal was given and a secretary slid from the room. The Administrator was sitting at a very large desk with two or three chairs scattered around. There were carpets on the floor, fine blinds on the windows and a lounge for special guests to sit in equality and comfort. The walls were decorated with native adornments but the most conspicuous position was reserved for the Australian flag and a large picture of Her Majesty Queen Elizabeth II.

I was nodded to a seat on the other side of the table and was gruffly asked the nature of my business. I felt like a hopeful borrower, facing a hostile manager of a bank, across a very large desk. This was the first time that I had been in the presence of the great. Dr Dina had said that there was no need for a big man to be rude. The man before me made me feel uncomfortable. Perhaps this was his manner and he did not know any better. Perhaps this was the way he was schooled to deal with natives. He heard my complaint out in silence, lifted a telephone and made a few enquiries. With a remarkable economy of words he then told me that he was sorry but there was nothing that he could do. 'Good afternoon.' No consideration, no talk, just a curt goodbye.

I took my leave. I was growing quiet inside like Dr Dina. As I neared the door, the secretary of the big man slid in again and was taking notes before I passed the door. I was depressed but, perhaps, I had made some progress. I had learned more than the Administrator had.

That evening, Dr Dina visited me at Hohola. He did not want me to spend a night with disturbed thoughts. He knew my mission was doomed to failure because the Administrator could not go against the decisions of his officers. That is, unless the matter was gravely political and he himself was threatened. This was the price of loyalty. Where I had made my mistake was in thinking that he was the boss, like an important chief. But he, like the rest, was just a servant of the system and his authority was limited. Dr Dina asked me how I got on. I did not tell him because he already knew. I knew him as well as he knew me. I was in no mood to play with formalities.

'I found the Administrator rude. I wonder what would happen if I had been as rude to him as he was to me. I felt like a piece of furniture. He asked me nothing and knew nothing.'

'Don't judge him too harshly,' said Dr Dina as we sat on a low concrete wall outside the house. There was no privacy inside and a cool breeze was blowing outside. 'The Administrator is a bit like that with everyone. Not just you. It's his manner. Some of the European officers like him. They think that he is a loyal man and will stick by them. He also sticks by the PMC. He stopped obstructionists getting in our way during the early years. He was very helpful.'

'Well, if he helped you with the PMC,' I said, 'I'll forgive him but that doesn't help me get to London.'

Don't panic so early,' said Dr Dina. 'Remember our advice to the students. If one road blocks, try another. You can still go to London University as a private student. We will arrange your entrance ourselves. I shall recommend you. We will raise the money ourselves. You must go on and get qualified, otherwise we haven't got a chance. We'll borrow the money if we can't find it ourselves.'

Backed by Dr Dina's recommendation, my education and years of work at the PMC, I was admitted to a diploma course at London University. I was granted leave of absence, without pay, and I left my family to Dr Dina who was to arrange transport and leave them at our new home at rural Sangara. I collected my papers, received my injections, packed my bags and left for London.

Dr Dina came with me as far as Brisbane. In the afternoon we shopped and bought an overcoat and underwear suitable for a sunless climate. I did not believe that such a place could exist but Dr Dina insisted that I buy the clothes just in case. The next day I boarded the plane for London. Halfway up the gangway I turned and waved. He should have been with me. I had not been so alone before. I took my seat and stared out the window. Except for essentials, I did not speak or move until the plane touched down in London. I had had this feeling before when I was on the bare brown rock but that was different. There, I was with my own. Lonely but not alone. Now I was desperately lonely and desperately alone.

* * *

In England, the cannibal image was flourishing. A few Londoners had heard of Australian Papua. The people were still in the trees. How were the cannibals? The anthropologists were the most knowledgeable. They had been forced to sweat over us to pass their examinations. They were grateful to see one in the flesh. It was a pity that I was not more primitive.

From professor to street vendor one interest dominated. Do we still eat one another? One Englishman, addressing our class at the University, directed a question at me.

'Are all of the people in New Guinea cannibals? Do you still eat one another?'

I was embarrassed by this fixation on cannibals so I said, 'I did not eat anyone for breakfast but I am looking around for dinner!' The learned discussion ended. I don't know who was responsible for selling us off as a race of enthusiastic cannibals. Whoever it was, they did a good job.

Unexpectedly, one day, I was asked to address a meeting. I was terrified and tongue-tied, so I fell back on the cannibal image and the audience were most impressed. I relived an experience that I had had with Dr Dina at Okapa in the Highlands of New Guinea. Dr Dina and I had travelled all day over mountain roads in the highlands of New Guinea until we reached the remote area of Okapa, the land of 'laughing death'. We were supposed to be escorting a VIP, but the professor travelled by plane leaving us free to explore the country by truck. It was here that I heard of and saw *Kuru*, whose mystery was unravelled by an American scientist and several collaborators. The American won the Nobel Prize for Medicine. It was here that children were eating the brains of their dead relatives as part of a tribal ritual and, later, developing a terrible illness that always led to death. The American discovered that the virus escaped to a new victim when children were compelled, by customs, to do this, eventually settling in the brain of each child, there to live and multiply. In a few years, usually at about the time of early maturity, the new victim became progressively more clumsy until he or she became a helpless dying cripple. Death was swift and sure for the victim but not for the virus, for it was liberated by the next generation of children who were compelled to eat the brains of their elders.

We walked among the victims of the disease. They were

girls and boys and young adults. Women more than men. A constant uncontrollable smile transfixed the faces of those seriously afflicted, adding to the sadness of their condition. Victims of a bizarre ritual, they died to preserve a tradition that they did not understand. Foreign kindness was the only treatment and civilization was the only cure. Young girls in the beauty of their spring showed the signs of early death: a dropped pot or a clumsy movement was enough to warn. The people knew before the victim. In a few months, the face would fix in a big smile and they would succumb to the laughing death. Once again I felt ashamed of my comforts and affluence. I wanted to make myself fit to give something back.

Sealed in the tombs of their final victims, the viruses now perish with them and the disease should soon vanish. Eating human brains is now forbidden by regulations.

Our cannibal image overseas touched all of us. It also touched many of the white professionals who worked with us and tried to make good elsewhere. The bizarre can still be found for those with a purpose to seek it. Mud men will still dance, for a price. The story of *Kuru*, the laughing death, was as strange to me as it was to a Londoner. The only difference was that I had seen it.

The first day I was in London, I caught a taxi to London University for I knew no other way to get there. The taxi driver swore at me, insulting me because I did not give him a tip. I was shocked. I had not met a white beggar before as I had thought that all whites were rich, even taxi drivers! In my innocence, I would have given him my whole purse if I had thought that he needed it.

In London, I learned to be a health educator; saw Her Majesty; stood in the cold for hours to file past the dead body of Winston Churchill; visited bishops; saw the Bridge, the Tower, the Palace, Piccadilly Circus and Soho. Out of London I saw the countryside, castles and Shakespeare land; the lonely moors, the lakes, and the Sunday villages. I saw everything but the sun. It seemed possible that the whole earth had slipped behind a cloud to block the sun forever and that a place called Papua no longer existed.

Then, one day, Dr Dina arrived! Trembling with excitement, I waited in disbelief at London Airport. There he was! He looked so different in London clothes. I had only seen him in shorts and shirt before. It must be him. Confidently I walked with him. It was my Dina. No more make-believe. No more lonely days. I could live in his arms.

Dina had resigned from the PMC and was reviewing clinical medicine, which he had had to neglect to establish medical education in Papua and New Guinea. After London, he was to go on to the Philippines to study for a Masters degree — as planned by us on a star-filled night at Sangara, long ago.

Together we reviewed my work. He said that I was doing well. Laughter was cheap and beauty was everywhere. The days were short, with too much to see and too much to be done. There was only one world and that world was Love. We were secure and happy. For tomorrow there were plans, but today who cared: tomorrow was born of today and today was ours. Christmas came and together we saw the world.

We went to St. Johns Wood and bought a car. In violent weather, we crossed the Channel and laughed at the contrast with our sun-drenched home. Was this a cyclone that threatened to destroy us, or was this weather natural to these parts? Nobody was alarmed so we shared their disregard.

Together we plunged into Europe and winter, a light car all that existed between us and destruction. Holland, Belgium, Denmark, France, Germany, Switzerland, Spain, Monaco and Italy all passed beneath our wheels. We explored the ice and the snow, the cities and the country, the wonders and the riches of an ancient world: Rome growing out of the stumps of the past, the dancing feet of Paris lost in the art of forgetting; the lonely mermaid of Copenhagen with heart grown cold in a sea of frozen love.

We tried to make Venice by night and became lost in heavy snow. We spent the night on a wharf because we could not tell the difference between cement and sea. With the aid of a tiny lamp and the physiology of our bodies, we survived. In the morning, the car was an igloo completely submerged in ice and snow. The beauty of the ice and snow touched my senses most. Here was natural beauty on a grand scale that

filled my heart with love for my own. I was also touched by
the shrine of Bernadetta. If God created miracles for one girl,
he might create them for another. We romped through history together, confident and alive. I was happy and I was in
love. A day late back for lectures. A day less to think.

'Did you enjoy your holidays, Miss Abaijah?' asked a sar-
castic lecturer accustomed to post-holiday blues.

'Yes, sir,' I replied. 'I saw the world. I am sorry to be late.'

'Well, Miss Abaijah. We would all like to be happy for an
extra day but it is only the privileged who can afford it.'

Was the lonely mermaid still washed by the freezing sea? I
would not see Dr Dina again for a year but it was worth it.
And at last the year was spent. With a diploma in my hand
and a skin too pale to be recognised, I went to London
Airport for the last time. Then, back to joy and my native
land.

4

Love magic

*B*ack to Papua — to the sun, the tropical rain and the stars. Back to native markets, street vendors, floral shirts, ramis and sarongs. And, beyond Port Moresby, the lagoons, the canoes, the brown villages, the palms and the people. Everywhere the eternal blue. And everywhere strangers on the move and Papuans in the shade watching a quicksand swallow up their native land.

Things had not changed much in the year I had been away. The colonials had divided themselves into those who were going and those who would stay to see it through. The demand for newspapers advertising jobs in Australia had increased several fold. Rabid native-haters were beginning to see the errors of their ways: the colonial sloth was stirring though so far it had only stretched its legs.

The main thing that had changed was me. I had been as unprepared for the violent assault on my mind by blacks in London as I had been for the bitterness of colonialism in Port Moresby. A philosophy of hate could not grow in a heart that longed for love. I was a reject of the blacks in London and a reject of the whites at home. I must steer a middle course.

Dina was at the University of Philippines and I was in Port Moresby with a Diploma in Health Education. I was the first. The first Papuan to be qualified in Health Education, and that could spell trouble. Previously, Health Education had been a small preserve ruled by colonials and their minions. Now, a foreign usurper had slipped in. I was interested to see what ingenuity would be called forth this time to keep me down. I had learned to expect nothing. Dina was away for a year. What would happen in the meantime?

I did not have to wait long. I was to be banished to Lae, a large town on the New Guinea side. My reunion with my son and my family would have to wait. My house in Port Moresby would remain an additional source of income to help pay off my debts. I was to be attached to a senior colonial at Lae to be *inducted* for a year, a special courtesy that was not extended to any of the Australians who had gained the same qualifications in the past. I was singled out for special caution again.

While in Lae, I took part in a secret love magic that, to date, has given better results than my sterility rights at Misima did.

This time, a New Guinean girl was my senior. She was a nurse and I, as a lone, unattached native female, shared quarters with her at the nurses' home. For the magic ritual we had to go to a secluded, black sand beach and there discard our clothes. We then had to walk a short distance into the bushes to seek the youngest leaves of a certain tree that grew in the area. The leaves, which emitted a sensuous aroma, were then rubbed between our hands and, at the same time, we repeatedly recited a prescribed incantation. This completed, we cast the leaves like confetti upon the sea.

The ritual was concluded by swimming several times, back and forth, underneath the leaves until our endurance matched our desires. My mind had to be filled with thoughts of elegance and beauty so that my body would capture the fragrance of love that would bind my lover to my body forever in spiritual fulfillment of his senses and of my desires.

Several times, during my stay at Lae, I repeated the love

ritual with my New Guinean companion. We were earnest to succeed and we both profited by our confirmation in love.

* * *

I wrote to Dina every day—pessimistic love letters of gloom and frustration. He was never comfortable when I was unhappy and I was determined to be unhappy now. I would kill that man when I saw him. His letters were irregular, impersonal and optimistic. He even made mention of the virtues and attractions of some of his new Filipino friends. A slow death would be too kind for such a thoughtless creature. And me rotting in hell! Dina asked me how I expected him to complete a Masters degree and write a daily dissertation to me as well. I persisted, nevertheless, and at last I got my message through. I was lonely and depressed. I had tasted the sweet life and was not thriving on my present fare. This produced the desired results and, as of old, the plans began to roll and purpose and confidence were restored.

Dina made immediate plans for me to study in New Zealand while waiting for his return as I was only wasting my time in Lae. I had a matriculation and a Diploma from London University so the rest was easy. I was to be attached to an institution in New Zealand particularly suited to my needs and all I had to do was to get my papers, collect my ticket and go. The money from renting out my Port Moresby home had accumulated while I had lived rent free in the nurses' home in Lae, and would be adequate to keep me while I was away.

I promptly applied for leave. It was refused. What I needed was more practical experience, I was told. But I was only playing around in Lae. I applied for leave without pay. It was refused. The needs of the country came first, I was told.

Dr Dina wrote,

'Leave and go. Damn them. Qualifications are the only things that count in the long run. The people who are blocking you now will be out of the country or working for you in the future. Just go.'

Weak and alone, I was still a coward. I could not stand up against the will of the masters. I signed the papers but went

home to my bed and cried myself to sleep, not only for the
opportunity I knew to be lost but, also, for the empty days
ahead. I did not write to Dina for a week. When I did, this
was the reply:

'You are a fool listening to those idiots and for playing
games at Lae. Don't worry, I'll cancel the arrangements for
New Zealand and say that you are sick. That's as good an
excuse as any other. Don't worry, we shall start again some
time.'

I closed my eyes and went to sleep. Papuans sleep when
they want to forget.

* * *

Lae was in New Guinea. New Guinea was the short name for
the United Nations Trust Territory of New Guinea, a country
that was lost to Germany during the First World War.

Everywhere I travelled in New Guinea, I was simply
known as *Meri Papua*, which was pidgin English for 'Papuan
woman'. Being a Meri Papua led me into some strange
experiences and the strangest one was in the mountainous
interior of New Guinea, where the people had never seen a
Papuan girl before. It came about because in Lae, I had very
little work to do, and in order to break the monotony I took
part in any permitted government activity that appealed to
me. On this particular occasion, after much consideration, I
was permitted to join a government patrol going on a special
mission to the mountainous interior. I was warned of my
foolishness but still wanted to go. I had never been on a
really difficult patrol before.

A 'patrol' was a colonial institution used to count the
people, provide a service, show the flag, collect the people's
votes, catch a fugitive or perform some occasional administrative function. Between these patrols the people looked
after themselves. There were two methods of patrolling. One
method was to travel light and live off the country. The other
method was to carry everything imaginable and employ
native carriers to do the hard work. Loads were usually
packed in tin trunks which were slung on a stout pole cut
from the bush, and carried by two natives. In the past there
had been many unpleasant incidents when village natives

had refused to toil all day, carrying the white man's burden in return for two or three sticks of trade tobacco and a long empty return journey home. In efforts to obtain carriers or to teach people who was boss, houses had been burned, native treasures lost, pigs killed and guns used. Native carriers had been handcuffed to their loads, to themselves, and to numerous other things, occasionally with serious consequences.

The patrol that I travelled with was small by white standards. Only about twelve carriers were used. The carriers were villagers who carried out loads from one resting place to the next. They were then paid, and retraced their steps back to their own homes.

In the mountains, the carriers had a hard time. They had to struggle up and down the steep, slippery tracks with their loads and ford numerous, swift mountain streams, strewn with rocks and boulders. I made sure to walk between carriers, as we were warned that if anyone was going to disappear it was likely to be the last person in the line.

Worst of all were the leeches. Thousands of these creatures lurked in damp places on the moist leafy carpet of the jungle tracks. As we walked near them, their thin worm-like bodies convulsed into great activity and, if they touched a person, they immediately pierced the skin, liquified the blood and gorged themselves until they were many times their original size. They would then dangle helplessly, like giant bloated slugs, until something caused them to fall to the ground. The leeches were misery to me. I continually scraped them from my skin with a sharp knife but, at times, one would attach itself unobserved and remain undiscovered until it fell.

Every day, we moved higher and higher into the mountains and the patrol strung out in single file. An experienced government officer walked in front. Next came another foreigner who was a new recruit and was attached to the patrol for experience. Then came half-a-dozen native government workers, like myself, who were attached to the patrol to do some special job. I was to assess the health education needs of the inland people with the purpose of organising a programme appropriate to their needs. We all had duties to perform which were additional to survival. I was particularly anxious to perform well as I wanted to establish myself in

my new position free from the handicap of being a woman.
There was also the constant wonder of the pristine beauty of
natural things.

Many mountain streams had to be crossed and we usually
paused to discuss how the stream was to be negotiated before
we started, and to drink a few mouthfuls of the cool mountain water which we scooped up in our hands. The colonial
officers were constantly reading their maps and discussing
the reliability or otherwise of the person who made them. No
matter who read the maps or who gave the orders, experts
and beginners alike matched footprint to footprint as the
patrol moved on to a village of forgotten people at the top of
nowhere land. Only the masters knew where we were going
or what we were doing. They talked earnestly and privately
and when they moved, we followed.

At last the distant village of forgotten people was above
us, where the mouth of the valley closed its lips in green
slopes spotted with brown houses. I stood in prayer. I had
arrived with no great harm and, with the help of God, I could
return with the stronger men. Clouds slept in the valleys.
My heart was full of yesterday. My body was close to the
stars and my senses close to the fragrance of summer love. In
isolation, Dina did not seem so far away.

When we arrived at the village there was an obvious
emptiness. As we later learned, the people had seen us
coming and had fled. Two or three old men, who were too
feeble to leave, had stayed to face the enemy. Interpreters
told us that there were two feeble women lying concealed
somewhere in the bush. The other village people were beyond
our reach.

The old men, calmed by kindness and suitable gifts, began
to talk freely. They told us that they had been visited by the
government white men two or three years ago and, following
that visit, several of the people had become sick with coughs
and fevers and some of them had died. After hearing this the
masters held private discussions and made their plans. We
stayed in the village for two days and, during that time, the
village tracks were baited with beads, knives and axes to
encourage the people to return. The bait regularly disappeared but the prey was never sighted.

The masters were very disturbed by the failure of their mission. On the third day we left, but before leaving, further gifts were prepared and given to the old men for distribution. These gifts were to convince the other villagers that the white government was interested in their welfare and that the government would return to greet them on another day.

I did not know why we went to this remote village and I did not know why we left. The colonials were very secretive about such things. I think this was an exercise in colonial propriety following complaints from a lower valley tribe that the village of forgotten people had been responsible for lessening of their numbers in recent years. It was also suggested that some of their wives had been called upon to replenish the losses of the village of forgotten people following the last visit of the representatives of the colonial government.

In some of the villages that we visited on the return journey, I received more attention than I bargained for and, in one remote village, the people had never seen a Papuan girl before. I was seized upon by a crowd of curious women but the crowd was liberally sprinkled with equally curious men. The rest of our party had wandered off elsewhere. Before I could escape, my body was literally taken over for inspection. There was no threat to my safety, but there was to my dignity. Just the same, I was terrified and did not know what to expect next. I did not have to wait long to find out. A mature woman, carrying a baby in her arms, approached me and began to lick my arms. This seemed to be the signal for all and sundry to follow suit. My body was then licked by eager tongues, most of which, I think, belonged to women. Later, after I had related my experience to my companions, the knowledgeable master informed me, with firm conviction, that the natives were merely trying to get the salt from my skin. But I wasn't the only one with salt on my skin!

The licking finished, then came the inspection. My dress was held up and discussed. My hair was parted and searched. Clothes were no impediment to the satisfaction of their curiousity. After all, they were all but naked themselves. After the people had satisfied their curiosity and obtained their minerals, I was allowed to breathe again with ease.

I was then escorted on a tour of the village and greeted many people with silent signs. Everyone wanted to see me. After the tour I was taken to a small clearing and seated on a stool fixed in the ground. I exchanged smiles and silent greetings while the people kept a respectful distance away. I did not know any language that they could understand. Eventually, an old man approached me. He had a ceremonial stone club in his hand which had a well-worn look. The old man (age was a distinction) came towards me and made several ceremonial gestures. Through an interpreter, he told me that he wished me to take his old war club and keep it with me. He then held the club out for my inspection. It had a nobbly stone head chipped in two places and a long, strong, ebony handle. The old man told me that he had used the club in tribal battles, and because of this, he had been known as a distinguished warrior. With toothless prose, he told me that the club was heavy with magic, and that he had been worried for years about what to do with it after his death. Now the spirits told him that it should rest with me. He wanted my spirit to rest with his people and he wanted the spirit of his people to rest with me. His people were backward and deprived, but I belonged to the new generation and represented the future. Man was born through a woman and a great tribe would be born through me. He was a great warrior of the past, but I was armed with the weapons of today. He had never met a native woman with education as advanced as mine. I would be a great woman and his happiness would be fulfilled to know that the symbol of his strength rested in my young arms.

One unhappy consequence of my experience in recent years was that I wept too readily. Women only weep in ceremonial rituals. Sadness belongs to the heart and does not have to be revealed to men. I wept now. I embraced the old man as closely as convention allowed. He was happy and fulfilled. He had passed his war club to the new generation and hoped that his people would benefit from the exchange.

We slept in the village that night. The next day, when the time came to leave, I was given more food than eager hands could carry. With my war club over my shoulder and the spirit of old courage by my side, I walked confidently into the future. Both are with me still.

* * *

The sun was high when we walked into the small settlement where we had been told to hail the bus. My first thought was to seek out a trade store and squander a few dollars on luxury soap and exotic food. With light steps I walked through the open door, feeling like a hero returned from a lost world. As I made my way to the glass showcases filled with the luxuries of civilization, a harsh Australian voice shouted at me.

'Kanakas cannot come in here. This is for whites only. If you want to buy something go around the back. That's the kanaka store. You natives never learn. If you can read, why don't you read the notice on the door?'

Without looking at the owner of the voice, I turned and retreated to the street. I had lost my appetite. I sought the other members of the patrol and sat down to wait for a truck to take us back to Lae and normality. The patrol was over. The results were nil.

* * *

Back at Lae, there were several letters from Dina waiting for me. He had recovered from the disappointment of my cancelled New Zealand tour and was already into new schemes for my perfection and occupation.

Firstly, being experienced in the methods of medical research, he had designed a research programme for me to carry out in Lae. This would keep me busy for all of my remaining time at Lae and would be stimulating and rewarding as well. Secondly, he had decided that I had grown out of the New Zealand exercise already. He had arranged for me to attend a post-graduate Health Education course at the University of the Philippines instead. He would be back from his Masters course soon. I would have to be ready to leave for the Philippines soon after.

'Don't apply for leave. Don't apply for anything. You already have a passport. Just sit on it. Nobody will stop you this time.'

'The man is definitely mad,' I said to myself.

In one of his letters there was a scribbled verse. Dina liked to do things like that when the going was tough. 'Don't expect too much,' he wrote, 'I do have to pass a few examinations you know. In the meantime, I wrote a song for you. It has something to do with our time in London together. A few lines to cheer you up.

> Hair of winter black, you're that.
> Eyes of summer brown, you're that.
> Laugh of autumn gold, you're that.
> Love of spring unfolds as your lips I hold,
> Sounds of yesterday never walk away,
> Mine for every day, you're that.'

But what could I do with a stupid song but forget it? I wanted something that I could feel and remember.

I was convinced that I would be leaving for the Philippines in about three months' time. Dina worked out the details of such things carefully before he spoke. His careless speech concealed the value that he placed on words, often to the undoing of the unwary. Because I was brought up in a society where actions never matched words, I had frequently made mistakes by attaching too little importance to what he said.

Dina had told me that I should have at least three years' overseas experience. At the time I did not believe him. This was to be the second year. To soften the blow he promised to visit me in Manila, as he had to make scheduled trips overseas during the time that I would be there.

I was now happy with my work at Lae. I was working on Dina's study programme and that was the nearest I could be to him. The work was on understandings of foreign words and of visual art material among rural people. This sort of work was basic for the establishment of a professional health education service in the country. Each day I travelled with nurses and other workers and carried out studies among the villagers while my companions attended to their own work. I was surprised at the results. In the past, too much was taken for granted. Hundreds of misconceptions of common words used in teaching adults were disclosed, and 'conventions' in graphic art materials were not recognised at all. 'Health' was heard as 'help', so the Department of Health was the Department of Help. Lines used to denote wrinkles in drawings were seen as worms or sticks. Light reflected off bright hair was seen as greying or signs of age. Later, the studies were repeated in other parts of the country with similar results. My ideas of native concepts and perceptions of foreign conventions were altered and the results of these studies became a basic part of our work during the next five years.

* * *

The great day arrived. Dina was back in Port Moresby. I was still in Lae but I received a letter almost every day now. Books to be studied, formalities to be completed. I went to renew my passport. Papuans were issued with Australian passports as, officially, we were Australian citizens. But that was where similarity with white Australians ended. Passports for white Australians were issued for five years. Our passports were issued for the exact duration of our journey, or perhaps an extra week added for good measure. The colonials wanted to keep a strict check on every Papuan who left the country. They did not want to lose count of their children.

After the usual wait, I was ushered into the presence of an Australian seated behind a very large desk. A heavy ceiling fan rocked overhead. I wondered if these things ever crashed.

I was questioned on where I was going, what I was going to do, where I would get the money, the use of the experience, who would I travel with, who would guarantee me, where my ticket was, where I would stay, whether I would go somewhere else, whether someone would deposit a bond for me, and whether I could produce a bank statement. I was especially warned that, if permission to go overseas was granted by the Administrator, I was not to wash a dish, sweep a floor or do any kind of domestic work for anyone, anywhere. The colonials were very protective. They wanted to keep the exploitation for themselves. I cautiously asked the gentleman how I would live if I did not help myself or the people I was living with. I should have known better. This extended the lecture by fifteen minutes. Natives were not to work anywhere for anybody. Especially they were not to do domestic work for other people. I meekly suggested that this was what we were doing for the whites here.

The climax to the encounter came in a manner that surprised me. After going into details about my education overseas and my intention to study in a university, the colonial gentleman asked me if I could sign my name! Old habits died hard in colonial Papua.

As I left the office I thought that I had wasted my time testing the unsophisticated village natives. It might have been more revealing to have studied some of these whites instead. They did not seem to be able to do anything graciously. Everything seemed designed to lower our dignity. Servility was our second name.

When I travelled to Port Moresby, my reunion with Dina was like old times. I was only in Port Moresby for a couple of weeks but we managed to spend most of that time together. I was more confident now that he was here and I was developing a career of my own. I was coming to terms with my new world.

* * *

I had been separated from my family for two years: one year in London and one at Lae. As transport by plane was easy from Port Moresby, Dina and I decided to visit them before I left for Manila.

The plane touched down at the outstation airstrip, some kilometres from Sangara. The country was unbelievably rich and green. This was my first real visit to my Sangara home. My first and only previous visit, two years before, was when we visited the site and arranged to buy the property. Dina had settled the family here while I was in London. He had improved the old native material house, where we once slept, and had had a concrete floor and high concrete piers put in as a start on our new home. He had not seen the place for a year, the time that he was in the Philippines.

Our family reunion, this time, was disturbed by the health of some of the children. My son, Robert, was up to my shoulder now but he was not well. He was anaemic and his spleen was as large as a football — tell-tale signs of heavy malaria. All of the children had enlarged spleens and it was evident that malaria carrying mosquitoes were thriving in the area. The next day was devoted to the children's health and we became engrossed in the small industry of keeping my family alive. Blood films, on small pieces of glass, were taken and specimens of stools were collected in improvised coconut shell containers. The blood was to be examined for malaria parasites and the stools for the eggs of worms.

At about noon we managed to get a lift on a truck going to a small rural hospital a short distance away. When the microscopic examinations were carried out, it was found that the children were heavily infected with malaria and hookworm. We were able to get some medical supplies at the hospital and were able to return to the farm on a hospital vehicle returning to the Popondetta settlement. We now had to give top priority to health: one of my married sisters had already lost a child to malaria here. The position was urgent and our stay was short. What was intended to be a family reunion turned out to be a medical clinic.

Life in a Papuan wonderland could be hard and dangerous but a few elementary precautions could protect against the most serious threats to health. No man can live without blood. The children had been exposed to the bites of malaria-carrying mosquitoes and their bare feet exposed them to the penetration of hookworms, and so they were hosts to thousands of parasites which were destroying their blood. Dina and I worked with the family to correct the situation. We dug a hole, the diameter of a 44 gallon drum, deep into the soft volcanic soil. This was to be a pit latrine. Scraps of war metal were plentiful. With parts from a war-time jeep we made a firm platform over the top of the hole. This was our first permanent toilet and it functioned for several years. This got rid of the hookworms while a weekly dose of anti-malaria tablets kept the malaria parasites at bay.

We returned to Moresby a day late, a day that I could not afford as I was about to depart for Manila where I would stay for a year. We had not done the things that we had intended to do at Sangara, but we were grateful that we had returned home in time.

Many things were left undone and many things had not
been discussed yet. Everything was rush now. How was I to
live in Manila? How was I going to handle medical subjects
new to me? What contacts would I have in Manila? When
would Dina come to rescue me? I had a feeling that I was
about to be thrown into a big pool to sink or swim. I felt that
Dina was over-optimistic about me.

We were sitting in Dina's car at Ela Beach, overlooking
the blue Pacific. The Australians had removed their large
signs on the main road, which had prohibited my presence.
'ELA BEACH. EUROPEAN SWIMMING BEACH. NO
DOGS ALLOWED.' We thought that we would take advantage of the new era and enjoy the white sands and the blue
sea that had been my constant companions during my growing years.

There was silence for a short time while we looked over
the sea and sorted out our thoughts. We never felt a need to
talk continuously while we were together. This may have
been why we could tolerate our own company for indefinite
periods. Dina took my hand in his and said,

'I'm sorry, Jo, that things have been so rushed. I thought
we would have had time to go over everything quietly and
discuss the subjects as well.'

'I am frightened,' I replied, showing my feelings.'I'm not
ready for an experience like this on my own.'

'You don't have to do it if you don't want to,' Dina said
patiently. 'You can pull back if you want to.'

'It's not that I don't want to. It's just that I don't know
what I'm doing. I rely on you so much that I need exclusive
rights to your time to succeed. Sometimes, I think I should
just marry and settle down and produce children like my
mother and sisters and forget about education or success.'

'It might be tough,' said Dina frankly. 'I thought it would
be better for you to get experience quickly rather than drag
it out for years. There are some subjects that will be hard. I
have repeated some of these courses three or four times.
Other subjects you will handle all right. With your smile you
will have more people on your side than against you. You
have a lot going for you, Jo. Don't underestimate yourself.'

'Do you promise to come and help me as soon as you can?

You still have some leave due?' I said, turning to Dina with a broad smile to indicate that I had received the message. I also had a message of my own. 'Where am I going to stay in Manila? I have been rotting away for the past two years. This is the last time I'm going to be on my own, career or no career.'

'I have given that careful thought,' said Dina.

There was no need to tell me that. He gave everything careful thought. It would be wonderful to do *something* without thinking for a change!

'While I was in the Philippines, I cultivated a Filipino girl so that you would have a companion there. You might call it combining business with pleasure but it was a lot deeper than that. She is a university student. She comes from a large family. She knows exactly what your needs are. I became heavily involved in her affairs and am helping to pay her university fees now. She will not let you down. She will meet you at the airport and will welcome you into her family like a sister. Her name is Josephine, Josephine Ramos.'

There was no need to inquire how this deep and touching friendship had developed. After all, I had been the recipient of the same treatment myself. I was sure that my Filipino namesake would be as steady as a rock. I was relieved to know that I had a Filipino counterpart who had been touched by the same gentle hand and had been strengthened by the same abundant confidence.

The sun was sinking behind the town. It was time to go.

'Okay,' I said, 'I always end up doing what you say. I am just clay in your hands. Just remember to come to Manila quickly. I might be in trouble otherwise.'

Port Moresby airport was crowded as usual and the Manila plane was ready for the next stage of its flight. Dina was with me and Dr Sidney, always thoughtful, had come to wish me well.

'I'm surprised that there are no Papuans here to see you off,' Dr Sidney said. 'Foreigners seem to be monopolising your company.'

'My son and my family are at Sangara,' I explained.

'What about all of your uncles and aunts? I thought that there would be a plane load of them here,' persisted Dr

Sidney, who was really puzzled by the absence of native well-wishers. To him it was abnormal to see a lone Papuan on such an occasion. He wanted to maintain the status quo.

'You may be surprised to know, Dr Sidney,' I replied, 'that I have no close relative left, other than my own family and they are all away. Of my twelve uncles and aunts only one survived, and he is in Milne Bay. The other eleven were dead before they married.'

'It is unusual for a Papuan to have no close relatives,' said Dr Sidney sympathetically.

'Yes it is,' I said, 'and it does not say much for the medical services that were provided for these people in the past. Mostly they died of elementary diseases that were easily prevented or cured.'

Dr Sidney, always ready to defend the reputation of the colonial administration, came back at once, 'But most of the diseases in Papua and New Guinea are diseases of poverty or diseases of ignorance. It is not easy for a government to do much about ignorance and want.'

'But did they try?'

The final call for the Manila flight sounded over the loud speaker. The people began to shuffle off and I was on my way.

I shook hands with Dr Sidney and Dina, gathered up my handbag and walked towards the plane. I turned and waved. Dina was the only one my misty eyes could see. Both doctors responded. My only thoughts were on my lips: 'When will I be back again?'

As I settled into a seat on the plane, I thought of Dina. 'Life has to be lived, not talked about. It's a waste of time to live for one day and then spend the rest of your life trying to recapture the magic. There is magic in every day.'

Lunch in Port Moresby and dinner in Manila. It did not seem so far away. In Manila, I cleared the customs, went through the gate and, as Dina had predicted, went straight into the arms of Josephine Ramos.

5

The road to Hula

I went to the Philippines to spend a year, but I did not expect to last that long. But I did, and I ended up returning there four times to spend more than two years studying in the University of the Philippines, the International Institute of Rural Reconstruction, the International Institute of Malaria, World Health Organisation programmes and with departments of the Government of the Philippines.

I found the University of the Philippines as tough as I had expected. Without Dina's help I could not cope with some of the technical subjects in so short a time. The course was a multi-discipline one with plenty of options. I learned all that I came to learn and a lot more. The things that were of value to me were not all in universities. There was plenty to learn in the streets and homes of Manila and in the barrios of the countryside.

It was in the Philippines that I first glimpsed the image of a new world that was relevant to my own. I developed an awareness of a natural evolution of cultural development that had proceeded for hundreds of years. I experienced the awakening of a new vision undreamt of before, and caught the first glimpse of a new direction to my own destiny. A new beauty to add to the old. It now began to dawn on me why Dina had planned for me to go to a country in South East Asia. He did not want me to study in the University of the Philippines. He wanted me to study in the University of Life.

In Australia, I was a carefree child. In England and in Europe, I saw but I did not understand. In the Philippines, I looked at a panorama of cultural changes that had purpose and meaning. Changes came despite the industrial revolution and through poverty, where it was necessary to seek out non-material values that enhanced the quality of life. Not that everything I saw in the Philippines was good. Destructive elements in Filipino society restricted the capacity of the people to enjoy the richness and beauty of the culture that had evolved.

The first thing that struck me about the Filipinos was their smartness and the care that many of them took with their appearance and dress. I do not know what I expected. Soon after I arrived, a thoughtful lady doctor told me that I should smarten up my appearance and try to look the part if I wanted to impress anyone around there. This was about the worst thing that could have happened to me at the time as I *was* doing my best to look the part! But I promptly took her advice and smartened up and, later, was even glad that it had been given.

One of the qualities that impressed me was the status that the women seemed to have in the community. There were some occupations largely reserved for men but it seemed to me that the women had a status unimaginable in my own country. Mixing with the Filipino women developed in me a sense of pride and satisfaction that I had never known before.

Accommodation was no problem. That was Josephine R.'s department. There were many Filipino homes where the people were happy to earn a few extra pesos accommodating a foreign girl who was unlikely to make heavy demands on their resources or their privacy. Clean, austere, with good food, I didn't know why I had lost so much sleep worrying about accommodation.

Josephine R. was a constant visitor. She took me every-where, showed me everything and did everything that I was too helpless to do myself. Dina had a good eye for women. He selected carefully and they worked out well. A satisfactory deal all round.

In my room at night I rocked gently in an old cane chair, surplus since the death of its last occupant, and I reasoned that I was some sort of a freak. No other woman ever did as many first, yet ordinary things as I had done in my country. I was a constant fugitive into Tomorrow. No traditions, no destination. I was not a normal girl looking at normal people. My eyes were blinded by the sun outside the dark cave of my ignorance.

Drugged with the soft poppy, Australia slept, and in the generations no-one stirred. Like a fat cat, in the warm sun, the colonial usurper slept and dreamt of its next meal. Shame was rising in my mind. Not only for indifferences and neglect but, also, because the maladies caused by indifference were now being used against us. A witch-doctor maiming with his own cure. Why was I the first of so many things just because it suited Australia to quit now? Why didn't my parents, my grandparents and those before them have a chance to grow? Why didn't my country have a chance to mature and think. It was so easy; why wasn't something done? The people queued all day and, when the game was over, the gates were opened to let them in.

The next few years were the most productive of my life. I spent my time between studies and travel in other countries and practice and teaching at home. I was now a woman, scarred and damaged, but I kept what I could intact. I had learned to live with what I had and, at last, was learning how to give.

In the meantime Dina had successfully stormed the fort and was now in charge of health education, as well as medical research, for the colonial administration. We were together again. In Port Moresby, more out of force of habit than from any pressures from above, we established an Institute of Health Education and introduced a course of studies leading to a Diploma in Health Education. Dina became the Chief of Division and I became the Principal of the Institute. The diploma course was post-graduate and covered one academic year. The Institute received support from the World Health Organisation in Manila and some of our students came from overseas.

We developed enough resources to live in comfort indefinitely and enough teaching materials to last a lifetime. We commandeered the disused female living quarters, complete with fence and conveniences. There was ample space for teaching, storage, administration, workshops and privacy. What we did not have we built ourselves. The Apex Club gave us a 4-wheel drive Land Cruiser, and we were left in peace to sow and multiply.

* * *

Dina and I were seated in our office which was adjacent to the large teaching forum where the students were. The diploma students were in session and we were following their activities through a thin partition wall. Dina paused for a moment in his preparations and said,

'You've got a good job here for life, Jo. You couldn't get a better job than this in the entire administration this side of independence. After three diploma courses, you know this work like the back of your hand.'

I looked up in surprise at the remark, and said,

'Sure, I couldn't get a better job than this but that doesn't say that I am going to stay here for the rest of my life.'

'You could do worse. Life is not only lived at one level. You could become a writer. Start a literature, write a philosophy or something. You could do that in your spare time. You have been with the first so many times it should be a habit now.'

Dina was warming up and I knew that his latest scheme would soon be revealed. He became bored when a job became too comfortable. I took this as an indication that he was finding the present job too easy. I became anxious as I did not know what to expect. My mind was going to stay blank until I heard more. Dina was fumbling for words. This was a prelude to introducing something that he thought was important.

'I saw an advertisement in the gazette, today. The Administrator wants a communications officer to be an advisor to him on communication with the people. There's nobody in this part of the world who can outclass you in this.'

It was my turn to fumble for words.

'And what are you going to do if I get a job like that?'

'I'll keep this job going for you here in case you don't like the new one,' he said. 'If the job is any good, you can look around for a job for me, too.'

'All right,' I said sharply, because I was not confident about anything dealing with the colonial administration. 'I'll apply for the job just to see what happens. If by any chance I get it, I can easily turn it down if I want to.'

I read the government gazette carefully, turned to Dina and said,

'They don't want a native for this job. They're too immature for that. They want a fancy colonial to write big reports that they can file away. They don't want to communicate with anyone but themselves.'

Over the next couple of days, I gave thought to the wording of the application. It was an area where I was confident. I had been teaching and practising communications for three years. The completed application had all the information and testimonials that a long experience at the PMC had taught me were necessary. I delivered the application personally.

The closing date passed, then a few weeks more, but no word came. This was unusual. Then, one day, the press and radio announced that the Administrator had said that nobody suitable had applied for the job and there would be no interviews. This was the second brush that I had had with colonial administrators, and I was not impressed. Dina made excuses for the other one. I wondered what he would say this time.

'I hope he chokes for forcing me to make a fool of myself with these idiots. This is the last time that I expose myself to their ridicule.' With these thoughts I went to bed and was soon asleep.

We had five good years. Years of consolidation, teaching and outdoor activities. We organised courses of studies and established principles. We were learning about needs, motivation and change in village communities. The village people taught us and we taught the students. Then we wrote it all down in reports. Dina wrote reports on principles, I wrote reports on practice and the students wrote their assignments. After the people, the love, the tears and the laughter were turned into notes, they were all filed away. We both knew that there would be no continuity to our efforts. Most of it would be destroyed. We did not expect anything beyond the happiness of the day and what survived in the minds of the people. And our own development.

Individuals grow according to their own needs and step to the beat of their own destiny. For me these were five years of beauty and compassion, five years of growing and adventure among the rural villagers. I felt my spirit soften. I had now bathed in the deep waters of my native land. I was suspended in motionless time, clean and refreshed. Fulfilled, warm and in love.

Dina was with me always. For another five years our lives were plotted on the same course. We shared every bump on every road, every mosquito in every swamp and every star in every sky. Our cultures eternities apart, we were permitted to worship at a common shrine before stepping into the confusion beyond.

* * *

There were no vehicular roads built in Papua during the main of Australian colonialism. A few bushmen, with a good bullock team, could have achieved more in the time. A few short stretches of road leading to nowhere radiated around government and mission stations, or where foreigners had invested in primary industries such as copra, rubber, coffee or timber and needed roads to get their produce out. The beasts of burden in Papua were the native women. With strong muscles and bent backs they carried the produce of the land in slings attached to their heads. Travel was limited to a few small aircraft serving primitive airstrips scattered about the country. No outstation was in contact with any other outstation or the capital by road. The few major roads that were eventually built began to appear during the dying years of the Australian authority. This was part of their effort to decolonise and get out.

The roads that we used were pioneer, experimental bush tracks that emerged before there was any regular traffic to the villages. Our aim was to get as far away from Port Moresby as possible. Our basic vehicle was a 4-wheel drive Land Cruiser. This was loaded with most of the rescue gear that experience had taught us was necessary. The Land Cruiser had eight forward gears, a comfortable cabin and a small, one tonne truck body. The truck carried more people and the cabin separated us from the passengers, which was often an important point. No matter how much you like the country, it is not a relaxing experience to travel for hours with an axe or a decrepit shotgun poised at the back of your head. On muddy or swampy roads, we sometimes travelled in convoys. Mud, swamps, landslides and rising rivers were all part of the day.

I had to do my share of driving. Dina and I were the only ones who drove our own vehicle and we each took our turn. I was not spared and had to cope with whatever came my way. Where I suffered most was in trying to stay close to the seat. It may be true that the bigger they are the harder they fall but, in a vehicle, it is also true that the lighter they are the higher they fly. I don't know why we didn't fit seatbelts. Perhaps they were another hazard if we had to jump for it.

Dina and I, with Erlinda, a Filipino visitor, were on a trip to Hula, a large coastal village east of Port Moresby. Erlinda was a community development officer whose visit was sponsored by a United Nations agency. I first met her as a classmate at the International Institute of Rural Reconstruction in the Philippines and the last time that I saw her she was giving injections to pigs and showing the Barrio people new techniques for their care and propagation. Now we were taking the students to an important rural area for field work. They were to work in threes in different villages where they would live with the people and gain practical experience. They were all experienced rural workers and keen to try out their new techniques. We had been driving for about four hours and now crept our way through bogs towards the big swamp which was only a few kilometres from our destination. The vehicle rolled like a ship at sea and I tossed like a cork on the waves. I found it safer driving as there was something to hold onto, except when the wheels took over as they slipped into deep holes and the steering wheel spun dangerously. This trip from Moresby would have taken two hours if the road had been reasonable. As it was it could take a day or a week.

We reached the big swamp and slowly made our way. This section of the road was a two-kilometre stretch of mangrove logs. The logs had been cut from the swamp and, unmatched for size or fit, were laid together to form a continuous loose decking to the road. Except for the infrequent occasions when a vehicle attempted the crossing, the mangrove logs rested peacefully beneath about half a metre of swamp water.

Slowly, we edged our way into the last stretch. By this time, Erlinda had her rosary out. Night was coming closer and the swamps were well stocked with mosquitoes and evil spirits. A night in a Papuan swamp came close to Erlinda's idea of a bad nightmare and she did not hesitate to share her thoughts with God and us. Yet she was as tough as the vehicles we travelled in. As long as we got through, she enjoyed every hazard on the way. She thrived on difficulties. Her skills had been developed in a hard school.

The twisting vehicle edged forwards, feeling its way over each log. I controlled the engine and little else. The constant splash of the water made the vehicle sound more like a sea serpent than a land craft. As we rounded each curve, I hopefully looked for a rise that would herald dry land and rest. The rest of the journey would be easy. Switch on the headlights and away to Hula, food, safety and rest.

We turned another bend — and then it happened. Ahead was the welcome rise and dry land. But there was something disorganised about the road ahead. I coaxed the vehicle forward gently until, suddenly, the road disappeared into the swamp. The students were glad to get off the back of the truck onto firm land, even if that land was under a foot of swamp water!

The men edged their way into the hole and tried to map out the bottom with their feet. By now the other two vehicles had crawled up behind us. Amid shouts and general uproar, we planned a course of action. We decided to construct two narrow tracks under the water using twenty pairs of willing hands and what mangrove logs and rocks we could find. There were plenty of rocks on the higher land and we could cut timber. The vehicle was to be emptied and I was to drive it across. With one vehicle over, it would be easy to tow the other two to safety and dry land.

It was now night, and battery torches and kerosene lamps provided us with light. The men were soon saturated and covered with mud. They were no strangers to this work. It was part of the preparation. They would not find any better roads anywhere else. They had to learn the rules or stay at home.

At last the road builders had finished and there was a general consensus that this was the best that could be done in the dark. It was worth a try and I had to drive. Dina would not let me quit when the going was tough. If anyone was going to fall into a hole it may as well be me. It was good for the soul and made us a part of the same team. We had to learn to make it together. I was to put the 4-wheel drive vehicle into a low gear to prevent the engine from stalling and then was to move forward as quickly as possible, to get what benefit I could from the momentum. As we would only be in flight for a moment, we disconnected the fan belt to stop the spray. Then we were ready.

The land serpent roared in the lowest gear. Then, away we went, trying to gain momentum as the vehicle pounded over the last few mangrove logs. I went on to the newly made tracks under the swamp water. They held for the first part of the crossing. Then, some obstruction and the front wheels began to churn to the side. I could feel it going. Should I stop and start again? Use the back drive only? It wouldn't be any better later so I decided to keep on. I had already given up hope.

Then, suddenly, the end came. The front wheels continued in their sideways descent and we slipped off the track with a bump, nose down into the primordial mud.

Almost without speaking, we decided to work into the night and dig ourselves out. It took twenty people about four hours to get that vehicle out of the swamp. Winches alone were no good as the angle was too acute. We had to work for every centimetre with block and tackle, while winches consolidated every gain. The men were wet and muddy but the warm weather kept the conditions tolerable.

We decided that while the vehicle was being hauled out of the swamp a quick meal could be prepared. Rice, tinned meat and native vegetables was a standard meal and easy to prepare. Erlinda volunteered to do the cooking and I attached myself to her. The glow of the fire added colour and comfort to the scene and the anticipation of food made work lighter.

'Can you speak Spanish?' I asked.

'I can speak some Spanish,' Erlinda replied, 'but I do not get enough practice to speak well. We are all supposed to learn some Spanish but English has taken over now. Why do you ask?'

'The Spanish were in the Philippines for a long time. I think they contributed a lot to your culture. Your present life-style has got a lot of Spanish influence.'

Erlinda looked at me and said, 'They were there for a long time. They were very cruel, sometimes.'

I was thinking of our own colonial experience and cautiously said, 'Perhaps cruelty or suffering is an experience too. We avoid unpleasant things. Sometimes they are destructive and sometimes they make us grow.'

'What do you mean by that? All cruelty is bad. It is bad to make other people suffer.'

Touching the drying rice with a stick, I said, 'Yes, but that does not mean that all kindness is good. Indifference is a form of cruelty, as is neglect.'

Erlinda looked up from the food and said, 'Some of our great heroes were born through opposing the Spanish. We are very proud of them now.'

'We have no heroes,' I said.

'The Americans taught us how to make money but the Spanish taught us how to live. It's hard to imaging the Philippines without the Spanish influence.'

'I can imagine it,' I said, playing with new political ideas that had come into my head. 'Nobody knows what destiny has in store for us. Some day we may be invaded and ruled by another foreign people. I hope the next one shows us how to live.'

'Who would invade your country?'

'Filipinos may take it. Who knows?' I replied.

'Don't be ridiculous,' laughed Erlinda.

'What about Indonesia, then?' I suggested, 'or some in-
dustrialised country exploiting our resources and controlling
our lives at the same time?'

'I don't know which would be worse,' said Erlinda.

'Or the best,' I suggested. 'That might be more important.
We might even be taken over by ourselves.'

'What do you mean? How can you be taken over by yourselves?'

'Easily,' I said. 'Do you think that all of the people of this
country are the same racially and culturally? The strong can
dominate the weak internally as well as externally. You
should know that.'

'You sure have some weird ideas tonight, Jo,' said Erlinda.

'Not really, we have national elections next year. Probably
the first where the Australians will not run everything. We
have to grow up some time.'

'You should put up for parliament yourself, Jo,' said Erlinda
cheerfully. 'You are talking like a politician now.'

'Has any Filipino woman ever been elected to the Parliament of your country, Erlinda?' I asked with a smile.

But Erlinda had gone. She had just thought of her rosary
and was making her way to the vehicle which was in the
final stage of rescue. She would find it threaded on the hand
grip. I did not want it to be lost while I was driving out of the
swamp. We weren't home yet.

At last the vehicle was hauled to dry land amid cheers and
shouts. It was soon cleaned and ready for the road again. The
other vehicles were hauled across the swamp by the first
Land Cruiser. When all was ready we sat around the fire and
ate the meal that Erlinda had prepared.

Soon it was all over and we were on our way. Erlinda
played her guitar and serenaded us until we reached Hula,
tired and wet, but safe.

* * *

Erlinda, Dina and I stayed together for a week, in a village
home in Hula. The students had to work and live in the
surrounding villages. Our hosts, an elected village official
and his wife, were our old friends.

The Hula villagers were typical south sea islanders, living

on the beach and from the sea. The sea was their second home. They were more robust and flamboyant than the gentle Misima people I had grown up with. The Hula villagers had been isolated with their church for a century and they lived with gusto and colour when not involved in the drudgery of survival. If they built a church, it was big; a sail, it was high; played games, they were strong; and when they danced, the flowers laughed and the earth trembled. Some of them bore Chinese sounding names like Alu (Mr Lu) and Awong (Mr Wong) and many had straight hair. If some ancient mariners landed here and had escaped the pot, they could not have found a more enduring shrine for their ancestral tablets, or a more beautiful repository for their seed.

A week of village life. Tourists in paradise. A week of sun and sea. As visitors, we lived in grand style. We stayed in a large open house full of life with plenty of daytime shade and wide verandahs to catch the sea breezes.

And then we reached the final exercise: The Happy Party. The village women had attended meetings with me for a week. This was to be an exercise in motivational selling — Hula style. The women met each evening when, amid laughter and self-expression, we identified needs and expressed our purpose. We formed a mutual admiration club based on warmth and beauty; the warmth of the common touch and the beauty of song, dance and self-expression. I identified with what I admired in them and they identified with what they admired in me.

At the Happy Party each woman dressed in her best clothes and was decked with some of the bright flowers which grew in great profusion. She was a *hane-namo* (a princess) for a night that she would always remember. The event was fixed in the memories of those who took part by a certificate and a photograph. During the evening, each woman expressed herself in her own way and then the night flowed with food, dance and song. It was our habit and our need to share the happiness of the night and then, while hearts were full and spirits were high, we departed and left the women alone to finish the celebrations.

This was how we brought the market-place for Western health to the village, but the only ones deceived were the sellers and the only things sold were us. They paid in the love and affection that they had to give and we were mortgaged to a dream.

After we left the Happy Party, Erlinda, Dina and I walked in silence over the white sands to the water's edge. With feet bare, we walked through the warm water until we picked up the kerosene light of our village home. We then climbed onto the fallen trunk of a coconut palm and used it as a bridge to cross to the grass beyond the beach. Then, along a hibiscus lined path to our favourite verandah.

We did not speak for a while. The cool breeze, the bent palms and the brown figures moving around in the clearing below did our talking for us.

'Village life will go on,' I said. 'But I don't think that much of our traditional culture will survive in its present form.'

'It's hard to change a whole country,' said Erlinda. 'The Spanish were hundreds of years with us.'

'We should not resist change,' I said. 'I think what we need is a much closer contact with a strong culture that can enrich our own and teach us how to live with our poverty. Just teaching a few people how to make money is not going to solve anything.'

'There you are, off on politics again,' Erlinda laughed, 'you sound more like a politician every day.'

'Yes,' said Dina, as he put his cup on the floor. 'I agree with Erlinda and lately I've been thinking.' Dina and I had been together for eleven years. Nobody had to ring a bell to tell me that something new was cooking in his mind. He began to speak at last. That slow, fumbling voice again. I wished he would get on with it. Nobody was fooled by that fake voice he reserves for special occasions.

'I have been thinking, Jo, that you should stand for Parliament.'

I was stunned into silence. Such an impossible idea had never entered my head. What was Dina talking about? He never joked about such things. Perhaps he is just showing off in front of Erlinda. I would not put it past him. She is his type too. I am glad she is not a Papuan.

'What do you say, Jo?' Dina ventured.

'You must be joking,' is all that I could find to say.

Dina stretched out in his chair, locked his hands behind his head and said,

'I am not joking. I am deadly serious. I was not game to bring it up before but Erlinda said it for me. So I can blame her, now.'

'Don't blame me,' Erlinda cut in. 'It's I who was joking. I never thought of Jo becoming a politician. Don't blame me.'

'I will blame you,' said Dina. 'You can handle Jo better than I can. I shall just say that I am backing you up.'

'Keep me out of it,' pleaded Erlinda. 'I really don't know anything about politics.'

'Why don't *you* stand for Parliament?' I said, looking at Dina. 'You would be a certainty in the central district. You can speak Motu and they all know you. They still think a master must be better than a native. Nobody would have a chance against you.'

'Not me. I thought about that, too. It's too late in the day for that. I might get in but what then? Just wait until they kick me out again. This is your show, not mine.'

I was now certain that Dina had considered this carefully. Not a point had been left out. This was just a final announcement to a detailed study. I was intrigued by the novelty of the idea and was complimented to think that one man, at least, thought I could win a seat in Parliament. Of course, Dina was prejudiced. I should not count too much on his opinion. After a silence, I said,

'I am a woman. No woman has ever been elected to Parliament before. This is a man's country. The men run everything. The women just do what they are told.'

'Yes, I thought of that,' said Dina, nodding.

There was no need to tell me that. He was a careful planner who thought of everything. 'Also, I am from the Milne Bay district. I don't even come from the central district. It's impossible.'

Again Dina nodded.

'Yes, I have thought about that, too.'

'Why do you keep saying, 'I thought of that'? I know that you have thought of everything. But what have you thought? That's what I want to hear.'

'I have thought of all the difficulties and I still think that given a properly organised campaign, you will get twice as many votes as your nearest rival.'

'You're impossible, Dina,' I said. 'I can't talk about this any more tonight. You have spoilt my sleep already. Now I'll be tossing around all night thinking about it.'

Dina looked towards Erlinda and said,

'Erlinda can get her guitar and serenade us. That'll soon put your mind at rest. You'll be asleep in no time. I know you better than you know yourself.'

'That's an uncomfortable truth that I have to live with,' I said with a smile, and sat back in my chair to think.

Erlinda was soon serenading us with Filipino songs. My mind closed to the worries of the day. Dina was right. In half-an-hour I was asleep.

* * *

We had not spoken again about Dina's suggestion but I knew that my days at the Institute were drawing to a close. Six of the happiest and most productive years of my life had passed here. I could have wished it to go on forever. Dina was always by my side. We made the journey together and we forgot about the time. Senior Health Educator and Principal of the Institute. There was nowhere else to go.

Then, after eleven years of service at the Papuan Medical College and the Institute of Health Education, the colonials panicked. The writing was on the wall. I was still there and they were moving out. At this closing hour they offered me a World Health Organisation fellowship to study for six months in South East Asia and India and the Pacific. I accepted it as a tribute to my tenacity. I had paid my own way and now it was over. I had outlasted them but they had not been convinced until they were packing their bags to go.

* * *

The Institute was jammed full of pastors from the United Church. We had collected them from rural areas outside Port Moresby to attend a special course to provide them with material to help them in their work with the villagers, and to give them the satisfaction of having completed a health course. The course was successful beyond our expectations.

The closing ceremony arrived when we handed out group photographs and certificates. Shortly before it began, Dina came to me and said,

'What about the Parliament thing we were talking about in Hula? If you have decided to do it, you could not pick a better time than this to make an announcement, to see how the pastors take it'

'All right,' I said. 'I'll just try it out and see how they take it.'

The pastors were assembled in the teaching forum and a murmur had spread around the room. A successful course was drawing to a close. Then, the long trip home to the rural villages. I picked my time and then I told the group that I was resigning from my work with the Government and going to stand for Parliament at the national election.

There was a hush in the room. A woman standing for Parliament! My heart stood still. I wished Dina would not make me do these embarrassing things. I thought, 'They must think that I am stupid standing for Parliament and a Milne Bay girl at that — I don't even come from this district. I wish they would say something.'

Then, suddenly, the silence broke. An eager murmur spread through the room and the pastors clapped and cheered. I had not cried much lately but I began to cry again now. A bad start for a woman politician!

Then a deep resonant voice began to sing the opening words of our Motu song, *Papua*. The sound rolled on like a giant organ until it rested in my heart. The curtain was coming down on the work that I had come to love. There could be no turning back.

PART THREE

The silent wonder

1

The Cherokee

*T*hey said that it was impossible for a girl to be elected to Parliament in a Papuan electorate, a traditional society in which men had few privileges and women had none. They said that it was impossible for a native from Milne Bay to be elected to Parliament in the central district. The Europeans would swamp the credulous villagers with their money and their propaganda. As we were still a colony of Australia, any resident could stand as a candidate for the national Parliament.

I had no great ambition to become a politician. It was more a challenge to be elected desire than a desire to play the game. It was a desire to achieve the 'impossible' and to prove the colonials wrong that drove me to do something that I had little heart for. Perhaps I wanted to repeat a long colonial experience of being the first: this time, the first woman to be elected to Parliament. It was excessively easy to be a first in colonial Papua.

But there was another voice too. I was a prodigal returned to the native beauty and love of my childhood years. The innocence of my dark vigils with the sea and the stars had matured to form the as yet unexpressed compassion for the innocence of the village people who accepted their share of nothing with a passive acceptance as deep as the dark night. I now felt fit to share their company. I was not a complete fake. I had shared poverty with people who had nothing to give when I sheltered with my son on the bare brown rock. I too had bent to the insults of colonials as they smeared my dreams with dross.

I had resigned from the colonial administration and had nominated myself as a candidate for the Central Regional Electorate, which included the capital of Port Moresby and the rural district of central Papua. This covered an area of nearly 20 000 square kilometres of mountains, swamps and fertile plains; 400 kilometres of palm-fringed coast, extending eighty kilometres back into the 4000 metre high mountains of the Owen Stanley Range. An area larger, alone, than any other Pacific Islands country. The population figured 185 000, including those of Port Moresby town. There were also several small local electorates in the area covered by the central region.

Seven candidates had nominated for the contest for the hearts and votes of the people. Five Australian men, one Papuan man and one Papuan woman. An Australian was the favourite.

This was to be the third House of Assembly and the last before independence. Up to date everything had gone according to plan. The first House of Assembly had been manipulated directly by the colonial administration and the second House of Assembly was manipulated by the Australians by other means. The tail wagged the dog and it was business as usual. The third House of Assembly would be the first time that Papuans and New Guineans would be free from direct Australian rule, although it would still be an appendage of the colonial government, a part of the process of the colonials getting out.

New Year's Day 1972: Dina and I were sitting on the verandah of my house. The night had been noisy with the beating of drums and other disturbances that passed for celebrations — the unco-ordinated groans of a restless town that had lost its identity and had lost its soul. A town where, a few years ago, bare-breasted girls played at love as the moon turned the night to day. Now, the old culture had moved to the villages outside, and here, fear came with the night and no-one walked alone. Now it was a city of barking dogs, security lights and barred windows, a city of broken cultures, broken languages and lonely hearts — civilization's parting gift to primitive man. A lesson for the nation to learn.

The louvred windows of my house were wired and barred and there was a two metre chain wire fence isolating us from the rest of the world. Six cattle dogs roamed about the yard and all had the habit of hurling themselves at the wire fence if any stranger looked like ignoring the warning, 'BEWARE OF THE DOGS!'

'I suppose that the first thing to do is to work out a policy,' said Dina.

'What policy?' I replied, apprehensively.

'Well, in politics you are supposed to have a policy,' Dina said firmly. 'As you don't belong to a political party you will have to develop a policy of your own.'

'Look,' I said, defensively, 'I don't know why you talked me into this. I was quite happy at the Institute.'

'I talked you into it, as you call it,' said Dina, 'because I once told you that you could be the president of your country if you wanted to.'

'What president of what country?' I said, fumbling for words. I did not connect our casual conversation of many years ago with my venture into politics now but the truth was beginning to dawn. Dina had really meant what he said that day and had been working on it ever since. What a man. A ten-year plan!

'I don't know anything about politics,' I said, as calmly as I could. 'You know that. I just want to do something with the people. I was doing that in the job I had.'

'It will be just the same as your old work,' Dina said. 'You have been through it dozens of times. Identify the people's wants and this will give you the basis for a policy. Then a few slogans and you are in business. The rest is just hard work.'

'What are we doing this for?' I asked, seriously. 'Haven't we got enough happiness as it is?'

'We are doing it because we are what we are,' said Dina.

'What are we?' I asked.

He hesitated for a moment and then said,

'I don't know what we are, Jo, but I do know that something brought us together and something keeps us together. Twelve years is a long time and its likely to be another twelve years at the rate we are going.'

'Do you believe in destiny?' I asked. 'I have always felt that something was guiding me along the path that I had to follow.'

Dina nodded. 'I believe what it is good for me to believe, and it is good for me to believe that destiny brought us together. I believe in you and you believe in destiny. I will believe in anything that keeps us together.'

I patted a young dog that had settled at my feet as I searched for an answer.

'Too many strange things have happened in my life to be coincidental. Something controls what I do. I have done all sorts of things that I was not ready for. Passed examinations I should have failed. God is by my side. I can feel it always. I could have been a doctor now, knowing medicine and little else. Instead I have been prepared to stand for the Parliament of my country. A big dream for a small girl hunting fish in a blue lagoon on an island adrift in time.'

In faltering words I expressed to Dina every picture that came to my mind, the clear and the distorted. Together we explored the world we lived in and the world that lived in us.

'Do you know, Jo,' he said, 'I was in your village the day that you were born like a turtle on the sands. I stayed in the house next to yours for a week. Not bad judgement considering that you lived in a pretty remote place. I stayed for a rest in your village to recuperate during a sixteen hundred kilometre walk from the mountains beyond Kokoda to Milne Bay. I made a note in my diary that a baby girl was born that day. I knew your village language before you did. As soon as you left school you came to the PMC and we have been together ever since. We could have parted a hundred times but it never happened.'

'I am frightened that this new work might take us apart,' I said, 'I don't want to touch it if that's going to happen.'

'Why should it do that? Times are changing. We have to keep up with the times,' said Dina.

'Well, what happens now? How do I become a politician? Where do we start?' I asked, resigned to my fate but far from sure that we were doing the right thing.

Dina handed me a sheet of paper with a number of steps set out. It was written in the language of my profession so I knew exactly what I was required to do. I had to identify the needs of the people, develop a policy based on these, and plan an election campaign using slogans, motivation and fresh ideas. I had to project a personal image and never forget that I was a woman — not a substitute man.

My companion liked to give his opponents the impression that he was dithering around. This was what he was trying to do now. He would lull the opposition into a false sense of security, and then his efficiency would reveal itself when it was too late to run.

Dina was still with the administration and was occupied at the Institute. I selected suitable companions and, with our Land Cruiser for transport, devoted myself to the preliminary surveys. There was no difference between this and the work that I had been doing for the past six years.

I travelled west to the Mekeo, north to the Koiari and east to Rigo and beyond. South was the sea — and Australia, the errant colonial power that had decided that the future of our land and ourselves was not our concern. On paper, Papuans were Australian citizens. It said so in my passport. We were a part of Australia. Off paper, we had no such rights. We were like animals in a zoo and less expensive. We were grazed on our own lands and told what to do. We were the inmates of the first open zoo. No economic development, no political development, only the raw beginnings of education, no interest. And now, interest only in getting out.

We could not enter white Australia without a permit and, unless we got mixed up with the Torres Strait Islanders who were sitting on the resources that Australians wanted, we could not work. Australia had a large immigration policy to attract southern Europeans and others to fill the empty country but their policy towards Papua, their own colony, was to conduct their business in whispers and to keep the 'paper Australians' well and truly where they were.

Back in Port Moresby, I was questioned by Dina. 'Well, what did you find?'

'I found plenty,' I replied excitedly.

'Where are the results?' Dina asked impatiently.

Confidently I handed him a paper with three words on it:

PAPUA – TANO – MAURI (Papua – Land – Life)

'Is that all you got?' he said with a smile.

'Yes, that's all,' I said, happily. 'You don't want all of the padding to you? I put it in the rubbish basket the same as you do.'

'I'm proud of you, Josie,' said Dina, taking up a pen. 'When you can reduce a political policy to three words, you are getting somewhere.'

I had been pleased to discover that I was able to apply the methods of my old professional work to my new role as a politician.

'I went through the routine with the Mekeo, Rigo, Koiari and a few of the settlements in Port Moresby. What they want is to control their own country, Papua, to preserve their lands and to safeguard their life-style. Basically, before everything else, they don't want to lose their land or have their communities weakened. Everything else is secondary.'

'Were you surprised at the results?' asked Dina.

'Yes I was and I still am,' I said. 'I thought that it would be all schools, roads, hospitals and bridges. But they don't come into it. They are not basic.'

I walked up to the chalk board that was in the teaching room, took up a piece of chalk and wrote.

PAPUA – TANO – MAURI

This was our usual routine. We reduced developed ideas to simple terms and then put them into slogans, songs and messages that appealed to the people.

I scribbled slogans on the board as they came to mind. Dina did the same thing on a piece of paper left behind by the students. Two Papuan women were in the room with us and they commented on our efforts. This was how we worked. We played with slogans and called them out. After several attempts and polite approvals we produced a simple slogan.

PAPUA DAINAI – TANO DAINAI – MAURI DAINAI
(FOR PAPUA   FOR OUR LAND – FOR OUR WAY
                                                          OF LIFE)

The response from the women was immediate. They repeated the slogan and committed it to mind in seconds.

This would be our slogan for the campaign. It would be my policy, too. It said everything that the people wanted in a few words. I had no separate policy of my own. I would only represent the views of the people. Their policy would be my campaign.

With surveys and slogans completed we were on our way. Time was short and some of the candidates had started months before. We now had to produce our material and get going. We drafted the materials, took photographs and in forty-eight hours they were with the printer. The machine was oiled and running smoothly. The campaign was under way.

* * *

We went to a local aero club and managed to charter a small Cherokee, a single-engined aircraft, to do early morning runs for us. We intended to saturate the whole of the central district with my name, photograph, new image and political slogan, by flying over each village and showering the people with leaflets and hand calendars.

During my surveys, I found that my greatest appeal to the village people was as a modest Papuan girl supporting traditional Papuan values in the new era. The people were hungry for non-material values that gave meaning to their poverty. The image I had to present was one that they could identify with and understand. I was worried about my short dresses and my western style. There would have to be changes. I would be the person they wanted me to be. I would not let them down.

I did not come from the central district so I would just have to be a Papuan girl. I could not be catalogued, so the people said that I looked like a Fijian. This was their way of accepting me from an area outside local village politics. A smiling, modest, coastal Papuan girl who belonged to no-one, came from nowhere and was acceptable to all. I had made a good start and one problem seemed less formidable. Some of the other candidates kept beating the drum about me being a usurper from Milne Bay and not a native of central Papua. But the people shook their heads and said that I was a modest, coastal Papuan girl who looked like a 'Fiji'.

Each morning we loaded our materials and ourselves into the small Cherokee and flew into the crisp dawn. The villages stained brown the endless green carpet below as aloft in the sky we sought out our prey. We opened the windows and our flesh threatened our bones as we abandoned our messages to the sky. Too early for wonder, too quick for fright, the white bird paused in its flight and the image of a smiling, modest Papuan girl showered onto the bewildered villagers below.

We skirted the coast and palm-fringed beaches, traced the streams, challenged the light mountains with our tiny lungs and returned to Moresby to start the work of the day. Within a week, every man, woman and child in central Papua knew the name and the face of a Papuan girl and had heard the words, Papua dainai, Tano dainai, Mauri dainai.

After the first day, the doors were taken off the small plane so that we could more easily throw our messages into the sky.

On the first day without doors I was caught unawares. I wore light clothes and had no protection for my head. The wind blew against my face like a hurricane. The pilot was protected by a windshield but Dina and I took the force of the wind as we shared the single seat behind. The wind was in my face for hours as we twisted and turned in the sky. I tried to get some relief with a light scarf that I carried but it was blown away. Sometimes, as we passed low over a village, I could scarcely manage to get my hands outside the plane and, at times, I really thought my skin might be blown off my arms.

I was sorry to find out later that some of the villagers were terrified and had run for the bush as they thought that the plane, which suddenly dived out of the sky, was going to crash on them. Some of the more thoughtful ones grabbed a baby or a pig before they plunged into the deep foliage that surrounded every village. In one village the native pastor and the congregation were gathered in the church for morning prayer. They were reciting the Lord's Prayer as the plane roared towards them. As we passed overhead, the prayer came to an abrupt end and minister and congregation abandoned their praise and dived for the nearest cover.

In another village, one of the white candidates was addressing a gathering of village people who had been coaxed to hear his words. He had worked hard to get an audience. As we came over the village and dropped our pamphlets, pandemonium broke out. Caught by the wind the pamphlets showered on the village in a fine display much to the delight of the people. The gentleman was gracious enough to smile about it later when he told me that this was the beginning of the end for him. For the first time it had dawned on him that it might be a disadvantage to be a foreigner in PNG. His only regret was that he had not received the message earlier.

It was the beginning of the wet season and our small, single-engined plane played a game of dodging the monsoon rains as they charged at us from behind the sun. Day after day, with one eye on the black clouds and the other on the fuel gauge, we sought out the villages of the central district. The price that we paid for the hire of the plane did not include any communication with the pilot. In any case, with the wind howling in our faces, it was almost impossible to speak. I contented myself with using hand signs with Dina. Without doors on the plane, the well worn seat-belts gave us little comfort. The strong magnet of survival bound Dina and I together as we huddled in the middle of our small seat. Occasionally, as the plane banked steeply, we locked our arms together. I am not sure if this was to keep us in the plane or to ensure that we hurtled to death together. We zigzagged up the rivers and the deep gorges. When we reached the headwaters we climbed up to the ridges and followed them until they were lost in the plains below. As we followed along the course of a river, the pilot began to show some concern. He broke his professional silence with reluctance and began shouting at us and pointing to the back of the plane. With the hurricane wind blowing in my face I turned with difficulty to look towards the direction of his distress. To my surprise, I saw that hundreds of our pamphlets, singly and in bundles, had settled about the tail of the plane like pigeons at lunch in Trafalgar Square.

I conveyed my findings to the pilot by holding up bundles of pamphlets and pointing to the back of the plane. I was pleased at my usefulness for once but if the pilot shared my feelings he did not show it. Instead, he said something which, from the shape of his mouth, I was sure was an explicit foreign obscenity.

The complacency of the pilot had been disturbed and he revealed this by communicating with us further. It seemed that, for better or for worse, we were going to land at a small airstrip that a young foreign patrol officer had just cleared out of the jungle. It had been opened a day or two before and was near a government outstation, about one hundred kilometres from Moresby.

The pilot landed us safely and he appeared to be pleasantly surprised that the plane and the airstrip were both unharmed. As the plane lost momentum, hundreds of pamphlets disentangled themselves from various parts of its anatomy and, with the aid of a stiff breeze, distributed themselves widely over the brand new field. I was appalled at the mess that the pamphlets made, and was anxious to make a speedy departure but, unfortunately, the pilot had other ideas; he announced that he thought that we could afford to rest for ten minutes. As expected, this gave the young patrol officer, who had cleared the airstrip, time to get transport and dash in our direction to see how his masterpiece had fared following the invasion. I am sure that the sight that met his eyes surprised him more than if the Cherokee had been in two pieces. There were pieces of white paper littered from one end of the strip to the other, each with a large photograph of a modest, smiling Papuan girl who looked suspiciously like the one who was grinning at him now from beneath a large motorcycle helmet.

* * *

'Where do we go from here?' I asked as I tried to get some relief by lifting my bones from the seat bouncing beneath me on yet another journey.

'I was thinking that the best way to visit the Goilala would be by helicopter,' said Dina, staring at his feet. 'There is no chance of you going to those mountains any other way.'

'Do you think I'll get any votes in the Goilala?' I asked.

'Perhaps,' said Dina. 'I don't know. They are pretty backward, but there are 20,000 of them. The Catholic mission has done some good work but other than that they have been forgotten and left behind.'

'The Goilala is too primitive. I could not go there alone. I wouldn't do any good if I could. They will never vote for me.'

'I agree,' said Dina. 'But we might be able to land a helicopter near the villages and test them out. Nothing would surprise me.'

'An exercise in futility,' I said, as I searched the coastline for familiar signs, 'but, if we have any money left, it might be worth it.'

'Okay, a helicopter it is,' said Dina. 'We'll go and see about it tomorrow.'

Silence again. It was not easy to talk in the lunging craft. I felt a bit better now. The thought of the helicopter had taken my mind off my discomfort. It would not be long before we were home again. During the campaign I had walked the lonely trails to isolated villages, travelled by plane, car, truck, tractor, speedboat, schooner and native canoe. Now a helicopter. I wondered what Dina would dig up next? About the only thing left was a balloon. As it turned out, a balloon would have been as useful as a helicopter, but we had to learn that the hard way.

We arranged to hire a helicopter for a day. We followed our usual routine of rising at dawn to take advantage of the early good weather, and went to the airstrip to join the helicopter for our assault on the mountain villages.

This was my first trip in a helicopter and I was impressed

by the immense power as we were lifted off the ground to look down on the city below. The sun heated our capsule as we bathed in a cloudless sky and my eyes roamed over the ageless beauty of my native land, the blue sea fringed with white, the brown villages, the palms, the plantations, the jungle patterned by swift rivers and the mountain sentinels behind.

After about an hour we swung into the deep mountains and were lost in time. The earth closed around us like a cave and we touched the mountain sides and twisted over perilous gorges. We were mocking the great mountains with our restless bubble and nature's indifference to our small intrusion was the only protection that we had.

The people of the Goilala mountains were served by three Government outposts clinging to small airstrips and a scattering of Catholic missionaries living in symbiosis with their primitive surrounds. Our plan was to seek out Goilala villages in their mountain fortress, and then to try to sight a clearing large enough for our strange, unearthly bird to land.

We came in slowly over a village and my heart stood still as we manoeuvred towards a small clearing at the valley's edge, scarcely big enough to contain our restless machine. For centuries the Goilala had lived alone with nature, enduring thunder, lightning and the ever-present magic that threatened from beyond. A small machine drifting in the sky was one thing but a snorting monster poised over head and home was another. I could almost call to the people but they were terrified and scattered into the bush to watch while the ungainly bird settled onto their land.

We soon learned that a helicopter was an unsuitable vehicle for landing close to a village. As we began to descend the closest houses convulsed in the wind and the light, paper-thin roofs began to flap and disintegrate. They could withstand volcanic eruptions but they were never made to withstand the draught from a helicopter blade. We touched the ground and I was relieved when peace and quiet were restored.

'We sure made a mess of those houses,' said the pilot, curiously inspecting the effects of the wind on a house nearby.

'Yes,' I replied with concern. 'I never thought that the landing would be so rough on the houses. We'll have to land further from the village next time.'

'I guess so,' laughed the pilot. 'The next time we might blow the whole village off the mountain side.'

'You can laugh,' I said, looking inside the damaged house. 'You're not putting up for Parliament. I'll have to leave them some money. With a few dollars they should be able to repair them.'

The pilot was a citizen of the world, a cheerful, casual fellow and I guessed it made little difference to him whether he was flying in Papua or Brazil. He was not an Australian but what he was I did not know. I was bad at accents and only had a vague idea of where people came from. All white people were either Australian, American or European. I walked around the empty village with the pilot while Dina went beyond the village to try and make contact with those who had fled to the safety of the thick bush.

'Do you like flying a helicopter?' I asked the pilot, in an attempt to make some sort of conversation.

'I guess so,' he replied after some thought. 'It's the only work I know. I don't belong anywhere, anymore. It's a pretty useless existence but it suits me.'

The pilot was a thoughtful man with an easy relaxed style that invited confidence. He felt no need to sell himself and this suited me. I had nothing to sell, either.

'We all lead pretty useless existences,' I said, thinking of my own ambitions. 'Some of us like to hide our simplicity in heavy camouflage. At heart, there is not much separating us from the people who live and die on this mountain-side.'

'I wish that I could live and die on a mountain-side like this,' said the pilot with feeling. 'Life to me is a clear day, a safe landing, pleasant company, good food and a warm bed. As I said, it's a pretty useless existence but that's me.'

It was good to listen to someone else for a change. Two strangers meet for a moment in the wondrous isolation of a clean world, exchange a few words and part, never to cross again. That was life too, and a necessary part for me. I wanted to be free to love and to be loved in a clean world. Not alone in the narrow restraints of a sexual embrace but in the wondrous isolation of the whole world. Love as a measure of the world, the compassion of Buddha, the meaning of Christ, the love that passes from human to human whilst bathing in the daily streams of life.

Dina returned to the helicopter and, waving towards the heavy foliage that surrounded the village, said, 'They are there. I don't know where, but you can be sure that they are looking at us right now. They probably expect us to burn the village down. Except for missionaries, all white people carry guns as far as they're concerned.'

'Well, we have no guns,' I said, 'and we are not going to steal anything from them either. We just about wrecked the roofs of those houses over there. How much money do you think I should leave?'

'Not much, here,' Dina said. 'These people have very little cash. Any money is likely to be a windfall to them. It is important to leave it properly. It should be a bit ceremonial and it should be visible so that everybody in the village can see. It could even turn into a social event.'

'How much will I leave?' I asked again. Dina had more experience in such matters.

'If you want to be generous,' said Dina as he carefully looked for signs of life around the village, 'leave ten dollars for each house. I have ten dollars here if you have the same.'

'Okay, that sounds all right to me,' I said. 'I would not like to try to repair a roof in Moresby with ten dollars, but I suppose things are different here?'

'They certainly are,' said Dina with a note of concern. 'And it is time we got out of here. We don't really have any guns you know. Not like the last time I was here.'

I took the ten dollars from Dina and said, 'How do I give the money?'

'Something like a Chinese dragon dance would be okay,' said Dina, moving towards two long poles leaning against a pig fence.

'Tie the money to one end and then lean the pole out from the house, over the village, with the money dangling from the top. Let's move quickly and get out.'

Dina tied a pole, with the money, to one house and I did the same at the other. Then the dragon roared and its symbols clashed as we slid off the mountain-side exchanging one danger for another as we proceeded through the day.

We landed at about fifteen villages and at an isolated mission station as well. After our first experience, we approached the other villages with more caution. We waved greetings from the air before we attempted to land and sought a landing pad a discreet distance away. We had more success this way. The people came to us at the helicopter and we walked with them to their village. Motu, the Papuan language, could be used. Interpreters eagerly translated to those who did not understand.

The materials that we produced for the campaign were distributed in each village and I was subjected to the usual curiosity. I did not know how to identify with these people, and a coastal girl in their midst was more a source of natural wonder than of any political significance. The mission gave me encouragement but I did not expect to win any support on election day. When the polling teams trudged to their villages, they would point a skinny finger at the face of a familiar man and then retreat to the safety of their homes. They eagerly seized the materials that I gave them but, beyond that, I did little else but defend myself. My materials went up all over the village without discrimination. Even paper was a novelty.

We landed on a small clearing about two hundred metres from a village. Below us a track turned down into a mountain abyss where gardens hung like giant pots suspended from terraced walls. I walked to the village holding two small girls by the hand so as to distract the attention of the adults. But, in the end, the inevitable happened. The women, all but naked and with skin coarse and hardened by unprotected contact with the sun and hard work, could not resist trying to make closer inspection of my body. First, they began to lightly caress my skin and then, like fish at live bait, they darted forward to sample other parts of the anatomy. This was my signal to move off, for next comes the licking and I had reached the stage where I could stand no more.

We rejoined the pilot at the helicopter who, alert to the possibility of an accident, made extravagant gestures that convinced the people that it was wise to keep a safe distance away.

The blade turned slowly as the batteries grudgingly parted with their power until the engine exploded into life and we slid off the mountain-side into the sky.

After a few days the monsoon rains began to close in and the pilot had had enough. Our aerial campaign had been successful and, now that it was over, we were pleased with our start.

2

Campaigning in Moresby

My next job was to visit the people of the urban villages, slums and housing settlements. Time was running out. There were only a few weeks until the elections. We were the last to start in the race and there was a lot of catching up to be done.

In 1972, Port Moresby was a town of about 75 000 people. About 16 000 of these were white foreigners and the rest were mainly Papuans and New Guineans. The Papuans and New Guineans lived in squatter camps, low cost housing settlements, or in urban villages. They also lived in the 'boy houses' attached to the houses of the masters, and in the hostels and dormitories attached to institutions.

The squatter camps were the refugee slums of Port Moresby. Refugees from poverty. Those who had nowhere else to sleep or call their own finished up in the squatter camps. There was no limit to the capacity of these slums other than food. Like giant, sleeping cows, they accepted everyone who could stay alive on the sustenance that they had to give.

The low cost housing estates, the next step up the social ladder, were the attempts by the colonials to transplant foreign suburbia to Papua and New Guinea, but scaled down to the pockets and the status of the natives. Some of the houses were so small that they would not cage a half-grown crocodile while others were the size of an average village house. They were built with cement floor and walls, an iron roof, and very little else.

For the most part, the people liked these housing estate homes and they housed many of the newly emerging urban class natives. New gardens and fruit trees began to emerge from the small plots of land and these were nurtured by water from the single tap or by the overflowing sewage from the septic tanks. After a time, the estates began to take on the green softness of a tropical village.

The next group was the urban villagers. These came from the six or seven traditional Papuan villages where the lives and lands of the people had been swallowed in the urban growth of Port Moresby. These villagers were adapted to urban life but they were still the custodians of many aspects of the local language and culture. These Papuans lived in communities where generations of families had lived and died on the same sands, whose people were the first to greet the white invaders and the first to hear the salute of their guns. The introduced Church and the established community institutions had played a big part in their lives; they were nostalgic for their lost lands and for many of the beautiful things that western urbanisation had taken from them.

Another large but intangible group were the domestics living in the 'boy houses' close to the residences of the masters. Most Australian homes had servants' quarters at a discreet distance down the back, but not so far that the popular call of 'boy' could fall on deaf ears. Some of these 'boy houses' were elegant by local standards, while others were no better than modified tool sheds.

The final group of native urban dwellers were those in the Government hostels and dormitories connected with education and training institutions. These were young men and women preparing for careers in the finance sector or public servants improving their career prospects. These residents were short-lived blooms on the Port Moresby scene and had few roots in its urban life. Some of them formed temporary cult groups of young men or women, but most of them were window shopping for Tomorrow. They contributed to local sport and movie attendances and freely tossed their few coins into the local economy. They were involved in studies, institutional life, boy meets girl situations and Saturday morning window shopping among the material wonders of the world. Cargo for a civilised life. A source of satisfaction to the colonial masters. A sense of security to the Chinese trader, sitting by his cash register, patiently waiting for his share of life and immortality. The students sometimes formed social action or pressure groups, but mostly they were conservatives waiting their turn in the queue.

The colonials lived in large sprawling houses mostly provided for them by the colonial government or private business firms. The foreigners did not form into communities well and were happier in pubs, clubs or small interest groups. The white wives, who did not work, amused themselves as best they could. With no television but plenty of cheap labour for laundry and housework, some of them lived the life of forgotten days in brash and apologetic ways.

There were a few hundred Chinese in the town. They formed their own loose communities of friends and foes and unobtrusively fitted into the life of the town. Mostly, they were descendants of Cantonese-speaking Chinese who were imported into German New Guinea to fill gaps in the labour force.

In Port Moresby, foreigners travelled from place to place in Japanese motor cars and so escaped many of the unpleasant realities of life in the town. Still, many foreigners felt threatened by individuals or gangs who broke into their homes, stole their property and did much damage. Security bars were standard equipment on all homes where they could be afforded. It was in these situations that the poverty and affluence of the town came together in ugly forms. Not that foreigners were the only ones who suffered from loss and violence. I was attacked by foreign natives twice in situations that could have led to murder. Murders were not uncommon among native groups but, unless a white foreigner or a prominent native was involved, the incident received scant attention. Political overtones of violence were also played down.

This was Port Moresby, 1972. A pleasant enough town if you could take it. It was the only town that the Papuans knew. Foreigners liked it or disliked it according to their mix. Some found status and authority here that they could never find at home. Many used it as a stepping stone to other things or to finish off their education. Professionals did well if they didn't stay too long and many of them added to their degrees, publications and lists of overseas junkets. The curriculum vitae of smooth relationships. The colonials were most generous to themselves. Servants and taxes were cheap but 'decent' food was expensive. Even so, all could afford an extended holiday of three months or more, on full pay and fares, every two years. On the whole, the benefits outweighed the unpleasantness and there was always someone to blame if something went wrong.

Port Moresby was still very much a colonial town and everyone who was a resident had a right to vote. This meant Australians, Chinese, Papuans and New Guineans. I was an unknown in Port Moresby but I would have to get some of the votes there if I was to have a chance. I expected most of my votes to come from the urban and rural villages and settlements.

I listened to the experts in the town and everything pointed to failure. But then I went to the villages on the white beaches, by the clear rivers and in the cold mountains and I returned with new hope. Among the villagers I looked for signs of rejection but I did not find them. Perhaps I was blinded by bias or perhaps the villagers would not reject a modest, traditional Papuan girl as readily as many of the experts had predicted.

Back in Moresby I rested like a bird rescued from a storm. I was with Dina every chance that I had. He was busy at the Institute doing my work as well as his own. It was wonderful to be reassured in the face of so many doubts, to have someone who believed in me. What I was doing had meaning only while I was with him. I was growing as my political ideas were being moulded by the people but the rest was an exercise in selling an image. I was not exposing myself to this rough experience because I liked it. I was looking for love, not for thrills.

An English missionary, who had been influenced by a life of involvement with traditional Papuans, lent his name and his voice to my cause. In so doing he displayed more kindness than discretion and I was worried that his attachment to my cause might attract some harm to him. Perhaps the image of a modest, traditional Papuan girl, which was aimed at the hearts of the villagers, had unintentionally wounded him as well.

Except for Dina and the pioneer missionary, the colonials kept well clear of the action and took no unnecessary chances. With but a few very modest and cautious exceptions, the colonials who gave me their support confined it to the polling booths, where the cramped silence of a confessional was the only witness.

* * *

At week-ends I did my campaigning with Dina and we visited many rural villages in our own 4-wheel drive vehicle, and many coastal and island villages in speed-boats that we hired. Using a small speed-boat we could visit several villages in a day that would otherwise take many days. Safe hands steered the boat over the blue waters, through the coral reefs and into the quiet lagoons. Then the beach, the palms and the village.

The villagers were accustomed to a lot of attention at election time. It was the one season when their worth to the society was fully appreciated and their rights given plenty of air. When I visited a village I only brought the simple message of *Papua dainai, tano dainai, mauri dainai*. I tried to avoid village meetings and developed a routine of visiting each home in the village. It was hard work but it was effective. Each person could talk to me in the intimacy of their own home. Much of village life is lived on the verandahs and this is where I met the people. Everyone was involved; those who spoke and those who listened. They carried on the daily routine as they listened to my story and summed me up for value. Motu was understood everywhere and, as the people did most of the talking, I gained more than I gave.

I moved from house to house with little disturbance to the routine life of the village. No house was too grand or too mean to distract me from my purpose. It was time consuming, but I could not have done it any other way. I did not have the confidence yet to speak for the people. I had to spend more time with them before I could understand what they were saying. I listened to their ideas for three months and this gave me the confidence to develop political policies of my own.

The routine in the speed-boats was to go as far as we could with the fuel that we had and leave enough for the return journey, with some reserves in case of accident. A risky procedure, but fuel was not the only mishap that could befall a small boat in these waters. It was better not to think of the other possibilities or no work would be done. Still, before pulling out from Moresby, I always checked the life-belts first.

When the day finished, we would board the speed-boat again and head for Port Moresby. Every afternoon the wind came up and changed the sea from a placid, yielding pool to a restless obstruction.

We were on our way home to Moresby and had been snapping through choppy seas for about three hours when I wiped the salt water from my face with a towel and said,

'I don't know how much longer I can carry on like this. It's getting harder and harder. I'm really tired. I must be getting sick.'

'The strain has been too much,' said Dina, draping a towel over my head. 'We'll check your temperature when we get back to Moresby.'

Dina must have noticed how dark my skin was from exposure to the sun, so I quickly replied,

'Yes, and I'm going black too. I've never been in the sun and the wind so much in all of my life. Bumping about on these boats is killing me.'

'I didn't put the towel on your head to stop you from going black,' said Dina. 'I was thinking of the heat. What's wrong with going black, anyhow? You will have plenty of company.'

'There's nothing wrong with it,' I said, resting my elbows on my knees and staring at the bottom of the boat that was all that stood between us and eternity. 'It's just that I can't

take this much longer. I'm not as young as I used to be. I'm
not made of steel.'

The boat we were in was fibreglass, but we had travelled
in everything from hollow logs to luxury yachts. The spartan
fibreglass hulls were fitted with powerful outboard motors
and carried nothing that could be done without. Motorcycles
of the sea, they provided their owners with recreation but
little comfort. They were symbols of easy money and easy
days and could change hands several times before they ended
up in a watery grave or left on some forgotten beach.

'I'm too tired to think straight,' I said wearily. 'I don't want
to use these boats again. I can't see everyone in the region.'

'I think that you should ease up a bit,' said Dina. 'There
are two or three weeks to go. We can give these boats away.
You have time to do all you need to do.'

3

The image and the soul

*T*he election was coming closer and excitement was mounting as the media fed the news and predictions to the people. I spent three or four days in Port Moresby making final visits to settlements and villages around the town. The reactions of the people gave me hope but all of the candidates seemed to be confident that they were going to win. Papuans are naturally courteous to strangers who are usually told what they want to hear rather than the unpleasant truth.

I was weary with the strain of campaigning. For two months I had been on the go, using many kinds of transport, walking and even swimming to where I had to go. I ate and slept under all sorts of conditions and lost a lot of weight. I was also weary with doubts and predictions and the worry about the future. Then, with what energy and enthusiasm I could muster, I decided to set off on one final trip. Together with a Papuan girl, *Hisiu* (star), I caught a small plane and travelled to an outstation airstrip west of Port Moresby, which was the centre of a large village population. This was the country where men dominated political thinking and it was the area where the experts had consistently predicted that I would not get a vote.

The light plane bounced and skidded over the wet field which was no more than an elongated playground and eventually, with some luck and some good judgement, came to a halt. The pilot, who was upset by the landing, quickly regained his composure and taxied the plane to a small white box marked on the ground, the work of some faithful colonial subordinate who was sweating it out and serving his time.

'These bastards'll kill me one day. I didn't know the strip was like that,' muttered Mr Watson-Jones, the forthright young pilot who was trying to gain hours and experience without killing himself in the process.

Watson-Jones was angry and had been aroused to full consciousness by the unpleasant landing. In a few strides he bounded from his small craft with a new-found mobility, leaving Hisiu and me to follow in his wake, and confronted the first human that he came to who was pale enough to be classified as 'European'.

An unsuspecting 'European' sauntered towards him with an unmistakable Australian gait and an unmistakable Australian 'ow ya mate' expression on his sun-tanned face.

'What the bloody hell do you think you're doing,' shouted Watson-Jones. 'This bloody field isn't fit for a cat to piss on, let alone for a bloody plane to land. Why don't you bloody well tell someone what gives before you kill someone?'

'Steady up, mate,' shouted the 'European' more in surprise than anger. 'This bloody strip ain't nothin' to do with me and yer bloody kite ain't nothin' to do with me neither. The bastard that looks after this bloody outfit ain't 'ere so save yer lip for im.'

'Why ain't he 'ere?' shouted Watson-Jones in defiant retaliation.

'Aw, pig's arse,' said the 'European' who had regained his composure and had begun to walk away.

'What a bloody kanaka,' said Watson-Jones in an undertone that could be heard by the six foot 'kanaka' but not understood.

'Aw, drop dead,' shouted the 'European' over his shoulder to keep the score even.

'Culture,' I said as Mr Watson-Jones turned towards the plane.

'I don't understand them when they talk like that,' said Hisiu as she summed up the human hazards of our immediate surroundings.

I had never visited this area before and I was frightened that we might be chased away by the men as predicted by the experts. This was the big test. I would not get any votes from the Goilala mountain people and the foreigners in Port Moresby would vote heavily against me. I had to get some votes here if I was to have a chance to win.

When we entered a village and the people became aware of who we were, there was great excitement. At last they could see the Papuan girl who everyone was talking about and who had swooped over their village in an aeroplane several weeks before. I had left this area until late but now I had to face reality. The moment of truth would soon be at hand.

I approached the people carefully, observing all of the points of etiquette and customary behaviour that I knew. My image as a modest, traditional Papuan girl would have to come through loud and clear if I was going to impress these people. The value they placed on traditional behaviour was high. I ignored the women and spoke only with the men. I displayed the restraint that I thought was required of a woman in the presence of men. Gently and quietly I tried to win their confidence.

We had arranged that Hisiu would contact the women while I talked to the men. In this village, my practice of going from house to house did not work as the men migrated to their own meeting place to greet strangers while the women collected in groups elsewhere.

Hisiu was a modern Papuan girl who was educated in the ways of the colonials, but she was as much at home in a grass skirt in a village as she was wearing the clothes of foreigners in an insurance office in Port Moresby where she worked. Her body was tattooed with traditional village designs and this, together with her native Motu accent, were assets to us now.

The men were quiet and courteous, which was not always their nature but, on the other hand, they did not wish to appear too enthusiastic while talking to a girl about important affairs of state. My slogan 'our Papua, our land, our life' had impressed them deeply as had our exploits over their village in the tiny aircraft several weeks before. I knew that some of the other candidates had received hostile receptions in these villages. At least they were friendly to us. Perhaps I was making progress. Only time would tell.

We were asked to spend the night in the village. I was weary with the strains and uncertainties of the day and close to the stage when I would have to face up to the reality that I couldn't take any more.

Hisiu and I stayed in the home of a village councillor. The councillor had a handsome house of native materials standing in a central position among the twenty or thirty houses in the oval-shaped village. He had two daughters, both approaching marriageable age. They were the last of several children who had grown in the cool shade and stern austerity found within the security of the palm-thatched walls. Outside the house, they had shared the sands and the stars with the generations of the thousands of years since time began.

We were shown to a small, open room where we were to sleep for the night, and then given mats and mosquito nets to serve as our beds and protection.

'I heard that these people have a lot of taboos with women,' I said as I took a bed sheet out of the small shoulder bag that I carried. 'I was told that a man will not drink water if a woman has stepped over it and a woman must not walk up the steps of a house if men or children are underneath. Do you think that this is true?'

'I suppose so,' said Hisiu, laughing as she dragged her shoulder bag under the net with her. 'We'll have to be careful what we do.'

'There are too many customs to remember them all,' I said with a yawn.

'I follow the good ones and forget the rest,' said Hisiu. 'That's the best way.'

'*Bamahuta* (go to sleep), Hisiu.'

'*Bamahuta*, Josephine.'

I felt like I did as a girl on Misima Island when I sometimes fell asleep soon after the evening meal was finished. Hisiu was soon asleep. Everything she did was deliberate.

Hating, making love or going to sleep. All were incidental, secondary pauses in the journey through life. I loved Papua for her beauty and her people but Hisiu loved her for her spirit and her soul; a spirit buried deep in the animal soil of her being that held the spirit of all her people, all of her future and all of her past. By professional deceit I had extracted the people's thoughts. Papua, land and life. I was puzzled by its meaning and puzzled by its success. I was puzzled why a Papuan girl could influence so many people with three words. Words that I did not know the full meaning of myself. A meaning that was locked in the tempestuous spirit of the tattooed Papuan beauty who lay breathing by my side.

I was envious of some of the things that Hisiu was. I was a detribalised Papuan who had been lured from my native soil by the empty baubles of a directionless materialism that I mistook for the new Christ. Hisiu did not have to rationalise or justify. She belonged to the earth that I sang about. I lived with beauty and compassion and sought love and a gentle touch. Hisiu was the beauty and the spirit of my native land. She felt emotions I had never known. Her passion flowed in her belly through the still night and beyond the dawn. If I was going to be a politician then I must go back to the soil and learn from the people. A new emotion was born in me from a dormant seed of time. I had to be exposed and fulfilled. God would give me the courage to play my role.

My thoughts wandered as I tossed on my mat: 'What is Dina doing now? He sits up half the night. Here I am going to sleep and the night has just begun. I don't really like working on my own. I hope I will be successful. For his sake as well as my own. He has more confidence in me than I have in myself. But I don't want to be alone. I must share to be whole. I don't know anything about politics. Everyone seems to want to be elected to Parliament. It must be a big honour. I wonder what clothes they wear in Parliament. We'll wait and see. They might be wrong and I might win after all. Look after yourself, Dina, wherever you are. You should learn to relax. The nights will be long and lonely. Take care. Hisiu is lucky. She can just turn her mind off and go to sleep. I think half the night.'

I sat up, secured the mosquito net tightly under the mat to

deter the spirits and the mosquitoes, placed a towel over my plastic bag to make a pillow, pulled my sheet over my head, closed my eyes and waited for sleep.

* * *

At one stage we travelled by foot into the low hills that framed the Owen Stanley Range. Here we met a French missionary who lived close to the people. He had spent twenty years in one spot and thanked his God for the privilege. He lived in a clearing above a large village, in a large, well-verandahed house which spoke of primitive elegance, positioned so that the front looked over the green hills and plains to the distant sea, while the back looked down the throat of the village.

The cloaked missionary could have been a frugal monk or a feudal lord. What he did not know about the villagers was not worth knowing. He heard most things on the village grapevine and what he did not pick up there was whispered in confession. He was French, scented, accented and nativised and he spiced his native fare with wines and nourishments from Europe, so that his table, now framed in a silhouette of Papuan mountain grandeur, could have passed without comment on a Paris boulevard.

The missionary was the first normal European we had met on this excursion. The abnormal ones included colonial officials who tried to discredit me at village meetings. The priest not only offered us the keys to his house, but the keys to his church as well! At this stage we could appreciate a little spoiling so we ate in the house, held our meetings in the church, slept in a teacher's house, and accepted the offer of our host to stage manage our affairs in the village.

The priest told us that the local people had been undecided whether to vote for me or for a *taubada* (big man) who was known in the area. But, since my arrival in the district, the tide had turned in my favour. I represented the things that were of value to the people but they did not know if a Papuan girl would be strong enough to stand up in a man's Parliament. It would take time for a consensus to be reached among the villagers but our kind host thought that I would win in this area.

Tears came to my eyes. It was the first confident word that I had heard from a foreigner who worked with the village people.

When our work was done, the missionary blessed our endeavours and arranged for suitable protectors to see us safely through his private Eden to the lowland villages below.

* * *

A few days later a change came over the campaign in the villages. We had reached the final stages and expected to return home in a few days. I needed a rest. This had been the final effort. The central district, with its hundreds of villages spread over thousands of kilometres of rough and rugged country, had been difficult to cover once and was beyond thought to do again. This was all I could do. I had done my best.

I had these thoughts in my mind as I held Hisiu by the arm, as we bounced together on the back of a village truck which we shared with pigs, fish, rice and copra. It was late afternoon when we arrived at a large village which was the home of an important chief. The front of the village was decorated with palms, flowers and streamers stripped from the jungle.

The pigs in the truck snorted with discomfort as the driver unexpectedly braked at the village entrance. He was surprised to see the village dressed up for a special occasion. It crossed my mind that the ceremonial welcome may have had something to do with us, but I did not entertain the thought seriously until I noticed an impressive looking man striding towards our vehicle. With him were a group of village elders.

We extricated ourselves from the fish, the rice and the pigs, gathered our shoulder bags and jumped from the high sides of the truck to the ground below. Hisiu laughed impolitely as her unexpected arrival on the ground dispersed a group of eager men who had closed in on the truck. It was now obvious that these were the big men of the village.

I had been well-schooled in handling situations such as this. Separating a chief from the commoners, in a Papuan village, was by no means easy. In most villages, chiefs did not exist and important decisions were reached by common agreement. Even where chiefs did exist, they voiced the will of the people and absolute authority was unknown. Autocracy and the gun were colonial innovations. Papuans ordered their affairs through talk, traditions, shame, magic, and occasionally with the knife or the spear. They existed for thousands of years without money, policemen, armies or bosses.

After sorting ourselves out, we were escorted to the meeting place of the men, which was the usual palm thatched shelter situated in the middle of the village. There, in loud voice and with much repetition, three or four spokesmen for the chief told us that the people, after much thought and deliberation, had decided to vote for me in the national elections. I represented the traditional values of the people which were in danger of being destroyed and they repeated what I was to hear many times. Christ was born of a woman and Papua would be born of me. Here was a myth in the making, but no harder to digest than the stories of origin of these and others who held a woman, in some form, responsible for the origin of the people.

This declaration meant that a consensus had been reached at last, and that the people could now openly show their support. It also meant that it was probable that most of the other villagers in this area were thinking the same way.

I would smile my way through the celebration that had been planned for us, but I had to get back to Moresby soon. I had had enough. I wanted to tell Dina the news and I wanted to hear what news there was of other places.

* * *

The earth had been fed, the sun was down and now the confusion of the night. Banana fruits bent the stout poles and banana leaves glazed the hot food. The earth was our host and our oven, mother of all things. The cord of life and eternity.

Hisiu and I were women of Papua. We were conditioned to give as well as to eat. To expose ourselves to the emotions of the hour was the measure of our sex. The drums, quieted by the hour, were restless now. Laughter and food were wine to some while some stirred to other things. The drums beat restlessly, the stars turned bright and bodies turned to the glory of the night.

A murmur, and the drums gave way to the whisper of the palms, as paradise paraded from beyond the trees and beyond that night, and the heads of the dancing dandies were fused with cane crests hung with feathered remnants from the walls of heaven. Beauteous men, bursting with sap and coloured beyond their pride, circled the small earth and intoxicated our senses with the aroma of passion and the breathless beauty of birds of paradise. Gentle feathers, fallen to vanity and the unfettered search for love, yielded to the sensuous rhythm of delight. Coloured mausoleums of death-less beauty which mocked man to contain his sap beyond the moment of the night as they mimicked his carnal drudgery.

The dancers beat their own rhythm now with constant hands on seasoned drums as they swirled in fine display. Many people dispersed from other interests to unmask their excitement and daub their bodies with the colours of the dance. The men went through their pageantry of love and war while we stirred to other things.

My eyes fixed on the sprayed feathers of the birds of paradise moving with practised motion on the dancers' heads. Tiny bodies, attached to lethal beauty which casts a spell over the dreams of men and drives the birds to vibrate and display in deep and lonely solitude. Why should a little bird, less than a cat's meal, raise such envy in the minds of man that he bids yellow gold for red death in a search for an elusive love that breathes dormant in his own soul? Why copulate with death while life lies unfulfilled and waiting? Since days of dazzling flowers and bright coral reefs, beauty has been my weakness and colours as plentiful as my dreams. The dancers were by my side and exotic herbs were in the air. A small canopy of feathers fanned my face and there, ringed in a flush of black parrot feathers, was a red-plumed bird of paradise. Yellow cap on a band of gold. Emerald throat pulsing on a lilac breast. Sienna wings resting on plumes redder than a blushing sky and more

sensuous than a lover's touch. If you had not been so beautiful, little bird, you could still have filled the world with
beauty, and death would not have been your fate.

Hisiu had slipped away and a grass skirt had been hung
around my hips as the male display gave way to the spirit of
the night. Men and women narrowed the periphery and
grass skirts swirled to a new rhythm as songs of the islands
joined hands with the past. This was the signal for me to
slowly edge towards the moving people and join them in the
dance.

There is a natural segregation of the sexes in Papuan
dancing and this now gave me the chance to laugh with the
women and cement the bond of our sex. The women knew
that, in politics, I must be preoccupied with the men. They
were anxious for me to succeed and knew the rules of the
game we played. Now, in the romance of the dance, it was
different. Now we were one. In love, in motherhood and in
drudgery we served a common god.

Hisiu was once more by my side. She had dressed for the
dance and was now moving with the grace and freedom of
her people. She wore a coloured grass skirt, garlands of
flowers, amulets of herbs, armlets of pearl and a pig's tusk
between her breasts. Proud of her tattooed body, her grass
skirt was hung low on her hips showing her light brown skin
and the symbolled symmetry of her tribe.

A vivacious community of desires, we shared our sensi-
bilities as the moon rode through the night and the spirit
returned to its temporal tomb and veiled for the coming
night. Sensing the disposition of the people, the chief stood
on his platform and raised his hands and the drums rolled
his command.

'We are here tonight because *Dirava* (God) has called.
With us tonight is Abaijah *kekeni* (girl) who will become the
mother of Papua.

'*Dirava*, help our *kekeni* to be strong in the face of temp-
tation, as evil men will use money, magic and power to
corrupt her mind and corrupt her body so that she will be a
slave to their comands.

'Our ancestors lie beneath our feet where all of the spirits
of all the generations lie in peace. Now they are restless and

move among us. They cannot rest because our lands are in danger and our ways are being replaced by dark and evil things.

'Once we could walk in safety but now we must walk with the knife and the axe. Once our women walked with their eyes straight, but now they walk with restless eyes and fear violation and death.

'The *taukurokuro* (white men) came and told us that they were our *tamana* (father). We trusted them when they said that they would protect our way of life. 'We now know that this was *koikoi* (lies) and soon our people will sleep like *matabudi* (turtles) on the beach.

'They educate our girls so that they can steal them from us. They teach them to disrespect their parents and turn away from their own land. They send them far away to live with foreign ways and fill their *bogana* (bellies) with foreign sap.

'The *taukurokuro* smile when our children are lost, they smile when our land is lost and they smile when we are full of beer and smokes and are slaves to their money and beggars to their desires.

'*Momokani* (true) *natugu* (my child) Abaijah I am no longer a young man. You have been educated and you are still one of us. God has kept you to be the mother of Papua and the mother of our hopes. We will vote for you to go to Parliament and God will be by your side and you will win.'

Strong arms lifted me on to strong shoulders and I was carried forward to join hands with the chief.

There was a hushed silence. All were moved by the emotions of the moment but none as much as I. None of them knew of my frailty as a person and as a woman and that the image that I projected was only a part of me. Their faith alone could not carry me to a Parliament that was the preserve of men. None of them knew the sterility of my purpose or that they were committing their future to the belly of a coward who had yet to prove herself.

I turned to the stars and the pale moon and then to the people below. I went on one knee and prayed aloud an old familiar prayer,

'God, always by my side, don't desert me now. You are the

way and the light and through you I walk the path of my
destiny.'

Then I stood, turned to the people and said,

'I don't know what lies ahead but I am the servant of the
people. I shall serve you in every way that I can. God will
show me how to protect our beautiful land and how to
preserve the good ways of our people. If you are with me, I
shall not be afraid of any man. Your women walk in fear of
violation and death. Why should I do less? Your praise, your
faith and your dance has made my stomach warm. Your
magic can match the magic of our enemies. I love the beauty
of our land. I love the ways of our people. I love you all.'

Hisiu was standing beneath me. I gave her my hand and,
with the agility of her age, she vaulted to the platform and
stood by my side. She was the tradition of the past set in a
modern frame. Her light brown skin, unmarked by wound or
parasite, carried the deep blue of her tattoo over graceful
swells to disappear in capricious cavities. A *hanenamo
momokani* (a true village beauty) stood before them and
their hearts swelled with hope and pride. The humble people
of the soil cheered our presence and we, embarrassed by the
attention, jumped from our pedestal to the earth below and
slipped quietly into the shadows of the night

* * *

In the morning we were still unrested and wearily faced the
labours of another day. We travelled in a 4-wheel drive
vehicle that took us to some of the more difficult-to-reach
villages. A vine-lashed raft ferried us across a wide river
that carried crocodiles, snakes, vegetation and waste to sea.

Our visits to the villages grew shorter. Smiles replaced
words. We established our identity, gave out our materials,
made our excuses and went on our way. Everywhere we were
greeted with happy faces and invitations but I was nearly
exhausted and could not take any more. It had been a long
campaign and, win or lose, I was finished.

At last the work really was finished and we prepared to
leave for Moresby and home. We waited on the outstation
airstrip for our small chartered plane to arrive. I had mixed
feelings of relief and satisfaction as we searched the morning

sky. Then, out of the east, came a faint drone, an arrow, a bird, a small machine.

'Had a nice holiday, girls?' Out bounced a smiling Watson-Jones, speaking with jarring freshness.

'It's good to get away from Moresby,' said Watson-Jones. 'I must try it sometime.'

'And its good to get back home, no matter where it is,' I said, anxious to get on the plane.

'And what are you going to do when you get there?' asked Watson-Jones with a smile.

'Sleep,' I said with a yawn. Young Watson-Jones was beginning to get the message and he beckoned us to board the plane.

'Any luggage?' he asked, less enthusiastic now. 'Most natives coming back from the villages are loaded with food and other rubbish.'

'No luggage, no food, no rubbish,' I said, and holding up my battered bag, continued, 'only this small shoulder bag.'

Watson-Jones, remembering his upbringing, helped us to board the plane. In the middle of this business he paused and said, 'Did you see that white kanaka again?'

'What white kanaka?' I said. 'There are plenty of them around.'

'The fellow who was on the strip the morning I dropped you down.'

'No, we didn't see him again.'

'You're lucky,' said Watson-Jones with feeling.

'You've got to be lucky sometimes,' I said.

'But you need only be unlucky once,' said Watson-Jones thoughtfully.

The small engine roared and dispersed the crowd of foreign and local natives who had gathered around. We were soon droning our way to Moresby and home.

4

A politician in the making

*P*olling for the national elections was to start the following
Saturday in Port Moresby but it would take several teams of
workers three weeks to collect the votes from the whole of
the Central District.

During the week, Port Moresby came out in a rash of
posters. Busy workers stuck photographs and exhortations of
their favoured candidates on anything that would hold a face
or a smile. Some enthusiasts were busy putting posters up,
while others were busy defacing them or tearing them down.

As for me, I sat at-home with a sick feeling in my stomach
and felt too ashamed to speak about the elections. I could not
do any more work and was content to sit out the awful
suspense of waiting for the judgement to be pronounced. I
had never exposed so much of myself to anything before.
Now, I braced myself for the hurt that my wild indiscretion
would create. Other than Dina and the family, I did not want
to see anyone. Especially, I did not want to talk about the
elections. Newsmen were anxious to get a story, but I had
none.

Polling day in Moresby came and went. A sole helper at a polling booth was not encouraged by his experience and reported little evidence of support. Motu-speaking Papuan villagers confronted Pidgin English-speaking electoral officials with mutual confusion and distrust. The battle was fought hard and there were casualties on both sides as a fragile democracy was put to the test.

A surname can be the given name of the person or of his parents. A name may be drawn from the whole vocabulary of heavenly bodies, earthly entities or spirits. Nothing was too delicate for a name except, perhaps, the name of a dead relative who was still a spirit in their midst. In the daily round of work, persons could be confronted bearing such names as dog, pig, knife, lost, water, star and intimate acts of sex. When an important occasion like a national election came along, finding a name often became a battle of wits. People who could not read or write searched for their names through strangers who could not understand or be understood.

In Port Moresby, polling day was extended for a few days and this was a signal for candidates to hire trucks to coax people to vote for them. In the end this became too tiresome and voting came to an end. Many teams in the rural areas trudged and bumped their various ways to the remote villages in a gallant attempt to keep their appointment with the national count that was to commence three weeks after the first polling day.

* * *

Three weeks passed and, at last, counting day. It was a Saturday night and preparations were on a grand scale. The Sir Hubert Murray sports stadium was the nerve centre for the count. Results from all of the electorates were relayed to Port Moresby and then broadcast to the people. In the centre of the stadium was a huge tally board that provided a running summary on the state of the game.

I was too embarrassed to confront so much publicity so I arranged to travel with Dina to a quiet outstation, 100 kilometres from Moresby, to check on the counting there. In this obscurity I could hide my face until the trial was over and I knew my fate.

It was night when we arrived at the outstation. We parked the car outside the counting hall and prepared for the long night. I locked myself inside the car with a radio and a blanket as candidates were not allowed inside, while Dina went inside the counting hall as a scrutineer to supervise the counting.

The counting at this outstation was in the charge of a Papuan, but the counting team was well braced with colonials. As it turned out the counting was well conducted and the only serious error detected by Dina was when a foreigner failed to post a few hundred votes to my credit.

The night wore on. Dina came out now and then. I was holding a good lead. The only other candidate who was getting votes here was a local planter. Through my radio, I learned that I was doing well in other parts of the district also. However, the votes in the Goilala were split between two Australians and a Papuan man. I got none. These candidates had done all right in the Goilala but they were not doing so well elsewhere. The central district was extensive and nobody could succeed who only had local support.

By about 2.00 a.m. on Sunday morning, the counting was finalised at the outstation where we were.

'Let's go,' said Dina. 'It's all over here.'

'What's the latest?' I asked.

'You won easily here. Have a look at the figures.'

'I'm relieved,' I said wearily. 'I'm too tired to be happy now.'

'What have you done to make yourself tired?' asked Dina, 'I have done all the work tonight.'

'Sometimes its worse waiting than being in the thick of things,' I said.

'You drive the car,' said Dina. 'You can then say you did some work.'

'Okay, that's fair. Let's go.'

'What did you hear from Moresby?' asked Dina as the car rolled towards Port Moresby, about two or three hours away. Kilometres meant nothing here in the land of tomorrow. Hours are the only things that made sense.

'The commentators in Moresby seem excited,' I said. 'I'm

thousands of votes in front according to them but counting is not finished yet.'

'Are you pleased?' asked Dina cautiously, as he knew I would not tempt fate by presuming too much.

'I'm more pleased than I was,' I said, easing the car over one of the ditches in the road. 'But I'm not counting my chickens before they're hatched.'

'You might have a lot of chickens to count,' said Dina philosophically.

'Then you'll have to help me count them,' I said.

Then our conversation gave way to thoughts. It might be time to start thinking about a new life, but I wasn't prepared to admit that possibility yet. The road was wet with a recent shower, the corrugations dictated our speed and animals of the night scurried in urgent flight. A typical drive home on a typical Papuan night.

* * *

We arrived home in the heavy dark before the first light of dawn. I hushed the dogs, opened the door to the house that Dina and I had built ten years before and went inside. I made my way to the kitchen to make coffee.

'There's nothing like a cup of coffee on a night like this,' I said, stepping between my brothers and sisters who were sleeping on mats on the lounge floor. My son was with them and fast asleep.

'I'm glad that the *taukurokuro* taught you that,' said Dina wearily.

'Yes, I suppose they taught me how to live in their own way,'

'Cheer up, it can't be that bad,' said Dina.

'No,' I said, 'when I travel to other countries I always get the feeling that Australia is a pretty good place to live.'

'Does that include Papua, too?' said Dina softly.

'No, it does not,' I said with feeling. 'I can't explain how I feel about Papua. It is part of me like my skin. These feelings have become worse since these elections when I opened my heart to the voice of the people. I might have bitten off more than I can chew. I'm on the back of a crocodile and can't get off.'

'The back of a tiger, I suppose you mean,' said Dina.

'No, I mean the back of a crocodile. I think a crocodile is a bit more realistic than a tiger.'

'You're the only crocodile that I know,' said Dina. 'I am glad that you are a bit softer than your sisters in the rivers. The water's boiling.'

'And the sun is turning on its lights,' I called, looking out the kitchen window.

We drank our coffee in silence and then we went to bed.

I slept the rest of Sunday away. I was warm with a feeling of satisfaction. The village people had supported me, and the experts were running for cover and trying to work out what had gone wrong. I had not made a fool of myself and that was good.

I was not taking anything more for granted, yet. I had a healthy suspicion of anything that colonial officials were mixed up in. Twenty times bitten twenty times shy. I was a brick wall. A block of ice. I would never expose myself to their insults again. If there was any way of keeping me out of Parliament they would find that way for sure. I had no faith in them.

For twelve years I had diligently served the colonial administration. I was young, educated, slightly bewildered and the first of the few. Many times in the past I had swallowed my pride and held out my hand as a mendicant or as a friend and as many times I was rejected, admonished, humiliated or told to go to hell. In the end I really felt unclean in their presence. A leper without a bell. A beggar without a tin. Without the constancy of a few close friends, I would have been a casualty of the system, a statistic, a story without an end.

Luckily for me, my defences had me prepared for the anti-climax of the next couple of weeks. Results were coming in from most of the electorates but not from mine.

Monday came and election fever was still around. Seats were declared won and the numbers game was on. But still no mention of the central district of Papua. What was wrong? Josephine Abaijah, the modest Papuan girl, was thousands of votes ahead of her nearest rival but there was nothing more than that. So the delay went on from day to day from one week to the next. Everyone knew their results and seats were declared all over the country, while I sat home and waited for the next humbug to raise its head.

At long last the primary count was completed in the central district after a recount of the votes from Kwikila, the place where the Papuan had been in charge and the place where Dina witnessed the count.

The Kwikila votes were laboriously recounted by a team of faithful officials and, when the task was completed, they wiped the sweat from their faces and declared them correct. Josephine Abaijah was confirmed as being thousands of votes ahead on the primary votes but now, weeks after the election, the counting of preferences began. The preferences might tell a different story. To the undisguised surprise of some, my lead continued to increase. This was the picture until I was ten thousand votes ahead.

After two weeks of needless anxiety, Josephine Abaijah was declared the winner of the regional seat of the Central District — the first and only woman elected to the PNG Parliament.

* * *

About six weeks after the first vote, the counting and re-counting for the central regional electorate was completed and the officials were finally satisfied. I ended up with twice as many votes as my nearest rival. The unbelieveable had happened. An unknown girl from Milne Bay had been elected to the influential electorate of central Papua.

I was to be declared duly elected to the national Parliament the next day which was the Wednesday before Easter. Not knowing what to expect, I asked Dina to come just in case. I had very little trouble with colonial officials when he was around. I dressed in my best for the occasion but, as usual, I was wasting my time. Nobody would have noticed me if I had worn dogs' teeth and a grass skirt.

We always let the colonials call the tune and usually ended up making fools of ourselves. We let them create the image of our country and what a mess they made of it. We tried to show our visitors beauty and love but, cheated, they turned away to continue to seek the primitive and the grotesque.

It was a stinking hot Port Moresby day. We walked across a small, bare rocky compound towards a tin hut where the declaration ceremony was to take place. The hut was the usual type of temporary office built to house the colonial administration following the war. This meant that it was a low, rectangular, out-of-date cowshed with corrugated iron roof, concrete floor and unlined fibro cement walls. It was as hot inside as it was in the sun but inside, some relief was provided by a battery of noisy electric fans in various stages of disintegration.

Six Europeans and one native worked in the office, so there were six standard sized tables covered with files and papers and each table was provided with a standard, tubular aluminium chair and a standard filing cabinet. These, together with ball point pens marked Commonwealth of Australia, an ash tray and enough light to see by comprised a standard employment kit for one Australian clerk. We knew the office well because we had spent hours here while they counted and recounted the votes.

By the door was a table half the size of the others. It had a chair but no filing cabinet. In place of the filing cabinet was a small cupboard. The cupboard housed six cups and saucers, a teapot and the ingredients for making coffee and tea. Above these was an untidy collection of envelopes and other office stationery. This was the table and accessories for the Papuan member of the staff who amused himself between 7.45 a.m. and 4.06 p.m., Monday to Friday, performing useful tasks for the Europeans such as making tea, cleaning up and buying the daily newspaper. The newspaper was thoughtfully distributed by the publishers to coincide with the start of the working day.

The office was as colourful as a police lock-up and the reception was just as chilly. Dina, who was more experienced than I was, wore shorts and an open necked tropical shirt, which was the only thing in the room that was not grey. Between us, we managed to draw attention to our presence and our purpose and three or four colonial officers sauntered up to a clearing near the door to witness the ceremony of declaring the first woman elected to Parliament. Then a small sheet of paper was produced, a few words read out and that was it. The clerks wandered back to their desks and Dina and I wandered out. I was now a duly elected member of Parliament and had a licence to be heard on any subject from the economy to the price of sweet potatoes. In addition, I would be given a small office at Parliament house, a reasonable salary and a soft job. The awakening was to come.

* * *

My next official duty was to meet the press and it was not long before the gentlemen of the media arrived at my house for the first press conference. They represented local and overseas interests.

I knew little about politics and less about reporters. This was the first time that the gentlemen of the media had considered me worthy of attention. Before the press conference, I took the precaution of locking my dogs under the house and so, by prearranged plan, the reporters arrived in a block on my front verandah. But, to the disappointment of some, they got no further. Thus started a continuous love-hate relationship that eventually made me the most publicly abused Papuan in our history.

Trembling with apprehension, I squeezed my way out of my partly opened front door and, accompanied by Dina, sat down on a garden seat that we had placed on the verandah for the occasion. When I appeared, notebooks and tape recorders flashed to the ready like soldiers presenting arms, and practised hands began recording the interview before I had time to sit down.

'What is your name, Josephine?' said reporter No. 1. 'May we call you Josephine?'

'I would prefer to be called Abaijah, if you don't mind,' I said timidly.

Some of the reporters stopped writing and began tapping their books in slow rhythm while others, who saw opportunity in my weakness, began to write faster.

'The village people only know me as Abaijah and Abaijah I

want to be. The people don't know me by any other name. It is only reporters and a few people around Port Moresby who want to call me Josephine.'

'What is wrong with Josephine?' asked reporter No. 1.

'What is wrong with Abaijah?' I asked.

It wasn't a very good start but I did not feel like trying to play the good little girl. The only one who knew my story and my limitations as well, was the man sitting by my side. Nothing else mattered. Some of the reporters saw me as a smart opportunist but not as a serious politician. Good copy but poor prospects. Others saw me as something different to the political crows that they usually had to deal with. A laugh or a sigh but never an issue. Josephine, never Abaijah. A nice little lass to show to the girl friend. A misguided Papuan who had the blood but not the brains, the smell of frangipani not the smell of war. The concubine but never the queen.

'How does it feel to be the first woman parliamentarian?' asked reporter No. 2, who represented an Australian paper. 'It probably feels strange to be the only woman in a parliament of a hundred men?'

'I don't feel anything being a woman. I don't think politics is a time when you specially feel like being a woman. I don't think it has much to do with sex. I have been the only woman many times before. I didn't feel anything then. I would like to feel something special now but I don't, sorry. You probably don't feel anything very special about being a man. Life can be beautiful, man or woman. The men might have to make a few adjustments. I don't think so.'

More tapping on the paper and more scribbling as words flowed onto pad. The professionals sweated in the steamy heat as they worked for their next meal.

'Do you support women's liberation?' asked a reporter who was hanging over the rail on the verandah steps.

'I don't really know what women's liberation means,' I said, wondering what all of this had to do with politics. 'Personally, I am as liberated as I want to be. It might be unhealthy to be any more liberated than I am now. I don't want to become a man. I don't think women's liberation means anything to Papuans. It is not relevant. It might be relevant in some foreign countries where the people have enough to eat. But it is not relevant to us. We don't want men to carry our burdens for us, we want roads and transport to relieve us of our drudgery. Some men need liberating just the same as some women do. Some of them are selfish or lonely. They spend their lives chasing dollars, smoke or booze and are starved for beauty and love. I really don't know what women's liberation is. That is something I have to learn about.'

'You were elected on a fair go for Papua. How do you expect to achieve that?' asked a quietly spoken Papuan employed by the colonial administration.

I felt less hostility now. Perhaps, I was overreacting to these foreigners. I had better cool down. I could feel Dina by my side. The next time one of these foreigners asks me a question I will bring him into it. That will take the pressure off me. I wished that they would go. I turned to the Papuan and softly said,

'I don't know what I'll do. I have only been a Member of Parliament for about an hour. I'll have to work it out. I don't really know anything about political matters. I only know about the people. I'll do what they want me to do. I was thinking I might start something like Papua Besena (Papuan family). Not a thing for politicians, just a thing for the people. I graduated at the International Institute of Rural Reconstruction and I was very impressed. I would like to start a Papua Besena here something like that, a rural reconstruction movement based on the people. I would like to do that on a large scale. It is what I know and what I can do. Time will tell. I hope I can. I shall also speak for the people. Not for myself. I shall not take any soft political job and forget the people. I am sure of that.'

'Were you helped in your campaign by Europeans?' asked one of the Australians impatiently. 'Where did you get all of your money from?'

I had better answer this myself, I thought. Dina is still in the colonial administration and some of these people will try to get him into trouble if they can. My good intentions

forgotten, I now became hostile again. I always became
hostile when they tried to get at me through personal matters. Creeps like this would like to make a crime of love.

'Two or three of them helped me,' I said icily. 'One Australian and one Englishman to be exact. Is there anything
wrong with that?'

'No, there is nothing wrong with that,' said the impatient
one, 'But surely they were not the only Europeans who
helped you?'

'There were plenty of other foreigners who helped me,' I
replied, trying to remain calm. 'But most of the others were
too scared to show their faces. They live in my country with
my people but they won't publicly support us. They are
frightened for their businesses or their jobs. After all that is
what they are here for.'

So the questions went on. I could not see how this was of
any interest to other people but, then, I had not read the
stories. I grew tired of the mental tug-of-war. They asked me
all sorts of personal questions that I had to talk around and
some political questions that I had never thought about. I
signalled to Dina with a touch that I had had enough and
wanted the trial to end.

'Do you favour a unicameral or a bicameral house, Miss
Abaijah?' asked one smart guy, giving me an examination
question. I gave Dina another nudge and turned to him and
said,

'What is a bicameral house?'

Dina fidgeted in his seat and said,

'The gentleman is talking about the structure of the House
of Parliament. Do you prefer it structured into upper and
lower houses or just one house as it is at present.' Then
turning to the reporter he said in a low restrained voice,

'Miss Abaijah has never given any serious thought to such
matters. I don't think it is under consideration so nobody has
thought about it much.'

'How do you know what Miss Abaijah thinks?' said the
smart one. 'We would like Miss Abaijah to answer her own
questions if you don't mind.'

I gave Dina another nudge. I wanted this thing to come to
an end.

'I don't mind, but we don't always get what we like.' Dina said smartly. 'Sometimes we have to be satisfied with what we can get.'

'What is your policy towards multinational corporations?' asked another reporter quickly, sensing that the session might quickly come to an end before he had asked his special question.

'Papua has not had any experience of multinational corporations.' I said. 'We need foreign money to get off the ground. We will have to encourage investment. Beggers can't be too fussy about how they get their money. Many countries could never have developed without heavy overseas investment. I don't suppose we can be any different. I would like to see some multinational corporations in Papua. It would be a sign we are alive. Now we are dead. We have never been developed.'

I had never really thought seriously about multinational corporations. Just now they seemed a far cry from the humble village people. They had never seen a multinational corporation in Papua but they still had to struggle to get enough to eat. I leant heavily on Dina to signal that I was finished.

'Could you give us some idea, Miss Abaijah, how you would control foreign investment so that it did not bleed the resources of the country and increase the poverty of the people?'

Dina rose from his chair and said,

'Miss Abaijah has already told you that she does not think that the poverty of the people can be increased. What they get now they get from God and nobody is likely to take that away from them. Miss Abaijah is tired. She has been here for an hour. It has been a big day and it has been her first interview. I think she would like a break. Let's call it a day.'

'Do you decide what Miss Abaijah thinks?' said the smart one who wanted to write a 'Beauty and the Beast' story and was enjoying himself.

'I do just at the moment,' said Dina, 'and she thinks that she has had enough.'

I stood up and moved close to Dina.

'How do you know?' asked the smart one.

'Because she told me,' Dina said.

By this time I had opened the door and had slipped inside while Dina stayed outside to see the men down the steps.

The reporters exchanged puzzled glances and soon were on their way to the desk, the telex or the pub. Port Moresby can be a stinker at this time of the year.

* * *

That night I tossed restlessly in bed. Around me were the records and trophies of yesterday. What use were they now? I was flattered by the new attention and warm with the feeling of satisfaction that followed success. Yet I was not at ease. I was uncertain about the future and about myself.

In my job as Principal of the Institute I had felt adequate; the only time in my life that I had reached such a stage. I knew what I was doing because I had been through the mill. I had prepared myself methodically and professionally. We had planned it all one starry night at Sangara eight years before and it had all come true. Step by step we had followed the plan. But now I was turning my back on the past and starting a new life full of doubts and unknowns. Where would it all lead to? My confrontation with the reporters had done nothing to lessen my fears. There was one thing that I was sure of. I would not do it alone.

Twelve years was a long time to spend in the constant companionship of one man. Warm rich years of growing and feeling, an exotic experience of intemperate adventure and love. I had tasted the best of two worlds and, avoiding the disagreeable, had cheated in both. I enjoyed the excitement of freedom — freedom from drudgery and bondage, and my world was heavy with the fragrance of love. Freely, I had surrendered to the orgasms of life and fulfilled, was jealous beyond reason to hold onto what I had. Isolated and oblivious, I was spoilt, selfish and satisfied. Passion at its peak must flow through the sublime moment into the night, and reaching the dawn refreshed, bud again to recklessly flaunt its vulgar beauty as a woman in love.

I didn't know much about politics but what little I did know made me think that it was a mean little world where liars and humbugs could thrive, a man could grow big by the destruction of his enemies and such menial tasks as character assassination were left in the competent hands of police drop-outs and frustrated clerks.

Whenever I felt the need to think things out I always thought of my rural home at Sangara where my parents and family lived. Sangara was across the mountains but only 30 minutes flight. I could be a person and, unthreatened, I could think. Then and there, I decided to go to Sangara the next day and spend Easter here. With these thoughts my mind lightened and I went to sleep.

PART FOUR

To travel alone

1

Easter at Sangara

I was up with the dawn and fresh thoughts came with the new day. Never had our whole family been together at any one time. Three of my married sisters were at Sangara holidaying, so together with the children at Moresby and Sangara, it was possible that we could all be together as a family for the first time.

We managed to get on a special flight and I arrived at Sangara, with the children, in the early afternoon. Sangara was wet and abundant, as always, yet still a shock to me after being mesmerised by the dry brown of Moresby town. Mt Lamington, the smouldering giant, stood beyond time surveying its creation — the multitudinous green life of its rich soft land spread before it from the cloud-capped mountains to the blue seas. And our small cell, half way between.

The first thing that I did was to hold a family roll-call. There were twenty-nine of us in all. My parents, their thirteen natural children, four adopted children and ten grandchildren. At last we had our whole family at one place at one time. Dina had promised to come over on Saturday, when we would take our family photograph. 'Such fecundity should not go unrecorded and it would be a pity to remove a statistic just to click a camera.'

We estimated that my parents would have between 50 and 100 grandchildren. They had done well to re-establish a family line which, through disease and poverty, had all but disappeared. They could have done better still if they had not fallen into the hands of an ardent conservationist who, thinking that my parents were placing too heavy a demand on the resources of the country, tied my mother's fallopian tubes. Nature diverted was not nature restrained and my parents ended up adopting a few more children.

Children gave us life and hope. Sangara would be quiet and lonely without the sight and sound of children playing in the cocoa or romping on the lush green grass. In our turn, this is where each of us should rest. We had already picked a spot near a tall kapok, by the edge of the cool cocoa and ringed by coconut palms that would drop their brown fruit onto the soft earth above our sleep. I was the eldest of the children but who would be the first to die?

Good Friday came quietly. Together we walked along the dusty Kokoda road towards the brown thatched church. The children ran ahead using their energy to gain distance for their games while we 'big ones' walked leisurely behind, watchful of the passing trucks and mindful of the harm that they might do to our Good Friday clothes.

The Church of England priests had taught us that, on Good Friday, we had to maintain silence until 3 o'clock in the afternoon. The children treated this vow of silence as a new kind of game but the adults maintained it with remarkable constancy, greetings and communications being made only by nods and signs. Papuans are good at observing vows of denial that only last for half a day! As it was Good Friday, a proper priest had come out to take the service. I wondered if the priest was going to observe the no-talk restriction the same as the people. To practise what they preached would seem to be more holy than to preach a sermon. Later I learned that special dispensations and leniencies were necessary lubricants to keep the church of God in motion!

When the service in the church was over, the people moved

in procession to assemble on the green lawns outside for the
stations of the cross. In Church I had become lost in thought
and heedless of myself but, when we burst into the light of
the fierce high sun, I suddenly became conscious of the shape
and colour of our reality. I had known no real deprivation as
my hurts were of my own pride. I was too proud to be a
servant and too weak to be a slave. Here I stood among the
poor farmers and the deprived village families of Sangara
and wondered why God had singled me out to travel alone.
Christ was white but His poverty was black and His church
had flourished in Papua.

Then the drama of Christ of the Cross was re-enacted. In
silence and servitude we followed God's servant from station
to station over the green farms, across the silver streams,
along flowering jungle paths to our own Papuan Calvary. I
have no power to describe the moods and colours of the
stations of the cross, set in the natural beauty of my native
land. Each station was marked by a simple cross cut from
the pressing jungle or salvaged from the discards of civilization. At each cross we joined hearts in prayer or meditation
and traced the triumphant journey of Christ from His crown-
ing to His death. I was deeply moved and humbled beyond
my custom. Words made clean by the presence of God stripped
me of my vanity and made me cry out for salvation and my
soul.

'Oh God, always by my side, don't desert me now. Give me
the strength to honour your will and follow the path of my
destiny. You are the way and the light. Show me another
dawn, the trail to the mountain, to the sunset, and to hope in
your name, Amen.'

As we stripped ourselves of our own demands, our senses
sharpened to the fragrance and colour of life and to the
nature of our true desires. The hibiscus flowered brighter,
the frangipani sweeter with the scent of desire, and the
people and the earth were bursting with Hallelujah.

Then we came to Calvary. A green hill and on top, a simple
cross. Beyond the cross, in a hollow, was a half-buried heap
of rusting iron. These were the jeeps, the gun carriages and
the other machinery of a fierce and lonely war, fought by

young men and growing boys in the quiet jungles and treacherous trails where we now traced the stations of the cross.

Some of these young men never had a chance. They died defending this heap of rust and a country that they never saw again. They did not feel victory or defeat. They did not feel anything for the country or its people. They only felt death in the primitive loneliness of a foreign hell.

I have travelled in the homelands of these boys who spilled their blood on the soil of my native land and I must have brushed past many who never saw their loved ones again. Everywhere I have gone I have tried to meet the people with laughter and happiness and carry to them the warmth of my country that the young soldiers never knew, and they, the people, have shown me a kindness that I or my country have not deserved.

The service over, our family walked back along the dusty Buna road. We were less mindful of the traffic now and we did not think of our Good Friday clothes. We were still quiet because of the restrictions of silence. I walked behind the others and thought of the day, the foreigners who had lived among us, and my own life, and I felt ashamed.

Dina arrived on Easter Saturday and we prepared for our first and last family photograph. We had trouble fitting everyone into the frame! We decided to arrange ourselves like a school class, twenty-eight of us in all. Our parents sat in the middle like teachers and we managed to stay still for a few seconds while the photograph was taken. Saturday was a boisterous day with everyone clamouring to be heard. We were pleased that the restrictions of Good Friday only came once a year.

* * *

Life was not the only thing that had progressed at Sangara. During the eight years, we had managed to build a house to the same plan that we had used in Port Moresby. Dina and I had travelled over here many times at week-ends and holidays and gradually the house had taken shape. On the outside it was basically the same building as my Moresby home but inside, it lacked plumbing, electric light and other

civilized refinements. Still, water was plentiful and there
was no trouble getting a bath. Also, we had progressed to the
stage where we had a hygienic, deep pit toilet about thirty
metres from the house. Our Sangara home had one big
advantage over its Port Moresby counterpart. Having learned
our lesson, we built this one on stout, 2.5 metre concrete
piers and these, together with a smooth concrete floor, gave
us a second house underneath. With twenty-eight of us
sleeping here at different times, with plenty more to come,
the double house had big advantages.

On our farm, beauty was everywhere. The deep cool of the
cocoa beckoned during the hot days. The bright green lawns
around our house were ringed above with graceful palms and
below with a colourful display of tropical flowers and shrubs,
while the centre was chequered with papaya, orange, banana
and other green and yellow fruits.

Easter Sunday was a peaceful day. A Christmas Day
without the tinsel. A retreat within a retreat. A return to
forgotten quiet and beauty. With Dina I was never idle —
even sleep was a refuelling in flight and not even a dream
was wasted. The family had returned from church and mountains of sliced bread, plain or garnished with a light spread
of vegetable paste or honey, gave a picnic atmosphere to our
family gathering.

Life in rural Papua was a labour-intensive industry that
called its own hours and its own leisures. The soil had to
replenish its own vitality, and when one land became temporarily exhausted we simply moved to another. We had
never been introduced to any moving wheel or machine that
would lighten our burden. Even the humble wheelbarrow
was a stranger. What we could not carry, push or drag, we
cut up into pieces.

Our twenty acre farm was mainly planted with cocoa.
Together with large plantations owned by foreigners, we
formed the Sangara Cocoa Project. There was a central cocoa
fermentary, under the management of a foreigner, which
bought our wet beans and prepared them to be sent to the
chocolate factories of the world.

Breakfast finished, Dina and I strolled together under the
cool canopy of cocoa, down the hill to the small stream, along

the dead log over the stream, up the steep incline on the other side, through the young cocoa to the jungle at the edge of beyond. It was small but it was ours and some day, please God, we two might lie here together when, parted from our skin, our bones would cause no wonder.

The cocoa was cool and restful. Beneath our feet were the soft humid droppings that carpeted the forest floor, and above, the cocoa trees brushed their leaves together like spring lovers. The cocoa pods — green, red, orange and brown — hung the forest like Aladdin lamps before they ended up as wet, slimy beans inside my father's bucket.

Everyone liked working the cocoa. It was cool, like a soft mountain breeze, and the pods hung close to the earth to invite easy picking. Cocoa was not only generous but also valuable. My parents also worked a native garden where they grew sweet potatoes, yams, taro, bananas, tapioca, pumpkin and sugar cane. There were many varieties of bananas, most of them for cooking, and they formed one of our important foods. For greens, leaves were used such as pumpkin tops, sweet potato tips, watercress and a loose-leafed cabbage. Papaya, watermelons, tropical oranges, sipora (lemons), guava and pineapples grew wild around the house and in the surrounding plantation.

The house was about one hundred metres back from the Kokoda — Buna road and between the house and the road was a small plantation of coconut palms. These palms gave us a plentiful supply of coconuts for food as well as leaves for making mats, baskets, skirts, brooms and walls, and timber for buildings, dams, bridges, paths and platforms. There was plenty of other timber on the farm from forest giants that yielded heavy timber used in building houses, making drums, carvings and building canoes, down to small saplings used for animal yards, small spears for dehusking coconuts, axe handles and a hundred other things. Nothing was wasted. As the trees died or branches fell, it was not long before young hands gathered them up to be used for firewood. We even grew kapok for our pillows, perfume and colours for our bodies, and betel nut and peppermint for our pleasure.

While I was working at the Institute of Health Education,

I had tried my skill at rural reconstruction and had established a small poultry farm that found use for our food scraps and gave us a constant supply of fresh eggs. Another rural reconstruction project was to recycle human waste, supplying us with fish, greens and other delicacies.

Two cattle dogs from my home in Port Moresby completed the family and I was in the process of establishing pigs. I had learned about these earthy creatures in the barrios of the Philippines where nothing was wasted. I knew about worms and other parasites, had been rehearsed in immunisations and pig obstetrics, and was almost hardened to the indelicacy of artificial insemination, Filipino style.

We were trying to come to terms with the new world and my parents, brothers and sisters lived accordingly. Everything was provided out of my earnings.

Of all the places on our Sangara farm I loved our small stream the best. It was a mountain stream that strayed from its parent course to wander through our farm about fifty metres from the house, to bring to us mountain fresh water all year round. It was at small stream like this where, as a child on Misima island, I regularly took the family dishes for their ritual scrubbings. On Misima, dishes were required to be kept cleaner than humans and, as old habits die hard, I felt that my young brothers and sisters were privileged to be able to wash the dishes now, with the same care that I gave them when the family was young and undetermined. A few times I had considered putting sinks and showers into the house and choking it with elaborate plumbing but, each time, I turned back from the brink and found some reason for denying the family the luxury of these innovations. The simple life was better.

It took Dina and me about half an hour to stroll through the cocoa to the edge of our property and, on our return, we came to my mother and the children washing clothes in the stream at a place where it had been dammed by large rocks and was deep enough for many purposes. There was a big log in an exposed position at the top of the rise above the stream, where my mother and sisters sunned themselves after bathing and clothes were spread to partly dry before gathering them for further attention. Sitting on this log, I turned to Dina.

'I don't know what lies ahead of us. Before, we were private and secure, now we seem to be public property. I hope things go all right.'

'Yes,' said Dina. 'It's strange to stand on the edge of a new life and wonder what lies ahead. Have you got any plans for the immediate future?'

'Really, this is the first chance that I have had to think,' I said, throwing a small stone to the water below. 'I wanted to rid my mind of some of the doubts I collected during the elections before I tried to think at all. What do you think? You know all the answers.'

'I don't know anything about this one,' said Dina, throwing a stone to follow mine to the same spot in the water. This was a game that we sometimes played when our vehicle broke down on some adventurous journey and we found ourselves suspended in time in lonely isolation.

'I knew something about having you elected to Parliament but very little about what comes now.'

'Me too,' I said, 'I'm really a fake. I had nothing in my mind other than to be elected.'

'You'll probably need some sort of an office to work in,' said Dina, thinking of the logistics of being a politician. 'You'll probably need a new car, too. Running around in all sorts of strange and dangerous places won't be any good if you don't have a reliable car.'

'I'll have to work out where I stand politically,' I said. 'Both of the main parties have offered me a ministry if I'll join them.'

'That's the numbers game,' said Dina. 'Parties don't seem to mean much. It seems to be one group of individuals against another. Money is the real strength. Whoever controls the money controls the country.'

'I think I'll stay out of it,' I said, 'I don't see how I'm going to talk for the people and play power politics at the same time.'

'Well, you'll have to decide before we return to Moresby,' said Dina, as he stopped the stone-throwing and scratched the ground in front of him with a stick. 'If you are going to be a big shot in politics, you'll have to join the club. Professionalism and grease will do the rest and you can turn on plenty of both when you want to. If you stay on your own you might end up a heroine or a martyr. Abaijah is Hebrew for "God is Father".'

'And Josephine is the feminine of Joseph and that's how I know that God meant me to be part of you,' I said, looking at Dina whose second name was Joseph.

'As long as God includes me it's okay,' said Dina, touching my arm. 'With God and magic you seem to be able to explain the whole universe.'

'Don't forget my second name, Maria, means bitterness,' I said seriously. 'My name is a trinity of God, love and bitterness. I know what the God and the love parts mean but the bitterness has not been revealed to me.'

'The bitterness could have been when you lost your coloured dreams,' said Dina quietly, as he knew that I took these omens seriously. 'It was a pretty bitter experience when you ended up alone in the slums with your baby. If you had not fought your way out of that, the bitterness would be still with you.

'I hope so,' I said with concern. 'Everybody has a share of sorrow and bitterness. God will show us how to bear it if we trust in Him.'

'What about love,' said Dina teasing me. 'Does God look after that too?'

'God looks after everything but magic comes into it. A New Guinean girl in Lae taught me some love magic and all the time I used it, I was thinking about you. If it wasn't for that I might have lost you before this, like white men who play around with native girls and then run away and leave them.'

And what about my God and my magic?' said Dina. 'Don't they come into it?'

'They don't as far as I'm concerned,' I said with finality, as I rose from the log and ran down the hill to the stream where my mother was washing.

'Is love magic true, *Alou* (mother)?' I said to my mother in my native tongue and loud enough for Dina to hear.

'If it wasn't true how would I get thirteen children?' said

my mother in a matter of fact voice as she continued kneading the clothes on the rocks. We did not always have soap for washing.

'I'm sure her name isn't Maria,' said Dina. 'She has no bitterness. She wasn't satisfied with her own thirteen children! She had to adopt a few as well.'

'No, she is not bitter. The missions called her Sybil,' I laughed. 'That means sorceress, so she should know what she's talking about when it comes to magic.'

'How do you know all these things about names?' Dina asked, joining me at the stream.

'I know, that's all,' I said. 'How do you know about medicine?'

'And what do my names means?' said Dina. 'I think you really believe all this rubbish.'

'I won't tell you,' I said, starting for home. 'But they suit me.'

'And when are you going to think about your new role?' asked Dina, as we walked under the cool canopy of the mature cocoa on our way back to the house.

'I've decided already.'

'And what's that?'

'I'm not going to join anyone or anything. I'm just going to speak for the people and learn about politics. The people want me to speak for Papua, land, and our way of life. If I join the government and live the sweet life of power and privileges I can only say what the government wants me to say and that mightn't be what the people want. You have proved your point. I could make it but I don't want to. I don't want to lose the things I love.'

'You're right, Jo,' Dina said, as we joined my father, who was shredding a coconut for cooking. 'It would be a mistake to embrace the sweet life and turn your back on the people, now or ever.'

2

Sebastian

*D*ina and I were sitting on the lawn a few metres in front of the house. The other adults were sitting on the floor underneath the house, indulging in the favourite Papuan pastimes of eating and talking. Banana leaves were spread like glazed tablecloths. Pineapple, bananas, and papaya were set out on the leaves as refreshments. When the fruit was finished the remains were rolled up in the banana leaves and the whole lot thrown into the rubbish pit a few metres away. The first disposable tablecloths! The young children were already asleep on their mats on the floor of the living room a metre overhead. Bugs had been eliminated from the floor boards by sweeping the floor with boracic acid powder and insecticide, so everyone could expect to sleep soundly.

Some of the adults were chewing betel nut. When chewed with peppermint and lime, it makes the tongue loose and the body warm. It also causes cancer of the mouth. It makes the colonials very angry when the rich, red, juicy bolus is spat upon their walls or floors. The ubiquitous graffiti of Papua, it enhances nature, defiles the rich and comforts the poor. As it costs nothing to produce and can be bought, sold or stolen, it is probably the only substantial Papuan industry that does not earn money for foreign business.

My father was holding court with the betel nut chewers. He was a small, wiry man with slightly bowed legs and bent frame. He had little hair left and his eyes were not that good but otherwise he was remarkably tough considering the hard life that he had lived in the hot Papuan sun. He spoke four Papuan languages and enough English to keep him out of trouble with the masters. He had a single eyeglass which was one of his few personal possessions that he would not barter for a smoke or a drink of beer. As he infrequently used his eyes for reading now, this relic of days of importance was seldom called into service. After working for the masters for thirty years, his total personal possessions were worth less than ten dollars. But he was rich in children and he could now look back with pride on the establishment of one of the largest surviving families in the district. Probably most of the credit should have gone to my mother as many Papuans died in childbirth. And further credit to her for insisting that we all lived together while he served the masters.

In the days of Sir Hubert Murray, my father would have been paid five shillings a year for every four children and a payout of ten or fifteen shillings a year was not unheard of. The five shillings was not to feed the children but to encourage the parents to try harder. He had seen service in war and in gaol so he was a respected member of colonial village society.

He was now holding forth on the qualities that he had instilled in me, his first born, that led to my success in the national elections. My own memory of him was as a stern and exacting parent who demanded service from his children and who considered it was natural and proper to sell his daughters in marriage to the highest bidders. As the oldest child, I withstood most of the wrath and punishment until Australia's decolonisation exercises slowly broke down the traditions of his family life and left him alone and unhonoured. He lived too close to the white man to survive unharmed. Serving the master brought rice and meat to feed

his family but he paid a heavy price in dignity and degrad-
ing servitude. My privilege now was to help my parents and
to show them the vista beyond the narrow horizon of colonial
servitude.

* * *

In the group with my father was a village man who, knowing
that we had many visitors over Easter, had come to enquire
if he could get transport for himself and his wife to return to
his village. They lived about sixteen kilometres away and
within short walking distance of the Buna road. I did not
know the man's native name but we called him 'Sebastian',
the name bestowed upon him by the foreign missionaries.

Sebastian wore a red, cotton cloth around his waist secured
like a beach towel. A *rami* was the usual garment of village
natives. They frequently wore short pants underneath which
provided them with pockets and enabled the rami to be used
for other things.

Sebastian was probably about thirty-five years old, though
appearance was deceptive because village Papuans often
aged quickly after they matured and married. There was
nothing unusual about Sebastian's appearance and he would
have passed anywhere as an ordinary village man. The one
unusual thing about him was that he was married to a
young Australian girl who lived with him in his village.

Sebastian's wife was squatting on a mat on the concrete
floor under the house. I did not know her name and it never
occurred to me to ask. Sebastian simply called her *lauegu
adavana* (my wife) and to us she was Sebastian's *hahine*
(Sebastian's woman).

When I first saw her in the village she seemed to be a girl
of sixteen or seventeen years. I had seen her a few times but
she never made any conversation and I never intruded on
her privacy. Sebastian's *hahine* (woman) was just another
native *hahine* and she passed unnoticed among the village
women. The story was that she came to Papua from Australia
on a holiday with her parents and, when they left, she stayed
behind with friends and later married Sebastian who was
working for practically nothing as a 'house boy'. She was a
slightly-built girl about my own size. This probably gave her

the appearance of being younger than she was. She had blonde hair that hung around her shoulders and gave evidence of attention but no particular care. Her eyes were blue, her skin was very fair despite the Papuan sun, she wore a loose cotton dress, clean but unstyled, and her feet were bare.

'It's strange that girl living the way she does as a native in the village,' I said to Dina as we leant back on our chairs enjoying the cool that always followed the heat of the day.

'Yes,' said Dina, 'I was thinking the same. She's the only white girl I know of who has really gone native.'

'There are a few white women married to Papuans but they are not like this one,' I said.

'Some of those women are just trying to prove something,' said Dina turning towards the girl, who seemed to be oblivious of her surroundings and to our presence. 'One white woman married a village native because she wanted to study the natives.'

'And some of them keep their jobs,' I quickly cut in. 'So that they can keep the cash flowing. Two earners are better than one, especially if one of them is on white wages.'

'Wages seem to be a sore point with you' Dina said.

'Not really,' I replied sharply. 'I've never felt jealous about what other people have. Why should I. I live in luxury myself. Why should I worry about them?'

'Are you cross with me, too?' said Dina with a smile.

'I'm often cross with you but I have enough sense to get over it quickly.'

Car headlights appeared in the driveway. We quickly vacated our seats, stepped to the side to get out of the lights, and waited to meet the unexpected visitors.

Five foreigners got out of the car. Dr and Mrs Sidney from the Papuan Medical College but now working in the Popondetta area; a visiting District Commissioner and his wife who had vaguely known my family in Misima; and a girl, Sandra Rowntree, in her early twenties who I learned later, was a Peace Corpsworker from Canada.

Miss Rowntree was a highly motivated foreigner of a type not unusual in our country. At times they sought to heal some personal wound by self sacrifice. She would have looked more at home as a glamour girl on a television show than she did sitting in front of my house on the Buna-Kokoda road. She had thick black hair, olive skin and green brown eyes. The fine lines of her delicate face and high cheeks had the appearance of marbled beauty that I had seen in Rome, but the open top of her pale orange blouse, revealing tight rounded breasts, the skin-tight fit of her sombre jeans and the starry sheen of her well-groomed hair gave evidence that she was no stranger to her mirror. I thought that it was strange for this black-haired beauty to isolate herself from her natural world to be contained with those who could not pay her homage. Nevertheless, I welcomed her as a pleasant change from the colonial stuffed shirts whom I frequently encountered.

Two of them were sitting in front of me now in the persons of Mr and Mrs District Commissioner. They called me Josephine and I called them Mr and Mrs. 'Mr and Mrs D C' were almost terms of endearment among the colonials. 'Mr D C' signified a man who upheld the traditions of empire and who held the powers of life and death in his small outstation world. And 'Mrs D 'C was not a woman to be trifled with, as she could be a source of danger to anyone who circled in her orbit. In his district, a Mr D C was the overlord of all material things emanating from the colonial authority, while a Mrs D C took charge of all VIPs who visited the station. She could dispense social justice with Belsen-like efficiency. As we were the last living museum and the first open zoo, VIPs and politicians were thick and heavy — particularly during southern winters.

Mr D C was seated next to his wife, in the best chairs as became their status. Mr D C looked relaxed in accustomed well-starched shorts and shirt with coloured tie, highly polished brown shoes and matching long socks. He had dispensed with the subdued green tie that he usually wore, so as to denote the informality of the occasion.

Mr and Mrs D C had given the best years of their lives to serving Australia's interests in primitive Papua and New Guinea. As rewards, they had lived fully, loved conservatively between tours and official duties, entertained import-

ant people and looked forward to a generous golden handshake when they left the country.

I knew Dr Sidney well from the Papuan Medical College.
He had finally married a Chinese girl. The Chinese in New
Guinea had invaded Papua when Australia had joined Papua
with New Guinea in an administrative union following the
Second World War. The Chinese now owned most of the
trade stores and small businesses in the country. Probably,
the Chinese were the ones who best profited from the union.
They were industrious beyond reason, counted their money
meticulously and sought fulfilment within shouting distance
of the family store. The easy-going, beer-drinking white
traders were no match for the resilient, thrifty Chinese and
they quickly and quietly disappeared from the scene.

Dr Sidney's wife was beautiful. She wore a black cheong-
sam embroidered with a red dragon and relieved by the ever-
present jade pendant. Miss Rowntree had the exotic beauty
of hidden desire and the promise of early spring, but Mrs
Sidney had the softness of moonlight, the clearness of water,
and the fragrance of jasmine fitted her translucent skin like
the cool of the evening.

My mother and sisters interrupted the small talk by serving sugared *sipora* (lemon) drink, quickly prepared soon
after the arrival of the 'superior' people and now served in
six clean glasses that we reserved for special occasions.

Stimulated by the arrival of our unexpected visitors, I sat
back with my thoughts while the others enjoyed the *sipora*. I
was thinking about Mrs Sebastian, the white girl who was
sitting a few yards away. Should I ask her to join us or would
that be stupid? Mrs Sebastian and Miss Rowntree were two
white women both trying to go native and both now sitting a
few yards apart, unaware of each other's existence. They
could have been from different species. The tiger and the
squirrel. I decided to leave Mrs Sebastian where she was for
the time being. If the party became dull, I might introduce
her later. It might do her good and the others good, also.

Mr D C remembered my family in Misima. He did not
remember me because I was only a small girl when he was
there. He had been firmly convinced that I had no hope of

being elected to Parliament but he was not going to say any more about that. He clearly remembered my father, so he said. All government officers seemed to clearly remember my father. By his misdeeds or miscalculations, my father had an unhappy knack of impressing himself clearly on the mind of every government officer who stayed on Misima for any length of time.

As a child growing up on Misima island, I was unaware of any conflicts between my poor family and our colonial over-lords. I would like to be able to regard ourselves as some sort of a pioneer revolutionary family but revolutions are not born on islands of love and beauty. They are brought there by other people.

'It's really beautiful out here,' Miss Rowntree said, as she looked at the wide expanse of the starry sky. 'There must be more stars here than any place on earth.'

'There are not so many buildings to shut them out,' Dina said, 'I like to come here when I want a break. Things are clearer away from town. I guess we all need some retreat to hide in. A private womb of our own.'

Mrs D C shifted uneasily on her seat and said defensively, 'I don't believe all this nonsense about wombs and things. A pre-school woman at Rabaul said we should build a pre-school like the shape of a mother's arms. I never heard such rubbish. All a child needs are three good meals a day and proper care. It makes no difference if the building is round, square or the shape of a mother's arms.' Then changing the subject said curtly. 'Is it true that you spent twenty thousand dollars on your election campaign, Josephine? My goodness.'

Mrs D C was a very fluent woman. It was unlikely that the present company would bring out the best in her. Some gin in the *sipora* would have worked wonders,

'You can't believe these rumours, dear,' said Mr D C politely. 'Some of those men like to talk big. In any case, it is Josephine's own business how much money she spent,' and, turning to me, continued, 'I don't suppose you stole the money did you?'

'I wish I could steal that much money,' I said quickly. 'I would not have to worry about work. Some of these Europeans get on my nerves. They spend all the money they like on themselves, but a kanaka like me can't spend any money on anything without them dragging in all the dirt they can.'

'What is a kanaka?' asked Sandra Rowntree. 'I heard it a few times but I don't know what it means.'

'It means a tramp, a hillbilly or something like that,' Dr Sidney quickly cut in. 'It was sometimes used by foreigners when they were talking about Papuans or New Guineans. It came from the New Guinea side. Pidgin. I don't like names like that. The natives use the term, too, but it would be better if we stopped using it.'

'It is commonly used,' I said. I was no longer the withdrawn, courteous little girl that Dr Sidney had known a few years ago. 'It would be better if they stopped but they don't. Once they shouted these names all over the place but now they say it to themselves. We should retaliate and start calling them names instead of *taubada* (big man) and *sinabada* (big mother) as we do at present.'

Mrs D C moved uneasily on her chair. She had never heard a native talk like that. Indeed, she had never heard a native talk at all unless it was in answer to a question from herself. Mr D C sat up straight in his chair. This would have been his cue to leave but, unfortunately, for once in his life he did not have his own car so he could not stage the one man walk-out protest that was almost traditional with offended colonial officials.

'It's getting a bit late, don't you think, Matilda? We should be making tracks,' said Mr D C to add substance to his concern.

'Yes, it's time for us to go, Douglas, I'm sure Dr Sidney won't mind,' Mrs D C said in a voice loud enough for Dr Sidney to hear.

Dina came to the rescue and tried to ease the tension. This was what I was usually called upon to do. Nobody took any notice of Mr and Mrs D C's request and the conversation continued. Dr Sidney did not like tension but there was no chance of him being intimidated.

'All people have unpleasant names to throw at others when they are angry or want to boost their own ego,' Dina said. 'When I was in Hong Kong, I often heard the Chinese call us *hung mo kwai* — red-haired devils.

Like a ripple on a lotus pond, Mrs Sidney smiled and said gently, 'And white apes, too — *pak ma lau*. That's a common expression.'

'Well that's fine,' cut in Dr Sidney, slightly offended that his wife carried such secrets locked within her mind. 'Here am I trying to persuade people not to call Chinese names and here you are calling us pak ma something — white apes.' He then turned to Miss Rowntree and continued, 'So now you know what a kanaka is.'

'I'll keep my big mouth shut next time I don't know what something means,' said the black-haired beauty. 'I have never really had a chance to talk to a native, a Papuan or whatever you call them. It would be great to break the barriers and share our thoughts. There are too many barriers between people. Every second word seems to offend someone around here. It's really terrible.'

This was dangerous ground for Mr and Mrs D C and so they retained the diplomatic silence that they reserved for such occasions. Unable to register their usual protest of walking off and leaving us, they had to sit and take it. Such things should not be discussed in front of a native.

'I don't get offended by words easily,' said Dina looking at me. 'I seldom concede anyone enough status for that. I think that words are like other hostile acts. Sometimes you have to defend yourself, but I don't think that this is the same as being hurt and brooding.'

'That's great,' said Miss Rowntree. 'I was just beginning to play with the idea of taking an advanced course in sign language. I'm learning fast and I'm glad I met you, Jo. You have given me fresh hope. Please call me Sandra.'

'I suppose you'll start to work hard for the women now, Josephine?' said Mrs D C, giving me a friendly nod.

'Not particularly,' I said as kindly as I could. 'It was the men who voted me into Parliament. I'll have to work for them too.'

'But the poor women have been so badly treated in the past. Somebody must speak up. It will be terrible if you don't speak for them first.'

'It might be terrible if I do,' I said mildly. 'I'll never be elected again if I don't speak for the men also. These people live in family groups. I want to speak for the whole family.'

Mrs DC was beginning to enjoy her first verbal confrontation with a Papuan woman. She had spent thirty years in the country and nobody had stood up to her before. She had won most of her arguments with her husband and he was a DC. She would soon put this Papuan 'bighead' in her place. It was woman to woman, white to black. This was her job. This was one argument that Douglas could keep out of. She would put me straight in no time.

'I'll be ashamed of you if you don't speak up for our women. This is what we all expect you to do. It is your duty.'

Dina shifted nervously in his chair. For him the day had already dawned and he did not want to be present at any painful awakening. He would have preferred to have seen Mrs DC pass quietly into oblivion. But I needed time to think. I had spent my life backing away from these colonials. I had no intention of backing away from this one.

Mrs DC was talking again. 'If I was a woman in Parliament I would not be afraid to talk up for the poor women. You'll let them down if you let the men push you around and treat you like rubbish the same as they treat their own women. I wouldn't let them get away with it. I'd tell them what I think.'

All the men were becoming uneasy now. Mr DC looked at his watch from force of habit. He did not want Mrs DC to flatten me with a verbal broadside. These new politicians could be dangerous. Dina was mortally scared for Mrs DC. He had occupied my body and my thoughts for so long that he could count the beat of my heart by the pulse of his own. Dr Sidney was uneasy because good relationships were threatened and, after infidelity, this was the blackest sin. The only people at ease were the impeccable Mrs Sidney, who showed neither joy nor sorrow as she serenely watched the scorpion and the spider choose their own death, and Sandra Rowntree, whose eyes shone like a wild beauty watching stallions match their power and pride.

Thoughts flashed through my mind that I would not dare express. I was not going to back away from this bitch without a fight. These colonials had hurt me for the last time. Their status was gone forever. I had apologised and backed down for years until I had lost myself in Dina and my work. It didn't mean much to me, but it would hurt her if a native stood up to her and made public the superficiality of her concern.

It offended me to know that my father was cringing, on the other side of the house, like a scolded dog just because these morons were lording it in front of his family. With a fury born of pride and aggression, I returned to the task of dealing with Mrs D C. This was something between Mrs D C, my father and me, and nobody else was concerned.

Oblivious of my intent, Mrs D C continued along the familiar path of her own fury. 'What we need in this country are women who are not afraid to speak their minds. Until we get them, the native women will be underdogs and they'll be treated worse than village pigs.'

I started to speak slowly with controlled words and mind. I thought I sounded like Dina but I wanted to sound like myself. 'Why do you keep talking about being afraid? I'm not frightened of anything that hasn't got a gun or poison fangs and, especially, I'm not afraid of you.' Dina always said attack the argument not the person, but then, Dina was not a woman. That was one thing I was sure of. 'You are afraid of making a fool of yourself so you take it out on me. You talk about me being ashamed. I'm not some little girl for you to lecture to. All you are ashamed of is the mess you colonials made of our country. I have been a Member of Parliament for about three days and you tell me what I should do. You colonials stole my country a hundred years ago. What did you do for the women? Nothing. They are worse off now than before you came. Once they only had to look after their gardens and their men. You introduced their poverty and gave them no means to fight it. To you it is better for men to get drunk and bash their women than it is for them to oppose your stupid colonial rule. You and your stupid colonials did nothing for us. You lorded it over us for a hundred years and now you are going to leave us with the mess you created.'

'I've never been spoken to in such a manner in my whole life,' shouted Mrs D C hysterically. 'At my age, I've never been insulted like this before. I'm the mother of grown children and old enough to be your mother too.' Mrs D C began to weep and her husband looked on in obvious discomfort.

'Thank God you're not my mother', I thought, thinking of my own patient mother who was sitting a few yards behind me and who had never raised her voice in her life and who, for the first time in her life, had her own thirteen children gathered around her.

'Then don't tell me to be ashamed and don't tell me I'm afraid until the facts prove it. You only cry when you get a bit of your own medicine. You didn't cry for our women in the past when you had the chance to do something for them.'

Mrs D C wiped her eyes with a neat white handkerchief and said haughtily, 'What could we do for you people? You would never let us. You work against one another. You can't work together. I started a woman's club at Lanirama once and was prepared to show the women how to sew and how to live decently but they all ended up fighting. I wouldn't waste any more of my time on them after that. We Europeans stick together, we help those in need, we support one another. We're not all rich you know. You natives are always against one another. We showed you how to live decent Christian lives; what more could we do? I'm not talking about you, Josephine, you went to school in Australia so you know better, but it's the others I mean. Sometimes I have been very disheartened.'

I thought that Mrs D C was going to cry again. One thing that I did learn in Australia was that women sometimes cry when they want to get out of trouble. It was much more difficult for a Papuan woman to get out of trouble by this simple method. Mr D C was mopping his balding head with a folded white handkerchief and had engaged Dr Sidney in conversation about the time. He was alternatively mopping his head and tapping his watch with his finger.

I had no intention of trading insults with Mrs D C. I had made my point that I was not going to be talked down and it was now time to end the discussion. Dina would approve of this strategy but I still had a couple of tricks that I thought would maintain my individuality as a woman. Dina would laugh about it in the morning after he recovered.

I suddenly excused myself from the gathering and made straight for Mrs Sebastian, the young Australian, who was still patiently squatting on the ground chewing betel nut and

looking in the direction of her husband, who seemed to be in
no hurry. I had never spoken to Mrs Sebastian but we had
exchanged friendly glances. She minded her own business
and I minded mine and unless our paths crossed to some
purpose that was how it would be. I approached Mrs Sebastian
with a smile and, sitting down beside her, said,

'These people are going to Popondetta now and I know the
doctor with the car. He'll give you and your husband a lift to
your village if you want to go. It will save messing around
tomorrow. I'll call your husband over. Do you like the idea?'

'That's good,' said Mrs Sebastian, holding my arm in a
friendly grip. 'I'm going mad sitting here. It doesn't matter
how we get home as long as we get there.'

'I'll have to introduce you first,' I said, touching her arm.
'What's your first name?'

'My name is Edna,' said Mrs Sebastian, rising to her feet.
'You can introduce us, it doesn't worry me. It's a free world,
isn't it? We haven't got any *gau* (things), we are ready.'

I nodded to Mr Sebastian, who was holding forth on his
latest exploits, and when he joined us he quickly summed up
the situation.

'*Namo, ita lau*, (good, let's go),' he said.

Mr Sebastian did not speak much English so he would
have to leave the talking to his wife. This suited my purpose.
He was rather proud of his young white wife and was not
reluctant to display her on suitable occasions. The three of us
walked into the circle together and I made my way straight
to Dr Sidney.

Dina was the first to become aware of the intention of my
actions and he sank back in his chair with his fist firmly
holding his chin, as though bracing himself for a heavy
explosion. Mr and Mrs D C were making movements towards
an early departure.

'Dr Sidney,' I said, 'This is Mr Sebastian and his wife,
Edna. Mrs Sebastian comes from Sydney but the Sebastians
are now living in Wanadu village. I know what a kind man
you are. I thought you might be cross with me if I denied you
the chance to give them a lift to their village. Mrs Sebastian
can sit on Mr Sebastian's knee so there should be room. Mrs
Sebastian is no bigger than a Papuan girl, they won't take
up much room. They don't have any luggage. As you know,

Papuans travel light and Mrs Sebastian is a Papuan *momokani* (true) now.'

I beckoned the couple towards Mr and Mrs D C. Mrs Sebastian, wiping red betel nut juice from the side of her mouth, came forward. Beneath her clean rags she was an attractive girl who carried the look of innocent childhood with unaffected ease. She must have been in her late teens but her unadorned simplicity gave her the appearance of a neglected schoolgirl. Barefooted and with unrestrained breasts, fair hair and white even teeth, smeared with red betel-nut stain, she could have been a jungle Cinderella.

'Mr Sebastian and his wife Edna,' I said with pleasant formality. 'Meet Douglas and Matilda Drinkwater. Mr Drinkwater is a visiting D C, waiting to go on holidays.' Then, turning towards the Sebastians, I said, 'Mr Sebastian is a village farmer near Buna and Mrs Sebastian is a Sydney girl but she now lives with her husband in the village.'

Mr Sebastian gave a wide grin, displaying a good set of jet black teeth acquired by years of chewing betel nut. He had his red rami pulled around his waist and plaited armbands on one arm, out of which stuck a half smoked cigarette and a piece of peppermint plant for chewing with betel nut. He thrust his small, toil-toughened hand out in willing comradeship and gave a vigorous pump of Mr and Mrs D C's right hands in turn as they were reluctantly offered in his direction. This was the first time that he had shaken hands with a real D C and he was making the most of the occasion.

Mrs Sebastian then came forward and, looking the picture of schoolgirl innocence, timidly shook the hand of Mr D C, which had suddenly grown limp and motionless. She then curtsied in front of Mrs D C whose queen-like stance and stern lines did not invite any closer intimacy.

'Do your parents live in Australia, my dear?' asked Mrs D C in a stern and commanding voice, but visibly affected by this unexpected confrontation with a fellow Australian. 'Where do they come from?'

'We come from Sydney,' said Mrs Sebastian quietly but without hesitation.

'And how long have you been living like this?' Mrs D C said with matronly dignity.

Mrs Sebastian was not unaccustomed to such interrogations

so she continued with ease, 'Living like what? I have spent
the last year with my husband in the village.'

Mr D C had become agitated. He did not want any trouble
in front of the new politician. He had spent a long time in his
department and he was not going to let his wife's lack of
discretion lead him into unwanted publicity.

'Do your parents know you are living like a er... er
...native in a village?' Mrs D C asked and then turning to
her husband, continued. 'This should be investigated,
Douglas. This young girl should not be exposed in this
manner without protection.'

'It is nothing to do with me, Matilda, and I will be investi-
gating nothing,' said Mr D C firmly. 'I am just a visitor here
and no doubt there is nothing to investigate. There is no law
against a girl living with her husband in his village. If there
are no complaints there is nothing to investigate.'

Mrs D C caught the note of stern warning in the official
tone of her husband's voice and withdrew to contend with
her own emotions. Mrs Sebastian seemed pleased to be getting a lift at the price of a little unpleasantness. Dina sat
immobile in his chair while Mrs Sidney and Sandra Rowntree
showed evidence of an enjoyable evening.

Dr Sidney, sensing the mood, sprang into action and was
soon ushering Mr and Mrs D C into the front seat of his car.
For their part, they quickly complied, dispensing with the
formality of bidding us goodbye.

Dr Sidney stood by the back door as the four squeezed into
the back of the car. Mrs Sebastian sat on the edge of her
husband's knee as it was not good conduct for Papuans to be
intimate in public.

Sandra Rowntree waved at me wildly from the door, 'See
you later, Jo, I hope,' she shouted.

Dr and Mrs Sidney were more formal in their farewell.
Mrs D C was crying again and her handkerchief was working
overtime. With an engine's roar and garbled calls, four
Australians, a Chinese, a Canadian and a Papuan, joined in
the common purpose of coming to terms with life and the
social discords of changing values, turned into the night and
disappeared along the Kokoda road in the direction of Buna
and oblivion.

'How do you think that they'll get on?' I said to Dina with a satisfied smile.

'A good average mix for a Papuan affair,' he said, laughing for the first time.

Together we walked towards the house and my father said anxiously, *'Purapura anatapuna i ai bo ega?* (Is everything all right?)'

'Anatapuna i ai, marina (everything is all right, now),' I replied.

My father looked up quickly and searched my face for a sign as the 'now' added feeling to my reply. But we had already settled down to enjoy the remaining hours of the evening with the family.

* * *

On Easter Monday we returned to Port Moresby to face the challenge of the new life. Many people wanted to see me. Poor urban villagers who had lost their water supply because they were unable to pay for the tap outside their house. Many people were distressed: evictions, violence, hunger, separations and all manner of things. There were many who could not communicate on elementary things with government departments.

Parliament had not met and there was intense activity to get numbers to form a government. Following my vow to keep out of all this, the contestants found me dull and unresponsive and looked elsewhere to cast their nets and choose their ministers.

Then on the 13th April, 1972, Port Moresby became a city. This was the most important civic event during the first couple of weeks since my election. As I was the elected Member of Parliament for Port Moresby and the central district, I received an invitation to attend the ceremony but, being unfavoured by colonial oficials, my new office received no special recognition and I sat at the back. The administrator put on his best for the occasion and, with suitable remarks, elevated the president of the local government council to the status of Lord Mayor and the town of Port Moresby to the status of City.

The ceremony was held at the reception room of the Sir

Hubert Murray stadium. Foreigners monopolised the seats while a handful of curious natives stood at the back, in replay of the annexation of Papua which took place in this same locality. I wondered what all of these foreigners had to do with this occasion and my thoughts went to my dear, dead Uncle Robert, buried by a gaggle of foreigners with a bright new Australian flag wrapped around an expensive coffin, whilst I, his only relative, was pushed to the background.

Declaring Port Moresby a city was another colourless foreign exercise as the colonials ticked off one more item on the shopping list for decolonisation. Less fuss than opening a shopping centre! In 1884, a British naval officer declared that Britain owned our country and our people. Now, in 1972, an Australian colonial official declared that Port Moresby was a City. I wondered when we would start writing our own history.

* * *

Next came the opening of the Third House of Assembly, the name the colonials gave to the national Parliament. The House of Assembly functioned under the authority of the Papua and New Guinea Act of the Australian Parliament and the final decision on the appointment of its ministers still rested with the minister of the Australian Government.

With as much ceremony as could be mustered and in the presence of Prince Charles, the Third House of Assembly was opened and the one hundred and one Members were duly sworn in, among them the one lady member.

At lunch time I walked down the town to meet Dina and we went to a small restaurant where we sometimes had lunch.

'How did it go?' asked Dina.

'Okay,' I said. I shook hands with all of the 'Europeans' and had my photo taken.'

An Australian woman, who was waiting on the tables, came to take our order. I chose a grilled steak, a luxury that I found hard to resist when we were near here at this time of day. A few natives patronised the restaurant but the customers were largely foreigners, and foreigners entertaining native guests with a novelty meal in the town. Very few

Papuans could afford the luxury of spending dollars on a single meal, especially in the middle of the day when they often did not eat anything.

The woman left to attend to our order and soon afterwards a commotion broke out in a dim corner of the restaurant. The Australian woman and a neatly dressed Papuan man were engaged in an argument. When the argument did not subside, I thought that it might come within my range of activities as a parliamentarian to investigate the disturbance.

I walked to the table where the dispute was raging and I spoke to the Papuan in Motu so that he could express himself in private.

'*Turagu, dahaka*? (What's wrong, my friend)'

Before the man could reply, the Australian woman said, with indignation, 'This 'boy' ordered a meal and now he says he cannot pay for it. I should call the police.'

Knowing that the man understood the conversation, I said, "*Inai hahine momokani ia hereva i ieva*? (Is this woman speaking the truth?)'

'Yes,' said the man, speaking in Motu. 'But these whites are full of tricks. I never thought that they would charge so much for one meal.'

I looked at his table and it seemed to be liberally scattered with empty dishes. I guessed that he had been guided more by his stomach than by his pocket, so I said,

'I'll pay for it. Forget about it. You'd better get out quickly. If the police come you will be in trouble. The police station is just opposite.'

I paid the bill, was surprised at the splendid nature of the dinner, and returned to eat my humble steak with Dina. 'It might have been a confidence trick,' I said to Dina. 'But it made me feel that I was doing something worthwhile. It was something to do with the people.'

3

Politician of the people

*M*onths went by. A government and a ministry were formed that nicely situated the designs of the colonial government. The largest party retreated into the wilderness of a perfunctory opposition to brood over their isolation while the energetic number seekers, helped by enthusiastic Australians, co-opted a variety of coalition partners to seize the government and with it the power and the money.

After the elections, the colonial government greatly hotted up its campaign to sell its idea of a politicial union between Papua and New Guinea without any reference to the options open to Papua. A committee was formed to further the Australian cause and to introduce the concept to the 'indigenes'. As an initial move, the committee introduced a Pidgin English slogan, '*bung wantaim*' (unite). To quote the words of a prominent Member this committee was a 'movement promoted by the Australian government to facilitate its own getaway'. The country became flooded with '*bung wantaim*' posters and propaganda.

Many other signs of hustling and bustling became evident.

Papua and New Guinea became Papua New Guinea and Papuans and New Guineans became Papua New Guineans. A constitutional planning committee was formed with the sole charter to develop a constitution for a combined Papua and New Guinea. Australia had already made the decision. A national flag appeared that survived and a national song that faltered. A rash of posters appeared throughout the country, which took on the appearance of a one-sided paper war to win the hearts of the people to the Australian decision to force a political union between Papua and New Guinea. No money or resources were forthcoming for any contrary option or opinion.

While all this was going on, my own attitude was hardening. The more contact I had with the tens of thousands of Papuan villagers the more I realised that the people were being sold a pup that they did not want to buy. Australia had assumed that because Papua was an Australian colony and we were paper Australian citizens, they could do what they liked with us and they could make all of our decisions. Cattle to be grazed on our own land for any purpose that Australia decided.

In Parliament, I made a maiden speech and set the scene for future conflicts. I also made other speeches, one supporting free education for the Southern Highlands, a much neglected Papuan region. I introduced a private motion of my own which was a detailed plan for the development of the youth of our country. I collected more than my share of abuse and hostility and became hardened to bearing a reputation of being a rebel voice of the people against the colonial plan for Papua.

Monday, 11th September, 1972, was set aside as the first National Day. This was a new holiday to replace the old Australia Day holiday which had been observed previously. We still observed Anzac Day, the traditional Australian soldiers' remembrance day. Papua and New Guinea was still fully controlled by Australia and a form of self government was more than a year away and independence from Australia was some time in the future.

For the National Day, the usual entertainments were arranged by the government to attract a crowd to Port

Moresby's Sir Hubert Murray Stadium. I was asked to make the key address in English, the Lord Mayor was to make the address in Motu (Papua) and the Australian Administrator was to make the address in Pidgin English (New Guinea). I discussed the speech with Dina. I wanted to give a message of hope to the Papuan people but, as I was to speak in English, I decided to make generalised statements that could apply to any group and not single out the Papuans. We wrote a speech of doubtful substance but managed to steer clear of controversy. Then, in due course, like a lamb to the slaughter, I went to deliver my speech to the nation. After the speech, the colonials were so relieved at my restraint that the speech was hailed as a major triumph—not a triumph for me, but for themselves. It was said to herald a new era.

Parts of the speech were extracted and played again and again until I became embarrassed at the sound of my own voice. After this, I resolved that I would temper my courtesy with more judgement.

* * *

This first National Day was a day of great personal sorrow. I made the address at the Sir Hubert Murray Stadium at 12 noon and, at 4.00 p.m., my youngest brother died at our rural home in Sangara. My brother was nine years old when he died and he was the last of my parents' thirteen natural children. The last time that I saw him he was a happy healthy boy. I don't know what caused his death. My mother said that they took him to the hospital at Popondetta because he complained of pains in the joints. Now he was dead.

After my brother died in the hospital my parents managed to secure a truck and, with his body wrapped in a sheet, brought him back to our home. He was placed under the house where we had held our first and only full family gathering at Easter. Nobody guessed then that our youngest would be the first to die.

My father, with some of his friends, went to a sawmill situated close to our home on the Kokoda-Buna road where they bought a few planks of freshly sawn timber and returned to the house to hammer together a simple coffin. When the coffin was completed my brother was cleaned, dressed in his best clothes and properly prepared for burial. When all was ready, he was lifted into the home-made coffin and the lid was secured with a few nails.

We then prepared for the burial. Months before we had selected a site for our family graves and this was where my brother would rest. He was the first. The site was at the back of the house, in the cool at the edge of the cocoa, under the tall kapok.

A Papuan Anglican bishop travelled to our home to lead the service and our neighbours gathered with the family to bury our boy. The coffin was lowered into the ground and the soft earth was replaced. Within a few months the earth would be restored to its level, the grass would grow green and there would be no sign of where my brother was, other than a small cement marker. The children would laugh and play over his grave, unrestrained by his presence, as the years passed in quick succession, and our parents would count his age as though he was still with us.

My young brother was a gentle boy of rural Papua. He had known no other home than this, and his were the trees, the earth and the stars of Sangara. The rural Papuans are gentle people who but lightly touch their environment. They live for thousands of years on one piece of earth and leave no more trace of themselves than the creatures of the jungle. They do not pollute the air, the earth or the seas and the generations of the past join with the continuous present in one communion. Generations use the same earth and, as each departs, the table is restored for the next banquet. The only harm they do is to themselves, and others are not threatened by their achievements. They are born into the world of nothing but nature and leave it as they found it. The threat to man is not from the over-used hands of simple people but from the idle brains of cultures perverted by the latent virus of material insanity. The poverty of Christ may be his final message. Our own sorrow was not that there were thirteen of us from one womb but that one of us was missing.

* * *

The people of the central district fell roughly into two groups. The first were sturdy mountain people from the rugged interior, who had reputations as good workers and fierce warriors. When they settled in small urban communities around Port Moresby, they brought their reputations with them and frequently lived up to them. These were my soldiers and my spies. They shadowed me everywhere I went in Port Moresby and infiltrated public political meetings, so I was well informed on what was being said and done.

The second group of Papuans in the central district were those who came from later waves of adventurers who settled on the coast and the inland plains. They were handsome, brown people who were good at sports, canoe racing, serenading, going to church and making love: all things that sublimated man's primitive aggressions and diverted him from sustained violence. These Papuans hang on to old breasts with optimistic expectations that new nourishment will flow along old ducts. That is until, reluctantly, they are forced to seek their nourishment elsewhere.

The aggressive drives of fierce mountain warriors and the sublimated impulses of the pleasure-loving coastals was the political blend that I represented, and they were all my people. I was nurtured by the blue waters of the warm Pacific, but in Port Moresby I had been confronted with the ugly aggressions of a competitive society and I was now regressing to primitive savagery. Old values were no longer adequate for the role I had to play and I found that I had as much in common with the mountain warriors as I had with my own blue water people. The tiger and the lamb of my own personality were both required.

* * *

In many parts of the Central District a substantial bride price was paid as part of marriage transactions. In theory this was paid to the family of the girl but, in reality, many people shared in the takings. Previously, a bride was paid for in native wealth and this was an important stabilising force in marriage. A man had to have status to raise the large amount of wealth required and a marriage, so dearly bought, did not break down easily. It was expected that the man would have daughters of his own who would provide an important source of wealth for him at an important stage of his own life. A part of the cycle of community life; but foreign money was now replacing native wealth and thousands of dollars could be involved. Many relatives were called on to contribute and goodwill was gained or lost.

The bride price was important to the girl as it brought her status and respect in her own family as well as stability to her marriage. The higher the bride price, the higher the prestige. It was not a sale of flesh. The greater the endowments the higher the price. All girls had their place in Papuan society and each was beautiful in her turn. There were other determinants.

A bride was a valuable person in traditional village society but the same could not be said of a widow. When a man died, his widow had to adhere to a strict ceremonial mourning. If she had a grown family or had a robust personality she could continue to live with status within her own family. A younger or more timid woman could be treated as a chattel in her late husband's extended family or, alternatively, if she was nimble, she might take advantage of a niche that became available to her in the village community or return to her family home.

Widows sometimes used their period of mourning as a breathing space to look around the village for a new arrangement. A Papuan woman might have many things on her mind besides the death of her husband. The outward grief could shadow a complex inward design for survival. She played her cards with caution but accepted the results with subdued emotions. Some widows developed loose sexual relationships that brought them some sense of purpose or security.

In some parts, where the status of women was low, a husband might hire out his wife for additional duties, like a rent-a-car.

Generally, the village women were a force to be reckoned with. After marriage they grew in proportion to their native affluence with minds to match their robust physiques. They had their own village institutions which usually centred around the church or sports. The government encouraged

other women's groups but none were more successful than
the village stream or pump.

* * *

The women of a village just outside Port Moresby were
opening a new cricket pitch and I was an honoured guest. A
women's cricket match was not only a game of bowl and slog,
but also a graceful exhibition of singing and dancing, inter-
spersed with refreshments and followed by a native feast. As
was usual the occasion was used as an excuse for a women's
festival, but this was only one side of the story. Underneath
was a severe rivalry between the opposing teams from two
different villages, and the men gave the cricket ground a
wide berth and left the women to themselves. One or two
men were given diplomatic immunity to act as umpires but
the others kept well away from the action.

The women of both teams sang and danced around me in
gestures of welcome and I was draped with garlands of
flowers and strings of shells. The cricket ground was a large
grass clearing ringed with coconut palms five or six lines
deep. Immediately through the palms was the silhouette of
the inevitable village church: the only tangible village institution.

The church was always the most imposing building in the
village and often the coolest. It was at the hub of village life,
a cool rest by quiet waters, a south-sea island picnic with
God. The native pastors were very much men of the people
and their white ramis and superior living were outward
marks that they were men of God. They had less need to sin
than the people, otherwise they tasted most of the pleasures
of village life.

The bowling team took their places on the field with much
shouting and laughter, while the batting team squatted on
the grass under a palm leaf shelter that had been erected for
the occasion. Scattered around the shelter were young green
coconuts that had been cut from the palms to provide light
refreshments for the players.

A woman bowler took the ball to the accompaniment of a
song and dance by all of the fielders. Then came a hush as
the generously proportioned woman gained momentum for

the delivery. The batswoman, facing the first ball, made a mighty swipe with the bat which was intended to loft the ball into the coconut palms. Unfortunately, she failed to time the stroke properly and missed the ball, which caused her to lose balance and almost stumble over the wicket. This caused a wild roar from the fielders as they took this as a good omen. Then they again burst into song and dance while the bowler prepared to make the next delivery.

So the game went on until the opening batswoman connected with the ball in a mighty swipe that sent it soaring into the coconut palms for six. Pandemonium then broke out among the women in the palm shelter who, so far, had been very subdued. They decked their hair with wild hibiscus and burst into wild celebrations which culminated with their own song and dance routine. A day of cricket was an exhausting affair, as was the feasting and celebrations that followed.

The cricket match was well on its way when I was approached by a young woman who was a stranger to the village. I was hot with the excitement of the match, but when she told me that she had made a special trip from Moresby to see me, I took her aside to sit on the long log that was all that remained of a giant from the original forest. This stout log was here when the people were born and it bore the marks of generations of axes. Every child had challenged and conquered its obstacles but, still, it remained the most permanent object in the village. The sun and rain produced and the sun and rain destroyed. An old man seldom died in the village of his birth. Every cell was changed. Nothing in a village outlived the life of a man. Only the earth and the log remained.

The woman at my side looked like a young girl but I guessed she might be about twenty. A patch of black cloth pinned to a faded cotton dress told me that she was probably a widow, not wearing the full mourning of a village woman but carrying a respectful gesture to a dead husband. Underneath her soiled rags she was clean and groomed. She did not have the approach of a village girl. Although she looked like a full Papuan, she acted and spoke like a mixed-race girl and had probably grown up on one of the missions.

She had straight hair, but many Papuans of the central district had straight hair and some mixed-race girls had fuzzy or curly hair from their native mothers. Many Papuans had lightly coiled hair which was teased with special combs to stand out far from the head, and some had hair wider than their shoulders. Carefully clipped to burnished black and domed like an oval fountain, it was a mark of beauty.

'I'm sorry to disturb you, Miss Abaijah,' said the slight girl who could have been one of my sisters.'

'Don't worry about that,' I said, vaulting backwards to sit on the top of the log.

'Why did you come to see me?'

'I came because I need help. I am very worried. The people say you are very kind. You're the only one I could think of.'

'What's your name?' I asked, helping her to gain confidence.

Papuans think that they must say complimentary things as an introduction to requesting help. Speech is circumspect and they may come to the point very slowly.

'My name's Lucy, Lucy George. My father's name was George. He was a mixed-race man who married my mother who came from Arima village.'

It was important to establish relationships first. The village, district, and family were all important. Lucy was filling me in on the details, some of which I guessed.

'What do you want, Lucy? How can I help you? You talk English like a mixed-race girl. Do you live in a village?'

'I don't live anywhere. My husband died last month and now I am staying with his people. They are very cruel to me and they say I made magic to kill him because I wanted to go with other men. My husband had tuberculosis and I looked after him in a small hut for two years before he died. I got his food, washed his body and cleaned his dirt while he died in our little hut. His relatives never came to see him or help him while he was alive, but now he is dead they say I have to live with them. They want to treat me like a slave and some of the drunken men want to use my body. They say I'm a useless widow and only fit for work and bed. I'm frightened. I want to run away but I've got nowhere to run to. You see, I was brought up as a mixed-race. I have no proper relatives and I have no village.'

'Where did your husband come from?' I said, looking for more details about her life and the background to her marriage.

'He came from the western district. He was a good man but his relatives live in Port Moresby. His brother is very cruel and I am frightened of him. He might kill me if I don't do what he says. My husband was old and sick when I married him. Now they say I killed him.'

'Why did you marry him if he was old and sick?'

'He wasn't that old. His sickness made him old. He couldn't work but we had three children.'

'Where are the children now?' I asked, trying to get to the bottom of the story. This could go on for half an hour unless some short cuts were taken.

'Two are in Moresby, in the house of my husband's brother, in an old tin shed in a settlement. The other one is dead. Her name was also Lucy. My little girl was the eldest. She died last night. They say I killed her too because I hated my husband. But that's not true. My husband gave her his sickness and she died the same as he did.'

'I am very sad to her about your little girl. So many of our children die. You are very young and you have had much sorrow. Where is your little girl now? Is she buried?'

'No, she is not buried,' Lucy said, wiping her eyes with her soiled dress. 'I wrapped her in my blanket and gave her to an old school-mate of mine to mind in her house. She did not want to take little Lucy but when I said I was coming to get you, she agreed. She is frightened too. She has hidden little Lucy under some timber, but she will not tell her husband or he might be cross. I want you to help me to take my little Lucy back to our house. It is at the side of a *niu* (coconut) plantation close to the beach. I want to bury her there near her father. I can't leave her here with these bad people. They say I killed her but she died of tuberculosis just like her father. She got a big fever, then she died. She had a big fever many times. I didn't know she was going to die this time. I think she died because we didn't get enough food to eat.'

'Where is the house where you buried your husband?' I asked, slipping off the log, for I already knew it was about eighty kilometres from Port Moresby and across one very difficult river that would have to be crossed by a raft.

'It's on the other side of the Aroa river though not as far as Angabanga. Our house is near the beach.'

'Okay,' I said. 'I'll help you some way. You can't do all this on your own. That's for sure. We'll do it together. The village people are lucky. They always have many friends to help them. You seem to be on your own. We'll get little Lucy and take her to my house where we will make a small box for her. Then we'll go and get your other two children. There'll be no trouble if I'm there. Then I'll go and get my friend. He's a doctor. He'll know what to do. He will help us.'

'Thank you very much, Miss Abaijah, you are very kind,' said Lucy, crying with relief. 'I'm most grateful. I didn't want to make so much trouble but I knew you would understand. I have no money to give you. I have no money at all. I hope my husband's brother feeds my two little boys. He is very cruel but his wife is kind. They are very poor. They have very little food. They don't want to feed us. They want me to sell my body to earn some food, but I'll die before I do that. I can die like little Lucy and my husband. I'm not afraid of death.'

'You have no money, I have no money,' I said. 'This is not a matter of money, it's a matter of love. Let's go to Moresby. We must hurry but first I have to do a couple of things here. We won't be able to leave Moresby until early tomorrow morning. Lucy will be all right. It will be nice for her to be buried where she lived. It is very lonely in Moresby.'

* * *

On the way back to Port Moresby I found out more of the details about Lucy's life and marriage. Lucy's father was some sort of a mixed-race man because his father was a native who came from an island in the Torres Strait. Lucy was the only child as her mother died at the birth of her second child.

Lucy's father died when she was eight years old and she went to stay at a mission school. When she was fifteen years old she ran away, and set up house with a native man who worked as a mechanic on a foreign-owned plantation. When her husband became too sick to work, the planter allowed them to live in a small single-roomed house at the edge of the plantation where they could get coconuts, grow native foods and catch fish.

Lucy had lived there for three years, until a month ago, when she buried her husband. Now, she was going back to bury little Lucy, her first daughter. This was her only home. She did not realise that the home, also, was dead. The plantation owner had not given them the house, he had only loaned it to her husband to die in.

Lucy was a curious mixture of holy restrictions and perilous living that invited disaster: a mixture that caused unprepared girls to grow in anguish before they learned to come to terms with life. Lucy urgently needed help with the other two children and a steady, undemanding hand to hold on to until the world stopped spinning.

The burnt earth of Port Moresby began to pass under our wheels. The first thing that we did was to collect little Lucy from a 'boy house' in Boroko, the suburb where most of the masters lived. When we arrived I was relieved to find that the native woman's husband had not yet returned. Relieved to see us, the woman ushered us into a small, open laundry where a large, wooden packing case was resting at one end. The woman and Lucy rolled the packing case away. Under it was a neatly wrapped bundle about the size of a small child. Together we gently raised the bundle and carried it to the truck where we placed it on the back. The woman and Lucy hurried back to replace the packing case in its usual position. Then we drove home.

When we reached home, I decided to leave the body where it was on the truck, while I went to search for Dina. It was Saturday so he would not be far away. Back at the house we decided on a plan of action. First, we made a small coffin out of dressed timber that we kept for this purpose, as a body was likely to turn up for disposal at any hour of the day or night. When the coffin was finished, we wrapped the bundle tightly in plastic sheeting and placed it in the small wooden box. Lucy put some religious pictures, a photograph and a small book inside and we nailed the lid in place. Lucy then said some prayers and sat down on the truck, alongside the box, while Dina and I went inside the house to discuss the next steps.

We had arranged a meeting in a village near the Vanapa river for Sunday morning. We would take Lucy and her dead daughter with us and later take Lucy on to her isolated beach home for the burial. We left Lucy's other two children with my family as a guarantee that she would return and not try any dramatic gesture, such as trying to live in the wilderness on her own, and set off.

When we arrived at the Vanapa village, the villagers were gathered around a huge live crocodile that had just been captured. Jungle twines and pieces of stick kept the dangerous reptile immobile. A stick propped the great mouth wide open. Villagers had caught the crocodile with nets. The skin was valuable and it would be removed with care and then the flesh would be distributed as meat among the villagers.

Occasionally, a crocodile carried a child or an adult away and, later, ate them. Women were sometimes victims as they carried out duties like washing clothes and dishes by the river bank. The crocodile slowly stalks its prey and in a final dash, seizes the victim in its strong jaws and then drowns them. They then carry them away to an island or isolated spot and eat them piece by piece as they become hungry. Crocodiles have been found with a whole woman inside with different parts of her body in different stages of decomposition.

This crocodile was a great monster that had been troubling the villagers for a long time. The hunters had snared it into the net and then manhandled it to overcome its defences so that it could be captured alive. As I felt the strong skin and the smooth belly, a shudder went through my own body. It could easily have swallowed me in one gulp without the need to take me apart.

Natives do not hunt for pleasure but they kill without pity. They can also be cruel if it serves some purpose and, perhaps, the only way to keep meat fresh is to keep it alive as long as possible. It is not all bad for the crocodile. Some of them are protected by law so that the swamps and rivers can maintain their fill and ladies can have their pleasures. In some parts of western Papua, crocodiles are the main native industry.

With the crocodile disposed of, we held our meeting with the villagers at the Vanapa village and then continued on our journey. The major obstacle was the Aroa River — a wide river that we had to cross by using a raft made from the jungle. We were lucky to find a raft that villagers had made the day before, and half-a-dozen village natives were willing to help us get across. All the lashings of the raft were retied and, after testing for buoyancy, we put it to the final test.

The first hazard was to get the truck onto the raft and then, when that hazard was overcome, we were on our way. Water lapped around the wheels and everyone was prepared for the worst, but we slowly edged our way to the other side, to a sloping site where the truck could be driven off. There was a rope secured to a tree on the side so we could haul ourselves to the right spot on the bank. By midday, we were on the other side of the river and on our way again.

The house that Lucy called home was a small one-roomed house with a verandah, at the edge of the coconuts and fronting to a white beach and the blue Pacific. Beautiful and lonely as a butterfly in flight. A brave attempt to deny the existence of humanity in the midst of learning life. An alternative paradise.

We dug a lonely grave in the sandy soil, buried the small child, and marked the spot with a cross. Dina and I walked for half-an-hour under the coconut palms at the edge of the beach, while Lucy walked alone with her past.

The story of our world would have to be rewritten if we were without the graceful ballet of coconut palms. Tambourines of the soft winds, harps of the violent seas, temptresses of the liquid moon, fragrant oils of yielding love. Rich as a lover's touch in the cool clean air of the virgin night. Beautiful palms of the soft sands you have seen me bared for love. I love you for your bounty, I love you for your strength, I love you for your passion, jealous lover, as you turn my head from the hot breath to take my eyes beyond the fantasies of love to the wonders of life.

When Lucy was ready to face the world we bundled the few bits and pieces that she called her possessions, onto the truck and set off to face the hazards of the long trip home. If we were lucky, we might get back across the river the same day, and be home that night. If not, we would sleep by the river. Much depended on the raft abandoned at the river side. It belonged to no-one and would soon disintegrate and be swept out to sea with the other droppings of the lush jungles.

* * *

Monday was business as usual. Lucy and her children were settled into their new poverty. A few dollars bought a lot in a shanty town — warmth, safety, food, and space to breathe. There would be little meat or fish but there would be sweet tea to moisten the dry bread or rice, and there would be native vegetables. The village people often brought me native fruits and vegetables. There was enough to go around and we had our own economy.

Here, Lucy could meet humanity on her own terms. She made little use of her body or her emotions, but twenty years was too short a time to live. A woman must learn to love once before she is born to die. A refuge from life, Lucy had to learn to live again. There was no such thing as romantic love but, some day, there would be a new rag, a smile and a hibiscus in her hair. A few dollars a week and a few sweet potatoes was not an unreasonable price to pay for three bodies complete with mind, senses, warmth and the seed of love in the human image of the sacred Christ.

* * *

The first part of 1973 passed quietly. Dina took my place and commenced the last of a series of Diploma courses for local and overseas students. This was my work and I found it difficult to part company with it. I joined in as much as I could. I also wanted to be near Dina. We were complementary and everything went better together.

I wanted to move away from the injustices and personal casualties of the new society to do something more productive. Moves were made to commence a rural reconstruction movement in the central district. A small loan fund for village people was established to advance short-term money, enabling them to repair outboard motors (needed to power their canoes for transport and for earning cash from fishing), or to complete deposits on trucks so that they could get on with the business of living and earning some cash. The coast of the central district was littered with outboard motors needing repairs, and often these were minor. Because of the past lack of development, no pool of mechanical skills existed in the native villages. We purchased many trucks for the people and were involved in numerous small scale village undertakings. Large ice-boxes were made for the storage of fish and lobsters, dinghies and outboard motors were obtained, village community halls built, and assistance given with the building of village churches.

We worked on the transfer of land, plantations and sawmills to the people. We acquired two large trucks of our own so that we could participate in rural development by the transport of materials for buildings. We arranged for the purchase of materials at the best prices, and transported them to the villages. We bought a concrete mixer, an electric generator and power tools as part of our equipment for the villages. We acted for the people with the government on building airstrips, roads and transferring properties from foreigners to the local people.

There was always some sort of a crisis with floods, deaths, cyclones and village emergencies. We raised money, supplied food and transport, and helped in whatever way we could. Our trucks were available to village groups for sports, social activities and work. Village funds were started for all manner of things such as tractors, trucks, boats and buildings. Money was invested for individuals and groups and we held a lot of money for village people. These funds were handled with care and accounted for in terms that the people understood. The people learned to trust us and we were swamped with demands that we found impossible to handle.

In the towns we bought old rags collected from the garbage of the city and washed and sorted by women of the settlements. We sold these to the government store which was importing rags from Australia, for supply to private firms for cleaning machines. Our trucks were used to transport empty bottles, rags, animals and all sorts of things for the poor people. And we had to find time to deal with the bashings, deaths, poverty, courts and pathos in the daily life of the new ghettos of Port Moresby.

Port Moresby was a conglomerate of new rich and old poor set on a lake of failed experiments and fouled by malnutrition, drunks, violence, poverty, house breakings and community disintegration. The urban villages clung to their communities and cultures but lost their land and their freedom. These were the people who were promised that their lands and their women would be protected. These same people were the first to become landless and their women became the most threatened. The first Papuans to end up on the beach.

Most of the people in Port Moresby now received some education. They were left on the streets for six or seven years, given six years of indifferent primary schooling, and then put onto the streets again. A few completed four years of secondary education and fewer still went on to matriculation and university.

A primary education in Port Moresby, which was the usual, led to the classification of 'drop-out', 'failure', 'rascal', or 'criminal' depending on the sex and drives of the recipients. The numbers of these swelled each year and became social evils when they threatened the comforts of the new rich and the foreigners. Some sought remedies while others withdrew into the isolation of their homes and motor cars and accepted the phenomenon as part of the new order. So a new generation began to grow who knew no other life, and Port Moresby was becoming an unpleasant city. Papua was passing from a sleepy, do-nothing police state to a national crash programme in decolonisation with the hurry of a batch of newly-hatched turtles.

I worked hard to have a sound national plan introduced for our young men and women so that they could occupy a dignified place in the new society, but my motion was defeated in Parliament by a few votes with the government and most of the foreigners voting against it. I introduced a plan to give an adequate transport service to a neglected newly created outer suburb, Gerehu, by using my own vehicles. This was rejected by some board or other. I spent countless hours fronting up to government departments on behalf of the people but, slowly, I turned my attention to projects outside the influence of colonials and politicians, and turned my mind to other things.

Much of the political work that I was doing was alien to my nature. It was too involved with violence and poverty while I had been conditioned to laughter and living. This was the other side of the coin, the reality I had tried to turn my back on. I never had cause to doubt my success as a politician of the people but I doubted my usefulness. This kind of work took up too much of my time and prevented me from doing more productive things. I also needed to reassure myself that I was not completely wasting my time. Leadership was a lonely retreat, a fanatacism of holy orders. My failure was a failure of leadership not a failure as a politician. I wanted to trust and to share with a flower, a dog and a man. A cause grows cold in bed and has to be warmed in the morning sun. I needed to feel the warm shaft of life more than I needed an ego trip to the moon. For me there was no alternative paradise.

My son was twelve years old and I was still living with my brothers and sisters in my home at Hohola. I had now adopted three small daughters of my own, one girl from each of my married sisters, so, as was natural to our kind, my family was substantially growing.

Dina was my constant companion. He was the father of my children and their doctor as well. He was an interesting man and life was always interesting when he was around. He expanded every sight into a vision, every picture into a scene and every conversation into a dissertation. I never had a chance to grow tired of his presence because the path lengthened with every stride and I was always committed to a future that I could not face alone.

He was an intellectual man who was well versed in several disciplines outside of medicine, his 'meal ticket'. He had an abiding desire to build and not to destroy and whatever he touched was intended to last. He learnt five languages and we could speak together in three. His main conflict was in deciding what to do with his time. He could make his living in science, business or the arts and I am sure, if I had whispered the word, he would have made me a millionaire. I was equally sure that he would have no such urge on his own behalf, and I was too busy trying to maintain the illusions of my own perfections to dare to consider uttering such a vulgar suggestion. It would have been so much easier if I had accepted a portfolio, joined the club, tripped around the world at public expense, met the right people and wined, dined and laughed my way into a self-centred coma — and by carefully concealed cunning, planned and manipulated myself into the best jobs in the country, and Dina could have worked with me in honourable respectability. As it was, I had made up my mind to stay with the people.

PART FIVE

Harps of the violent seas

1

The Indonesian alternative

*T*he proposed political union of the Australian Territory of Papua with the United Nations Trust Territory of New Guinea had been of academic interest only. What little had been said about the matter had not filtered down to the people. It was the calls of Australian politicians and their servants, after the 1972 elections, that first alerted the people to the issue. In 1973, the central theme of Australian political policies was to unite us with U N New Guinea and to incorporate us into its economic development.

While I was occupied with my pursuit of an identity in political life, I became concerned at the spate of crash programmes that Australia had introduced, which were aimed at its own getaway without proper thought for the quality of life or the nature of the new society. To me, this was characteristic of the disregard and neglect that distinguished the colonial experience in Papua. Australia was an extremely inadequate colonising power in Papua. It had nothing to give but money and concern, both of which were denied during the vital years for our development. The only voice that

Papua heard during the dying stages was one saying that we would be cut off from all aid and support if we did *not* make a political union with U N New Guinea. There was also talk of possible bloodshed and violations.

Papua would have been infinitely better served by a rich country that contributed something to our economic or political development, or by a poor country that had well-developed non-material values in education, music, socialisation and labour, and which had the zeal to impart some of these values to its subject people. Australia valued democracy and a 'fair go' ideology, but these values were not brought to Papua. They were replaced by a political philosophy based on white supremacy and the social fear of dark people — white bigotry, an assumption of white supremacy, which found practical expression in Australia's rejection of any permanent association with Papua, and a blind insistence that they, and only they, were fit to make every decision about Papua's welfare and political destiny. We were never educated to make a free choice. We were only manipulated to accept what was already decided.

Australia's sincerity may have been more convincing if it had established some sort of an economic or political basis for an independent Papua. As it was, Australia had the destitute colony of Papua on its hands due to its own disregard and neglect. So when the Australian Army, during the Second World War, decided to administer the two countries together for military purposes, the Australian Government seized the opportunity to take advantage of the superior development in ex-German New Guinea to dump Papua in a new political set-up and, at the same time, rid itself of its own colonial embarrassment. The whole dilemma of Australia, in Papua, was caused by its neglect of any economic, political or educational development. The government education of Papuans, that started in my time, could have been started just as easily at any time in our colonial history. Papuans were docile subjects and pacification of the Papuan coast and islands was carried out with ridiculous ease by a handful of white men almost without any serious acts of organised aggression.

To the Australian Government it was abhorrent that

Papua should pass into the influence of Indonesia by uniting with Indonesian New Guinea (West Irian), but it was entirely acceptable to them that we should politically unite with U N New Guinea. Australia found Asia threatening but not the small island nations of the Pacific.

I found the ambivalence of Australian arguments hard to stomach. It was bad for us to be dominated by Indonesian strength and culture, but it was good for us to be dominated by New Guinea culture and land shortage problems. New Guinea highland dominance of Papua was good for us but Indonesian dominance of Papua was bad for us. But, because of their failure we were not fit to govern ourselves or control our own lands and economic development.

While Australia was busy demanding that we must submit to exclusive U N New Guinea dominance, they themselves were packing their bags to holiday in Indonesia to bask in exotica. Those few Australian tourists who strayed to PNG came with cameras looking for cannibals and primitive savages, and were kept busy photographing their own neglect and failure.

I lived in Australia for long periods and everywhere I enjoyed warm relationships and I lived among my white contemporaries with ease and comfort. Still, I have been puzzled always by their complete inability to recognise where I come from. In England, I was usually identified as an Australian but, in Australia, I was invariably identified as coming from some other Pacific Islands country. It seemed to me that any Papuan who had had a bath must come from some other country. It would be revealing to know what the white Australians really thought of us. They must have fallen for their own promotions.

Australian theorists were fond of the argument that Papua must politically unite with U N New Guinea. Their arguments centred around catch-cries of cultural and racial affinities of border tribes; big is beautiful, might is right, colonial borders and bigger markets. I sometimes suggested to these people that Papua also shared a colonial land border with Indonesia and that all of the arguments advanced by them also applied to Indonesia, so therefore union in that direction could be an acceptable alternative, and should be considered rationally in terms of our welfare. At this stage, the arguments were dropped and further discussions, if any, centred around undefined abstractions like freedom, democracy, human rights and other emotional issues. These were issues to Australians, but not necessarily to Papuans whose freedom had always been at the dictate of a master, were democracy had been the right to choose what Australia had decided, and whose human rights consisted of an introduced material poverty and a subsistence economy unrelieved by a century of colonialism. In any case, the choice open for Papua was not between freedom and bondage, but a choice between one dominance and another. Over-protection or under-protection. Strength or weakness.

When it was suggested that Papua could not have fared worse under Indonesia which was well versed in the cultures of poverty, and that had this occurred we would now be more attuned to our future reality, blood pressures jumped and red-faced men spluttered *ad hominem* arguments and whispered subversion, foreign influences, evil men, spies, guerilla warfare, threats to security and a lot of garbage about gratitude, freedom and democracy. Brotherhood with ex-German New Guinea or small Pacific countries was of a different quality to brotherhood with large Indonesia. It seemed that Christ spoke all of his words looking north to U N New Guinea, but never turned his neck to look to the west to Indonesia.

Australia assumed a god-like omnipotence in proclaiming one colonial border rubbish and the other sacrosanct. Nobody is likely to accept such bigotry. So the question still has to be answered, or, as some hope, it will never be asked again. The ultimate wish of people calling for love and unity is union of the whole island of New Guinea. God is not only looking north, he is also looking west. There is nothing on the present artificial border with Indonesia that is worth spilling one drop of Papuan blood for. There is no border war that would ever be worth fighting. What matters most is what arrangements will best preserve and enrich our lands, our communities and our cultures. If we are denied the freedom to govern ourselves, we must seek the best from our next bondage. Short-term foreign political expediency is not good enough.

We must learn to live with Asia. To live with Asia or to die with Asia is our destiny. Why not a foreign policy of our own to meet the big adventure halfway? Something unique to our own. Why not learn Indonesian as a national priority instead of spreading the old colonial Pidgin English? Indonesian is understood in 200 ethnic groups representing 130 million people in Indonesia, and reaches from our western border through the 3000 islands to the mainland of Asia. The Malay languages are in consonance with many of our own.

Why not unite with the Papuans of Indonesian New Guinea (West Irian) to form one island state, within the Republic of Indonesia, and remove the obsolete colonial border before the trickle of death has a chance to become a flood?

Why not put our self-reliance of thousands of years to the test in the present scene instead of living with the narcotics of dependence and death?

Why not use the hundreds of millions of dollars in untied grants to develop education, health, infrastructures and governments that can survive?

Why not prepare the poor people now for survival in their own clime?

Bend with the wind and survive.

Don't leave your land and your food or you will die.

In rich men's wars, don't provoke or be provoked by any side.

Don't set Asian against Asian on our own land.

Have the courage to be what we are; use the English language as an asset to ourselves and not as an instrument to keep us down; develop our skills for the export market overseas and throw off the colonial heritage of isolation and dependence.

* * *

In the early months of 1973, while politicians and their servants were shouting their threats and planning their departure, I was occupied with thoughts on the political realities of the Papuan people. It seemed to me that Australia was making a big mistake but that nobody was supposed to talk about it. There was no doubt about Australia's intention to deprive Papuans of their Australian citizenship and to manipulate a political union.

The more that politicians and officials shouted *'bung wantaim'* and the country was flooded with posters of dark and light-skinned natives holding hands together, the more Papuans told me that they did not want any political union. They wanted to govern their own country, spend their own money, control their own lands and communities and plan their own economic growth and development.

Nothing short of violence or sabotage would have stopped the Australians in mid-flight. They were going to solve their Papua dilemma by making us part of U N New Guinea come what may. Any thought of free political education in Papua or of explaining the options and alternatives to the people was out of the question.

It takes a long time for a colonial power of any colour to convince itself of its own failure. Self-interest and sabotage are the only languages that it readily understands. Otherwise, it prefers to be lulled to sleep with the opium of its own illusions. Nurtured in introverted self-interest and in the traditions of force and violence, it can regard restraint as a sign of weakness. The overt agency of violence is the army and the concealed agency is the network of corruption and authorities which may be used to sustain power or privileges. And when a cult of violence is introduced into a society a cult of resistance is never far behind.

Australia's aims and aspirations in its dealings with Papua did not have origins in moral rectitude, as the Australians liked to believe, but deep in fundamental Australian political philosophies and experiences. Australia had become so accustomed to bossing us around, wasting vital time while making all of our decisions for us, that this is how it continued right up to the bitter end. Australia's failure as a colonising power in Papua was the important determinant in its final attitude towards its destitute colony.

The main era for Papuan development was up to the end of the Sir Hubert Murray era and the Second World War. Up to that time, there was no government education in Papua of any sort. Any education available was through the missions and this did not usually proceed past three elementary primary grades. The two or three solitary white doctors working on government medical services, were confined to Port Moresby and to one or sometimes two small centres. A large part of their work was caring for whites in special European hospitals. There were a few European travelling medical assistants (dispensers), some of whom more or less had a roving commission to go anywhere they liked in the country. The government medical services to the rest of the country were rudimentary or non-existent. Late in the era, Native Medical Assistants (dispensers) were attached to the Government outstations where there was a white government official. They were supposed to provide medical services to hundreds of rural villages by constant patrolling; in fact, they could do little of value and spent most of their time collecting useless data and giving ineffective preventive injections for a tropical disease, yaws, using a cheap single injection of bismuth in peanut oil. My parents lost all but one of their twelve brothers and sisters before they reached marriageable age. And all probably from elementary diseases. If Australia had introduced a reasonable medical programme or established a basis for reasonable economic growth and development, the population of Papua would have been two or three times that what it is today and we would be that much stronger, more secure and independent.

There was no native political development. Rule was through native policemen under white officers. The Australian government officer acted as policeman, magistrate, tax collector, welfare officer and anything else that came along.

There was no reasonable economic development due to Australian government effort. A few coconut and rubber plantations were scattered around the country and these were all owned by big foreign companies, missions and individual foreign planters, and were situated on the best available land. The incentives were cheap land and cheap labour. Land was a few cents an acre. Papuans worked as labourers on the plantations for one dollar per month plus basic survival rations and a wooden bunk in a communal 'boy house'. After two years, a native would collect what was left of the twenty-four dollars and buy an axe, a knife and a few trinkets, keep enough to pay his tax, and return to his village.

For practical purposes, there wasn't a motor road of any sort in the country. The roads out of Port Moresby were no better than those in the rest of the country and ended a short distance out of the town. 150 000 square kilometres of nothing. Hence the small aeroplane and the outstation airstrip were very popular. I doubt if there was one substantial bridge in the whole country.

The Australian grant to Papua was between 15 000 and 30 000 Australian pounds a year, or from 2500 to 5000 Australian pounds per year for each Papuan district. The rest came from a small amount of native copra, a small head tax and what could be extracted from the foreign planters and the local economy.

In considering the Papuan situation now, it is basic to understand that this was the state of Papua at the time it was occupied by Australian and American armies during the Second World War. The Australian army relinquished control in 1945.

To summarise the situation as it was then: Outside of the work of the Christian Missions, there was no government education and no useful health services to the great majority of the people. There were no roads, no economic development outside of foreign plantations, no native political development of any sort and no welfare services. The country was run as a police state under the control of white officers and native policemen.

As the northern part of the Australian colonies became settled, pearlers, traders and blackbirders began visiting what later became Papua. From 1822 on, the Australian colonies pressed the home government in England to annex parts of the island of New Guinea. This was held up because the British Government was not enthusiastic and wanted the Australian colonies to help to pay the cost. Britain was not interested in annexation and repudiated the attempts that were made. The Australian colonies became more alarmed when Germany began to settle into the northern part of the island but, as late as 1882, the British Government still

refused to do anything about it. A German presence in the
area made the colonies more dependent on Britain.

In 1883, the Queensland government sent an emissary to
take personal possession of what became Papua. The Australian colonies of Victoria and New South Wales supported
the action but it was disowned by the British government.

The colony of Queensland then agreed to contribute 15 000
pounds a year to the cost of the administration so, at last, in
1884, a British Protectorate was proclaimed over what became Papua. It was proclaimed a crown possession later. The
first ceremony was conducted above the sands of Hanuabada,
the big village, and later, on other parts of the Papuan coast.
Then, Britain administered the new country on behalf of the
Australian colonies.

A month later, Germany annexed what became German
New Guinea. Papua came under full Australian control
when the Australian colonies became independent to form
the Commonwealth of Australia in 1901, and they celebrated
the occasion by adding an extra point to the stars on their
flag.

Thus, the eastern part of the large land mass of New
Guinea became divided between Germany and Australia.
The western part of the island was already under the control
of the Dutch, and thus passed to Indonesia as Indonesian
New Guinea (West Irian). So Papua came to have a land
border in the north with ex-German New Guinea, a land
border in the west with Indonesia, and a sea border in the
south with Australia. When Australia decided to get rid of
its undeveloped colony of Papua, it chose to solve the problem
by casting Indonesian New Guinea adrift in space and creating a fantasy island of its own which it called Papua New
Guinea, but which Indonesia called Irian, a part of an old
Indonesian empire.

The grand Australian delusion was that if they had not
forcibly occupied our country to secure their northern shores,
we would have remained in glorious isolation forever, and
that they did us a great service by having a hundred-year
sleep in our land. Those years were vital to our preparation
and the welfare of our communities. Instead of political
progress and economic development, Australia slept through

in a heedless stupor until awakened by the march of events in other countries.

* * *

The era up to 1945 was the era of my parents and their parents back to the time that the colonials first looked across the straits of Torres to the land of gold and mystery.

The story after the war was my story. I was a late starter but I still caught the first ride. Inside and outside my country I was in the first of everything. Government primary, secondary, and tertiary education, and everything else. When I closed my books, I was no longer puzzled why this was so. It all started with us.

It would be a mistake to think that Australia immediately sprang into action following the Second World War. I started primary school on the first day of the first government school on Misima Island in 1950. The Australian Government had decided that something had to be done in Papua but it administered the whole thing with a yawn.

After the war, the Australian Government appointed a Minister to look after Territories but his main portfolio was Transport on the Australian mainland. He visited my country only once as did his successor.

Then in 1951, there was another election in Australia and a Minister was appointed as a 'tail ender' to look after Australia's internal and external Territories in a newly created Ministry of Territories. This was a new ministry, the most junior ministry in the Australian cabinet, with the job of establishing an Australian Department of Territories for the first time. This was the start of the real Australian effort in Papua and New Guinea.

In an account of this period, the man who was the first Australian Minister for Territories, Paul Hasluck, described the bedrock conditions in his book, 'A Time for Building'*, and the struggle of creating something from nothing.

When the new Minister was appointed he had little knowledge of colonial territories and no particular interest. He

---

A Time for Building by Paul Hasluck, Melbourne University Press, 1976.

accepted the appointment more in anger than with grace and he felt, '... That the creation of the new Department of Territories had not been an imaginative stroke with a clear purpose behind it but a matter of convenience to find some rail to which another untried pony could be hitched.'

The author, describing how he stuck to the job for the next twelve years, up to 1963, said,

'More probably the reasons were some lack of confidence on the part of others that I was capable of doing anything else and very largely the fact that no other Minister would touch the job with a barge pole.'

In July, 1951, he visited Papua and New Guinea for the first time, and he described his first impressions:

'It was much more ceremonious than I had imagined. One very vivid first impression that accounted for some of my subsequent actions was that the habits and outlook of colonialism permeated the place. I had read about colonialism of a comic kind in other lands and had seen a little of it before the war but had not expected to meet it in an Australian territory... The Administrator was saluted as his car went down the street, native passers-by 'standing fast' at attention by the roadside until he had passed...

'... When we went on our tour away from Port Moresby, the local people all travelled in 'spotless whites' with a native 'boy' carrying a big bundle the size of a bishop's swag... At each senior residence or district office there were native messengers standing at the doors and doing nothing much except standing and coming to attention when a white person passed in or out... The house boys were eager, docile and mostly sleek. They lived down the garden slope in 'boy houses' that seemed no better than huts. They were cheerful in the way in which pets are cheerful. On the New Guinea side, the younger boys were called 'monkeys'. 'Master' was the common term for a white man.'

If the first firm foundations of colonial administration began in 1951, it would be a grave mistake to think that anything happened then. It was not until ten years after that that any turning point was recognised in the colonial history of Papua and New Guinea. The Minister wrote, 'The year 1962 seemed to me at the time to be a turning point in the history of Papua and New Guinea. Hard work below ground had been done and progress seemed to quicken.'

While the Minister was busy with his ten years 'hard work below ground' I was busy with my primary education in Papua and secondary education in Australia.

The graduation of the first nurses at the Papuan Medical College, in 1961, that the Minister saw as 'something stirring at last', was the graduation that Dina and I shared as the first fruit of our own durable intimacy. I watched the ceremony with tears in my eyes — not of Australian sympathies but for my own comforts. The main thing that was quickening for me was the fruit of my own womb, and the tears were for the unfilled passions of my damaged emotions.

Since the first graduation of nurses, another twelve years had slipped by. The colours of another thousand dreams were forming. I had been allowed to touch the stars but had withdrawn in fear to the security of the people. A politician without an identity accidentally caught up in the history of her country. Adrift in an earthly paradise where angels are few and virgins hide in legends.

2

Papua Besena

Sunday, June 3, 1973, had special significance for me because on this day Papua Besena, a Papuan anti-colonial movement, was formed. At 2 o'clock in the afternoon, hundreds of Papuans met in the grounds of my political office in Hohola to protest against the forced political union of Papua with New Guinea.

It was a tense, rowdy meeting, where speaker after speaker condemned Australia for its neglect of Papua and its present attempt to force an unwanted political union. I was surprised at the intensity of the meeting. All of the Papuans spoke Motu so they shouted and gestured without restraint. They did not want to be exposed to internal aggression or pressures and they wanted to control their own country, to govern themselves and plan and direct their own economic development.

We were angry with Australia for not giving us our independence, for not allowing us to determine our own future. At the meeting it was decided to start an anti-colonial movement to oppose all forms of colonialism in Papua. The movement was named *Papua Besena*, the name that I had previously selected for a Papuan rural reconstruction movement. The meeting continued until the sun went down and the sky gave warning of the coming of the quick tropic night.

* * *

I went with the two Papuan girls, Hisiu (star) and Rara (blood), to my house, where I found Dina building a car shelter at the back. I told him about the meeting and our decision to start an anti-colonial movement.

When the meal was prepared, the four of us sat at the table while my four children and my brothers and sisters sat on mats on the floor. The only difference between this and the old days in Misima was that there we all sat on the floor, as we had no table. Instead of a nervous village boy making eyes at me across the room, trying to clinch our arranged marriage, I was nervously eyeing a man of an alien culture who had stepped into my life and confronted me with the challenge to reach for the stars. It was flattering for a weak woman like me to be confronted by high demands beyond my intelligence and my moral fibre. Unchallenged, I would have taken the easy path and lived in fruitful oblivion. A child, a rest, a weaning and another child in faithful rhythm until someone severed my ducts and separated me from the usefulness of my existence to wither like a dry tree; and then the short winter.

The two Papuan girls were my political companions. Hisiu had accompanied me on my election campaign when our only thoughts were on winning a political race and not on what came after. She had given up her job to work with me, as she thought she would see more of life with me than she would in an insurance office. She was to marry soon. A man was busy cajoling his relatives into collecting the thousands of dollars for the bride price which was a necessary preliminary.

Rara was another attractive girl. She came from Hula, which was outside the Motu area. She had not long left school and her cool untattooed skin and straight black hair contrasted with Hisiu as an alternative in Papuan beauty. The Hula were vigorous, industrious people who tamed the sea and the land sufficiently for their purpose and developed

a gracious culture in harmony with the beauty and colour of
their *kone hanua* (village on the sand).

'What are we going to do now?' I asked, as we proceeded
with the meal.

'Do about what?' asked Dina.

'This *Papua Besena* business?' I said. 'Are we going to start
some sort of a revolution?'

'Why shouldn't we?' said Rara. 'If we don't, we'll lose our
lands and other people will walk all over us. Our people will
never give their land away. Land is the only thing worth
fighting for and the only thing worth dying for. Our land
doesn't belong to us; it belongs to our past and to our future.
Why can't we run our own country? Why do we always have
to have foreigners telling us what to do?'

Papuan girls from the Central District are not backward
at expressing their opinions in a direct and forthright
manner as many *taukurokuro* (whites) and foreign natives
have learnt to their embarrassment.

'Who do you call foreigners?' Dina asked timidly.

'Anyone who wants my land is a foreigner,' Rara said
quietly.

'We don't know what the colonials will do in the future,' I
said. 'We don't even know what the future is. If they feel
strong enough they might say it is Crown land or declare it
unclaimed and vacant. Either way, they just take it. They
then move in outside people who gradually take over. Our
land, our stores, and the government. Once they get the men
hooked on their beer, cigarettes, motor cars and things,
money becomes God. They say that nearly every man has his
price. They believe that with their money they can buy
anything. There are always some weak ones. Some who they
can buy.'

'Have they bought you, Jo?' said Dina.

'Not yet,' I replied, 'It would have been easier if they had. I
wouldn't be sitting here with a revolution on my hands.
What do you think we should do?'

Dina thought for a while and then said, 'I don't know. This
is one of those situations where whatever you do will be
wrong. In which case, wise men shut up.'

'White men shut up you mean,' I said, angrily. 'You people

created this mess. Now you want to run and leave it all to us.'

'I didn't do it all, personally,' Dina chided, looking at the two girls for support.

'No,' said Hisiu. 'That's what you all say. You're not responsible. Now and always. You can't get out of it by always running away and pointing to someone else.'

'I'll do my best to,' said Dina. 'We've been doing it for a long time now. It might still work.'

'You call us black bastards,' said Hisiu. 'I wonder what you call yourselves?'

'Gentlemen, what else?' said Dina.

'They mightn't get away with this one,' I said, putting my hand on Hisiu's arm. 'They may find that all that they have done is given us to Indonesia. Indonesian New Guinea is the same as UN New Guinea. The only difference is in the heads of colonials who are still using us as their doormat.

'I don't see that the Indonesian culture is any worse than the cannibal image that they have given us. I don't want any bloodshed or violence in Papua for a thing that should not have happened.

'It is quite unrealistic for us to ignore our border with Indonesia or the presence of Asia. Fifty-seven percent of the people of the world live in Asia and less than one percent in the whole of Oceania, including Papua and New Guinea. The population increase in Indonesia, each year, is more than double the whole population of Papua and New Guinea and this will continue to be so indefinitely. And Papua alone is bigger than any other Pacific Islands country.'

We talked into the night about the establishment of *Papua Besena*, the anti-colonial movement of the Papuan people, and the future of Papua. At about half-an-hour before midnight, we drove Hisiu and Rara to their homes. Hisiu, to the large marine village of Hanuabada. Her family and clan occupied one row of houses built on stilts and extending out to sea. As extra houses were required, there was only one way to extend — further out to sea. All of the houses in one sea line were linked by a companionway, like a sideshow alley built over the sea. The companionways were made of an assorted collection of timber, some being custom-made from local sawmills and some being from trees cut from bush and swamps around Moresby.

The village called Hanuabada was made up of four different villages and numbered about 6 000 souls. To the casual observer it was just one large native village. The logistics of its survival and disposals were a complete mystery to all but the fully initiated. To most it was a seething mass of inter-personal relationships that a team of sociologists could not unravel in a lifetime.

The men and women of these villages upheld some of the best traditions of our native cultures as they withstood the onslaughts of a brazen city. It was here that Papua was declared a British Protectorate in 1884 to placate the nervous Australian colonials but, before the warships of Queen Victoria's navy arrived, the people were already safe in the arms of one of Britain's most successful colonial agents — the London Missionary Society. The church, resplendent in its robust, white-garbed poverty and vibrant alleluia had flourished with little change, except in names, up to the present day.

Hanuabada was also like London in other respects. If a stranger had money in his pocket he could buy almost any-thing, but it was no place for the innocent or the earnest student of Papuan culture. A stranger looking at a Hanua-bada girl seldom realised the value of the merchandise that he was eyeing. She could bring $10 000 on the local marriage market or a broken skull for a clumsy pass in the deceptive light of the soft, romantic moon.

We paused in the cool air of Metoreia Mission, above Hanuabada, on the earth where a white pastor had added souls to a church and a white sailor had added subjects to a crown. We looked over the roof of the village as 'Star' slid down the slope to the safety of her home.

Hanuabada, on a harbour of pacific blue. The shining brown of a *tiger's eye* in the tiara of a soft, Papuan night. I stood in silent wonder as old deeds and new visions drifted to my mind. Here a *haroro tauna* (pastor) talked of a new *Dirava* (God). Here a *taubada* (big man) talked of a *hane vada* (spirit woman). Here *tatau* (men) fired *ipidi bada* (big guns) and Papua bowed to an empty sky.

Hanuabada fought the fight of all Papua. It felt the violence of poverty, disease, rape and war but, refusing death, was permitted to survive. Choked by the consumption of her lover and her sight shadowed by the dark night, she lifted her body from the corpse and learned to live again.

Beyond the village a rusting ship torpedoed the sea, fixing the agony of war in the heaving frame of the restless night. The foreign masters left their ship in the despair of death but Hanuabada rose from the sea to survive on the rubbish and debris of a foreign war.

I loved this village for its spirit and its pride. It was the spirit of all Papua and if we were equal to its measure we would rise. Tested by threat and violence, it had learned how to bend with the wind and how to survive. It had lost its land to foreign pique and a sprawling dinosaur, but the people loved their earth and waited in patience for its return. There was beauty and hope for us all in the lightly flowering brown earth and the green mangroves beyond. This was not the extravagant beauty of Misima Island, but it was the beauty of enduring love and the vibrant ardour of life.

* * *

Over the next few days we worked out the details of the new *Papua Besena*. It had to be non-violent. I was no soldier primed for war. There was no glory in what I had to do. I was a simple Papuan woman who had a conscience and this was the only command I could obey.

It was obvious now that some of the people would express themselves in one way or another and, knowing the feelings in Port Moresby and the villages better than anyone else, I had few doubts about what would happen. They knew how to loot, burn and damage the same as other people and, like other people, the technology of violence and sabotage was within their reach.

Port Moresby was a very vulnerable town. If there was any threat to foreigners, within a week half of them would have their bags packed for departure. Port Moresby was never their home. It was just a place to pay less tax and save money. At best, a break from Australian suburbia and, at worst, a dreary spell in a dry dusty town. Their motor cars, glass houses and other instruments of their isolation made them easy targets. They were there on sufferance.

Sabotage and damage brought the most publicity because its news had the highest price and the widest coverage. Usually, it was the only language that a colonial power would try to understand. Still, I could not involve the Papuan people in sabotage. I knew the power of the emotions of the people. I must lead them in a peaceful way.

We had plenty of experience and did not underestimate the task ahead. If *Papua Besena* was to remain non-violent then this had to be built into it from the start. It was useless to sow the seeds of failure at the start and complain when the inevitable occurred. We had to plan for success, and success was a peaceful movement. This would not be easy and nobody could control the tides of change. There would be no oaths, initiations or subscriptions, so the cults and corruptions would be kept out.

Papua Besena would have only one objective: the freedom of Papua to determine its own future and control the land, welfare and development of its own people. In doing this, we would oppose all forms of colonialism in Papua and work towards informing the people of their rights and freeing them from the slave mentality òf subject people.

During the remainder of 1973, we held more than one hundred *Papua Besena* meetings in all manner of places. Tens of thousands of Papuans raised their outstretched hands in a 'hands-off' salute and shouted *Papua Besena* slogans: 'Besena is Best', 'Papua is Big, Rich and Beautiful'. In the following months, *Papua Besena* received much publicity and I became the most reviled person, ever, in the history of our country.

Some of the colonials gave me fatherly sermons on my misguided notions and pointed out with controlled patience the purity of Australia's intentions towards its Papuan colony. But we also received many communications from persons and groups in Australia and elsewhere, offering money or services to our cause against the common enemy.

* * *

Mr Douglas Drinkwater was the first of a succession of government agents who paid me the courtesy of a visit. He was now engaged as some sort of a government trouble-shooter in Port Moresby. He came to see me in my political office at Hohola, a concession to changing times and decolonisation. He wanted to see me privately but this was against the rules. I only saw white Australians on my own terms, now. I no longer interviewed anyone without a witness and this particularly applied to government spies and agents.

Hisiu and Rara sat with me while Mr Drinkwater and I engaged in conversation. With slow speech and studied concern, Mr Drinkwater told me how he had strong sympathies with our cause and hoped that some day Papua would have the freedom to determine its own future. Some officials saw this as the best line to take when dealing with me.

'I don't see much hope of your achieving anything immediately,' he said, with a quick brush to each side of his moustache. 'As you know the New Guineans are numerically much stronger than you are and a large population of New Guinea highlanders are sitting right over the top of Papua.'

'What has that got to do with Papuan freedom?' I said, wondering about the reason for his visit. 'Populations of every country with land borders have different population concentrations. I don't see what that has to do with us.'

Drinkwater had brought a map of Papua and New Guinea for my education, and he produced it now and placed it on the table with deliberate care. We gathered around the familiar map and he continued,

'You see the mountains here and all the rivers? This is where the big New Guinea populations are and you can't stop people from spreading down the valleys and rivers.'

'Don't they also spread up valleys and rivers?' I asked; 'If they are short of land they go anywhere the land is, up or down. They also spread across borders if they are strong enough.'

Drinkwater ignored my remarks as they were contrary to his thesis and continued, 'I suggest that you should welcome a lot of these New Guinea Highlanders into Papua. They will become Papuans like you are and just as anxious to retain their land and identity. You will then have the strength to establish your own independence as a country.'

'What about Indonesia?' I said. 'Couldn't we just as easily

join with Indonesia and achieve the same thing? That would make us a hundred times stronger than we would be through a union with New Guinea Highlanders.'

Drinkwater was caught unawares. He thought that Indonesia had been safely laid to rest behind the old colonial boundary of our western border and he was confused to suddenly find that his theory might have some holes in it. But, he was too experienced to be put off balance for long.

'I don't see how union with Indonesia is a possibility,' said Drinkwater, quickly recovering from his surprise. 'It would be very messy. The suggestion would upset many people.'

'It would only upset them because they have never been allowed to look at the possibility. They have buried their heads in the sand. Of course it'll upset some. That goes without saying,' I said, pointing to the map and the large expanse of Indonesian New Guinea on the western border of Papua.

'Wouldn't it be better to join people of your own race and culture than with people of a different race and culture?' Drinkwater said, persisting with his argument.

'Some of the people of Indonesian New Guinea are closer to my race and culture than the New Guinea Highlanders are,' I said. 'Indeed, many people of Indonesia, generally, are probably much closer to my language, race and culture. Anyhow, nationality does not depend on such things. An Indonesian influence could make Papua very beautiful and colourful. It could be the tough experience that we need to make us grow and develop our aesthetic values instead of being drawn into a loser's game with western materialism.'

'Do you mean to say, Miss Abaijah, that Papua should join up with Indonesia?' asked Drinkwater, as he fumbled in his pocket and produced a notebook. 'Do you mind if I take notes of what you say? I find it most stimulating.'

'You can send a telegram to the Australian Prime Minister if you like. It makes no difference to me. I'll tell him myself if he comes up here. This is part of Australia you know. We are supposed to have free speech.'

'Certainly,' said Drinkwater. 'You are part of Australia and you are an Australian citizen. I am certain nobody will stop you from saying what you want to. But, also, please

remember that Australia plans to give Papua its independence when it is ready, and so it is proper for us to know the
opinion of the leaders. May I ask you again: Do you think
Papua should join with Indonesia? Needless to say, you don't
have to say anything to me if you don't want to.'

'Yes, *taubada!*' I said with a smile. 'I didn't say that Papua
should join Indonesia. I said that this is one of the alternatives open to us and we should examine it and not put our
hands over our face and scream murder. You suggest that we
flood Papua with other people so that we can get a bit of
muscle. I say that we could get much more muscle by joining
Indonesia and it might not be so damaging to us. It might be
better for all of us if we were all influenced by the same
power. We could be equal then. With the inevitable spread of
refugees from Asia we could be safer under Indonesia.
Internal aggressions and disintegration may be bigger threats
to us than external conflict. What I say is that these are
alternatives. They should be examined. This country cannot
stop Asians coming here, either as refugees or aggressors.
The new migration of Asia across the Pacific has already
begun. We might be safer as part of a large Asian country.

'It is not Australia's business to force us into something. If,
after a hundred years of Australian dominance, we are not
fit to make our own decisions or govern our own country
then the shame is Australia's not ours. There are several
alternatives. We should look at them.' Then, looking at
Drinkwater, I said, 'Did you get all that down on your paper?'

'What are the alternatives?' said Drinkwater ignoring my
last remark.

'There are Australian alternatives and Papuan alternatives,' I said. 'Which ones would you like to hear?'

'We earn our living by writing,' said Drinkwater, more
relaxed now. 'I wish we were paid for thinking but that's an
impossible dream. Can you tell me what the alternatives for
Papua are?'

'We can unite with Indonesia and become strong and
powerful and save future border troubles and bloodshed. We
can join with UN New Guinea as the Australians are forcing
us to. We can work for a larger Pacific federation. Or we can
negotiate with Indonesia for union with the Papuans of

Indonesian New Guinea to become one united island in federation with Indonesia.

'Of course the main alternative for us is to govern our own country and control our own lands, our own welfare and our own economic development. We can be small and part of the Pacific islands or large and part of Asia. These are the alternatives. No Papuan blood should ever be shed fighting Indonesia.'

Drinkwater paused for a moment and said,

'You mentioned Australia's alternatives. What do you see them as?'

'That's easy,' I said, as Drinkwater folded up his map and made ready to depart. 'But another day. Australia's dilemma is adjusting to becoming part of Asia. It's white Australia policy has already failed and new techniques of migration will evolve on the weaknesses of democracies.

'If Australia uses its present position to get a soft deal on the Torres Strait-Papua border — an Australian Alaska with oil, gas, ship passages and airspace, all free — then it could be manoeuvering itself into a dangerous position. It does not believe the lessons of history.'

'I think you are a bit hard on Australia,' said Drinkwater. 'While some of the things you say are valid, Australia does not see it the way you do. They think that they are uniting similar people across an old colonial border and that this will be the best for you as well as the best for themselves.'

'Do you think Papua will be dominated by New Guinea, especially the New Guinea Highlanders?' I said, standing up as Drinkwater indicated he was ready to depart.

'Yes I do,' said Drinkwater, rising to his feet. 'I think most of us think that. But it won't happen suddenly. It is something that you will just have to get used to and live with. That is the sensible thing to do, I think.'

'Perhaps,' I said, moving to open the door of my louvred office. 'That's is if there are no alternatives.'

'And do you think that *Papua Besena* will enable Papua to choose its own alternatives?'

'Not in the short term. *Papua Besena* is a peaceful organisation and quick results only come with direct action. But in the long run it might. God will decide.'

'But you have to deal with men, not God,' said Drinkwater, putting his broad-brimmed Australian hat on to protect himself from the burning sun.

'I don't deal with men. I follow my destiny.'

'Goodbye, Miss Abaijah and good luck. It has been a pleasure talking to you.'

'*Bamahuta taubada* (Go to sleep, big man),' I said, pleasantly.

'And, with a touch of his hat, he was gone.

* * *

Dina and I were returning to Port Moresby after a visit to the Vanapa on one of our usual village meetings. We soon realised that all was not well. The roads were littered with smashed windscreen glass and groups of New Guinea natives were rampaging through the streets. The mobs were on the lookout for passing cars with Papuans in them, as unsuspecting drivers drove their vehicles into the town. As soon as they spotted me, sitting in the cabin of the Land Cruiser, they began to shout.

'*Meri Papua, kilim, kilim.*'

The New Guinean mobs did not know who I was but I was easily recognisable to them as Papuan. We increased our speed to avoid rocks and bottles that landed behind us and, when one native separated from others to run to the side of the road to throw a rock straight into our windscreen, Dina changed direction and headed the Land Cruiser straight at him as though to run him down. In fright, the native carelessly threw the rock and dived for safety off the side of the road.

After this, I slid to the floor of the cabin out of sight and Dina drove through the mobs unharmed. We drove to my home at Hohola, past scenes of a serious uprising. At the shopping centre a large group of Papuans, caught unawares, had banded together to fight their way through rock-throwing, bottle-wielding New Guinea mobs.

We arrived home to safety behind our high fence and our team of cattle dogs. The children were locked in the house. They did not know what had happened but they had seen the shouting mobs of New Guineans passing on the main Hohola road about fifty metres below our house.

After our arrival, we immediately became concerned about Rara, who was doing casual work on the cash register at a shop that was open on Sunday afternoons to sell newspapers. Dina decided to drive to the newsagency to see if Rara was all right. Although the mobs only seemed to be attacking Papuans, we decided to attach riot screens to protect the glass of the Land Cruiser, just in case. He passed through several mobs in the streets, and when he arrived at the newsagency it was closed.

Rara had been attacked by a group of New Guinea men who had entered the shop and she had been rescued by half-a-dozen foreigners who had been there at the time. The shop closed and Rara was hidden in the residence at the back. When Dina found her, she was still recovering from the attack and, because of the uncertainty about what was happening, she wanted to rejoin her family.

The New Guinea uprising against Papuans commenced at a New Guinea versus Papua football match, an event that had taken place, twice a year, for more than twenty years. The uprising was not unexpected by the Papuans and only 7 000 of the expected 14 000 turned up, so New Guineans were in the great majority. Due to difficulty of assembly and scattered housing, mobs did not have great durability and found it hard to survive beyond the next meal. In this uprising, some violence continued into the night and Papuan houses in the suburbs were attacked. A Goilala settlement, sheltering in a small valley, was stoned several times during the night. After dark we drove to some of the Papuan villages round the town to see what had taken place. These were like armed camps and the mobs gave them a wide berth.

We expected the uprising to end on the Sunday but, to our surprise, on the Monday some large contingents of New Guineans assembled in the hills and marched in force on the town. The scattered nature of the housing favoured this sort of manoeuvre, as no large population concentration of Papuans was threatened at any one time.

On the Tuesday, the Papuans began to mobilise and I led a demonstration by thousands of Papuans which was blocked by riot squads of police. Dozens of large truck loads of armed village Papuans began to converge on the town and these were stopped by police roadblocks, where arguments continued for hours. They finally decided to turn back when prominent Papuans, who were rushed to the scene, convinced the village Papuans that there was no longer any threat to Papuans in the town.

After the uprising, many Papuans were reluctant to venture into public and reveal their injuries, and we treated many in their homes. Papuans girls were vulnerable; some were kicked, bashed or hit with rocks or bottles, while others were rescued by people not involved in the attacks. Some were seriously injured.

People from many parts of New Guinea were involved on the first day of the uprising when the violence was at its worst. On the second day, the mobs polarised into New Guineans from certain areas who acted as though they were having some sort of a tribal fight.

In the meantime, the Australian Minister for External Territories treated the Australian people to the usual political 'claptrap' when he publically announced,

> There was the throwing of bottles — there were no weapons involved. It was a riot that first developed out of some disgruntled supporters but there was no evidence to show there was fighting between so-called Papuan people and New Guinea people.

This announcement, which was relayed from Australia, embarrassed many Australians and one of them wrote in the national press,

> I have just listened with an equal mixture of disgust and incredulity to the ignorant, self-opinionated remarks of the Minister for External Territories on the radio... how does the Minister, from his secure place of vantage in Canberra, really know of the violence and lawlessness which was experienced by local Papua New Guineans and Australians in Port Moresby during the past few days?

The national government of PNG acted in a typical way by directing that all football and other sporting events between Papua and New Guinea should cease.

The part of the Australian Minister's announcement that interested me was his reference to 'so-called' Papuans. Papua was part of Australia; Papuans were Australian citizens; Papua was named by the Australian Government, which also bestowed the name, Papuan, on us; and the Australian flag still carried an extra point on its star which was put there to signify the acquisition of their Papuan territory. Now we were Papuans — 'so-called'.

The uprising was caused by inflated ego and primitive ideas that Papuans could be subdued or dominated by muscle or numbers and that Port Moresby could be cowed by mob bashings, stones and bottles. Some colonials in New Guinea, and especially in the New Guinea Highlands, were fond of saying that, some day, New Guineans would walk all over the soft and easy-going Papuans. This prophecy may well come true but, following this uprising in Port Moresby, it was the Papuans who became more aggressive and the New Guineans who became more subdued.

The Papuans in Port Moresby knew that an uprising by New Guineans against them was due. That was why only half of the expected number turned up at the football match. There was a similar uprising of New Guineans against Papuans in 1968. On both occasions, the Papuans took no part other than to defend themselves if caught on the streets at the wrong time. Only the colonials were asleep.

* * *

A few days after the New Guinea uprising, a television team arrived from Australia to film a current affairs special on my political activities. A lady was in charge and they were all cheerful and professional and I was impressed by their style and performance. The lady gave an impeccable display of diligence in the pursuit of a story, and the only time she got ruffled was when we lost her and her colleagues on a dangerous mountain road in the dark interior! Such events had been a part of my life and I thought little of them. Many times in the past I had knelt in lonely vigil through the silence of the night.

When the team arrived in Port Moresby, we asked them if they wanted to film around Port Moresby or if they really wanted to go out and see the people. They opted for both, so both they got. There was plenty of activity around Port Moresby and they worked there first. We called a large open-air meeting by the sea, at Konedobu.

The police seemed anxious to break up the meeting by the familiar method of creating a disturbance themselves. The white police officers seemed to become disturbed on seeing the television cameras and the enthusiasm for breaking up the meeting waned. They advised the television crew of their displeasure at their presence but, at the same time, redirected large police vans to other parts of the town. At last, the Papuans were left alone to hold a meeting in their own country in peace.

We introduced the television crew to a cross-section of the urban and rural areas but avoided the more rugged experiences. They worked for about ten days and a film was produced that faithfully recorded some of the spirit of my work and the beauty of my native land. The film was shown overseas but, unfortunately, its essential truth and beauty was marred, for me, as somewhere between the taking and the showing a couple of bits of inaccuracy managed to creep in which distorted the reality. By dextrous use of the scissors, a tiny fragment of a two hour talk to university students on the political and economic development of Papua, when shown, appeared to some as though we were advocating the introduction of guerilla warfare! We were really advocating the building of a road between New Guinea and the Papuan coast which was a highly unpalatable suggestion to Papuans at that particular time. Overseas newspapers took up the guerilla theme and some are quoting it still.

Another small segment of the film was presented in a way that many interpreted it incorrectly as exciting further violence. We were trying to quiet the nerves of remote villagers, who thought that several Papuans had been killed in the New Guinea uprising, by giving them an accurate account of what occurred. The New Guinea uprising was harder on the villagers who had to wait and cope with rumours, than it was on those in Port Moresby who knew what was taking place.

These presentations finished up with our being accused of

planning guerilla warfare in Papua. Eventually, the story
became blown up until we had become collectors of tactics of
the Latin American revolutionary, Che Guevara, for use in
Papua! I did not wish to appear disrespectful but I had to
admit that I had never heard of the gentleman. I had never
heard of him as his life's work was not required reading in
my education. Why the Latin American connection, I had no
idea. We had plenty of healthy guerillas in South East Asia,
some of whom leant heavily on giants of the destruction
industries.

* * *

These cheerless experiences increased my resolve not to be
pushed around by foreigners and to increase my efforts to
oppose Australia's efforts to whitewash its failure, in Papua,
as a colonising power.

Following the New Guinea uprising, I was told that I
would not be permitted to teach at the Institute of Health
Education because of my politics. Perhaps I might contami-
nate the post-graduate students by telling them fairy stories?
It was a fitting end to the thirteen years of graceless co-
existence with the colonial administration. I was sad to be
tossed out of the Institute I founded as principal, and I
missed the work that I had grown to love. An individual that
started off as a smiling, modest Papuan girl with a thousand
coloured dreams had ended up as a dangerous politician, a
wicked witch and a 'revolutionary'.

I was now introduced to a sleazy world of narrow meanness
— phone tapping, bugging, snooping, break-ins and professional seducers. The world of liars, pimps and licensed
sinners. The swamps of the poisonous snakes and wide
jowled crocodiles were unsoiled sanctuaries compared with
the cesspool of sick white politics. I still had plenty to learn.

Police surveillance became a familiar facet of my existence
and, from police cars, I sometimes had a running commentary
of my own locomotion like a public broadcast of an English
cricket match:

'Subject turned into street A.'

'Subject heading south.'

'Subject stopped.'

'Subject in, subject out.'

I was under surveillance by the police, by secret agents, by groups interested in my harm, by groups interested in my well-being by, Abaijah's soldiers. I made a pale blue flag and pulled it up a steel pole outside my home patrolled by six short-tempered cattle dogs that roamed freely around my grounds. The flag was our *Papua Besena* flag. Its background was our background of pale blue sea and sky. There were six white stars for the districts of Papua and these circled the cross of Christ. In the centre was a scarlet Bird of Paradise holding a branch, the land of Papua. To some it was the flag of defiance and violence, but to me it was the flag of native beauty and the law of Christ. Christ the tiger and Christ the lamb.

* * *

My next objective was to inform the Australian people. With Dina and Hisiu, I then set off for the Australian mainland. This barnstorming trip was not to win Australians to my cause or to arrest the Australian political machine in mid-flight, as it thundered through the fog towards a harbour in the night. I was an Australian citizen the same as they were. Papua was still a part of Australia but we were on notice to quit. At the end of the year, a self-government of sorts, under Australia's direction, was to be granted to Papua and New Guinea combined. Two years later, in 1975, Independence was to come.

We went to the capitals of the three eastern states. God made Brisbane to feel, Sydney to see and Melbourne to reproduce in, and on the fourth day he either rested, went on strike or had a sickie.

Sydney harbour is the jewel of Australia set in a city of delight. A roused peacock flaunting the glory of its erection in a deception of sustained love. Let me be fulfilled by your beauty and not beguiled by your pride. My passions rise, saturate and subside to the lucid colours and fluid contours of disneyland waters long before the unconvincing demonstration of the sexuality of man. What absurdity makes man

think that the climax of beauty is sex. The climax of beauty
is God. There is nothing to prove little man. Be gentle with
my dreams. Let me go to sleep.

* * *

When we arrived in Australia I was already news something
different to the politics that the reporters were accustomed
to. Australians wanted to have a look at the first female
politician to come out of the jungle. A female Tarzan trying
her luck in civilization. In addition, I was a revolutionary,
one of the few genuine revolutionaries in their tepid history.

The members of the media were kind to me and I was
given a million dollar publicity campaign, free. They said as
many nice things as they could about me and published the
best photographs that they had. The eulogies were liberally
embellished with blood, wars and prophesies of failed causes.
Australian academics ponderously informed their clientele
that I was talking through my hat. After serious journalists
had taken most of the meat from the bones, a few jackals
came in for the pickings with the old 'Beauty and the Beast'
story.

I visited a few government ministers in Canberra but they
did not know what I was talking about, and in turn, I
didn't understand them. With this mutuality we stayed
on good terms and ate and drank to my downfall and my
early departure from politics. I was told with reassuring
finality that the Trade Union Movement and the Returned
Soldiers' League were firmly behind the government's plans,
so any thought of self-determination in Papua was completely
out of the question. Naturally, the big threat, unite or starve,
was repeated. Unless Papua united with ex-German New
Guinea it would get no Australian aid and would be allowed
to rot in the poverty of development which Australia had
created.

The television special about my activities in Papua had
already been shown around Australia and with it the snip-
pets on blowing up bridges and the story of the New Guinea
uprising. The people had also heard a good deal about my
anti-colonial *Papua Besena*. Thus they were receptive to
stories of blood and revolution and the media and politicians

fed their appetites. The Chief Minister of Papua New Guinea, at the National Press Club in Australia, said, 'Miss Abaijah threatens to spill blood and sacrifice lives in her attempt to attain her impossible dream.' One Australian newspaper came out with the headline, 'Fiery Papuan beauty is too busy to think of love' and this was immediately followed by the declaration, 'Miss Josephine Abaijah, the most feared woman in Papua New Guinea, yesterday spoke of love and war... and came down in favour of war.'

Another thoughtful feature writer declared with eloquence,

Josephine Abaijah is slight, soft, polite, sincere, winning. And she is frightening in the way of all people who live beyond compromise...
Her smile is a small sun, her movements elegant with a grace that delights. But when the smile goes and the brown eyes flash darkly, when the language of commonplace gives way to the careless eloquence of the politician, Josephine Abaijah is an echo of Belfast, a terrifying mirror of Biafra...

While in Australia, many groups invited me to address them, but with the pressure of television, press and radio I could only accept two of these. I was attracted to the Wayside Chapel in the heart of Sydney's sleazy King's Cross. The pastor of the Wayside Chapel, Ted Noffs, wrote in one of his books, 'Small is Beautiful' and this is what Dina had quoted at our first meeting as medical students.

For survival, therefore, the world must heed the lesson of history. Bigness is dangerous. Simple is beautiful. Those things survive which have the flexibility to change and adapt to new circumstances. Small is beautiful.

I went to the Wayside Chapel to speak, and to see if small *was* beautiful. I found that it originated in 1964 from the Methodist Church, with the present pastor, and grew out of four empty, run-down apartments in a side street by the busy thoroughfare of Kings Cross. A chapel, a coffee house, a small theatre, a crisis centre and a dozen other organs pulsed in a body dedicated to the universality of God and the goodness in man.

I am a Catholic, but I am also a Protestant;
I am a Jew, but I am also a Muslim;
I am a Buddhist who also happens to be a Hindu;
I am a Sikh and also follow Confucius;
For I am a Human Being.
And nothing human can ever be alien to me,
We are all stamped with an imperishable divinity.

Walking down from the 'Cross', the Wayside Chapel seemed like a Teahouse of the August Moon and on the inside it was a workshop for God. And small was beautiful. The chapel was painted in the colours of hope and flowers were rich with the persuasions of Spring.

In the service we were invited to hear God and mix with a cocktail of his people. Guitars played the songs of Australia and an organ played the songs of God. The breathless spoke of the beauty of the heavens, the lame climbed the mountain top and I knelt in communion between Dina (sun) and Hisiu (star), close to the fragrance of a woman in love.

The Wayside Chapel in Kings Cross is one of the beautiful churches of the world. Its first beauty is warmth, its second beauty is love and its third beauty is life. I have been in the great cathedrals of the world and their beauty was of domes, columns, windows and faith, but sometimes I was too cold to pray, sometimes I was too lonely to seek a friend. Now I was a woman of blood and violence and needed a quiet place to rest.

But in this cathedral of lost sheep, princess of elegant beauty, I could reach my God and ask why he had singled me out to travel alone and where it would all end. And then the benediction:

> Go forth into the world in peace, be of good courage; hold fast that which is good; render to no man evil for evil; strengthen the fainthearted; support the weak; help the afflicted; honour all men; love and serve the Lord, rejoicing in the power of the Holy Spirit. Amen.

Out again into the bleak winter day, off to the airport and back to my native land.

3

God saved the Queen

When I returned from Australia the Parliament had just commenced its budget session. I got on well with most of the politicians and most of them were pleased to have a woman in their midst. The one in one hundred mix did little to threaten the male monopoly. Most of them accepted me as a politician and did not try to get cheap advantages. Occasionally a frustrated man tried to handle things more personally and, when he failed, would became a suppressed volcano of simmering rage.

Filled with Dina's attentions, I was a poor target for those who sought to cancel me out through a simple equation of sex. I also expected that some day someone would try to separate us. I was an unwilling martyr waiting for the sounds of death. At times, I wanted to quit before it was too late, but when I thought of my commitment to the village people I could not turn back. I could only pray that when the time came God would take my hand and lead me back to my dreams. The price for my dreams was more than I could pay.

In Parliament, I tried to give as much as I had to take. An

occasional politician, unrestrained by leaders or sanctions, would splutter out personal insults in a riot of pidgin English verbosity. When I did not want to listen, I turned off the translations, sat back and enjoyed the show. It was not unexpected that a few rough men would think that they could intimidate a woman by yells and threats. But, this was their problem, not mine. Survival in this environment made me develop a certain amount of callous disregard for my personal safety and feminine refinements.

Outside of Parliament, I was counted by friends and foes alike as a formidable politician. Among the voters I found that being a woman was more an advantage than a disadvantage. They put me on a pedestal and said that, being a woman, I was beyond the corruptions and foibles that afflicted many men. The people talked and I listened. They chewed their betel nut and nodded their heads. They were very impressed. The daughter of Papua with her blue flag of hope had not let them down.

For my part, I had to preserve the image of a modest Papuan girl who was educated in the ways of the white people, but more than that I was an intermediary between villagers and a white fantasia far removed from the realities of their own existence.

Then, suddenly, Dina was suspended from the colonial administration. The pioneer of medical education, tertiary education, nativisation and a dozen other innovations in my country was unceremoniously kicked out. The dying stages of the decaying colonial administration was the beginning of the era of the faceless men. A white professional who put the simple love of a simple Papuan girl before the club and the cocktail party was very exposed. He was sacked from the colonial administration because of his association with me.

They did not find anything to charge him with, but they told him that if he did not bow out they would sack him just the same. They wanted their pound of flesh and they would have it anyway. A few years earlier I had expected to be sacked because of my association with Dina. Both of us had now suffered the same fate.

Looking back, I regard it as an honour — the only honour that they had left to bestow! This Australian pioneer in medical education, government nativisation and a dozen other fields was now seen as a despot with a 'freaked-out' mind. It took them a long time to find out. After all, high ranking Australian politicians had said that I was being misled by white adventurers. Freed from this evil influence, I would be as harmless as a lamb. I had no mind of my own and, of course, the Papuan people who guided me were as meaningless cattle quietly grazing on their own land.

White Australians in Australia had always treated me pleasantly and I mixed easily with them. I never had an unpleasant experience with them in their own country. But to deny us the right to decide our own future or to govern our own country, because of their own failures, that was a different matter. I was pleased Dina was sacked. Now he could spend more time with me. I had long ago lost respect for the colonial administration and was glad that we had been honoured with a premature goodbye.

The only thing left that the Australian administration had control of was Dina's entitlements. After appropriate research it was decided that he had been a temporary, day-to-day, employee for the last few of his twenty years and, thus, some of the thin entitlements had been whittled away.

We went together to the slaughter, in the person of a young foreign woman who now dispensed accounting justice to temporary employees. Dina's records had been stored in Australia like those of the other contract and permanent officers but, now, they were hurriedly rushed back to this hot little office near Koki market, to rest posthumously among the dead files of the temporary foreign employees.

As we took our leave, the wind from Koki point was heavy with the smells of the day. No humiliating farewells, no fond goodbyes. Just a handshake from the latest temporary employee. It was time for us to go and start again.

* * *

There was no summer and winter, just hot and hotter, wet and dry. A traveller from a cool country, stepping off the plane in Moresby, could think that he had walked into a waiting room for hell. For a moment he might think that his survival was endangered, and then his body would recover

from the shock, take over and become acclimatised. The
only cool places in Papua are in the mountains and in the
sea. Over the rest is sun and shade, but over Moresby there
is mostly sun. The native Papuans lived in beauty by the
cool waters or in shady retreats but the foreign concept was
to fight the earth and make it flower to their command.

At Christmas, the wet season begins, the thinly timbered
brown hills take on a coat of green and the trees give a
promise of Spring. Freed from starvation, they ripen for the
seed. Up to the middle of the year, the town struggles on in
reasonable array, and then the dry sets in. Centimetre by
centimetre, the vegetation retreats into the dry land until
the earth cracks and wrinkles as it closes its eyes forgetfully
to await the coming rains. Rain is Spring and the cycle
begins again. Port Moresby is a freak in Papua, but it is the
sort of place that foreigners pick for capital cities, having a
good harbour for ships, good land for houses and plenty of
water for light and power. It was also close to Australia.

Port Moresby was growing in stern beauty as foreigners
fought the long dry, but ugly human values were replacing
the cracked clay and Papuans bowed to the passing of the
pleasant days. Papua had retreated to the villages a few
miles away. There was talk among the foreigners that the
city was to be cut off from the central district to become the
national capital district. A tropical Canberra. An ugly foreign
enclave on Papuan soil. The home of the wallaby and the
cassowary had become the home of the fox and the crow.

It was a hot day. Two of my daughters were home from
school so we decided to take them for a swim. The Port
Moresby swimming pool was fairly new. It was similar to a
council swimming pool overseas and was named after a
colonial administrator. The pool had been built in recent
years, under the strict decree that it had to be open to people
of all races. In plain English, this meant that it had to be
open to Papuans and New Guineans as well as whites. The
colonials did not want any additional embarrassments during
the dying stages of the game. Up to recent times, most of the
swimming pools in the country had been reserved for whites
or near whites. During the same era, the Papuan picture
show in Moresby was a white preserve.

We sat in a shady spot at the pool watching the children play in the water. I still had a curious feeling that I was doing something wrong sitting in a European swimming pool and I turned to Dina and said,

'I still feel strange sitting in these places. I have a feeling that I should not be here.'

'I thought you were getting over that by now,' said Dina. 'You're a big shot now and I'm nothing. You see they sacked me because of your political success. Things have changed.'

'What is going to happen to us now you are out of the administration? I think this politics business is a mistake. Before, we could be happy on our own and nobody worried, but now people think they can interfere with our personal lives as a way of getting at me.'

'I don't think anything will happen to us yet,' said Dina 'There's still a hangover that this is a free country. They would like to leave the dirty work. What do you think is going to happen to us?'

'I don't think they'll do anything to me,' I said. 'They would if they could but they don't know what to do. They can only send me to goal and that will make the people turn more against them. Some of these people will do anything to get their own way, always in the name of some political hogwash that nobody knows the meaning of. They fence their own abstractions to suit their own desires.'

'We will do nothing,' said Dina. 'We will just keep on going. We will fly into the storm together. We never turned our backs on what was right before. Why should we start now?'

I looked at Dina, then towards the children and said,

'I could not stand to be alone now. Everywhere I go and everything I do is with thoughts of you. You are always by my side. I never want to let you down. You are the only man who ever believed in me. With you I could go to the ends of the earth. Without you I would wither and die. It's foolish to take so much from one man. It's foolish to know only one paradise. It's foolish to give so much that there's nothing left behind. We ask too much of the gods. They can become angry at too much happiness. Love that knows only one sunrise must circle the earth to cheat the dying day. We have been

circling the earth for fourteen years now and I want to keep
it that way. We should get out of the sight of people and live
our own way. We have that story to write in the Philippines.
Why don't we go away?'

Dina was not accustomed to running away from difficulties.
He thought that the greatest successes come out of the
greatest difficulties. He put his white arm alongside my
brown skin as I leaned on the arm of the chair.

'I don't know what brought us together but we're not going
to quit now, no matter what happens. We grow closer as the
years go by. I'll be safe for awhile. Papua is still an Australian territory. Reporters and public servants are always
telling us what they are going to do, but nothing has
happened yet. Politics is a dirty game and there will be
plenty of dirt yet. There are many alternatives. Whatever
you choose suits me. We have many ways of making a living.
We don't want the sun to set yet.

'Josie, you know my life turns around you. I am intrigued
by your timeless beauty and bedecked with garlands of
desire. God deprived the red hibiscus of its perfume so he
could mix it with your love. You complete my flower and you
complete my life.'

I looked down at our two arms resting together, one coffee
brown and one milky white.

'You probably only like me because I am a problem you
can never solve. The harder the problem becomes, the closer
you want to get to it. You want to analyse it and tear it
apart. You know you can never give in, especially where I
am involved.'

Then, looking at our two arms again, I continued,

'Do you like your coffee black or white?'

'I like it coconut brown, 160 centimetres high and weighing 42 kilograms.'

'Why don't we go to the Philippines and write? Life is
always exciting when we are together. I don't think I've had
a dull day since we met. Except when you sent me off on
those awful trips alone.'

'We have to write a story about you first, but if we start
now, there'll be no end,' said Dina, as Kaia and Boio ran up
and pulled at my arms. I got out of the chair and as I was

pulled towards the small refreshment shop, I turned towards Dina and said,

'Okay, I'll see this through. I know I can't give in either. That's something I learned from you, but after I do what I have to do, I'm signing off. The rest is up to the people. No leader will ever rise while I am keeping them down. The people think that our country will be born through me. I may not be able to do that, but I can release them from the slave mentality of colonialism and show them that they can be free. You pushed me into politics, you'll have to pull me out again.'

I then let the two girls pull me towards the shop.

'Buy us some sweets, mummy,' said my smallest daughter. 'You promised you would some time.'

'Papuan children should not eat rubbish like sweets. You should know that. They are just for the *taukurokuro* (white people). That's why they have poor teeth.'

'Go on, mummy,' said second daughter, who was cheekier than the others, 'and Papuans don't call their mother, mummy, but we do. Times have changed since you were at school.'

'Yes, changed for the worse. I'll buy you an ice block this time but don't ask me again. I don't like you getting all these European bad habits.'

'Okay, mum, just this time.'

Dina joined us and we went out to my white Japanese car and drove home.

* * *

Most of my working time for the rest of 1973 was spent in the villages and settlements of central Papua, working with the people and leading marches and demonstrations to protest against Papua being denied the right to determine its own future. Even though I was repeatedly attacked by the government propaganda machine and strenuous efforts were made by committees and special workers to undermine my influence, I was more at peace now than I had been since the fateful day that I decided to take up politics as a living. Everywhere I went, Papuans cheered and supported me and I felt that I was doing something worthwhile.

Dina could be with me now so I no longer felt abandoned and alone. When the shouting died and the dancing stopped, there was no solitude. I was always happy with the village people but I could only touch them lightly in my journey to the thousand villages and the lonely, forgotten homes. I was now secure and happy. It takes the quiet of the night to reveal the noises of the day and it takes love fulfilled to disclose the empty heart.

We could now take our vehicle to many places that I could not have reached alone, and being bogged on jungle roads to sit out the lonely night, lost most of its terrors. We ventured further afield and took greater risks. It was the life I liked and had lived.

At last, I had made up my mind what I wanted to do and this calmed an alien restlessness that I had felt since becoming a politician. I would carry on the meetings and demonstrations until Australia cast us off. A short time before that date, I would make a unilateral declaration of independence on behalf of Papua. This would give us an alternative history and save us the final indignity of our colonial misadventure. Then it would be up to the people. New leaders would rise and the people would determine their own future. There would be no problem with maintaining the support of the people but the big task would be to prevent sabotage as a means of being heard, speech being the only weapon freely available to the people.

* * *

On December 1, 1973, Papua and New Guinea, as a combined unit, were granted a form of self-government. Independence was to come in 1975. Then Papua would be granted its independence by Australians, and ex-German New Guinea by the United Nations. It was planned that the two countries would be governed under one constitution to form a single country known as the Independent State of Papua New Guinea. But, today was self-government day not independence, and a dreary day it was. Papua Besena provided the most excitement and some foreign cameramen, starved of any sign of celebration, followed me 120 kilometres out of Port Moresby to try to get a story.

The self-government ceremony in Port Moresby was conducted almost in secrecy in a minor government department building. The Chief Justice swore in the Australian Administrator as the Australian High Commissioner. The new High Commissioner congratulated the Chief Minister and the Chief Minister congratulated the High Commissioner.

An Australian newspaper reporting the subdued event, recorded,

Papua New Guinea took the reins of self-government today — but there was double trouble. More than 2,000 people waited in vain outside the wrong building as the formal ceremony was held. And three miles away, 1,000 Papuans raised a rival flag to the Papua New Guinea national flag. Police patrolled both potential trouble spots and a riot squad was on alert. The historic break from Canberra rule was witnessed by fewer than 100 people in the Department of Information headquarters. Only a small crowd — most of them official drivers — waited outside the Department of Information building.

The colonial government was very jittery on the occasion of self-government. They did not know what action we might take or if the ceremony would be sabotaged. The self-government ceremony was very low key and without any celebrations.

I drove to Bereina, an outstation about 130 kilometres from the town. There, we raised the pale blue Papua Besena flag at a large rally of village people from the surrounding villages. Chiefs and village leaders gripped the flagpole in symbolic gesture as I raised the flag of Papua to the cheers of the people and the clicks and whirs of cameras. We then recited prayers, sang songs and spoke words of hope. My thoughts were with the village people and that was why I was there and not in Port Moresby.

* * *

The rest of December was spent visiting the settlements and villages around Port Moresby. The people were accustomed to me visiting them in their homes and I went from house to house and again spent time with each family. I spent one or two days in a large village. In the smaller settlements, I followed the house to house visits with a group meeting but, in the large villages, I liked to meet the families separately.

Wherever I went I was trailed by Goilala mountain tribesmen who lived in settlements in Port Moresby and who had become my permanent bodyguards. This precaution was unnecessary in Papuan villages but I was intrigued by their constant presence. They tried to keep in touch with where I was going and what I was doing and if they missed out on this information, they picked up my trail and attached themselves to their 'duty'. Previously, I had never particularly noticed Goilalas in the streets of Moresby, but now they seemed to be everywhere. Nobody argued frivolously with them. I had seen similar groups to these overseas, protecting exposed people.

It was my nature to approach all interpersonal relationships with gentleness. I was not aggressive by nature and was only at ease with happy, uncomplicated people. I had to constantly reassure myself that I was now free from the slave mentality of colonialism. I was not going to transfer my mind from one colonial master to another. The next time I was colonised I would attempt to retain my dignity. While I never met a New Guinean who did not want Papua joined to New Guinea, many New Guineans respected my work and voted for me.

In the months before self government, many people suggested sabotage as the only means of obtaining justice quickly. I also received communications from individuals and groups overseas offering assistance with money and know-how. Port Moresby was an open target and very vulnerable. Outside the settlements and villages, the suburban sprawl invited housebreaking and other aggression. Village people suggested direct action and waited on my command. Roads were vulnerable and trees plentiful. I was the image of *Papua Besena* and the people would not listen to anyone else. They had put their faith in me.

But I would not take direct action. I was a representative of the people not an undercover agent. I sought love not hate. I was a poor revolutionary. I wanted to protect, not to destroy, as I sought to free the minds of the people. I failed them because I was a woman who did not believe that the end justified the means. Dina counselled me not to break the law.

'If the establishment is going to gaol you, force them to do it on a trumped-up charge. Don't hand it to them on a plate. Don't break the law. This is still supposed to be a free country.'

'If they put me in gaol because of Papua, I'll become the first national hero,' I laughed.

'And if you're killed, you'll be a dead dog, hero or no hero,' said Dina emphatically.

'Nobody wants to die,' I said. 'But we've been running away from colonials for a century and I'm tired of running. Gaol or no gaol, I'm not running any more. Die or live, I'm finished running. If they try hard enough, they can corner a dog sooner or later and force it to show its teeth, even if it is only seeking a friend.'

'Yes, Jo,' said Dina. 'And a dead dog is a poor companion. I'm not much good at living on memories. Memories are like toast. They are best when they are freshly buttered.'

* * *

I was not only receiving attention from the people but also from Government agents. Her Majesty Queen Elizabeth II was due to pay the country a visit and it was rumoured that *Papua Besena* might sabotage the ceremonies in Port Moresby. We received visits from high-minded white officers who espoused our cause but appealed to our better natures to exercise restraint and tolerance during the royal visit. My political office was broken into and ransacked but we kept no records. The usual spies appeared among us but we said nothing to anyone that we did not say in public. I only spoke with confidence to the village people, and then always in the open and in Motu, which agents found frustrating. I assumed that all telephone calls were tapped and I had no telephone in my own house. A white neighbour became worried about this because he thought that they had tapped his phone instead of mine as a substitute activity! Despite the attention, I had not given any thought to the Queen's visit.

Dr Sidney came to see me. He was back in Port Moresby again and a government officer, concerned with security for the Queen's visit, had asked him to come and see me because of our previous association.

Dr Sidney's attitude had changed since I had become a politician. He was not as secure as he was previously and no longer took my friendship for granted. He had not come to the country to play politics, and he was more comfortable 'uplifting' us than he was facing present realities. Like many foreigners, he thought I was unduly critical of the colonial effort and that I did not understand their good intentions. He was still courteous but less relaxed. He was more at home rejecting the old master-servant relationship than he was at acting as either. He did not like the role of professional foreigner. He wanted to be fully accepted. Patiently he told me of the functions of royalty, and that I was to be honoured from an invitation to dine on the royal yacht, *Britannia*, as well as attend other functions that the Queen and Duke would be attending.

He was surprised when I told him that I would not accept any invitation to attend any special functions. I would only attend public functions with the people.

Dr Sidney indicated, in his roundabout manner, that he thought I was carrying my eccentricities too far in not accepting the royal carrot. To him the Queen epitomised all that was good and noble in his cultural heritage. He could not understand that I did not feel the same. Especially as I was a woman. I told him that perhaps I did feel something like that as a woman but I preferred to stay with the people. I had already turned away from the new world of privileges, political junkets and royal honours.

* * *

Papuans in Port Moresby and the rural villages were restless and wanted to take action to support their cause. There was no chance of obtaining recognition from a colonial power bent on a course of action, without direct action of some kind, but I could not personally lead a movement organising sabotage. Also, I had Dina constantly telling me not to break the colonials' laws. I did not keep the right company.

'You're not God,' he said. 'What they did to Kenyetta in Kenya they can do to you in Papua. It's no good rotting in gaol to establish a point that is already obvious. Some crude-minded people think that if they can get rid of the visible symbol of dissent they will get rid of the dissent as well. Those who hold the money and the guns hold the power. Keep to your original plan.'

My original plan was to stage numerous public protests so that nobody could say they didn't receive the message; to work to free Papuans from the servility which was the main gift of colonialism; to make a unilateral declaration of independence for Papua so that we could have an alternative history.

The rest would be up to the future. I could enter history as a revolutionary or a martyr but I decided to keep to my original plan. After all, as Dina had said, I was not God. I was a woman with a conscience who had applied a well-groomed professionalism to a dangerous political game.

Numerous protests and demonstrations were carried out. Marches, public rallies, petitions and demonstrations. The police did not provoke any trouble at this stage and some-times, motorcycle police even led our marches. Because of this restraint, there was no serious trouble.

One of our numerous demonstrations took place on the last Saturday of January. Thousands of Papuans assembled at a public reserve and marched seven kilometres through the streets of Moresby, to stop outside the National Broadcasting Commission on the edge of town. We marched with the pale blue flag of *Papua Besena* in front, escorted by motorcycle police from the Royal Papua New Guinea constabulary. Outside the Commission, we burned a life-sized effigy of the Australian Prime Minister amid cheers and angry gestures.

Following this, thousands of us marched into the NBC grounds. The officials, including white Australians, met us and received our message with courteous regard. With one eye on the glass doors at their backs and one on the crowd of Papuans in front, they acted as though they thought that the revolution might have begun. Many Papuans also eyed the glass-encased building thoughtfully as several of them had suggested that the place be torn to pieces.

* * *

On the last Tuesday of February, the Queen and the Duke of Edinburgh arrived to pay us a three-day visit and Government agents were worried about *Papua Besena* demonstrations or sabotage of official functions. Personally I did not have my mind on any such thing. I regarded the Queen and the Duke as more or less beyond the range of our politics.

As the time for the visit grew close, Papuans came to me with suggestions to use the Queen's visit to demonstrate for Papua. The media kept close on the heels of royalty and anything unusual, during a royal visit, was sure to receive wide publicity. The Papuans had nothing against the Queen but they thought it was a suitable time to press their claim for the right to determine their own future as free people.

The trouble for me started just before the royal arrival. Several Papuan communities were alerted by organisers that there would be direct action during the visit. These organisers, who were influential in urban communities, planned to stage a large, dramatic demonstration. They avoided telling me until the last moment because of my opposition. But these enthusiasts could only get the people behind them by using my name and promising my presence.

The opening assault was to be during a mass gathering when many outside news reporters would be around and it would be difficult to cover up what happened.

Thousands of Papuans were to assemble at the Hubert Murray Stadium, behind a high chain-wire fence, topped with barbed wire, that had been hastily erected around the arena just before the Queen's visit. They planned to push the wire fence over by bending the poles flat, and then thousands of Papuans were to march and carry me around the arena singing a Papuan song, to culminate in unfurling our pale blue flag in front of the royal assembly. This was to have been the start of direct confrontation and Papua would have won its freedom.

I heard of the plan only the night before and was worried about it. My part was to attend at the stadium. Everything else had been arranged. I just had to attend and be at the head of the people. I was worried that when the people pushed the chain-wire fence over, Australian security agents or white police might panic and in the name of the safety of the royal party, start shooting. I also thought that with any kind of shooting more violence could break out, as some of our people react badly to any serious violence against any one of them that they think is unwarranted, and they deal with offenders summarily. I could not take part in any demonstration that could end in violence of this nature. I would not be responsible for the injury of innocent people under such conditions. There must be other ways. Our own short span is only a minute in history. I had caught the habit of seeing things in the long term. To the people this was eternity.

On the day, a messenger came to tell me that thousands of Papuans had assembled and that everything was ready. But, I did not intend to put in an appearance. The action centred around me. If I did not turn up then nothing would happen. They would only follow me and I thought that I served them best by avoiding what could have led to tragedy for individuals.

The day passed in quietness and the night wrapped around our emptiness. With mind unstained by battle and body unextended, I played dominoes with the children and postponed their hour of sleep. Then, late at night, we cooked some scones for supper.

'What's the matter, Mummy?' asked Rakatania, wearily. 'Aren't your eyes sleepy?'

'Yes, my eyes are very sleepy, and it's time for you and Boio to go to sleep. You see, Kaia? She's asleep already.'

'Would the Queen be asleep by now, Mummy?'

'I am sure she is. She is only human. She has to sleep the same as we do.'

'Does she have a gold bed?'

'Of course not. Go to sleep now and don't ask such stupid questions.'

* * *

Following the frustrated demonstration, several angry Papuans came to my house and told me that I had let them down. Their best chance to demonstrate for Papua had been allowed to pass because I wouldn't back them up. It was the first time that I had experienced such intense anger by Papuans, directed against me, and I was upset. This was to have been their first move in continuous direct action to obtain independence. It probably would have worked but it was too big a risk. Did I refuse to lead them because I was afraid for them or because I was afraid for myself? This was what they wanted to know, and it was what I wanted to know also. They asked me how I expected to get our right to self-determination without any risks. I told them that I did not know the answer to this, either. Perhaps God would show the way. We are only a minute in history. I was confused. History had overtaken me and when the big test had come I had failed. After this encounter, several of my compatriots parted ways to apply their industry in other directions.

As an image-builder I had been too successful. My image had taken charge of me. The feelings of Papuans to the new situation would find new expression. The unpleasant society had become a reality. Everyone would have to live with it.

4

The hibiscus crown

The idea of police state rule was firmly entrenched in the minds of the colonials and they gave little attention to the development of a community police force. The 'army of occupation' concept worked better in other places than it did in Port Moresby. The white police officers were tactful and restrained with me, but I was drawn into many incidents involving the constabulary and the communities.

One unfortunate consequence of this policy was that the people of the settlements and villages of Moresby were involved with large numbers of pidgin English-speaking police and a peculiar type of tension between police and community developed. Efforts were made to improve the relationships without any attempt to alter the practice of avoiding a community based police force in favour of one based on outside natives. Valuable time and experience were lost without any real progress being made.

Dividing communities and seeding new ones to get a new order of man, loyal to a new Caesar, was another colonial absurdity that indicated a preoccupation with colonial aims instead of with our progress and development.

I was involved in one incident where I witnessed a police car run a Motu family in a utility off the road, and then the police brutally bashed the man of the family as a bonus. In the same area, a week later, I was involved in incidents following a large police raid on a Papuan settlement in which riot squads were involved and a large number of tear gas shells were fired into the homes of unsuspecting villagers, causing mass panic and damage. Many of the villagers, including expectant mothers, ran to hide or dived into the dark sea to escape the peril.

Following these incidents, I led a protest march by Papuans through the streets of Moresby to the office of the Commissioner of Police. The colonial Police Commissioner received our delegation, where I read out a statement and handed him a letter. He promised us an early statement on the matter and then we departed.

* * *

At this time, I was called upon to hold several meetings with Papuan villagers living on the cool tableland of Sogeri. Sogeri is about 70 kilometres behind the city of Port Moresby. It is a land of high mountain streams, waterfalls, cool rubber plantations, polocross, schools and destitute villagers. On the other side of the mountain range was the small government outstation of Kokoda and from there a road to Buna by the sea. The Sogeri tableland was the official start of the Kokoda Trail, the springboard to the Owen Stanley Range.

The Japanese had planned to advance on Port Moresby over this single track mountain trail from the land that they occupied on the coastal plains on the Buna side. A contemptuous gesture to the enemy but an unpleasant miscalculation of the Papuan mountains. It was on this trail that a small part of the badly-stretched Japanese army succumbed.

The Koiari who lived in this area serviced a mean war that was fought over, but not for, their land. But when their usefulness in war was past, they were soon forgotten and their flag remained unfurled in an empty sky. The victory parades now echo to hard concrete beats in foreign lands but the mountain leeches stand in salute to the soft tread of forgotten feet in my native land.

Much of the Sogeri plateau was now covered by foreign enterprises and foreign seeds, while the Koiari had retired to the smaller bluffs and steeper slopes in the unserviced bush or by the new feeder roads. The developments at Sogeri attracted the white man who lived in his own style, drank in his own clubs, played polocross, and discussed the price of rubber, the impending disaster and the 'coons'.

The development also attracted outside natives from more advanced areas, who crowded the Koiari out of the better-paid jobs and whose children crowded out the disadvantaged Koiari children from the priority schools. In Sogeri there were two grades of national high schools. There were no Koiari children in the one of higher academic acclaim and only one or two in the other.

The developments were served by the best roads and services and those who followed the developments had the best jobs, the best transport, the best houses and the most food. On the other hand, the Koiari clung to the edge of the past neither looking forward nor looking back. They were suspended in a heedless present with no chance of retreating to the obscurity of the past. They were caught in a vicious cycle of poverty, poor education, low productivity and disease, with no chance of escape.

When whole communities are challenged to change because of the richness of their land, most easily they become servants, drivers, labourers or prostitutes in a new market place. It is only when the change that rich land brings is internalised through the structures of existing communities that these communities profit and advance. Deprived people who give up their lands for white developments have little chance to benefit themselves, as competition keeps them down. Revolution may bring redress, but family and community breakdown is part of the price they have to pay.

But this was Papua where the only tangible native wealth was land and the greatest native poverty was to be a landless man. All things pass but only the land remains. As there was pratically no chance for a village native to acquire land, 'my land' was synonymous with 'my ancestral land', the land that has been mine since the beginning of time. It came from the past and goes into the future in contiguous generations and a man may live several times on the same land.

Myths of origin were modestly restrained to explain only the origin of themselves and their lands and the world was confined to a few hundred kilometres of sea and land. Out of this simplicity we emerged into colonial hands.

* * *

We slept in a Koiari village near the Sirinumu Dam so that we would be ready for an early morning meeting of villagers that was to be held on a grassy clearing overlooking the retaining wall of the dam. This dam provided the water and the electricity to Moresby. In a village we were provided with an old kerosene lamp, sleeping mats and a small one roomed house to sleep in. The only furniture in the house was the floor and a few nails hammered into the lashed sapling frame that supported the palm-thatched walls. The man of the house insisted on sleeping on the small verandah that served as a second room, so that we could enjoy the privacy of his castle which was about all that he possessed. His wife and children were away in Moresby selling vegetables at the native markets.

Another family cooked food of boiled native vegetables and black fish from the dam, which they served on an old enamel plates, with a spoon. Hot sweet tea and sun-ripe bananas completed our evening meal. It was a simple matter for us to bring our own food on short journeys but the villagers got a kick out of our sharing their life-style during our brief visits. They were all familiar with our tastes and style and this understanding added to the pleasure of our journeys.

The people were up and about at dawn. Dina and I wandered off to the great concrete retaining wall of the dam to witness the spectable of lights in the quietness of the dawn. I stood on the wall of the dam and looked back at the tree-spiked, flat, grey waters that flooded the Koiari lands, and then forward to the white thunder that poured through the concrete wall to fill the mountain stream that carried the tamed waters to the stations a few kilometres downstream.

There is nothing cleaner than the hour of dawn in the crisp mountain air; nothing deeper than the sleep contained in love in the silent night; nothing firmer than the warm hand of a confident man in the dawn of another day. Is it wrong to feel so much pleasure? Should the senses be dulled until there is no pain? Is God in every star and leaf and rainbow? Where does the devil hide? Are the spirits still adrift in the village night? How mean is the magic of jealous men? I must not show too much satisfaction. I must suffer with the people. I must hide my heart inside.

By 7 o'clock the villagers had assembled for their meeting. Several of them had slept at the site by the dam, while others had left their homes in the early hours before the dawn.

There were many grievances among the Koiari of Sogeri and the mountains beyond: the lack of proper war compensations, payments for land, unfulfilled promises with the dam, inadequate education and health, poverty and deprivation while others grew rich on their land. The biggest culprit was the colonial government which represented the people's interests as well as its own.

Some Koiari talked of sabotage of the Moresby electricity and water supplies. It was freely spoken that the government or its authorities would never take any notice of their plight unless there was a threat to their own interests. There were always people standing between the government and bad news. Colonial officials sometimes thought that their own interests were best served by only feeding their bosses good news. This went all the way up the line, from the people to the highest in the land. The peaceful methods of the Papuans were easily rebuffed and dissonance quickly filed away.

Subsequently, a protest meeting was held in Moresby and, for good measure, the Koiari blocked electricity authority vehicles from going to the dam by felling trees across the roads. In Port Moresby, the Koiari carried a cement survey marker strapped to a pole like a pig to represent their lost lands, old rusted kerosene hurricane lamps to indicate their poverty, and plastic containers of kerosene.

We assembled in a public park near the electricity authority offices, the target of our present mission. We hastily erected a platform in the park and made speeches of protest to the large crowd of people and reporters who gathered around. After the speeches I led a march to the electricity authority building and, still carrying our rusty lamps and kerosene, a delegation of us went inside to register our protest and present our demands. We were quietly received by the men in charge who were anxious not to precipitate any further trouble. After presenting our case we departed, leaving a list of our demands.

Fortunately, the electricity authority bosses got the message quickly and acted promptly to see that most of the requests of the people were implemented or put in hand. The traditional colonial government agencies dragged their feet but, at length, they also got the message. The results were encouraging and something had been achieved. Roads were built, education and health upgraded, opportunities increased, new lands acquired, boats bought for transport on the dam, a few electric lights installed, and other benefits for the forgotten people appeared. This was the present but the future was in doubt. A beginning but not an end. An expediency but not a plan.

* * *

Close on the heels of the Koiari protests came the Women's Demonstrations in Port Moresby. These were to be the most boisterous and politically damaging disturbances that Moresby had seen.

It all started innocently enough. Papuan women at Hohola, the housing settlement where I lived, decided to hold a public meeting about some grievances that they had and I was asked to attend. I did not know what it was all about but the women knew that they could count on my support, and that I would see to it that their voices were heard. But, as things turned out, I failed to have their voices heard and that was the cause of the trouble.

At three o'clock on the first Sunday of June I joined the women at their meeting. A few hundred women were assembled on a public recreation area near the Hohola open-air market. This was the first women's political meeting that I had attended since I had become a member of Parliament two years before, so I was anxious to make a good impression. I identified easily with the women of the villages and settlements but I had never politically represented women as a group.

It was exactly a year since *Papua Besena*, the anti-colonial movement, had been introduced. I had avoided splitting communities into political units of men and women. Now I was at a women's political meeting for the first time and I was curious about the results. After my arrival I learned that the meeting had been organised by a women's fellowship in Hohola. These women had decided to call a public protest meeting about several major issues; being their low living standards (they had to keep a family and pay rent on a few dollars a week); the privileges that the white sections of town received in things like street lighting and the sealing of the dusty roads; and the extravagance of government ministers who made frequent trips overseas and had just acquired a rest retreat by the banks of a cool river a short distance out of town.

The meeting was a lively affair and many of the women made speeches. When men and students made public protests they were reported in the news which, otherwise, was largely devoted to statements and counter statements by politicians, and 'good news' of what the government was doing. After the protest meeting finished I took a few of the women to the National Broadcasting Commission for interviews and issued a press release on their behalf. The media ignored our requests for mention. They were too busy with other trivia around the town. As far as publicity was concerned the women's political rally was a non-event. The first Papuan women's political meeting in Port Moresby was of no consequence.

This was the first time that a group of women had called on me to assist them politically. My contribution was to get publicity for their protest but I failed. I had let them down which was something that had not happened before. I was upset and was determined to do something about it. It was this something that led to the women's riots in Port Moresby ten days later.

* * *

I went with some Papuan women to a few settlements and villages around the town. Using loud hailers and speaking in Motu, we called to the Papuan women to join us in a women's political rally at Koki Market the following morning.

Most of them knew nothing about the Hohola women's meeting held ten days before but they were anxious to attend the rally. The three issues raised by the Hohola women were common grievances of all Papuan women in the town so we decided to use the same theme for this demonstration. The women, like the men, were very restless and wanted action, so one theme was as good as another.

The following day, Wednesday, thousands of women assembled at Koki market and prepared to march on to town. At the market we could see the native foods and, beyond, the sea-going native canoes. Things that had played important parts in our lives. We were in our native environment and we felt at home and confident. I talked to the women over an address system and told them what we were about. When I called for their approval there were deafening roars of *NAMO* (good). The speeches over, we moved off together on a seven kilometre march, first along a road cut in the brown cliff face, then on to white Ela beach and to the centre of the town. I had always admired the courage of our village women but never more than now, not only because they were on the march for the first time, but also because I was with them and my identity as a woman was reinforced.

As we marched, the late morning air was filled with laughter and song. Papuan women, Papuan style. On the way we passed a few conscientious women who were out on the rocks and wading in the shallow waters of the low tide, gathering a few shell-fish to garnish the evening meal of sweet potatoes and rice. They looked at us in wonder and waved while we marched on like a vagabond army, taunting them for their industry and calling on them to play truant for just one day.

Eventually, the long procession of shouting and banner-waving women reached the main streets of the town. There we stopped the traffic, business and everything else as the business fraternity and shoppers rubbed their eyes in the bright sun and gazed in amazement as we marched through the town. Half an hour later we arrived at the main government offices at Konedobu, by the shores of Fairfax Harbour, where the British fleet seized Papua and promised us protection of our women and our land.

Now Papuan women were marching for their own rights for the first time. We had to put on a good show. We were emerging from a soul-destroying colonial experience and I felt that the spirit of Papua was on the march.

For the next two days thousands of our women made their presence felt in a manner never seen before, and which some officials hoped they would not see again. Buildings were besieged, windows smashed, police threatened, offices invaded, drapes and fittings destroyed, an airport invaded, doors broken, women arrested, and police harassed. There were scenes of pathos, anarchy and moral courage as our women asserted themselves for the first time, and the forgotten half of society made their presence felt in the restless search for a portion of pride and self-respect.

The white police officers in charge of the hundreds of native police did not know how to control the women without using force that would have taxed their dignity and brought wide adverse publicity for the colonial cause. They braved it out, mopped their foreheads, had their conferences and hoped that it would not happen again. The demonstrations were not against the police, who had no previous experience in handling a women's riot like this. Indeed, once the women took to the streets, angry and aroused, there was no way that they could have been stopped. Either the police would provide the publicity or the women would provide the publicity themselves. As it turned out, the police acquitted themselves well. They allowed politicians to take over and focus the spotlight on themselves by confronting the angry women with reasoned arguments and honeyed talk.

The women first marched on the building of the public service association where they had a special grievance to air. As the large, wooden stockade gates to the grounds were closed against them, they stoned the building, charged the gate and threatened to break it down. A shout then went up and we turned our faces towards our main objective, the offices of leading government ministers and their staffs. During this period of native self-government, before independence, it was business as usual for many of the white colonials except that they had moved from the front seat to occupy the room behind.

We reached the offices with their spacious colonial steps, wide verandah, coconut palm gardens and, beyond, the harbour lying lifeless and glazed in the noonday sun.

There were now thousands of women assembled and they were in an angry mood. I talked to them in Motu over a loud hailer and the women shouted their support while lines of police barred their entrance to the building. Then someone in authority in the building decided to be nice to the women and a senior white government officer emerged, looking paler than usual, and told the white police officer-in-charge to allow some of us through the police lines into the building.

With the police barrier broken, this was the sign for a general rampage through the building by hundreds of women who immediately started to dismantle the large conference room by tearing down fixtures and curtains. In the process they injured a white government official who tried to protest.

I was surprised by the intensity of the women's feelings, but I had no remorse. I was standing in the office where a few years ago a white Australian Administrator had told me in a few gruff words, that his colonial officers had informed him that I was not acceptable for training as a health educator and waved me through the door. That had been just one of the continuous stream of rejections I received from the colonials during my twelve years' service with them until, in the end, I was barred from teaching my profession and from entering the colonial government premises at all. I was well prepared and primed to be a revolutionary but, when I thought of my companion and my coloured dreams, I could not raise a hand. One word from me, and the women would have torn this place apart.

A large number of police were rushed to the scene and, with difficulty, the building was cleared. I walked quietly away from the office of unpleasant colonial memories, past the debris, to join the women outside.

The women then continued to demonstrate outside the office for several hours. The Chief Minister, senior government ministers and some officials came out behind the police to appease them, but they were all howled down. Finally, I was able to hand a petition to the Chief Minister summarising our stand. In the late afternoon, we decided to go home and to return again the next day.

The next day, Thursday, thousands of women returned and the demonstrations were on again but, this time, more active and enthusiastic than the day before. The night had done nothing to cool them down.

Some women were to wait for me at Ela Beach and we were to march through the business centre of town, and around the shores of the harbour to the sports stadium, where we would join up with women from the other side of town. The usual contingents of police were at Ela Beach and the stadium.

I was delayed by writing a new petition so I did not arrive on time. The police, who were good opportunists, told the women to disperse as I would not be coming. The women ignored the police and patiently waited. When I finally arrived, they broke into boisterous singing and dancing as was their custom when expressing themselves. I translated the latest submissions into Motu and read it to them over an address system. I had barely finished the last words when women started chanting, *raka-raka-raka* (march-march-march).

All went to plan. Then, on reaching the far side of the stadium, we were faced by a strong contingent of police who had their own prearranged plan to stop us from marching on the government offices again. They planned to divert us into the sports stadium where, according to the police, the Chief Minister and other government ministers and officials had promised that they would meet us. Also, they would have us caged where we could be tear-gassed or otherwise controlled. They had prepared their own ring for the next contest.

Some policemen were shouting that we should go to the sports stadium as the government ministers were waiting to meet us there. But, being once bitten twice shy, the women took no notice of the talk this time. Instead, they charged the police lines using very unladylike tactics to make the police forget about holding hands and defend their manly pride. In one spot the line was broken and the women surged through towards the next line but, at this stage, they noticed that I had been left behind. Some of the women then staged a rearguard action to drag me through the gap in the police line while other women kept the police occupied with body language (Papuan style), confrontation, hula dancing, beating them with tree branches and placards, taking police caps, and other unscheduled female pranks. Just as I was making progress through the break, a police officer grabbed my arm. The women retaliated by grabbing the other. Then a tug-o-war ensued that threatened to tear my arms from their sockets! There was no shortage of women, only a shortage of space to hold. They were winning handsomely until police reinforcements arrived and went to the aid of the officer struggling to restrain me and half a dozen other women at the same time. The tussle continued until I really was in danger of being torn apart. In the excitement of the tug-o-war, the police managed to regroup around the back of the women and form a new line.

At this stage, two young women had fought their way up to where we were regrouping for another attack and shouted to us that most of the women had gone into the sports stadium and that the Chief Minister and others were waiting for us there. On hearing this we turned and retraced our steps, leaving the police to regain their composure and their hats.

When we joined our sisters in the Sir Hubert Murray Stadium I was surprised to find that confusion reigned supreme. Women were everywhere and the whole place was in a state of seige. The police master plan, based on the experience of the day before, was to shepherd us into the large sports arena where we could do no harm, and then to make political speeches on the 'Melanesian' way of doing things, about how to settle our differences in a dignified manner and to go home and leave the country in their capable hands. But the women were intent on showing exactly how they felt, here and now.

The officials had their way of controlling us and we had our way of making our presence felt. There were too many gladiators in one arena for them to be controlled and we did not wait for the thumbs down. Instead of performing to their command the women attacked the 'aristocracy' and their bodyguards.

A political method sometimes used on such occasions was for politicians to keep cool, smile for the cameras and play everything down. If successful, this meant that, to the world at large, nothing had occurred. Our methods were the un-rehearsed actions of women who had spent a liftime fighting to survive and who could only express themselves in the ways that they knew how: irrational, emotional and close to the heart.

I could not hear a word of what anybody said in the stadium except for those at my side. The police had snatched away my loud hailer so I could not make any contribution to the noise. Eventually, the Chief Minister and others were convinced and sensibly decided to strategically withdraw. Others more difficult to convince decided to stay on, with police guards, to press their luck further and reason with the crowd.

The Chief Minister had to go to the airport to board a plane for Australia and, the next day, the press described his efforts thus:

> The women shouted down the Chief Minister's speech whenever it was translated into Motu. They constantly taunted the line of protecting police. Lines of police and a riot squad were used to protect the Chief Minister when he left the stadium. Women threw stones as they did when the Minister for Foreign Relations, Trade and Defence, left more than an hour before.

Those ministers and officials who did stay to appease the women gained little for their concern. They were shouted down and punched until they also departed and the women in the stadium made for their homes. Sometimes the best-intentioned plans of officials end in tatters. The women had proved the exception to the political rule that the man with the microphone always wins the argument.

Next morning, the front page of the press carried a large photograph of a government minister being thrown a mighty punch by a 'lady' demonstrator while he was protected by the highest-ranking white police officials in the land.

After the departure of the Chief Minister from the stadium a large group of women separated out and surrounded me.

They wanted to go to the airport to continue the 'war' there while the Chief Minister was leaving for Australia. A few hundred of us then left the stadium together while the rest of the women stayed behind.

Using my own trucks and any other transport we could secure, a few hundred of us managed to get to the airport. When the police woke up to the latest move by the unpredictable women, they hurriedly blocked the roads to the airport and searched vehicles for women and other contraband and blocked any more women from getting through. Police communications were being severely taxed.

By this time, the women with me were all warmed-up and ready for further action. We took over the airport and marched up and down singing and shouting slogans. The police, having been taken by surprise by the latest move, were mainly conspicuous by their absence. But the word had gone out and, belatedly, they began to arrive in large numbers to get the situation under control. When the women were confronted by the newly arrived police they stopped marching and began singing, dancing and shouting.

Several skirmishes with the police broke out and in one of them a young policeman had his cap knocked off and seized by a woman in the crowd. A matronly Papuan, a notable village dancer, donned the cap and began a song and dance routine of police on parade, which was part of her repertoire. This was greeted by shrieks of laughter. Another skirmish, with the police on attack, and the cap was recovered. A senior police constable then began to shout that police caps should not be treated disrespectfully as they belonged to the Queen. But all in vain, as the women defiantly retorted, 'I don't care. I'm the Queen of Papua. Put me in gaol.'

The Chief Minister finally got to the aircraft but not before further incident, as reported in the press the following day:

> Several grappled with police there and tried to force their way on to the tarmac.
>
> Two glass doors were broken and a woman was taken to hospital.
>
> Police lined the entrances to the tarmac and the Chief Minister was taken to the jet in a closed van, accompanied by the general manager of the national air carrier.

After the Chief Minister boarded the jet a riot squad armed with tear gas guns double-marched to the tarmac and stood guard until the plane taxied away.

One woman was seized by police and I grabbed her, repeating what had happened to me earlier in the day. Other women quickly came to my assistance. The tug-o-war between police and women was on again with the unfortunate Papuan woman suspended in between! Finally, remembering my own experience, I called to the women to let go so as to prevent further injury. She was then roughly treated as the police dragged her away and, unconscious, she was thrown to the floor of a police van. I started shouting that the woman had been killed and shouted to the police to take her to hospital.

The woman was driven off in a police van and I got in a vehicle and followed. It turned out that she was not permanently injured and, after a few days in hospital, she was discharged.

In the meantime, eight other women were arrested at the airport in different incidents and were charged with riotous behaviour and acting in an offensive manner.

The women wanted to continue the demonstrations the next day but I thought that we had gone far enough and should call it a day. The police, under the control of their white officers, had exercised as much restraint as they could get away with. Some white political advisers were advocating 'get tough' confrontations, while some senior experienced white police were advocating maximum restraint, based on their assessment of my background and real intentions. It was obvious for months that they were handling me with kid gloves.

The issues that I presented to the women at the first meeting of our women's demonstrations had long since receded to the background, and they were responding to the tensions within their communities to take active steps to gain our liberty and our rights.

The next step would have been open confrontation with colonialism on a large scale. This was the step, justified though it may have been for Papua, that I was not prepared to take. The women had made their point clear and I had gone far enough. It was time for me to cool the situation down. So I sent out word and told the women that there would be no more direct action until I called another meeting in a week's time.

Following this stage of the demonstration, the Commissioner for Police in PNG was quoted in the press:

> ...we have been reluctant to use strong measures because we have had faith in the overall common sense and community responsibility of the people of Port Moresby. But in the past two days police have been subjected to repeated acts of provocation.
>
> Continued disorderly behaviour and property damage would force police to use stronger measures.
>
> This will result in many people being arrested and being brought before the courts.

And the press reported the Chief Minister as saying that he had seen unarmed police taunted, struck with sticks and stoned by demonstrating women.

> I believe it was one of the most magnificent displays of courage and restraint in the face of very real provocation and total irresponsibility.

On the same day, an editorial in the Sydney Morning Herald appeared:

> ### MORESBY'S AMAZONS
> ...the political implications of the protests can be deducted from the leading role played by Papua's separatist firebrand, Miss Josephine Abaijah.
>
> ... They might reflect that the Amazons of Port Moresby are in no mood to bother with matters constitutional and felt that they have the muscle — literally — to make their criticisms felt.'

The next women's meeting was held on a public reserve at Kaugere, below the slums where I once had lived. The women were anxious to continue the confrontation and get on with the job but we marched five kilometres around the green grass of the old golf course instead. When the women first assembled and marched on Moresby, they did not know about the forgotten Hohola women's meeting or what the issues were. They were marching for their dignity and to demonstrate their worth. The men had done all of the demonstrating during the past months. The women had set out to show what they could do.

Standing on an improvised stage and using my damaged loud hailer which I had recovered from the police, I praised the women for their spirit and their victories. The women then took over the stage and testified through uninhibited speeches, songs and dances as to the nature of their feelings and their desire for involvement. I told them that this was a beginning and not an end. There would be another day when we would march and fight together. They were satisfied and we dispersed.

White police officers were pleased with the turn of events and they were loud in their praise of my initiative in calming the situation down. I was even congratulated on the standard of my performance — a sure sign that I had been a colonial 'good girl' for once.

* * *

I had no hatred for colonials and no love for the new democracy. Neither was worth fighting about. My only protest was that of a dog abandoned to consume the days with dreams of sultry vapours and wheeling, bleating sheep. My eyes no longer perceived the crisp dawn of a new day. My frame was lost to a spirit trapped in the recesses of my mind, dreary days of dreary time dragging back to abandoned memories.

Why not accept the hibiscus crown and feather my desires with paradise? Delinquency repaired can demand a stern price and can music its own fragility. The serpent tamed is more wondrous than the dove, the tiger bedded with the goat more wondrous than the hungry pig at the human breast.

Why seek purpose where none exists or follow the bird in its dance to prove that it must nest? Man will be man in any clime, will kill to favour a child, to pay for yesterday's follies, or build for tomorrow's dreams. Why *my* blood to paint an image for vacant minds whose keepers will breathe, eat and procreate under any bishop or crown, and shepherd their thoughts to any political jingle?

My image had taken flight to leave me in my present unreality. The soft down of the eagle's breast that coaxed love from the stiff armour of reality. Some aggression, love and faith must survive in every harmony. When God gave mind to Man he created the perfect self-starter. What was the nature of tyranny and what was the nature of justice?

PART SIX

Belly chasing back

1

Purify! Purify!

*T*he crocodile sighted its prey from the murky camouflage of the river, fetid with jungle offal and the atmosphere of impending violence.

In a secluded recess by the river bank, a village girl washed sago from the macerated pulp of a sago palm to the tune of dreams of the big city, important men, grand offices and escape from the oblivion of the nothingness of the swamp villages.

For a year her breasts had burst shamelessly upon her rounded body, first causing embarrassment and confusion but soon giving way to a warm feeling of unaccustomed value and attraction. Since she had been ten or eleven years old men had played at her seduction, but that was different. The games played by the boys and the limpid attentions of the grown men had given way to an awakening of a dangerous sexuality.

The girl smiled to herself as her eyes isolated her mother from the other women bent to their tasks further along the river bank. The mucilaginous extract from the sago pulp coursed in fine rivulets down the oil-moist skin to lap at the margins of the summer light rag hung deep on her hips. She was prepared for procreation but she dreamt of love instead. Yet eventually, she, like the rest, would absorb the passions as the sago absorbed the sun.

The crocodile had moved unobtrusively closer as its two motionless, beaded slugs of death held the girl in focus while the rest of the evil held its awesome power suspended in its mud-stained tenement.

An ancient magic of the river was bending to the incantations and red spit of a deep swamp sorcerer, who had been persuaded to dispose of the girl in return for a set of dog's teeth given by an angry man from another village. The girl, for her part, had turned her back on a family obligation that required her not to dream, but to move her unstained mat deeper into the swamp to be bonded to an unknown swamp dweller and to the swollen shafts of the matted sago.

The sorcerer and the crocodile were one. The soft scales of the reptile's belly now brushed the new mud of the river bank and, poised to strike, it was as motionless as death. As hushed as a maiden's thoughts, as swift as a lizard's tongue, the creature of violent death hurled its terrible head through space to crush the milkless breasts. One piercing anthem of death froze the river air and the girl was in the shallow waters pierced and wedded to death.

Round and round thrashed the crocodile, belly chasing back, in a wild exalted display of violent over-kill. The girl, beaten to exhaustion and deprived of breath, was now held with restrained savagery beneath the muddy water for an endorsement of death, as a red trickle pierced the colour of the muddy revelry.

The cries and commotions from the river bank drove the reptile to the safety of the deep where, with vain-glorious disregard, it surfaced with the dead girl in its mouth to sweep the river current with its tail and then make for the interior — a delivery to be made, a mission fulfilled.

Tyrants come in many forms — spotless, tailored dummies or bloodied warriors knee-deep in death. There must be resistance to tyranny or acceptance of slavery or death. But, is every resistance a violence? Must every violence end in death? Round and round thrashed the crocodile, belly chasing back, and the mucilage of love spermed the devil's child of death.

* * *

'Drive me to Paga Point,' I said to Dina. Lately, I had had an urge to do some of the things we used to do when life was less complicated than it was now.

We had returned earlier than expected from a village fund-raising drive to move a marine village to dry land. Sunday was the only day when we had a chance of being left alone. Sundays were great when troubles took a holiday. Not much happened on Sunday that could not be put off to the next day when the clocks started to tick again. Most Sundays were spent in the villages as it was the day the villagers spent together.

From Paga Point we could see the broad sweep of the Pacific on one side and the harbour, dotted with large and small craft of two worlds, on the other. Graceful outrigger canoes, with square canvas sails, skimmed the waters like flying fish while two large foreign vessels waited fretfully. These foreign ships looked huge here, but when I chanced to see them tied up overseas, they were greatly diminished in size. It was always cool when we were at Paga Point. It was the market of the sea breezes.

'You must be feeling sentimental,' said Dina as we walked to one of our old familiar spots. 'It's a long time since you've been here.'

'Not so long,' I said, slowly looking towards the white stretches of Ela Beach with Koki in the distance.

'I came here the other day. I had something to work out. Once I could not stand being on my own but now I'm beginning to find myself better company. Might be a sign of old age!'

'More likely a sign of growing up,' said Dina, always ready to respond when I was fishing for a compliment. 'You want to be careful wandering around places like this on your own. You might get yourself killed.'

'Oh, I didn't get out of the car,' I said cheerfully. 'Like in one of the lion parks we've visited.'

'Those animals don't smash car windows but some of the animals around here do.'

'I'm careful. You know that. That's something you taught me.' Then, changing the subject to something closer to my thoughts, I said, 'I walked into politics with my eyes open. But I'm not so sure now.'

'Do you want to run away?'

'No, I don't want to run away,' I said emphatically. 'There's nowhere to run to. I can't run away from myself but I must aim at something definite. Something I can achieve. I can't accept survival as the only political goal.'

'You can achieve anything you set your mind to, Jo,' said Dina. 'You have courage and single-mindedness to burn.'

Here, on this very spot, we had talked out the meanings of motivation, change, needs and even definitions. A queer sort of love talk. Some people listen to a juke-box or play pin ball machines and say nothing. We talked and planned the days away. Juke-boxes or selling ideas were much the same to lovers. It is knowing when and how to relax that paved the rocky way and kept you walking. Knowing how to touch and how to feel. Love without warmth was like a tomato without a skin. It didn't take long to fall to pieces.

Our conversations were never dull. Theories had to be fashioned into tools that could be used in the coming days. Always urgent and vital, they were our arms for the coming encounters. The logistics of life, the by-products of expression, love and belief, with bonuses of security, adventure, and success. It wasn't difficult to stay in love.

'Your greatest victory has been your victory over yourself,' said Dina, pausing to etch his shadow as it lengthened in the afternoon sun. 'You have never let the people down. You have never taken the easy way. You have never been easy on yourself. Your beauty is timeless, Jo, because you and time are friends. You don't bother one another. There's no need to sully yourself with any harsh deeds. You will be remembered, in the warm earth, for love long after cold marble has been scattered by the next wave of self-seeking humans.'

I played with the idea of denying that I was worried with the thoughts of 'harsh deeds' but this would have been too transparent a lie for him to have swallowed. So, instead, I demurely mocked him.

'I prefer to continue to grow in your garden, if you don't mind. I don't want to be dead in warm earth or in cold marble.'

'I don't mind; go ahead. While you're there I need not plant another thing. All you need is a little water. In you is all the love and beauty that any man can expect.'

'What about direct action to gain our freedom like many of our people want to take?' I asked, coming to the point of my conversation. 'Is force in any form wrong? There must be some limit to submissiveness. A point where it is right to defend ourselves.'

'Force is wrong if you think it's wrong,' Dina said, rubbing my forearm with the back of his hand to reassure me. 'There's no more violence in you than in that yellow hibiscus in your hair. Violent people may win a short confrontation because they are more willing to use a gun. You don't have to sink to their level. In politics between countries it's even worse as there are no rules to say who is the crook and who is the victim. They make up the rules as they go along. It's all a matter of self-interest. Right and wrong hardly come into it.'

I turned to Dina and said, 'I want to give our people an alternative history. That's the least I can do. Preserve for us the right to decide for ourselves in the future. The people have been bullied long enough. We'll carry out protests until I declare Papua independent and free from colonial humbug. Then I can let the matter rest. The people will grow strong in the future. Then it will be up to them to accept or reject our alternative history. Time will tell.'

'And no violence?' asked Dina.

'Not if I can help it,' I replied. 'But I'm not God, remember?'

Round and round thrashed the crocodile, belly chasing back, and I returned to my garden and to the safety of my love.

* * *

We headed for a white cruise ship that was anchored in the harbour. A small white cutter with crew dressed in ascetic white uniforms had ferried us from the jetty.

'You get what you pay for,' noted Dina, as our elbows were respectfully elevated as we alighted on the gangway.

The passengers had paid plenty for small doses of sun and exotica with much 'five star' refinement for the remainder. There had been three or four unscheduled deaths among the passengers and this had dampened proceedings for awhile. But now the travellers had accepted the inevitability of the final challenge and, in the meantime, were determined to get as much as they could for their money.

As we climbed the gangway, Dina looked over his shoulder and said, 'It's a funny place to find an Indonesian student, isn't it? I thought that they were as poor as church mice. He must be the exception.'

A feature writer with an Asian magazine had sought me out to tell me that an Indonesian, a fellow student I had met in India, whilst travelling and studying on a World Health Organisation Scholarship was on a cruise ship anchored in the harbour and that he was anxious for me to come to the ship to see him.

'It does seem posh,' I said as I put my feet on the deck and looked around at the spick and span ship. 'When he was a student with me he didn't have much money, but he did have plenty of talk about Indonesia. Some kind of a nationalist, I guess. I suppose he has been on an assignment and is now making his way back to Indonesia.'

We had arrived early and many of the passengers were still at dinner so we amused ourselves enjoying the novelty of idle comfort, one of the good things of life that we seldom had time to make use of.

'Howdy folks,' came a friendly voice over my shoulder. 'Sure is a nice breeze out here. I'm Edward Fowler, Edward D. Fowler, junior. Are you folk joining us for the rest of the journey? I hope so. Live and let live, I say. Personally, I like plenty of variety. Stirs the folks up a bit to mix with people different from their own. Travelling is education.'

'Sorry,' I said, addressing the flamboyant character who was complete with dazzling island shirt and broad accent. 'We belong here. We're waiting for an Indonesian friend who is still at dinner.'

'Thought you were an Indonesian or something with that

long dress. A sarong, Lil said it was. Mighty pretty.'

'May I introduce ourselves. I'm Josephine and this is Dina,' I said. Talking to some Americans made me sound almost British.

'How do you do, sir. Pleased to meet you,' said Edward Fowler, turning to Dina. 'We were admiring the sarong dress your wife is wearing. Mighty pretty.'

'That shirt you're wearing isn't bad either,' said Dina, brightly. 'With that around you don't need to take any pictures of the islands.'

'Guess you're right,' said Edward Fowler. 'When in Rome do what the Romans do. That's what I say,' our convivial companion laughed. 'The only sin, I say, is not to enjoy yourself.' More boisterous laughter.

'What did you think of Moresby,' I said to change the subject. 'Did you have a chance to look around?'

'Sure. It was fantastic. I took eight rolls of film. Some of the folks back home won't believe me. Boy, are some of those nig...er, er, natives, primitive. You know, some of them still wear grass skirts around here. Fantastic. Some of those gals aren't that bad to look at either. No wonder those thieving missionaries like the country. And on our money.' And more laughter. 'You won't believe this but I got a photograph of one of the women feeding a pig with her own milk. I bet you've never seen anything like that before. Fantastic. They warned me to expect anything here. Very primitive country.'

'Did you see Koki market?' asked Dina, pleased to be entertained by someone else talking for a change.

'Sure I did,' said Edward Fowler. 'I saw some of the most goddam awful food I've ever seen. A civilised man would die if he ate it. Strings of fish straight out of the water, bats, turtles, crocodiles, possums, pigs and every kind of creature. Fruits and vegetables on banana leaves, as cheap as water. I took a lot of film.'

'What did you dislike about our town?' I asked, anxious to get his reactions. I did not have the courage to call it a city.

'The goddam awful weather. I couldn't take that for long. Lil spent the whole day lying under a fan in the cabin, exhausted and drinking iced mineral water. Get up and face it I said to her but she wasn't listening.'

'Anything else you didn't like?' said Dina, more anxious to know what people disliked than what they liked.

Likes can be universal while dislikes are often personal. A Taj Mahal, fresh mountain snow or kindness to a stranger will not dismay many, but a smell, an unmade bed or a single tiny bug can release torrents of emotions.

'There's one thing I didn't like,' Edward Fowler said with conviction. 'I don't believe there's a toilet in this whole goddam town, if that's what they call it. As I said to Lil, when I got back, you can tell the friendliness of a town by the number of its toilets. Those natives must have exanding pouches, like kangaroos or something.'

Dina came to the rescue. 'The natives relieve themselves anywhere. Behind a bush, sitting in the sea, anywhere convenient. They haven't got expanding pouches. They also have plenty of 'boy houses'.'

'Well, I'll be damned. The critters. I'll know what to do the next time I'm in this country. Wait until Lil hears this. The next time we go out here we'll take our bathers.'

Lil had appeared in the doorway and Edward Fowler excused himself and left to join her. 'Have a good time in Indonesia,' he called cheerfully and left us with a cordiality as lively as his greeting.

I had met American missionaries. They were usually quiet, hard-working people many with leanings towards scholarly activities, but I had met more American tourists. We had often used them as a guide as to where not to stay. Not that we disliked their company, but we disliked competing with the American dollar. I must have heard every kind of American accent from those who sound like other 'Europeans', to those whose conversations, to me, was unintelligible. When I first went to the Philippines, I had trouble with the Filipinos because I did not have an American accent.

But the American tourists I liked best were the talkative ones. They wanted to be friendly, especially to people like me who were 'undeveloped'. They talked easily and were content if they got a smooth passage, a good hotel and sanitary water.

I wanted to be liked too, so we got on well together and I

could laugh as heartily as they could. But I always kept out of their way when someone fouled a booking, the bed-sheets looked soiled or someone delivered a cockroach with a breakfast. Themes such as these could provide non-stop conversation for the rest of the journey!

I found relaxation in easy talk and laughter. For this reason I often had regrets with journalists. Most of them treated me generously but some special feature writers took an angle and a line of conversation that was only an authority to print their own story. Some I could trust to a point but I found it exhausting to be continually on the defensive. Relax for a second and, the next day, the golliwog could pop out of the box with the latest fiction.

We were still waiting to see our Indonesian friend on the cruise ship. 'It's a romantic night,' I said to Dina as an outrigger canoe breezed over the surface of the water on its way to the village. 'It is easy to picture the *Basilisk* nosing its way into the harbour, and Captain Moresby and his men nosing their way into the villages, expecting cannibals and wild savages but, instead, losing their hearts to unexpected kindness and hospitality.'

'One of the pleasant experiences in life is kindness where it is unexpected,' said Dina.

I nodded towards the lights of the harbour village of Hanuabada and said, 'When I look at the lights of Koki as I drive at night or the lights of Hanuabada as they are now, my spirit thrills to the thoughts of what might have been and I am filled with wonder at our share of beauty. If I could have one wish come true, I would wish that the beauty of this moment would last forever.'

'The beauty of this moment will last forever but it can only be seen through eyes as clear as yours.'

'Don't you feel it, too?'

'I feel you. I feel no beauty beyond you. You are my frangipani perfume, my hibiscus crown, the sound of my music, my moonlit village, the falling star, the dew of my mornings, the dreams of my nights. My Venus, my Aladdin and all of my lamps of love.'

I held the growing moon in my attention for awhile and said, 'Love can be a set of chains that you have to drag through life. Love can be a thief that steals your moments and keeps you home at nights. It keeps you young for its own violations and makes you old with the shallow satisfactions of its own release. Perfume may be bought in bottles and pussy-cats are soft to touch. Love is a bait, not a meal. A means, not an end. A vice that dulls the senses and ties man to his wheel. Many follies can be bought with the satisfactions of love. Every time a man's virility is tapped and he sleeps in the night, the devil laughs and plans the next assault.'

Dina joined me in my involvement with the mood of the growing moon and softly said, 'You talk of beauty and I talk of love. Now you talk of sex, the thief of love. Is this my punishment for too much intrusion on your thoughts?'

'I am not thinking of anything but cold and warmth, hunger and food, dark and light, hardness and softness, a steady hand in the dawn of every day and the trusting breath of children in the quietness of the night. Am I an ungrateful lover because I look for beauty as well as love, for fulfilment as well as release, for the sugar as well as the spice?'

'Love is not the only cheat,' said Dina softly, audible only because of the stillness of the night. 'You keep a man a student of your beauty and feminine perversity for fifteen years and then deny him the diploma of his success. To you, how long is life? What does a man have to do to qualify? Does he qualify in death or does he qualify in flight?'

I turned my attentions from the moon to more fully observe the man by my side. 'I shall give you your diploma if that's all you want but I'll give you the lesser diploma of love. Beauty is simple. Love is complex. Simple things are hardest to learn. Beauty is the Taj Mahal by moonlight, love is the rocket's flight. I shall give you your diploma in love, but must hold the diploma in beauty until another time. If love is to know you always, before the dawn and beyond the night, across the earth and in the stars; to span the space and calm the flight, then I give to you the diploma in my love and declare you qualified.'

'Thank you kind professor of love and beauty,' said Dina, sharing my glance. 'I now have a certificate that entities me to be your slave and I must now study for the Diploma in Beauty, so that I can also understand this and the remaining barriers between us will be torn down. This isn't the Taj by moonlight, but it is you. As a graduate in love, am I now permitted to kiss you in the ordinary moonlight falling on Hanuabada's handsome palms?'

'You are now qualified to do what you like with me within the bounds of love, but remember the devil finds work for idle hands. Also, before we think of love we must now think of your additional responsibilities. You are now a student of beauty and it's time for the first lesson. Love is better enjoyed in the mornings for there is so much beauty in the night. It's time for the first lesson to start. I trust you will never cease to be a student by my side.'

'Proceed, Professor, proceed. My senses are at your disposal and my love has been sedated and sent to bed to dream. The wind drops and hot grows the night.'

'The first lesson in beauty starteth thus: In heaven and on earth there is no beauty equal to a Papuan moon on Papuan palms. Tambourines of the soft winds, harps of the violent seas. So to summarise the first lesson please write down and memorise: 'Beauty is where the heart is and a savage land has mine.'

'Thank you, Professor, I shall memorise. Will it take another fifteen years to qualify for the diploma in beauty?'

'Perhaps longer, my child. Perhaps very much longer. Simple things are the hardest to learn. As beauty is the most accessible of all, it takes the longest time. During the time that it took you to teach me how to fool my way to the top you have only just qualified in love, and beauty still remains. We have many years of study ahead. It may be disadvantageous to qualify in too much too quickly, or that which we see together may be lost in the separateness of our ways. Do you understand me fully?'

'I understand and accept your wisdom without reservation, Professor Venus. But, may I now hold your hand in this beautiful Papuan moon, most sensuous of lights?'

'As I told you, you are now qualified in love so you may do anything you like with me that you have already learned in your wide field experience, but please excuse, not now, for our Indonesian friend approaches. The object of our present mission is come and I have need of my hand to greet him with.'

'I hate all Indonesians,' said Dina as he wheeled around impatiently, almost falling into Mr Bukittinggi's outstretched hand.

'Hello, Miss Abaijah, nice to greet you after all this time.'

'Nice to see you too, Mr Bukittinggi,' I said cordially, shaking his hand. 'I never expected to see you in my country. It's a small world.'

Some Asians are no good at shaking hands. Their handshake is like an apology for something. They are better at bowing and keeping both hands ready for the next move.

'Please meet my companion, Dr Dina,' I said, turning to Dina. 'Mr Bukittinggi is an old school mate of mine. We were students together in India.'

'Miss Abaijah very smart lady,' said Mr Bukittinggi, still beaming but showing more of his teeth than before. 'She is very smart at communication. Her English very good, also. I do not speak good English, but good for Indonesian. I speak some Dutch, also.'

Dina looked at me and then at Mr Bukittinggi and said, 'Did they give you a diploma after your work in India?'

'Yes they did. Thank you. Only take few months.'

'You're lucky,' said Dina. 'Some of the diplomas we have around here take fifteen years, that's if you live that long.'

'My word, that very long. Good things take long time. Please come and sit down,' said Mr Bukittinggi, beckoning us to a table. 'Please come and sit down. Nice and cool out here. I came back this way because I like to see Port Moresby. You see, after I return to Jakarta, I have to go to Irian... West Irian to work. So I like to see you first. I hope you do not mind?'

We talked for a couple of hours about things of interest in Indonesia and in Papua New Guinea, particularly communications, politics and people. In India we called him Mr Tingi, for short, and used the rest of his name as a prefix on appropriate occasions. He did not mind the abbreviation. He was a mild mannered man who spoke from his heart, and was a transparently prejudiced salesman when it came to selling his own country.

'I am very interested in your country, Mr Bukittinggi. We share a common border. PNG only has three million people. We are very small. The whole population of Oceania is less than one per cent of the population of the world.'

'Our population is over 150 000 000,' said Mr Bukittinggi. 'Population control is my work now. We still increase by more than two per cent a year. It is too much.'

'Every year your population increase is equal to our whole population. Where is it going to end?'

'We can all live together but we do not know the future,' said Mr Bukittinggi. 'In Indochina almost every country is under pressure from China, Russia or America. My own country will be sensitive about what is happening here. Pressures are sure to occur. As one bloc we can work together. We must not work as though we are in separate worlds. Much trouble will come from that.'

'Do you think my country will ever join with your country, Indonesia? We are like the Papuans of West Irian.'

'It might be better that way. I do not know. I think it might happen some day. Together we would share the same problem. Everyone is forming blocs for trade and protection, like Europe and South East Asia.'

'Some white people here say you do not like Christians.'

'That is not true. There are many Christians in Indonesia. It is one of our biggest religions. Our constitution allows religious freedom. It is only when religion becomes political that there is trouble. The same with other things.'

I signalled to Dina and we got up to depart. 'Thank you for an interesting talk, Mr Bukittinggi. Thank you for being so frank with us.'

Mr Bukittinggi rose to his feet and said, 'I tell you these things because I trust you. I talk as an Indonesian. I do not think much about Papua and New Guinea. We think of East Irian as a part of one island, Irian. I think our countries can trust one another.'

'We will have to trust one another if we are going to live together.' I said making for the gangway.

'Of course I only talk as one Indonesian. Others may see things differently.'

'That applies to all of us.'

'Goodnight Mr Bukittinggi. Safe journey to Indonesia.'

'Goodnight, Miss Abaijah. My country is not far away. See you again some day.'

'Goodnight.'

The small craft nudged its way into the shore jetty and, ahead of the crew, Dina took upon himself the service of easing me to the safety of the land.

* * *

Days with my work, nights with my plight; I thought that I should take my love and go to my dreams. A touch, a look, a smile and I was lost in time. To awake and dream: colour of colours, smell of smells, laughter of laughter, freshness of raindrops, in love with love and frangipani sweetness. Papua was splendid now. The blue-green country was carelessly tinselled with reds and yellows, while down the straight palms came brown men and boys emerging from the sun, and from under the canopies of green and white came women and girls fresh with frangipani love.

The boys ran to the edge of the jungle where elephants, with yellow crocheted hats and twinkling bells, lifted them with supple trunks to their backs before ambling forward on sturdy legs to water in the limpid pools and curtsy to delicate, colourful butterflies.

The girls separated out, ran to the white beach and, discarding their scarlet rags to bleach, tripped over the uneven broken waves to plunge into the bluer deep, to emerge minutes later grasping multicoloured fish.

The women had gathered the children in a sand-flooded nursery, under a roof of palms, and were instructing them in the SDL of island education — song, dance and love.

Men were busy parting old coconuts from their shells and making copra of banana leaves drying in the sun. Others sat in council in a palm-thatched Parliament house, sipping coconut wine and, to the ancient rhythm of the drums, deliberated on how and where the country should be governed.

The fish, the copra and the council were dropped as village and nursery shouted 'Cricket!' and, one and all, joined together around a great television screen in the centre of the village. The annual cricket match between Papua and New Guinea for the Bird of Paradise Shield had begun.

The Papuan champion, Sisia Dau (Longway Dog) had connected with a heavenly swipe that deposited the ball fair on Sir Fairfax Moresby's marbled head, to bounce into the sea and be lost. The general store of Burns Philp and Co. had to be opened to get another ball before play could be resumed. The people danced in the villages and streets and all further work was suspended until the last ball was bowled and Papua won. Then the dance, the songs and the night.

The sun came up and we returned to our work, fulfilled and relaxed. The elephants were still at the water pools flirting with the butterflies, and a team of monkeys scampered back and forth feeding them choice herbs and grasses gathered from the jungle's edge. The fish that the girls had committed to their breasts as they dashed to the white sands, had turned to seductive dugongs, half fish and half women, and had slipped into the sea. The copra was twisting skywards as it toasted in the sun.

The only things that had not prospered in our absence was the national Parliament, which complained it had nobody to govern, and the empty nursery, which complained that it had nobody to teach the S and D of love as the children were still celebrating the cricket.

* * *

When I awoke, the sun was streaming through the eastern louvres of my room and the children were already absorbed with the task of getting ready for school. Why was everything so subdued? Where was the carefree laughter I had known? Where were my dreams?

The dogs in the front of the house were barking as sullen men shouted obscenities from the street below while they made their way to nowhere and the Port Moresby streets. Tired-looking people were already gathering on the grass outside my side gate with the coarseness of the night still heavy on their minds: men and women of the settlements and villages who had come early to be among the first to place their worries in my inexperienced hands.

Without Dina this part of my work would have been impossible and, as it was, it took up far more time than I could afford. Yet it brought me a lot of satisfaction and kept me close to the people and the real conditions under which they lived. Why were the people so depressed? Where had the laughter gone?

2

Dare to live

I first heard the voices of the Ancestor Spirits when I returned to my native village, Wamira, on the north-east coast of Papua, for the opening of a new village church. I was born on the sands of this beach but had grown to early womanhood on a romantic south sea island, adrift in the Coral Sea. My important memories were all of Misima Island and not of Wamira. Still, this was my native village and this was my first native tongue. In Wamira, I could see no sign of change or evidence of progress. Twenty years of sleep. Forgotten and forgetting. Every track and every pebble in durable mould. Changes were cell for cell and the features stayed the same. A stone replaced a stone, a sand a sand, a tide a tide, in endless changeless procession.

One hot afternoon, while the villagers rested, I felt an inner compulsion to return to the okari nut tree where I was born to purify my mind of present shames and find purpose for my efforts. And, sitting in quiet vigil, I heard the voices.

The wind dusting the okari tree with summer laughter and a pig squealing in anger were the only companions to my thoughts as I descended deeper and deeper within myself. The sounds turned to music, and the music turned to voices. I felt no fear or disquiet, only a detachment of my spirit. My spirit had deserted me to frolic with the strangers. Improper elf of brazen deeds, stranger than the strangers, ejaculate your follies. Then, in a trilogy of tongues — Misima, Wedau, Motu — the spirits spoke their drama.

Spirit Voices:
Daughter of the soil and sands of Wamira.
Daughter of the dreams and romance of Misima.
Daughter of the cross of Papua.
Speak and we shall answer.

Daughter of Papua:
I speak for guidance not in anger, my nebulous spirits of summer laughter.
I am your daughter of the soil, your daughter of dreams, your daughter of Papua, but I am lost in devious paths and need to know your answers.

I spoke in the unknown tongue of faithless, foreign masters which echoed back in vibrant song — my trilogy of Papua.

A depression of the spirit has spread its gossamer on the wind until there is no man or woman who does not feel it resting ponderous on his mind.

Spirit Voices:
In everything that is bought and sold seek out that which cannot be bought and sold and this is what you need to multiply. Seek out the men and women who trade for lust and gain that which is not theirs to trade. The heartworms of the tribe. These you must divide. They are the worms that ride the richest fruits and poison the cleanest minds.
Purify! Purify!

Daughter of Papua:
Once we spent little and governed little.
Now we spend much and govern much.
But we were happier before than we are now?

Spirit Voices:
The rulers should be ruled. Rulers should be people
    not parasites. No privileges, no gold, no pride. And,
    when they depart the obscenity, the only medal
    struck should be for self-effacing service and self-
    sacrifice. Freed and thanked, to limp to the
    obscurity of the crowd, to vanish and learn again
    how people live and children die.
Purify! Purify!

Daughter of Papua:
And how may the people prosper in the present
    climate?

Spirit Voices:
Some have already disgraced our people. Minds rank
    with distortions make virtues out of white man's
    evils. Fingers festered with larceny proportion the
    crops. Without love they spill their passions on the
    passing sands and achieve nothing. Those who talk
    with forked tongues forget their promises. Some
    who were to lead the way to the promised land are
    lost among the golden idols.
Papua must be cleansed.
Purify! Purify!

Daughter of Papua:
I, also, have seen these things. But, how do we cleanse
    ourselves of these evil things?

Spirit Voices:
Do not live on the garbage of other people's ways. Do
    not change one corruption for another, one master
    for another. Be free without distortion, happy
    without envy, proud without insolence and exercise
    authority with humility. Develop the people not the
    worms and parasites. Make idolatry an unprofitable
    luxury. Dare to live.
Purify! Purify!

Daughter of Papua:
I have no ambitions. I seek no place or pride. I want to
    serve the people. How may they develop the courage
    and the ways?

Spirit Voices:
Seek your own ambition and your own pride.

Develop your own courage and discipline first.
Do not talk with forked tongue.
Do not worship the golden idols of power.
Be mild and constant in your ways.
Write your message on tablets of stone.
The good of the chaste prophet is stronger than the
vanity of the false king.
Purify! Purify!

The voices turned to music, the music to wind, the wind to trees. A child laughed in the village and I was whole again. Wayward spirit of unchaste schemes, are you harnessed to my bones again? We must away on lonely ways, strangers to strangers, enigma to our dreams.

I did not have the courage to be a martyr so I chose a softer duty—I dared to live. I dared to do what I thought was right. On March 16, 1975, I made a unilateral declaration of independence declaring Papua a free and independent country and disassociated from any further acts of colonial perfidy. I did this not only to give my country an alternative history but to restore some dignity and pride.

March 16 was chosen for the declaration because it was rumoured that Australia was going to discard us in April and I was determined that our show would come first. As it turned out, we ended our demonstrations prematurely.

My threat of a unilateral declaration of independence for Papua worried the colonials and the pre-independence government, and severely taxed the policy of playing everything down and avoiding open confrontation; of avoiding anything that would bring publicity. They ended up playing it both ways. Some tried to play down my activities while, at the same time, firing their own guns. They were anxious to ensure that history was well informed on their propriety. We were already wrapped for delivery but they wanted to secure the future against the awakening. Doing what was ordered by the masters was an established way of life.

* * *

A hasty meeting was called by politicians for some Papuan senior civil servants and members of the PNG Parliament. At this meeting, a prepared statement condemning my actions was read out and accepted. Later this was formally read out in the PNG Parliament and recorded in Hansard so future researchers would be provided with the bones of history.

When the statement was concluded I was firmly denounced. Several times I attempted to make a counter statement but, each time, I was gagged or abused as was the custom in the white man's democracy. So the parliamentary records remained unstained by any hint of controversy.

Three days before my declaration of independence, the carefully prepared statement that was read and recorded in the PNG Parliament was published in the national press as a paid advertisment, duly edged in black. The statement was recorded in Parliament but no 'counter-statement or reply. This was an un-Papuan like gesture. A rejection of our ways. Our way was consensus where the voice of everyone was heard.

As the day of the unilateral declaration of Papuan independence approached the air was thick with condemnations of me, but after three years of abuse from colonials and politicians I had developed some immunity. Merit could be earned at bargain rates by denouncing me! The condemnation of anyone who claimed to talk for a church, a committee or a man was gladly received and given wide publicity. Still, any meeting or demonstration by village Papuans against me personally was noticably absent from the scene, and there was no counter to the witness of the hundreds of public demonstrations and protests that I had seen and the tens of thousands of Papuans who openly supported me and were ready to take action for their cause. It seemed that all a person had to do was to sit in an easy chair and abuse me to prove that Papuans were willingly committing their country into the hands of U N New Guinea without exercising any choice or considering any alternatives. Even those who did not and could not speak never made this choice.

Wherever I went the people welcomed me enthusiastically. Some of them spoke of influential people, talking of killings, kidnappings and starvation if we did not join up with the U N New Guinea: a return of the blackbirding days on a grand scale. This was spearheaded by the Australian threats of

'Unite or be starved' of money or any kind of recognition. All people in government work would lose their jobs, and all government assistance to villagers would cease. Abaijah had no money. These were the popular cries. This was political education in Papua after a century of nothing. Yet, in the hundreds of villages that I was able to visit, north, east, and west, the people raised their hands in salute for 'hands off Papua'.

There was no way for an individual to suddenly communicate with the whole of Papua at one time or compete with the funds and hundreds of workers in a government machine. But, despite the bombardment, the Papuans of the settlements and villages of Port Moresby and central Papua remained unmoved. The people whom I refused to desert during my years in Parliament.

The distant villagers who were beyond communication continued undisturbed, sleeping under the heavy mantle of colonial unreality. Unseeing and unseen they repeated a changeless scene. The sore of colonialism heals from the centre to the edges. The concentric spread of the awakening.

This Parliament was not a government of Papua. It was a government of Papua and New Guinea that had been granted a form of self-government dependent on Australian laws, money, technicians and advisers, and was heavily dependent on the assistance of Australian sympathisers who were working within the political machine.

Dina and foreign journalists warned me to go easy and there were plenty of threats, so I developed the habit of looking behind me constantly. My personal experience with the colonial police was reasonably good so I was mainly concerned with secret agents who might be let loose on me. These were the instruments of white civilization that I was warned about. I was already guilty of an 'unpardonable crime'. I dared to live with a conscience but I did not dare to die.

The *modus operandi* for the two countries of Papua and New Guinea to be jointly administered by Australia was approved by the United Nations in the case of U N New Guinea and the Australian Parliament in the case of Papua. The Papua and New Guinea Act of the Australian Parliament (1949–1971) declared the intention of the Commonwealth of Australia to maintain the status and identity of New Guinea as a Trust Territory of the United Nations, and to maintain the identity and status of Papua as a possession of the Crown. Papua was first declared a protectorate of Great Britain and, later, a possession of the Crown.

This was the state of affairs when I was elected to Parliament in 1972. It was the state of affairs when Australian government ministers were publicly stating that the Australian territory of Papua would be cut off from all Australian money and recognition unless we politically joined with U N New Guinea. Changes to this Act were pushed through the Australian Parliament as it tipped its hat to say good-bye.

* * *

The Port Moresby City Council was the largest and most significant freely-elected council in PNG. Members who represented the Papuan villages and settlements around the city supported a free and independent Papua.

On June 18, 1974, the Port Moresby City Council passed a resolution that Papua should be a free and independent country and that there should be no political union between Papua and UN New Guinea.

In February 1975, the Port Moresby City Council passed a resolution that the Council supported the unilateral declaration of Papuan independence to be declared by me on March 16, 1975.

In August 1975, as the PNG independence date approached, the Port Moresby City Council passed a resolution that its controlling members would make a trip overseas to declare their opposition to Papua being forced into a political union with UN New Guinea.

A typical colonial response to the Port Moresby City Council's action appeared in the Australian *National Times* of August 11, 1975, where the City Council was described as:

a thoroughly inept body which favours the city's Papuan communities in its public works program and which the Government can be expected to abolish eventually.

Elsewhere in the same article, it was reported that an Australian television current affairs program about me revealed that we were lecturing Papuans on 'how Papuan guerrilla fighters could forestall regular army units.' Heavy international intrigue fed to gullible Australians for consumption with their Sunday dinner of roast mutton, baked potatoes and green peas. The reason for the threatened abolition of the Port Moresby City Council was not mentioned in the *National Times* and was left for other writers to record. On August 23, 1974, the *Sydney Morning Herald* reported:

> The Chief Minister has ordered the Port Moresby City Council to cancel a $25,000 world tour planned as part of the council's campaign for Papuan independence.
>
> (The Chief Minister), in a letter to the Lord Mayor, said the government would suspend the council if the trip went on.
>
> It was more than apparent that the council was 'fostering a program of disunity' (the Chief Minister) said...
>
> ... 'It goes without mention that the Government has no alternative but to intervene in such an exercise as the proposed trip. I am now directing you to cancel the trip and demand an answer within 24 hours' (the Chief Minister) said.
>
> However, should the council remain adamant following this instruction the following will eventuate:
>
> Councillors will tour of their own accord as private citizens and not as members of the council and action will be taken to suspend the council'.

These requirements made impossible demands on poor Papuans who lived from week to week. The money squeeze. Following the Australian lead, 'unite or starve' was the order of the day in the months leading up to the union of Papua with U N New Guinea. There would be two independences. The United Nations would grant independence to U N New Guinea, and Australia would grant independence to Papua. The two countries were then to be united by a joint constitution! A complicated real estate deal.

So the Australians slept on. Nothing but the direct action

that many Papuans were calling for would have aroused
them from their indifference. This was my failure as a
leader. I should have accepted the people's way. I had dared
to live with my conscience but I could not meet the sterner
demands. Heavy demands for a Papuan girl raised to love
and serve all who came her way. I had travelled a long way
but not far enough to serve the people who had trusted me.
Many of them had been schooled in harder ways than I had.
In me, the tiger and the lamb kept constant company. I was
a failure but would not admit my shame.

I needed to think again and order my mind to ancesteral
ways. A daughter of cannibals and savages should be built of
sterner mind. I should heed the spirit voices and be purified.
I should sharpen my ambitions and be prepared to lead the
way. I had not shaken off the mentality of colonial servitude.
I had to dare to fight and dare to win. Dare to live and dare
to die: a lonely call to find a place in the heart of a woman in
love. I would have to learn to hate before they would chisel
me in stone.

Yet the gentleness of Christ was not a craven's mask. The
warm fire of His love was not spread by those who sought an
early paradise. Little by little, person by person, His love
was spread by those who dared to live and not by those who
sought to die. The whole world does not awaken to the same
sunrise. Truth has no existence until it fills a vacant mind. It
takes courage to love. Death is inevitable. It takes courage to
expect. 'Well done thou good and faithful servant' is earned
by the quick, not by the dead.

* * *

Before the unilateral declaration of independence, secret
meetings were held by a large number of Papuan senior
public servants, including some departmental heads. They
came together to support the independence of Papua and
issued a statement:

> Because of our positions in the Papua New Guinea Public Service
> and fear of reprisal action we cannot sign our names. We are
> Senior Public Servants who support the other Papuan leaders
> who call for Papua to be an independent nation...

... We have given careful consideration to the future of Papua and have reached the conclusion that we as Papuans have no choice but to give our full support to Papua and to help form its own government independent from Australia and New Guinea and therefore support the establishment of the Republic of Papua.

As March 16 approached the police began to close in on me and my movements were monitored. Spies appeared in our midst under different guises. We cut out all telephone conversations between our different contacts. Nobody knew how or when we were going to make the declaration of independence.

Despite the hundreds of marches, public meetings and demonstrations that I had held with tens of thousands of people, and the constant and repeated support of the Port Moresby City Council, the policy of the colonials was to whitewash the declaration of Papuan independence and play down the opposition of Papuans to their schemes. They planned a *fait accompli* and then a retreat to behind the scene.

It was not possible to hold a meeting of tens of thousands of rural villagers in Port Moresby as this would involve a major transport movement. One hundred trucks carrying fifty people would only shift five thousand people and the drivers would all be breaking the law for overloading. The police or the army would merely block the two main roads into Port Moresby, the same as the police did to the truck loads of Papuan villagers during the New Guinea uprising. Such a gathering was only possible when the people came to the city for another purpose, such as the Queen's visit.

First we set up a decoy to stop police from interfering with our independence declarations. They may have had no such intentions but there was no way that we could know in advance. By the way that they had been watching my movements there was something in the air. We had to give them something tangible to get their teeth into. We did this by calling a public meeting to be held on a public reserve in Port Moresby for the Sunday afternoon, while we intended to declare Papua independent on the Sunday morning in each of the large Papuan villages and settlements separately.

The meeting on the public reserve was to be just the final repetition of the ceremony. It was to be held for Papuans from a few housing settlements in the town. But, by the time of this meeting, independence would have been declared in many village communities, including all of the villages involved in the earliest events of our colonial history. The British, when they took control of our country, made the declaration in several different villages.

Early on Saturday, a group of us went to the residence of the Australian High Commissioner. In the group were two of the eldest Motu landowners whose lives went back to early colonial land deals. The house was the old colonial Government House that had been occupied by Sir Hubert Murray and a string of Australian administrators.

Here we delivered to the Australian High Commissioner, for transfer to the Australian government, a package of axes, knives, beads, calico, trade tobacco and ship biscuits similar to those used in buying our land. With the goods went our words, 'Take your goods back, Australia. We wish you well, but we are now free and we claim back our land.'

We returned to our Hohola home and I noticed that the police had already started to watch my movements in preparation for the events to take place the next day. The next thing was to put these police off the scent so that they could not block me on some pretext. By now I had gained some experience at the cat and mouse game.

Early on Saturday afternoon, I hid with my daughters in the Land Cruiser truck that was parked in the grounds of my house. My car was parked in a conspicuous position in the grounds to give the police something to watch while my parents and sisters carried on normal activities around the house. When a suitable opportunity presented itself, we were driven, unnoticed, out of the grounds and into the town. We travelled back roads to a small village of traditional land owners, a short distance west of Port Moresby. This was an unlikely place to find me, and beyond the last of the large Motu villages close to the town. In this village we collected a small bus that had been given to us for the independence declarations and our Land Cruiser returned to my home in Port Moresby. The small bus was unknown to the police and so I was lost in obscurity while the police kept up a vigil outside my house, watching an empty shell. It was planned that, the next morning, the bus would take our main party of Port Moresby City Councillors and myself from village to village to make the independence declarations. The City Councillors represented all of the villages and settlements.

The people of the village that we had chosen as a temporary hideout were among the original landowners of Port Moresby and part of the city had been built on their clan lands. Land handed down through the generations until the collision with colonialism had robbed them of their heritage. In the early stages of colonialism their populations suffered badly from tuberculosis and other introduced diseases, but now the battle was against poverty. Unlike other Papuans, whose material well-being centred around producing their own food, these traditional landowners were now dependent on the foreign money economy. They had to earn money to survive. The village was no longer the picturesque village of the past and sheets of iron had replaced the thatched palms. A dusty road ran through the centre of the village of un-relieved iron and dust. The soft beauty of the village had given way to harsh necessity.

We were met by the councillor and escorted to his house where we had arranged to stay until the declarations of independence the next day. The house was similar to a village house with two or three lightly partitioned rooms, a kitchen with a fire on the floor and a wide verandah in front. Eating utensils were piled to drain in a plastic dish in one corner of the kitchen. The main differences between this house and a village house were that iron sheets had replaced the native palm thatch and the natural beauty of our native villages was missing.

After we had settled in to our temporary home, the children went to play among the coconut palms that grew at the back of the house. There they amused themselves playing Papuan native games with coconut shells and stones. They never had any European-style toys. I did not allow them to play aimlessly for too long so, after a while, I sent them out with other village girls to collect firewood.

I had discussed land matters with the councillor many

times in the past and had helped the villages with petitions and protests. Their lost land, which was now the wealth of Port Moresby, was constantly on their minds and any conversation was likely to end up with land discussions.

As we talked, a car speeding towards the village caught our attention. It was a large black car like those used by government ministers and it left a heavy cloud of dust behind it which floated in the air to settle on the village. The car stopped, a few words were exchanged and then the car moved and turned in our direction.

The car pulled up and three people got out. The Minister I recognised. He was Mr Kisim, a New Guinean who was responsible for a Government department on the pattern of the Australian system of ministerial government. He was a member of the cabinet during this period of self-government before independence. As he could not speak English or Motu adequately and I could not speak pidgin, we could only exchange elementary greetings. He was always pleasant to me and we exchanged smiles when we met. He only got upset with me when I suggested that we Papuans should have the right to decide if we wanted to be an independent country. Once, I remember him shouting a mild rebuke, 'Tupela kantri bilong yumi mas stap wantaim. Tasol.' (Two fellow country belong you me must stop one time. That's all.)

Mr Kisim wore long trousers in Parliament but now he wore shorts and was barefooted. The heavy, cracked skin on his feet indicated that he was more at home walking his native paths than he was wearing unaccustomed shoes in Parliament. He was a short, muscular man about 120 centimetres and heavily bearded. The muscles of his legs and thighs bulged like footballs.

He had with him a young Papuan driver, Idau. Idau had worked in a copper mine in New Guinea and could speak pidgin English. He doubled up in assisting the Minister with pidgin-Motu translations.

The third person was a young white woman in her mid-twenties who, I guessed, was the Minister's English-speaking secretary, and was probably there to handle English translations and do any writing. The woman looked familiar. She was tall, had long black hair and was dressed casually in a red blouse and tight-fitting jeans. She was a good-looking girl who combined her looks with confident movements. Then, suddenly, I recognised her. She was the Canadian girl, Sandra Rowntree, who visited me at Sangara with Dr Sidney and Mr and Mrs D C.

Mr Kisim gave me a wide smile, revealing unstained teeth gleaming white beyond his heavy black beard. I returned the greeting and welcomed him to my electorate. He told me he would like to see me visit his village one day. He then sought out the councillor and went aside to talk to him with the assistance of the Motu interpreter.

'Hello, Jo,' said Sandra Rowntree as she climbed the wooden steps of the councillor's house. 'Fancy meeting you here. What's a nice girl like you doing in a place like this?' Sandra Rowntree seemed as frank and forthright as ever. 'This is my territory. This is how I earn my living,' I said.

'I was just thinking about you a few minutes ago,' said Sandra. 'I was reading about you in a pidgin-English magazine in the car. I have to practise pidgin-English now. I never thought I would see the day, but it's a matter of survival. The magazine is edited by a foreigner. This is a photograph of you and a few words in pidgin. They don't seem to like you.'

'I don't care who they like or who they don't like. They are still playing white masters telling the people what they should think. They get on my nerves. Let me see it.'

Sandra went back to the car and returned with a ten-cent newspaper, produced mainly for pidgin-speaking New Guineans. I turned the pages until I came to a large, quarter page photograph of myself. The caption to the photo read:

'Daunbilo: Mis Josephine Abaijah. Sentral Rigonal. Namba wan PNG meri bilong palamen. Lida bilong Papua Besena. I gat olkain bikpela edukesen na save. Pipel i save pret long tok bilong em o behainim maus bilong em.'

I read the pidgin three or four times and slowly an English equivalent emerged from the darkness like a photographic print slowly developing in my mind:

'Down below: Miss Josephine Abaijah. Central Regional. Number one PNG mary belong parliament. Leader belong Papua

Besena. He got all kind big fellow education now savvy. People he savvy fright along talk belong him or behind him mouth belong him.'

'I think this is pidgin-English for 'Beware of the dog, it bites,' I said.

'Something like that,' said Sandra, 'you would think they would mind their own business and not use the newspaper to turn people against you. That sounds like a personal opinion, not news. Anyhow, I'm on your side, Jo. Not that I know anything about the argument but it is good to see a woman standing up against the machine. You sure have them worried.

'I was going to come to see you. I was going to ask you something personal. I'm glad I caught up with you.'

'That's good,' I said, 'I'm glad to see you too. It's a pleasant change to talk to a foreigner who will speak openly and hasn't got an angle to sell me. It's really a relief to be treated like a normal human.'

'You will think I have a hide, Jo, but I would like to write a story on your life. You are the person who interests me most in this country. I would like to do something worthwhile before I go back home. It would be great if we could get together at my place or yours and work on your biography. It would take a couple of days or nights a week. I have plenty of time. I want to get my teeth into something.'

I felt attracted to this foreign girl. She had a sophistication and confidence that I admired in women and I was pleased to learn she had doubts and worries like me. But, mainly, I was relieved to be treated in a natural manner by a foreigner, which really was a novelty for me.

I did not intend to write a book with Sandra Rowntree but I was flattered by her attention and by her attachment to me. I always felt grateful to people who were nice to me, something I missed in the role I was now called on to play. Being grateful and trying to please people was a hangover from my colonial mentality. This was what I was born into. Some day I might free myself from this servility. It was hard to be born a 'primitive savage' and grow into normality. Some of the past stains were indelibly stamped on me. I would prefer to be this way than have to turn to hate to relieve my shame.

'I am flattered by your interest, Sandra, but my life is very involved at present. My life is not my own. I would need time to think about something like that. The way I live, everything I do is bought at the expense of something else. My children, my work, the people. There's a man in my life you know, and he's been around for a long time. Fifteen years to be exact. There is no way I could suddenly give up my time with my children and those close to me to expand other activities. These things are like the air I breathe. I must know that they are there and secure before I can feel comfortable elsewhere.'

Mr Kisim and the councillor were making their way towards us.

'I wonder if he got his land?' Sandra said, looking in the direction of the Minister.

'I don't think so,' I replied with conviction, 'but ask him yourself.'

Sandra Rowntree turned to Mr Kisim, spoke to him in pidgin-English, and then turned to me with a broad smile. 'The councillor told him the same as you told me. He would think about it and tell him later. You Papuans must have a conspiracy to tell all outsiders the same thing.'

'Perhaps,' I said, laughing. 'But I will really think about it. It was great to meet you again. Our talk did me a lot of good. We get too isolated from reality. See you around.'

Sandra Rowntree towered over her boss as they stood together on the ground below. 'So long, Jo. Don't forget!'

* * *

Several Port Moresby City Councillors had gathered in the village. They were going to stay overnight and would form the main party who would travel with me the next day. We sat together and discussed plans for the next day and ate a meal of fish and native vegetables prepared by the councillor's family. After the meal, I wanted to be alone so I walked to the edge of the mangroves that stood between us and the sea. I had not been there long when I saw a man approaching along a track through the mangrove trees. Soon I recognised

that it was Lau, a village pastor, who had been an enthusiastic worker for *Papua Besena*. Together we had attended
many meetings. I joined him and we made our way back to
the village. When we reached the councillor's house we
paused to look over the houses of the village.

'This village reminds me of the life of Christ and the bible,'
said Pastor Lau, speaking in Motu. 'It is not rich and extravagant with beauty like many of our villages. It is poor
and bare like the stable at Bethlehem.'

'Yes, it reminds me of the poverty of our people,' I said. 'I
am glad that tomorrow we will rise here. Nobody seems to
benefit much just by living close to the masters.'

'I cry to see our country growing in ugliness,' said Pastor
Lau. 'We must always be turning from something we already
love to love what they command.'

I looked around the tin houses of the village with the
kerosene lamps and cooking fires burning like hope in the
darkness of the night. 'Many times we have been told to turn
the people to action to gain our rights as there are no
peaceful ways. We will be forced to watch our country grow
in ugliness, but God will give us the strength to purify and
love in natural ways. We must not turn from our duty
because the road is long. Time is on our side. Our call will
not be to conquer or destroy but to Purify! Purify! I want to
think, tonight, in quietness and solitude.'

'Then come to my house by the beach and bring your
daughters with you. You can stay in quietness there until
you see the morning light. Many things are revealed in the
quietness of the night.'

I sat on the verandah of Pastor Lau's house, alone, looking
out over the soft waters to the lights of the town. The house
was at the edge of a coastal village a short distance away
from where the group of City Councillors were spending the
night. My three daughters were asleep on grass mats nearby.
Papuans like to feel that they are a part of something no
matter where they are. The native breast was never far
away.

Tonight was the end of a journey for me. I wanted to look
back undisturbed on the journey I had made. I wanted to be

alone with my past. I might never have a chance again. A prophecy fulfilled is no longer a challenge to the mind.

According to civilized man, I was a recent descendant of primitive savages; at worst, insatiable cannibals who ate everything except themselves, at best, simple childlike people who were discovered a million years too soon. More pristine than Adam and Eve. The palms moved restlessly in the night as I wondered if being the child of savages made me different from other human beings.

My mother was a young village girl when, unattended, she pushed me out of her squatting body onto a banana leaf, as close to nature as a turtle in the sand. Why was I still so servile? Why did I long to please? Was living close to natural things what they meant by savagery? Why did the whites move into the Louisiade Archipelago and the lovely islands of eastern Papua with such blood and savagery? Did they have no name for this in their dictionary?

I grew up in gentle ways but it was the whites who persisted in violence. One hundred and fifty thousand men died in Papua New Guinea during the Pacific war alone. Now we need cry for Papua as it grows in ugliness. Whose hands are bloodied this time?

Years of dazed surrender to the colonial machine and being a first in everything was the natural path of things. The failure of love then a colonial drop-out on the bare brown rocks of Kaugere. Years of stolen love. Feelings too exquisite to reveal, too delicate to think on and too transparent to conceal. I am born again to cleaner rags and washed of some of the scale of my slave mentality. Then wonderful years of loving, learning and growing. Oblivion and dangerous pursuits. I caught a glimpse of what it was like to be free and dared to forget that I was just a native girl born to serve and obey. Too conceited to read the future and too selfish to give up anything I had gained, I accepted the impossible challenge to be the first woman elected to Parliament. The silent wonder and the stars were within my reach.

Then the awakening. My heart was too big to be easily satisfied so I sought the love of a hundred thousand villagers and I was trapped again. A slave to my conscience and a slave to my past. But I could no longer accept the Judas pieces of colonial servitude. I had become a disciple of the people and my laughter was wrapped in sombre robes. Evils I had never known were revealed in the name of a Christian morality. And now, tomorrow. Fear for my love, fear for my flight.

The dawn crept from the hills behind Port Moresby and spread its fingers over the sea to sprinkle the sleeping palms with the light of approaching day. Tambourines of the soft winds; harps of the violent seas; temptresses of the liquid moon; fragrant oils of yielding love.

It was the first light of dawn and I had not closed my eyes. I now regretted that I had not slept because we were going to declare Papua independent in villages and Papuan communities continuously throughout the day. On other days we would go to rural villages and repeat the ceremonies.

We would start in the small settlement where we had hidden to escape police detection. The poverty of Bethlehem. A stranger to the natural beauty of our native villages, but a fitting place to start our pilgrimage. Our mission-soaked Papuans wanted to cling to the Christ analogy.

I stood in humility with the community, and flanked by our councillors and important village leaders, I declared Papua free.

I went through the motions of our well-rehearsed independence ceremonies but I was mesmerised by my vigil through the night and became occupied with a mystic spirituality detached in time and in a boundless infinity. I felt like the little girl on Misima who clutched her small sister as she ran over the green grasses away from the threat of a white man's indecency. I felt that I had been at this scene before. There was nothing new to me and everything had an eerie intimacy. Disorientated in space, I laboured to balance reality. I was trying to reach my home which kept receding towards a receding sea. I desperately wanted to get my small sister to safety until suddenly and without warning, I burst upon a pale blue sea where figures moved beneath the glossy surface in endless variety.

A firm hand caught my arm and I heard a resonant Papuan voice reciting our promises to heed the word of God, to hold our land and to make our country free.

Dirava ita kamonai
Itaeda tano dogoatao
Itaeda Papua goadalaia.

I returned to the safety of my natural senses as quickly as I could bring my thoughts under control and walked to a flagpole and lowered an Australian flag to the ground: the same flag that the colonials had wrapped around Uncle Robert's coffin. Willing hands detached it from its cord and replaced it with a pale blue flag of Papua. I hauled our new flag up to take its place at the top of the pole and declared our country free.

'Almighty God determined the creation of our beloved Papua, the same as He determined the creation of other nations of the earth. For a hundred years wicked and ignorant men have been telling us that God made Papuans inferior to other men; made Papua poorer than other lands; that Papuans must never govern their own lands or be free.

'Today I declare to all people that God made Papuans equal to all other men. Papua is big, rich and beautiful. On behalf of our people and in the presence of you my countrymen, I declare that Papua is now a free and independent country. We will not recognise the authority of any foreign or colonial power or institution or any person under threat, intimidation or privilege to make any decisions affecting the political future of Papua or Papuans.

'We pray to God for early deliverance from our foreign occupation and pray that the people who now control our lives and our land will quickly leave us to look after ourselves with peace and goodwill, so that we may begin with the haste of restless people the great task of building our own homeland to serve our own needs.'

After this simple ceremony, amidst the roaring, groaning cheers of the crowd I boarded the small bus and, with the City Councillors, went on to our next stop; a large island village joined to the mainland by a causeway built by the American army.

There was no significance in any special ceremony. We planned to move in geographical progression, repeating the ceremony at Papuan villages and settlements until the sun went down. We symbolically returned the biscuits, tobacco, axes, knives and cheap calico with which our land had been bought; lowered the colonial flag and raised the flag of Papua; made our declaration of independence; said our prayer; sang our song and moved on to the next community. Tens of thousands of Papuans joined in declaring Papua an independent country and we joined together to pray for an early end to the occupancy of our country.

So on we went through the day. We made the declaration of independence in the four villages of Hanuabada and Elevala and at the spot where Commodore Erskine declared Papua a British Protectorate in 1884. Then we went on again to the villages and settlements around the coastal fringe of Port Moresby. In the presence of the City Councillors and the village communities we repeated the ceremonies over and over again. We held our ceremonies in peace and with the participation of whole communities. A solitary police employee drifted around the edge of the crowd in one village trying to draw attention to his opposition to our cause, but otherwise the police were conspicuous by their absence. They did not put in an appearance until the decoy performance in the late afternoon.

As we proceeded I became exhausted through the exertions of the day. I had declared Papua an independent country with many thousands of Papuans and my first task was drawing to a close. In this I had not failed.

As the shadows lengthened on Sunday afternoon we held the final ceremony on a public reserve at Kaugere for Papuans from settlements and housing estates in the town. By this time I was taxed beyond my strength and I wondered how I could carry on. I had not eaten any food at all, and without sleep the night before, I was weary with fatigue. It was in these closing scenes that the police caught up with us and descended in force on the ceremony, with several white officers and many native police who had had their weekend leave cancelled. The TV cameras and the press also arrived in force. I became the price of a trip to Moresby and the justification for cancelled police leave.

White police officers took up strategic positions and agents and police took still and movie pictures during the whole ceremony. Thousands of Papuans were treated to their scrutiny. I longed for the peace of the respectful communities in the quiet villages. I longed for the Papua that I knew. Not this brazen intrusion into our privacy. I should have been flattered that my activities warranted so much single-minded attention during the past few years.

Finally, I completed my task and Dina came to pick me up. Exhausted, I slumped into the back seat of the car and, with my daughters, returned to our home. Back in familiar surroundings and with something to eat, I recovered enough to rest and dream away the apathetic night.

Australia had created a new country to contain us and had redrawn boundaries to suit itself. If we had to be forced into a union with the people of part of New Guinea, then we should consider uniting with all of our Papuan people on the whole of New Guinea and face the reality of our destiny. This could be less threatening than the present scene.

My declaration of independence for Papua was to expose the lie that Papua willingly gave up its rights or its political independence. The counter to the artifice. It gave to Papua an alternative history. Papuans of the future will determine the value of my deed. At least we had retained a semblance of our dignity. I felt cleaner now and slept soundly but a price would be extracted for my 'unpardonable crime'.

A BALLAD OF PAPUA

My love is waiting for the sunrise,
   And the sound of marching feet.
The happy laughing new days,
   As the sons of freedom meet.

Chorus
Paradise bird you're fly-ing;
   Yellow cap and band of gold.
Paradise bird you're cry-ing;
   Summer wings on lilac fold.
Paradise bird you're dy-ing;
   Redder than the blushing sky,
Carried in a lover's sigh,
   As dreaming times go drifting by,
With mem-or-ies of Pa-pu-ah.

My love is waiting for Pa-pu-ah,
   For the thunder of the drums
To roll from sea to mountain,
   When the victory has been won.

My love is waiting for the toiling,
   And the planting of the seed.
The axe and kai-ah ringing,
   As we fill our nation's need.

My love is waiting for the praying,
   The joy and sweat and tears.
As growing up together,
   We sing away the years.

My love is waiting for the dreaming,
   And the setting of the sun.
For the hearts that beat together,
   While the work was being done.

3

A pasture to my mind

Let then our first act every morning be to make the following resolve for the day:

I shall not fear anyone on earth.
I shall fear only God.
I shall not bear ill will toward anyone.
I shall not submit to injustice from anyone.
I shall conquer untruth by truth.
And in resisting untruth I shall put up with all suffering.

Mahatma Gandhi

I was with Dina on a 250 metre hill which was part of a ridge separating Moresby into north and south. The sun had lost its fierce intensity as it paused in the afternoon sky. South were the large Motu villages; the Port Moresby of the early colonials; the many splendoured sunsets; the harbour; and, beyond, the Great South Land. North was the challenge of the future. The new suburbs of the sprawling city; the Owen Stanley Range with the tiny thread of the Kokoa trail, stitched lightly to the mountain sides — the only link across Papua; and, beyond, northern Papua with its rich lands, deep sea port and active volcanoes. This rich, fertile belt of land across the top of the elephant's trunk of the island was the centre of Papua, the beating heart of the country. West of the centre were the dreams of vast riches from oil, gas, copper and hydroelectric power; sago swamps and crocodiles; and Indonesia. East of the centre was the end of the elephant's trunk: south sea island magic; and mild, graceful people. I was the exception.

Dina and I often came to this isolated peak, as it was close to my home in Hohola. The peak was named after a senior colonial official who worked hard to have a hole cut in the hill to join old and new Port Moresby together. 'Of all the places in Moresby, this is our place,' I said. 'It's the only place where we can be sure of getting away from people. All the places we used to know have been swallowed up in the city. If it wasn't for the dogs we couldn't spend much time here either.' Once, bringing the dogs here with us was an act of kindness to them, but now it was a necessity for our safety. To most people, now, this was a nice place to show a visitor for a casual few minutes, but no place for idling.

'Moresby has changed,' said Dina, as we walked towards an exposed rock where we could stand and look out over the harbour to the open sea. 'It used to be a pleasant place for foreigners and the Papuans liked it because it was the only town they knew.'

'And now?' I asked.

'Well, the sunsets from here are just as beautiful,' said Dina evasively. 'They grow more beautiful every day that I spend with you, but the human side of the town seems to be going sour. If it wasn't for you I would have been happy to say goodbye to it long ago. I'm not good at clinging to the past. Tomorrow is built on a lot of todays. You are my only today. You are what matters to me in Moresby now.

'Your declaration of independence was a real triumph. It showed how closely you represented the people. I don't think anyone will take your place in Papua. They have a special respect for you.'

'I was very tired in the end. I didn't think I'd get through the last ceremony at Kaugere. I was satisfied. I did what I set out to do. It was a kind of spiritual experience.'

'Everything is spiritual to you,' said Dina. 'God, ghosts and magic all meet in jamboree. You will probably end up as a prophet or an image of incorruptibility. A south sea island Gandhi. I can't see you sticking to parliamentary politics indefinitely. It contaminates many people. You are too much a romantic to live for long with an unpleasant reality.'

'We planted a seed in an uncropped field. We can now wait to watch the seasons and count the grain. I feel cleaner now. I could not have done less and contained my shame.'

'And what comes next?' said Dina, as he pointed to a black car slowly winding its way around the side of the hill towards the summit where we were. 'We have company. Probably visitors coming up here to see what Moresby really looks like.'

'I only have one more job to do to end this episode. I must read out our independence declaration to the Australian Government.'

The dogs were safely locked up as a large black government car pulled up close to us. The Papuan driver called out greetings. Dina was well known in central and eastern Papua. Papuans could speak to him with ease, and his colloquial Motu was often better than their own. A few years ago they called him Doctor, but now they usually called him *adavamu* (my husband), something like the consort of a movie star or a queen. Dina said he was flattered by the promotion.

I was surprised to see that the first one out of the car was my old friend, Dr Sidney. The Papuan Medical College had since become the medical school of the new university. Looking as spruce and hygienic as usual, he smartly opened the back door of the car and ushered a senior PNG politician, Mr Vetari, and a foreign visitor onto the hallowed soil of our 'Place of the Dogs'.

Greetings were exchanged all round and I was introduced to the visitor. Mr Handiside was a dark, distinguished-looking man who used his greying head of hair, ample frame and generous gestures effectively to convey an air of approachable affability. A ladies' man for sure. A mixture of a

father image and a Mister Smoothie. I liked his style and
smiled generously as I tried to put a tag on his nationality.
Probably a country in central Asia. I was advised in a few
words that Mr Handiside was the distinguished representative of some United Nations agency looking for worthy
ways to spend some money on our underdevelopment.

'I have just been admiring your beautiful country, Miss
Abaijah,' said the affable visitor, 'and now I have the honour
to meet the attractive lady Member of Parliament whom I
have heard so much about.'

'Thank you for the compliment, but I am sure that I don't
deserve it,' I said. 'Politics is giving me grey hairs and
putting lines on my face!'

Before Mr Handiside could carry the conversation further,
Mr Vetari hooked him by the arm and steered him off to a
spot about fifty metres away where he could get a better
bird's eye view of the harbour and the wharf facilities.

This left us alone with Dr Sidney. A fairly uncomfortable
situation for him. He maintained a close affinity with Dina
which had developed in the common moulds of medicine and
the PMC, but he was not comfortable with me. He had
retired from medicine temporarily to act as one of the many
behind-the-scene foreign advisers to the government.

'I have been wanting to talk with you,' he said to Dina and
then, turning his head towards me, continued. 'I'm sure you
don't mind us talking in front of Miss, er, er, Josephine. You
two have been like pepper and salt for so long now I am sure
you do not have any heavy secrets between you.'

'Go ahead, shoot,' said Dina. 'It is healthy to share our
troubles. Josephine's shoulders are younger than mine.'

'It's your association with Josephine that I want to
talk about,' said Dr Sidney slowly and, carefully selecting his
words, continued. 'That is, your political association. Everyone in Moresby, Papua if you like, takes you two for granted
after fifteen or sixteen years—almost as old as the PMC.
But this politics is a new thing. I wanted to warn you
confidentially that there has been serious talk about your
deportation recently. You have been blamed for everything
from the Koki riots to training a secret army of guerrilla
fighters to topple the government. I have argued where I can

but I am only one voice. Other experienced officers who know you, have also supported you but many of these new types moving in won't have a bar of it. Of course, many of the local politicians are very angry with Josephine and I think that they are now beginning to fear their seats at the next elections. I want to counsel you to move cautiously. Please remember that I can only tell you this in confidence. I have to serve two loyalties.'

'Thanks,' said Dina, searching for the right words to reply to his friend so that he would not sound casual and unconcerned. 'We have been told these things frequently by reporters and public servants. Some of them talk to us pretty freely. I'm telling you this because you need not have anything on your conscience. Of course, coming from you it is more authentic.'

'Those liars would make up anything to save their own skins,' I called out defiantly.

'No doubt that is part of it,' said Dr Sidney. 'But that's not the whole story. They can't subdue you and they feel that your politics are a threat to them and their policies. They just will not concede that they cannot handle you or the people. They are sure that if they get rid of your support that you will collapse. They don't think beyond that. You are a woman. They must be able to defeat a woman. They must get rid of the man behind you to kill you politically. In other words, get rid of Dr Dina and they get rid of you.'

'And what about the people whom I represent? Don't they come into it?'

'No,' said Dr Sidney. 'I don't think that they come into it. You must remember that the Australian Government has closed the door on any discussions on the future of Papua. It is fairly simple. Get rid of Dr Dina and they will get rid of you. You must admit that it could be an attractive theory for people under pressure.'

'What is not so simple is what we are supposed to do about it,' said Dina.

'You are just the victim of circumstances,' I said. 'There is nothing you or anyone else can do about it. They are angry with me and they'll punish me by getting at you. Once I was threatened because I was associated with you. Now you are threatened because of your association with me. No matter what you do or I do, it will make no difference. Even if I gave up politics it would be just the same.'

'Unfortunately, I think Josephine is right,' said Dr Sidney. 'But they don't rationalise it that way. They talk about foreigners being here on privilege but it all amounts to the same thing. They want to get at Josephine.'

'Anyhow the demonstrations and protests have stopped. That phase ended with the unilateral declaration of independence. I don't know what else we can do to cool them down,' I said, as Mr Vetari and Mr Handiside approached the car again.

'Well, I have done my duty,' said Dr Sidney making off. 'I have told you what I know. I see no answer other than something like joining the government. And I am not seriously suggesting that. Goodbye, for now. I hope it all sorts itself out.'

Mr Handiside was steered straight to the waiting car and Dr Sidney already had the door open ready to usher him in. As Mr Handiside approached the car, like a man under detention, he paused for a moment to bend his head graciously and then disappeared from sight.

'Bamahuta,' (go to sleep) called the Papuan driver as he waved us farewell.

'Bamahuta,' I replied, as this was the Papuan farewell, and the car began to make its way down the hill.

The sun had grown to a crimson ball that was slowly sinking to draw the curtain on the day into the valley of Asia — the valley of rest or the valley of death.

I stood, silent, looking at the formation of the sunset and then, half audibly, said to myself. 'If love it be to know thee always, before the dawn and beyond the night. Across the earth or in the starways, to span the space and calm the flight.'

We were alone. This was our last outdoor sanctuary in Moresby. The last place where we could be alone. We were running out of earth. As we sat down together on the ground, I said,

'I remember chasing a sunset like this once, when we were

flying towards the mainland of Asia and Vietnam. I was very superstitious then. I wondered what the omen was.'

'I know what the omen is now,' said Dina. 'Since I am a student of beauty under your care, may I make my meaning clear?'

I turned to my companion with tears in my eyes and said, 'We must hasten to make everything clear between us as time presses around us and we are threatened by our dreams.'

'Each colour is a line of memories passing back into time and beckoning us forward to our next folly,' Dina commenced hesitatingly.

'Yellows are the new flowers opening to the first breeze.

'Reds are reality and the depths of passions eased.

'Silvers are time from eternity to eternity. The quicksilver that we walk over so carelessly.

'The orange-golds are the fulfilments. The pendant of gold that remains from the mountains of greed.

'The blues of the sky are the dreams. The reverie of what might have been.'

'Those are the elements,' I said, hiding my head in the thick fur of Flashie, the prince of my dogs, who had run up to comfort me. 'What of the whole? I am hungry to see our love in everything beautiful. I feel you have cheated me. Please do not deprive me of my sunsets. There must be some hope for us in what you see.'

'There can only be hope in Eternity,' said Dina, drawing me to his side and touching my head to pillow on his shoulder, my favourite crying place. 'If God didn't want us to love, He wouldn't have loaned us paradise. I once trusted time to lead us to sweet partings, but that knave has no honourable intentions towards us.'

I slipped off his shoulder to lay on the soft ground and rest my head on the familiar cushion of his legs as we absorbed the colours of another dying day. Dina lifted me half towards his head and said, quietly,

'The sunset is you, the colours are you, the opening flowers and the passions of life, the memories, the fulfilments and the dreams.'

I turned away from the sunset to look at the blue of other skies and whispered my intimacies.

'I have a familiar warmth growing inside me that bids me press closer to you and press you for more urgent meanings to your words. Please tell me if the yellows of the sunset are turning crimson shades, for how else can I explain the changes that are possessing me?'

Dina raised me closer until I could feel his hot breath over me as he whispered on my lips,

'Delicate nymphet, you are every sunset and every dream. Slide away from me to the grass mat at our feet so that we may lie with greater intimacy.'

'No barrier remains between us now,' I whispered with my few remaining words. 'Touch me gently so that I do not flow too freely to the night. We must live beyond this sunset and every other day. Hold me so that you can never let me go. Press me close to the earth as it has suddenly grown soft with expectations.'

'Gentle, Josie, there is no touch within me that is not yours; no strength that is not held in your arms; no violence that is not released in you. Turn your head and thread me to your dreams. The sunset is crimson now.'

> And to myself, I said,
> Bared for love, there's no wonder beyond your touch.
> Bared for love, hold my heart and lead me to paradise.
> Where rainbows meet and music plays.
> I am yours, take me to my dreams.

* * *

We still had to present the unilateral declaration of Papuan independence to the Australian Government to complete the series of hundreds of demonstrations during the two years since the formation of *Papua Besena*. Early in May, the Australian Minister for Territories came to PNG for a five day visit, so this seemed to be a suitable opportunity.

We needed to get some publicity for the event, so on the Sunday that the Minister arrived we gathered together a group of Papuans to stage a demonstration. As the plane from Australia touched down, a group of shouting, placard-waving Papuans prepared to greet him. The placards carried slogans such as 'PAPUA IS NOT FOR SALE!' and 'NO UN COLONIALISM FOR PAPUA!'

As expected, the Minister did not front up to the demonstrators and departed in an official car from the side entrance. Still, we had achieved our purpose and we did not waste much manpower or time on the effort. By this time I had reduced demonstrations to a few simple principles.

We next fronted up on Monday evening, outside the Papua Hotel where the government was entertaining the Minister at an official banquet. There were a few hundred of us this time. We were building up slowly. There would be thousands the next time if the Minister kept turning his back on us. Things were going according to plan. If he wanted a full scale riot on his hands he could have it. We were in no mood to humour politicians just because they were white. Those days were dead. We had thoughtfully waited until near the end of the banquet before we descended on the Papua Hotel. We continued to disrupt the reception until the Minister promised to meet us at 9.30 a.m. the next morning at the main government offices at Konedobu.

The next morning, I turned up with some City Councillors and Papuan leaders to present our declaration to the Minister. But, alas, no Minister.

The Minister was unintentionally building up a news story. It was a matter of how long it took to dawn on him that he could not get out of Moresby without listening to us or without very serious trouble erupting in the town. We had come this far and there was no way that we would bow to the antics of a politicians who refused to spend a few minutes listening to what we had to say.

We sent off some scouts around the government offices to find out where he was. We had friends in every government office in Port Moresby. In less than ten minutes the answer came back. The Minister was at the old Government House on the hill having a meeting with white Australian farmers.

We soon smiled our way through the guards at the entrance at the bottom of the hill and, as we reached the top of the hill, we noisily stormed the residence, shouting our disapproval of the Minister standing us up in our appointment while he hob-nobbed with white farmers who were apprehensive about their future in our country.

When the disturbance broke out in the grounds of the old Government House, the Minister promptly changed his mind. Then and there he undertook to see us and we were promptly ushered into an appropriate office. We opened the conversation by informing him that we had no desire to listen to what he had to say. All that was required of him was to sit and listen, the same as we had been doing for the past century. We also gave him a brief opinion on Australia's sleep in our country while it frittered away all of our vital years. I then recited our prayer, read out our unilateral declaration of Papuan independence, handed him a copy and said goodbye.

'The Minister Listens to the Lady' story nudged its way into a wide coverage in the Australian media. The Minister, when pressed to reveal what had happened, confirmed that Miss Abaijah had told him that she did not want to listen to him. Having heard this he had decided not to 'impose on her'. He admitted that all he said was 'hello, thank-you, and goodbye'. A fitting end to an empty association.

In July 1975, the axe fell. Dina and I were working at my office in Hohola, trying to get a wheelchair for a man with paralysed legs when two sternly dressed gentlemen walked in and handed Dina a letter. It was from a Minister of the PNG Government advising him that his visa to remain in PNG would not be renewed and that he would have to leave the country by August 20. He had been granted a few weeks' grace because of his long record of service to the country.

The press claimed that it was the first political deportation in the country. It was handed out while Papua was still an Australian colony, and was to take effect one month before the official independence ceremony in September. Another first to our very long list. A parting decoration.

When the order came it was an anti-climax and we read the letter without comment except to note the dates. Dina was heavily involved in everything I did. We always worked under threat but, still, it was a matter of go ahead or die. Since becoming a politician, I had been introduced to the world of business by Dina, but it was a world that I could not fully understand. I had enough on my hands. Everything went smoothly while he was around and I devoted my time to the people, doing the work that satisfied me most. Dina was also behind most of the services to the people. An unpaid, full-time, professional worker. All of this work would have to go. I had a few weeks to disentangle myself from business and to bow out of our many services to the people. Sell our trucks, dismantle our plant, and then go on the road again.

We made no comment to the press and we made no comment to ourselves. We just did what we had to do. This was the great master-stroke at last. This was to be the end of Josephine Abaijah, the rebel politician who could not be bought. This would bring her to her knees. Our informants had told us everything but the day.

After months or years of rumours and bellicose threats, it was almost a relief to know the date. Public servants and reporters had kept us well informed. There was no official explanation for the expulsion, but one of the final popular stories was that Dina was organising guerrilla fighters to take over the country! This was said to have come through the army. I did not know and I did not care. One liar or another, it made no difference. In this avaricious little world, love is a hostage to buy submission and servitude, an expendable commodity, a weakness of fools.

The story of guerrilla fighters was printed freely in the Australian press and even beyond. In *Asia Week*, a news magazine that offers its product in twenty different currencies, an article appeared on June 24, 1977, headed, 'Papua's Daughter' and its readers in many countries were informed:

> ... Papua Besena got more serious though in the weeks before national independence on Sept. 16 when intelligence agents learned that Abaijah's Australian friend and mentor (...), was collecting information on the type of guerrilla tactics previously employed by Latin American revolutionary Che Guevara. (He) was bundled out of the country back to Australia.

Amen! So Dina ended up a threat to national security, a guerrilla fighter organising to take over the country. These were the sweet sounds of politics where it has been said, 'all political parties die at last of swallowing their own lies'.

In the meantime, we had to stop the threat of a spate of car burnings in the town from becoming a reality. After the announcement of Dina's expulsion, somebody lit a large fire under the petrol tank of a car with the purpose of blowing it up. The car was owned by a man associated with the Minister who issued Dina's expulsion letter and the owner of the car thought that the fire was politically motivated.

Then began the empty days of dismantling our lives together in Port Moresby. The sixteen years since leaving school had passed on wings of happiness. Now the loneliness. Political jackals moved in with crude suggestions that they could replace Dina. Some went so far as to call public meetings to proclaim the new order. I did not attend any of these and I don't think anyone else did. We made no murmur or protest and we never discussed the expulsion. We just went about our business. Spies and secret agents nudged closer and marked the days off on their calendars. After Dina had departed they would present themselves as secretaries and as all manner of useful people.

August 20 came and, almost without discussion, I joined Dina. I intended that we would travel to Australia together. We made a last-minute dash to the airport with just enough time to catch the plane but, at the airport, there was a guard of honour of Port Moresby City Councillors and we were delayed further. Then a run for the plane and goodbye, Papua. We might never see my country together again. Mean little men might stop us from lying together under the warm Papuan sun. This was the punishment.

In Australia we ran into a barrage of reporters at the airports. I made the usual protests that were expected of me but this part of my work had ended with the unilateral declaration of Papuan independence.

* * *

While we were in Australia, Papua New Guinea put on its elaborate official independence ceremony in Port Moresby. The Australian Prime Minister kissed Mrs Imelda Marcos in friendly greeting. The Australian organisers plodded up the last hill of noble endeavour. Prince Charles told the people that 'rulers are not feared by those who do good but those who do evil'. A famous Papuan rainmaker made magic to bring torrents to wash out the celebration. The dancers danced, the soldiers marched and the school children sang, but no sign of a spontaneous celebration by the people. Was this the most subdued independence celebration in colonial history?

The *Sydney Morning Herald* told its readers: 'Papua New Guinea became independent not with flourish and fanfare nor with exuberant nationalism, but quietly, shyly and soberly.' The Australian *National Times* said: 'The ceremonies were organised with military precision and the crowds in Port Moresby behaved with self-restraint normally associated with the British.'

* * *

Dina and I booked a world tour to revisit countries we had seen before and others that were new to us. We spent all of the money that we had saved out of the ruins of our Papuan enterprises. The future had lost its meaning and holding on to today claimed all of our attentions. We talked about everything but our separation, and laughed in the Australian Spring.

The travel agent finally admitted in triumph that ours were the most complicated tickets that he had ever written. We needed something complicated to keep our minds off things and we apologised for involving him in our mental aberrations. We both travelled on Australian passports as Australian citizens. My last act before I became a foreigner.

Westward to Perth we chased the sun, and over the Indian Ocean to see Mauritius. It was like old times again. A bonus to our injury. A return to the exciting days before I buried myself in politics.

Into the Africa of animals, market-places, wars and pyramids. In Ethiopia, I ran into trouble because I carried the name of an Ethiopian royal family. I was combed from head to toe eight times by various officials before I was finally allowed to put myself together and board the plane!

In Greece we sauntered through the towns and villages

stretching days and chasing the sun that we hoped would never set. Across Europe we did everything again. In Paris we stayed in a small hotel near the Folies Bergère where we had been together ten years before when I had been a trembling, tongue-tied student from London University. In Copenhagen, we saw the lonely mermaid, separated by the icy sea from the lover she would never see again. As my heart filled I quickly turned away, but I could not cry here in competition with the snow. London revisited, friendly and warm in the short, sunless days. No taxi driver to call me a black bastard this time. I was no longer alone and everything was half the fuss and twice the fun. The grass of Ireland was as green as their aeroplanes and, in the small hotels, we survived on hot water bottles and Irish blarney. People rich with love, the Irish treated us as their own and when I saw white women with small children begging in the streets of Limerick, I felt ashamed of my extravagance and emptied my pockets of all the coins that I had.

A green plane took us across a grey sea to New York. Broadway, cops, movie scenes, Liberty and volcanoes steaming in the streets. Safely wrapped in my sarongs, I drifted easily past the scene. At the United Nations Headquarters, a lady expert explained carefully to a curious crowd of tourists that Papua New Guinea had been a United Nations Trust Territory that had just been granted its independence by the United Nations. Nobody had heard of the country, but I timidly corrected the expert by telling her that Papua had been an Australian territory. Not so said the educated one. Australia only administered Papua for the United Nations, she repeated with authority. I agreed and we passed on to the next assembly.

Washington DC, with the medals of a nation and the decorations of a democracy. Florida, and the sun. The *sun and coconut palms*, were the best medicine to goad my spirits on. We looked at the mansions of the millionaires and rested in cheap hotels. The West Indies and romance. Quiet islands too close to home to feel. I closed my eyes and forgot the world between. Venuzuela and Panama and from there to bus our way through half a dozen countries and into Mexico. The east coast of the United States lived up to the claims of its roving salesmen we had met in different parts of the world.

Hawaii, the Pacific Islands, New Zealand and Australia. Four or five months of continuous locomotion. A few days in Sydney, its beauty towering above its mortal load. We talked about everything except tomorrow. Then, almost without comment, I boarded a plane for home, alone.

Each climber to the mountain top must map his own path and choose his own step. As on my first trip to London, I sat immobile with loneliness. Frozen to my thoughts I dwelt alone and, like the lonely mermaid, I was turning into stone.

* * *

Home, with my children collected from faithful hands, I retreated into an unaccustomed solitude and the intimacy of my dreams, while, to the world outside, I smiled and carried on my affairs unchanged and untamed.

What happened next is blurred in my memory, except that every day I communicated with Dina, as I continued to do, in an unbroken rosary, for the next two years. Erlinda had told me that I had not experienced life fully because I had not felt the pain of waiting and wanting. The petals dropping from the flower before the fall of Spring. Was this the way a woman qualified?

My most vivid memories were stolen visits to Australia and the return to Spring. The people still sought me out to help them in a thousand ways, but with my arms lost and my plant dismantled I was reduced in usefulness. A smile and understanding replaced many services.

During the year, I was forcibly withdrawn from my provincial electorate of central Papua to become the Member of Parliament for the newly created National Capital District of Port Moresby. The only sizeable town in Papua was now a cosmopolitan city that was rapidly slipping away from Papuan control.

* * *

The year passed and another year came. I exposed myself to the ideas of the people and lived among them whenever I could. My usefulness was curtailed by my punishment, but my image as a faithful spokesman of the people and my identification with their hopes and aspirations remained. Then, in 1977, came the first national elections following the foundation of the Independent State of Papua New Guinea in 1975.

To my surprise, the Deputy Prime Minister, heir apparent to the senior throne and the Minister responsible for the department that sent the expulsion letter to Dina, elected to stand against me. A few other optimists threw their hats into the ring. Five years in politics had been a long time.

The appearance of the Deputy Prime Minister to stand against me was a reflection of how cosmopolitan the city had become. I thought that it was a sign of over-confidence on his part, but one can never be sure. In the central province of the rural villages nobody of any judgement would have stood against me. But Port Moresby was different with its public servants, national institutions and people of many colours, races and creeds.

Polling day arrived and passed in the city, but there would be the long wait for the votes from the rural electorates. Counting day came and the votes from Port Moresby were counted and checked with painstaking care. At last the results! The Deputy Prime Minister and Minister for Immigration, Army and Foreign Affairs was defeated by thousands of votes and bowed out of Parliament. Josephine Abaijah, the lonely woman MP, was elected to Parliament for another five years on a policy of broken dreams and a promise of faithful representation without favour or privilege. In Gandhi's prayer:

> I shall not fear anyone on earth.
> I shall fear only God.
> I shall not bear ill will toward anyone.
> I shall not submit to injustice from anyone.
> I shall conquer untruth by truth.
> And in resisting untruth I shall put up with all suffering.

All of the other Members of Parliament, including three senior ministers from Port Moresby and central Papua, lost their seats. The only survivor was one from the primitive, mountainous interior. Every seat was won by a candidate supporting *Papua Besena*. So much for the politicians who oppposed me and spoke up for the Australian plan for the compulsory union of Papua with New Guinea. And now, eighteen months later, a clean sweep.

During these national elections, the Australian media gave me plenty of publicity, mainly because the Deputy Prime Minister had elected to stand against me. Mostly it was prophesied that he was due for an early departure from the political scene; in the meantime the media had been kind to me as a politician and had given me plenty of coverage.

There was also plenty of colonial reactionary material being fed to the overseas press by foreign journalists covering the local scene. In their isolation, the journalists decided what others should or should not read. In Dina's expulsion the *Sydney Morning Herald* retained its dignity while the Australian *National Times* published a tedious 'Beauty and the Beast' story. I had a pleasant experience with one Australian magazine, the *Bulletin*, which showed that Australians could rise above the level of colonial politics to deal at the level of human beings.

* * *

The men of a rural village on one of the inland rivers of central Papua went to a Government outpost to protest against neglect and poverty. During the demonstration, mainly based on noise, someone broke six small glass louvres in the window of a government building. Later, police were sent out from Port Moresby and all of the men of one village were rounded up and taken to Port Moresby about 65 km away. One of the villagers was accidently killed on the way. Left behind was a village of terrified women and children. This was the response to a political protest that the people had hoped would bring them some relief from their poverty.

In Port Moresby, a group trial was held for the thirty-three men. Some charges were read out and the people, unadvised, raised their hands. The magistrate gaoled them all for either five months or three months, including one man who was nowhere near the demonstration, because he had been in the village caring for his pregnant wife at the time.

All of the women and children deserted the village as they

were terrified at the prospect of staying alone in an isolated village for months without the men. By one means or another, they managed to get to Port Moresby and abandoned their gardens to raiders and pigs.

Even though I was no longer the Member of Parliament for central Papua, as I had been restricted to Port Moresby, I was the one they sought out to help them. They were begging and scrounging food around the town, going into debt with friends and relatives, and sleeping where they could. Many of them were hungry and, with children sick, were in desperate need.

When I first met the women and children they were sitting on an empty, dusty block of land in Moresby, holding their children around them and crying together as a group, as they did when they were in deep distress. I was ashamed to see the humiliation of these women, some of them grown old before they were forty because of the ravages of sun and poverty. Destitute and in rags they were in no state to survive five months while their men grew fat in gaol. A few men in prison would have been accepted by the villagers, but a village exposed for months without men was not a proposition. With hands coarse through work, they were no strangers to toil and drudgery. They were only strangers to the hostility of a city to destitution.

First, I took them to see the Prime Minister, but he was away, and so we went to the Deputy. We got as far as the plush carpet and then met the closed door. The government would not interfere. It was a matter for the courts not the government.

It would be a big undertaking to feed 180 people for five months. Their gardens were already abandoned and there would be no plantings for the next crops. I bought them a few bags of rice and some cheap tinned fish and caught the first plane to Australia. With no help from the government, I could not handle a thing like this alone.

In Australia with Dina, we examined the options open to us and decided to first approach the Wayside Chapel in Kings Cross for advice. The Pastor of the Wayside Chapel had been a friend in need and had his finger on the humanitarian pulse of the city. He promptly put us in touch with a fund called the Bulletin Thousand which was organised through the *Bulletin* magazine, which invited readers to subscribe some of their wealth to be transferred directly into action, without any intermediate costs, to relieve distress and suffering. They soon handed me a cheque for one thousand dollars and I was on my way back to Port Moresby on the next plane. We had reasoned that with a 25 kg bag of rice and 48 cans of fish, a family could survive for a month and this would give us time to organise legal appeals and obtain more relief.

As the result of our actions and the publicity, appeals were lodged and, subsequently, the sentences of the men were reduced from five months to six weeks which was little more than what they had already served.

The women rejoiced when the food came. They rejoiced again when the men were released from gaol after their vain protest. And the people did not forget. Nine months later, after the gardens had grown again, the villagers held a large dance and celebration to thank me and a Sydney newspaper that they had never seen and could not read.

* * *

Submerged in my work, I travelled alone for two years hobbled to a dream. No day was complete without a word to Dina. He was ever my first thought and my last breath. Like a caged bird, I longed for flight without sighting a tree where I could rest. Fantasies replaced reality and I sought substance to my dreams. But words soon lost their meanings and the breath turned acid in the travesty of love that wounded more than it healed.

Some offended men longed to see my image lying in the dust and liked to see me alone and vulnerable. A woman alone must surely fall to ridicule and pity. Weakened in the void of loneliness, an easy prey to vanity. A dual conquest of a body and a soul.

Influential persons, who twisted the knife most, invited me to a truce, and to taste the pleasures of their companies. Love was still a hostage to be bartered for a deal. Spies and agents

offered their services to my cause with guile and gallantry.
My punishment was an open-ended sentence from now to
Eternity.

The long night, outside of death, knows no rest or peace.
Was this the unbridled lash that Erlinda spoke about? What
spirit carries the lamp when the oil runs dry and who smiles
when the skin withers on the flesh? Was this the punishment for too much happiness? Was I a woman yet? Carry the
load, grind the grain, dig the hole, and then?

A woman risks too much who gives herself to love. Sex and
vanity are substitutes. A woman watches over the children
as they grow towards their foolishness while she washes and
irons her own passions away to spotless purity.

* * *

The second year of my punishment was drawing to a close
as I expunged the unquenchable sin of Truth. Still, every day
Dina was my first thought and my last breath and a blue sky
was the only barrier between me and happiness.

Then, as the new year steadied on its course, suddenly,
without thought and without warning, I packed a bag and
my three daughters and flew into the blue sky on the earthly
side of paradise. Had I suffered for the truth long enough?
Was two years of the lash enough to scar my mind? Had I
qualified as a woman yet? Had I won or had I lost? Death
was inevitable, but the challenge was to live.

With my three daughters in Sydney and my son at school
in Brisbane, I was mobile and complete. With all organs
functioning and a mind at ease, I floated in a familiar
security where I could move and breathe.

Soft warm waters of childhood memories. A lonely native
girl with a thousand coloured dreams. Curtains of coral
colours and festoons of kaleidoscopic fish. Unfrequented
ways in the shadows of obscurity. The laughter, the songs,
the memories. The reckless red hibiscus pulsing in my hair
and the blush and the shame of passions gently eased. I had
done enough thinking during the past two years. Now I
was going to feel.

'What are your plans?' said Dina.

'I have no plans,' I said, settling back into the comfortable seat at the airport. 'Do we always have to have a plan? Can't we just breathe?'

'I suppose so,' said Dina with a smile, 'but it would be a novelty. We can just sit here and talk until one of your spirit voices tells us where to proceed. There's no hurry.'

'I'm glad to hear that,' I said shyly, 'I thought you might be cross with me landing on you so unexpectedly.'

'Why should I be cross with you? I have never been cross with you before so why should I start now? You never surrender, but you are never far away,' said Dina as the children gathered around us trying to get a chance to speak.

'Can we go to the shops and have a look, Mummy?' said Rakatania, the cheeky one, 'are Papuans allowed to look at the shops here?'

'Of course they are,' I said. 'You should not talk like that here. You are stupid to say such things. Anyone who has the money can buy anything they like in Sydney.'

'I wish I had a cheque book like you, Mummy, then I could buy anything I liked.'

'You'll need to marry a millionaire if you are going to buy everything that you want.'

'I'm not going to marry anyone, I'm always going to stay with you,' said Rakatania, with a sad smile, as she turned away with the other girls.

'We'll see,' I called after her, and then turned to Dina and said, 'Growing old is growing in joy if your love stays young. There are many distractions in a big city. Perhaps you have grown accustomed to not having me around?'

Dina looked at me intently and said,

'For many years I have been engrossed with the unfolding of your courage and your love. Clean, rewarding years. As close to the dew on an opening rose as a man can expect to be.'

'I need to be reassured, that's all,' I said, ashamed of my weakness. 'I have had a hard experience and it has left some scars.'

'You were probably drawn to me first as a father figure who offered you security and, from there, developed a deeper satisfaction that supplied all of your needs. We have now spent a big part of our lives together.'

'We always analyse everything out of reality.' I said. 'To me, love is a tiara of a thousand coloured dreams.'

'With us it seems to be an inextinguishable flame,' said Dina, putting his hand on my knee.

I put my hand on his and replied, 'Or, perhaps, saying goodbye to self and becoming addicted to the presence of someone else. What are we going to do? It seems the world has no place for us any more. I'm now a foreigner here. I'm an ex-citizen and you're thrown out of my country to punish me.'

'Why don't we write a book?' said Dina. 'Have we got time?'

'What's time?' I said vacantly. 'What can we write about?'

'Write about you,' said Dina casually.

'What is there to write about me?' I said sharply, looking back on the last two empty years.

'Plenty,' said Dina.

'I can only think of the loneliness and the wanting now, but I suppose things will change. I'm game.'

'You must have had a bad time.'

'Yes, things changed when you were sent away. Some of them really tried to get at me and drag me down.'

'And did they succeed?'

'Not often,' I said bitterly. 'I told them to withdraw their advances as this vixen would not play out of place or season. Being a woman in politics is not that easy unless you have a man at your side.'

'I guess it's not easy for a man either,' said Dina.

'Perhaps,' I replied. 'But where are we going to sleep tonight? The pressure of getting away has exhausted me.'

'Can I kiss you now?' said Dina softly. 'People will think we are strangers the way we meet.'

'No, you cannot,' I said defensively. 'As far as I am concerned a kiss is an appointment with sex, and I am not making any appointment that I don't intend to keep. I'm not the restless young girl that I used to be. I'm a woman now. Very tired and very happy. I just want to sleep.'

For the first few days in Sydney it rained, but then the sun started to come out again. As the months passed we visited the parks, bushlands and waters of a beautiful city for dreamers. We lived again through the laughter of the children, but the loudest laughter was our own.

I thrived on the challenge and the unusual life. The clouds lifted from my mind and once again I was able to think of beauty and love and prayer. The fountain outside our window at Kings Cross spun circles of laughter by day and liquid suns by night. Beauty was everywhere and the smile returned to my heart.

A year passed on silent wings and I only returned to my beloved soil to attend meetings of Parliament.

In 1979, just as word came through that a *Papua Besena* provincial government had been elected to govern the central province — my old electorate — we put down our pens.

And to you, the companion of my years, every word and every page is a dedication to the silent wonder of a love that endured beyond the limits of reason or the dreams of a simple Papuan girl.